GIVE PEAS A CHANCE!

Organic Gardening
Cartoon-Science

by Peter Barbarow

LIBRARY OF CONGRESS CATALOGING-IN-PUBLICATION DATA

BARBAROW, PETER, 1950–
    GIVE PEAS A CHANCE!: ORGANIC GARDENING CARTOON-SCIENCE/
BY PETER BARBAROW.

    INCLUDES BIBLIOGRAPHICAL REFERENCES.
    1. ORGANIC GARDENING.   2. ORGANIC GARDENING—CARICATURES
AND CARTOONS.   I. TITLE.
SB453.5.B37   1990
631.5'84--DC20   90-5838
                                                      CIP

ISBN 0-87961-204-5: $17.95
ISBN 0-87961-205-3: $10.95 (PBK.)

Books for a better world

NATUREGRAPH PUBLISHERS, INC.
3543 INDIAN CREEK ROAD
HAPPY CAMP, CA 96039
U.S.A.

TABLE of CONTENTS

INTRODUCTION 8

ONE--COMPOSTING 17

TWO--PREPARING THE SOIL 41

THREE--SOIL CHEMISTRY 65

FOUR--FERTILITY 83

FIVE--GARDEN PLANS 101

SIX--PLANT PROPAGATION 125

SEVEN--WATERING 161

EIGHT--PEST CONTROL 183

SOURCES 219

LIFE ON EARTH

ONCE UPON A TIME, THERE WAS A BARE, ROCKY PLANET:

THERE WAS NARY A SIGN OF LIFE, AS FAR AS THE EYE COULD SEE. SO THEN HOW DID LIFE GET STARTED ON THIS FORBIDDEN, GOD-FORSAKEN WASTELAND? WELL, AS NEAR AS SCIENCE CAN RECONSTRUCT THE SERIES OF EVENTS, IT'S A BIT LIKE BETTY CROCKER. START WITH A BARE, ROCKY PLANET. ADD AN OCEAN, AND A DASH OF SALT. STIR WELL. TURN UP THE HEAT TO ABOUT 75°F. ADD LIGHTNING. PUT ON "SIMMER" FOR A FEW BILLION YEARS. LA` VOILA`: BACTERIA CONSOMME`!

THE IDEA CAUGHT ON LIKE A FLASH, AND SOON BODIES OF WATER EVERYWHERE WERE GETTING INTO THE ACT. LAKES, RIVERS, STREAMS, MARSHES, MUD PUDDLES, BRACKISH PONDS; IT BECAME THE "IN" THING TO DO. PRETTY SOON WATER EVERYWHERE WAS FULL OF ONE-CELLED CRITTERS:

THESE WERE THE FIRST CELLS, LITTLE GIFT-WRAPPED BOXES OF OCEAN ON THEIR WAY TO GEO-CULINARY IMMORTALITY. FOR MILLIONS OF YEARS THEY CAVORTED HAPPILY IN THE SWIMMING POOLS OF THE EARTH. BUT THE OCEANS HAD BIGGER PLANS. GROWING TIRED OF CONFINEMENT WITHIN CONTINENTAL SHELVES, THE OCEANS DECIDED TO SPREAD OUT OVER THE LAND.

TO DO THIS, IT PACKED THE OCEAN-BOXES INTO VARIOUS WEIRD-SHAPED SUPER-CONTAINERS AND SENT THEM UP ON LAND TO SEEK FAME AND FORTUNE:

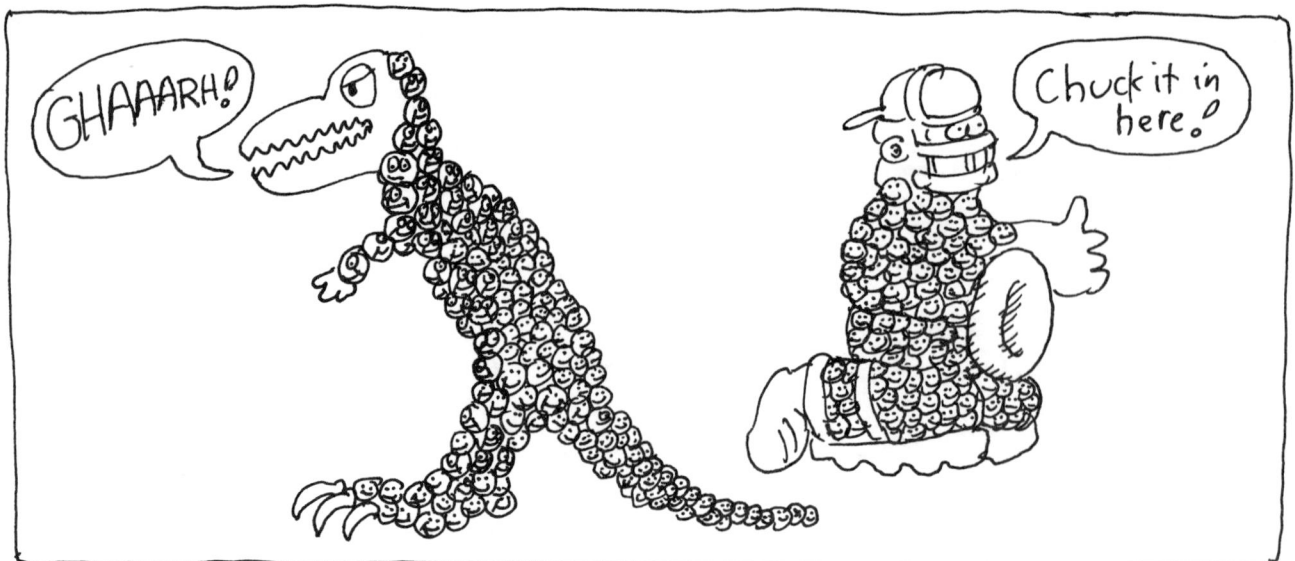

SO THE OCEAN HAD ACCOMPLISHED ITS GOAL, AND WAS GAILY CAVORTING IN CARTWHEELS OF DELIGHT OVER THE EARTH, EVEN THOUGH SOME OF THE OCEAN-CONTAINERS WERE BORED OR OTHERWISE PAINED IN THE PROCESS.

SOON, COMPLICATIONS DEVELOPED. ODDLY, THE OCEAN BOXES WOULDN'T STAY IN THEIR SUPER-CONTAINERS. THEY WERE CONSTANTLY BREAKING OUT, EXCHANGING NUTRIENTS (BY WAY OF THE NITROGEN AND CARBON CYCLES), VARIOUS GASES, PHEROMONES AND OTHER ATTRACTING CHEMICALS, DEFENSE TOXINS, AND EVEN PRECIOUS DNA, BY WAY OF VIRUSES. THINGS GOT SO PROMISCUOUS THAT SOON THE WHOLE AFFAIR BEGAN TO LOOK LIKE ONE GIANT ORGANISM:

A SHORT TIME LATER, THERE APPEARED BIZARRE BEINGS KNOWN AS "HUMANS," WHO IMAGINED THEY WERE SEPARATE FROM EVERYTHING ELSE:

BY TRYING TO DECLARE INDEPENDENCE FROM THE WORLD ORGANISM, THESE STRANGE APE-DESCENDED CREATURES ARE NOW THREATENING THE SURVIVAL OF NOT ONLY THEMSELVES, BUT THE REST OF THE BALLGAME AS WELL.

IF THEY DON'T MEND THEIR WAYS, SOON THE SUPER-CONTAINERS KILLED BY THE EX-APES' POISONS WILL SPILL OUT ALL THEIR OCEAN-BOXES AND DISSOLVE BACK INTO THE OCEAN. THE OCEAN, UNDERSTANDABLY VEXED, WILL NO LONGER BE ABLE TO WRITE SEA-FARING CHANTEYS ABOUT ITSELF, OR WATCH ITSELF STRETCH TO THE HORIZON AS IT WALKS ALONG THE SHORE.

AND THERE WILL BE NO MORE STORIES ENDING LIKE THIS:

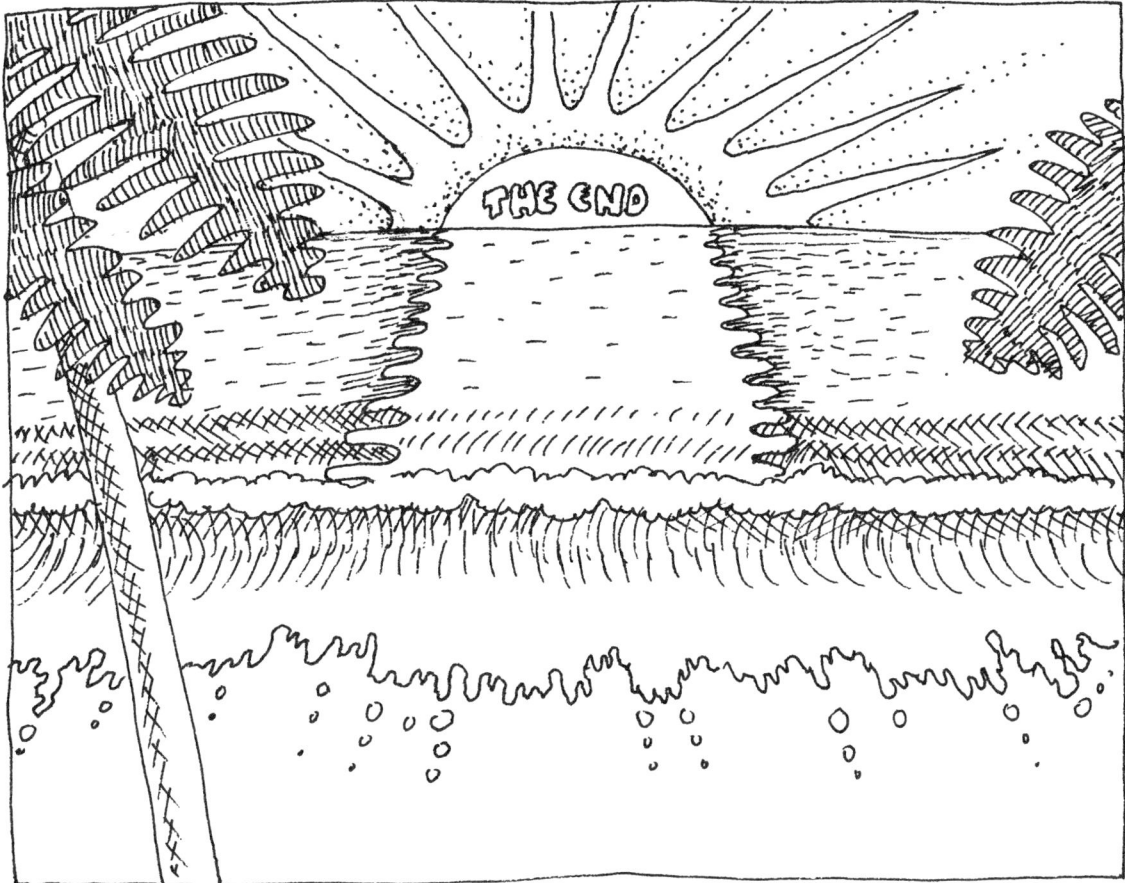

WHY ORGANIC? — PART ONE

SO THE MORAL OF THE STORY IS, IT'S ALL ONE BIG BOWL OF OATMEAL, SO YOU'D BETTER NOT SPIT IN IT, OR IT'LL COME BACK TO YOU SOME DAY WITH RETURN—TO—SENDER STICKERS ALL OVER IT.

SINCE WE ARE ALL (PEST INSECTS, PEOPLE, DOGS AND CATS) MADE OF NEARLY-IDENTICAL CELLS, ANY POISON DEVISED TO KILL ONE SET OF THOSE CELLS SOONER OR LATER HAS TO AFFECT THE OTHER SETS OF CELLS. AND THAT'S REASON NUMBER ONE FOR ORGANIC GARDENING AND FARMING. IN THE COURSE OF THIS BOOK, WE WILL SEE THE DETAILS OF HOW THIS PRINCIPLE WORKS.

WHY ORGANIC? — PART TWO

REASON NUMBER TWO INVOLVES LOOKING AT HOW NATURE DOES THINGS, AND TRYING TO EMULATE THAT EMINENTLY SUCCESSFUL EXAMPLE:

NATURE—
The World's Biggest Landscaping Company

MOST OF THIS BOOK WAS HEAVILY INFLUENCED BY OBSERVATIONS OF NATURAL ECOSYSTEMS. HOW DOES THE FOREST SOIL STAY FERTILE, WITH NO ONE RUNNING AROUND THE FOREST EMPTYING BAGS OF CHEMICALS? HOW DO SEEDS SPROUT, WITH NO ONE PREPARING SEEDLING MIX, CAREFULLY BURYING THE SEEDS, AND WATERING THEM? WHY AREN'T THE PLANTS STRIPPED BARE BY PESTS, WITH NO ONE SPRAYING CARCINOGENIC CHEMCIALS ON THEM?

ONE ANSWER IS **COMPOST**. OF COURSE, IN THE WOODS IT'S NOT CALLED "COMPOST;" RATHER, IT'S CALLED "DUFF," "LITTER," OR OTHER NAMES. IN ANY CASE, IT'S PIECES OF FORMER PLANTS AND ANIMALS, AND IT'S WHAT TAKES THE PLACE OF THE VARIOUS FERTILIZERS, PESTICIDES, HERBICIDES, FUNGICIDES, PH STABILIZERS, AND WHATNOT USED BY CHEMICAL GARDENING:

MULCH ON SURFACE
prevents weeds, conserves water, stabilizes temperature, prevents erosion.

SEEDING MIX-
Partly-decayed materials in soil aid seed germination

FERTILIZER-
The PERFECT balance of nutrients for plants

N P K

COMPOST
(REMAINS OF DEAD PLANTS + ANIMALS)

CO_2

CO_2 GAS from decomposition aids photosynthesis

Wastes (like manure) are USED instead of dumped into rivers, where they pollute

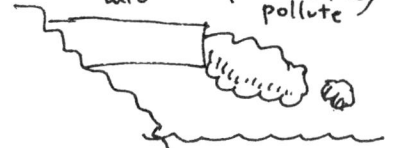

FREDDY FUNGUS SAYS:
SLURP!

PEST CONTROL-
FUNGI in compost eat soil pathogens like nematodes.

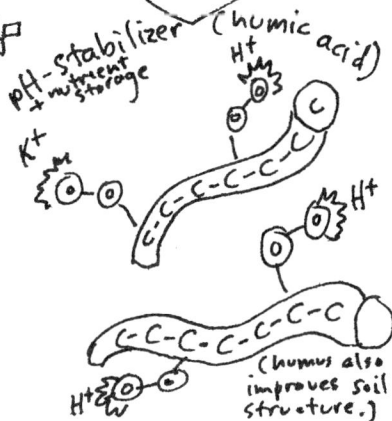

pH-stabilizer (humic acid) + nutrient storage

K^+

H^+

H^+

-C-C-C-C-

-C-C-C-C-C-

(humus also improves soil structure.)

BETTER FOOD-
Since soil is not polluted by excess chemical fertilizers (like nitrate), the food YOU EAT isn't poisoned.

A WORD ABOUT CHAPTER ORDER

NOW I'M SURE YOU'RE ALL ITCHING TO GET TO THE SEXY STUFF ABOUT PISTILS AND STAMENS AND SOWING SEEDS. WELL, HOLD YOUR HORSES! THE ORDER OF THE CHAPTERS IN THIS BOOK REFLECTS THE SEQUENCE OF EVENTS IN STARTING A GARDEN. FIRST, YOU'RE PROBABLY STARTING WITH A YARD FULL OF WEEDS. THAT'S WHY CHAPTER ONE IS ABOUT COMPOSTING; THE FIRST THING TO DO IS DIG UP THOSE WEEDS AND MAKE A COMPOST PILE. THE COMPOST YOU MAKE WILL BE USED FOR EVERY GARDENING OPERATION THAT FOLLOWS, SO EVERY CHAPTER REFERS BACK TO THE FIRST FEW CHAPTERS.

PUT ON YOUR THINKING CAP!

AS YOU READ, DON'T TAKE ANYTHING AS THE LAST WORD ON ANYTHING. THIS BOOK IS MEANT AS A JUMPING-OFF POINT FOR NEW DEVELOPMENTS IN THE ART OF PLANETARY SURVIVAL AND LIFE ENHANCEMENT. IT'S UP TO **YOU** TO GO OUT AND TRY NEW THINGS, AND IMPROVE ON THE METHODS ALREADY IN USE. FOR IT WILL TAKE ALL OUR COLLECTIVE MIND-POWER AND LOVE TO MAKE OUR WORLD WORK BETTER, AS WE MOVE THROUGH THE FINAL ERA OF THIS TEN-THOUSAND-YEAR DARK AGE INTO THE (HOPEFULLY) NEW AGE.

CHAPTER ONE
COMPOSTING

...OR, WHAT TO DO IF YOU HAVE PLENTY OF WEEDS, AND NOT MUCH....

...MONEY.

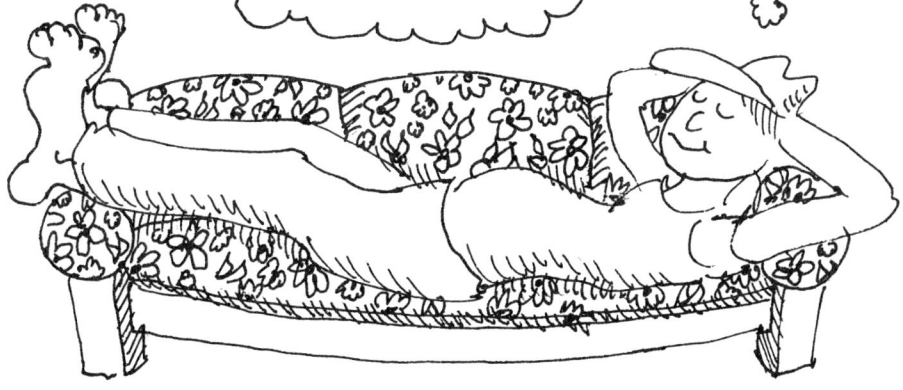

COMPOSTING

COMPOST IS ALL THESE THINGS!

- NATURE'S RECYCLING COMPANY
- YOUR PET ANIMAL
- A FREE LUNCH
- GOOD DIRTY FUN
- GOURMET DINING FOR YOUR PLANTS
- POTTING MIX

- GOOD-SMELLING (IF YOU DO IT RIGHT)
- PEST CONTROL
- SOLID WASTE DISPOSAL
- SOIL CONDITIONER
- FERTILIZER
- PH-NEUTRALIZER & STABILIZER

- SEASON-TRIGGERED PLANT NUTRIENT RELEASE
- NUTRIENT-BALANCER
- WATER-STABILIZER
- MULCH
- WEED-CONTROL
- COMPOST PROMISES YOU A ROSE GARDEN!

A COMPOST PILE is a PET ANIMAL

THINK OF COMPOST AS A LARGE ANIMAL YOU ARE FEEDING AND TAKING CARE OF. A COMPOST PILE IS ESSENTIALLY AN ENORMOUS COLLECTION OF BACTERIA (SINGLE-CELLED ORGANISMS), JUST AS ANIMALS ARE A LARGE COLLECTION OF THESE CELLS, WHICH WERE PROBABLY SEPARATE ORIGINALLY, BUT WHICH BANDED TOGETHER FOR THE COMMON GOOD. A COMPOST PILE BREATHES IN OXYGEN AND BREATHES OUT CARBON DIOXIDE, JUST AS ANIMALS DO, SO IT SHOULD BE TURNED ONCE A WEEK TO LET IN FRESH AIR. IT DRINKS WATER, SO IT SHOULD BE KEPT MOIST. BUT IT DOESN'T LIKE TOO MUCH WATER, BECAUSE IT CAN DROWN THE SAME WAY ANIMALS DROWN. SO IT SHOULD BE KEPT COVERED FROM THE RAINS. IT SHOULD BE AS LARGE AND COMPACT AS POSSIBLE TO CONSERVE HEAT, AND IT SHOULD BE GIVEN A HOUSE TO LIVE IN IF THE WEATHER IS VERY COLD WHERE YOU LIVE. IT SHOULD BE FED A BALANCED DIET. IT RESPONDS TO LOVE AND AFFECTION!

COMPOST:
The Original Fertilizer

COMPOSTING IS NOT ONLY GREAT FUN AND A REWARDING RELATIONSHIP, BUT IS MUCH MORE. COMPOST IS THE ORIGINAL FERTILIZER. WHEN FINISHED DECOMPOSING, COMPOST CONTAINS THE SAME CHEMICALS THAT ARE IN CHEMICAL FERTILIZERS, PLUS TRACE ELEMENTS NOT ALL CHEMICAL FERTILIZERS HAVE, PLUS HUMIC ACID (HUMUS), WHICH RELEASES PLANT NUTRIENTS WHEN THE PLANT NEEDS THEM, TRIGGERED BY THE CHANGING SEASONS.

WHEN YOU THINK ABOUT IT, IT MAKES SENSE THAT THE OLD DECAYING PLANTS AND ANIMALS WOULD BE THE BEST "FERTILIZER" OR GROWTH-SUBSTANCE FOR THE NEW PLANTS. THE OLD PLANTS CONTAINED JUST THE RIGHT PROPORTIONS OF ELEMENTS (CARBON, NITROGEN, ETC.) THAT THE NEW ONES NEED. THE DIFFERENCE IN ELEMENT-COMPOSITION BETWEEN **TYPES** OF PLANTS IS VERY SMALL; THE DIFFERENCE IS MAINLY IN HOW THE ELEMENTS ARE DISTRIBUTED IN SPACE AND TIME--IT IS THIS SPECIFIC PATTERN OF ELEMENTS THAT MAKES ONE SPECIES DIFFERENT FROM ANOTHER. THIS PATTERN IS ENCODED IN THE PLANT'S DNA, WHICH TAKES ELEMENTS FROM WHATEVER SOURCE AND TELLS THEM WHERE TO GO IN THE NEW DEVELOPING PLANT.

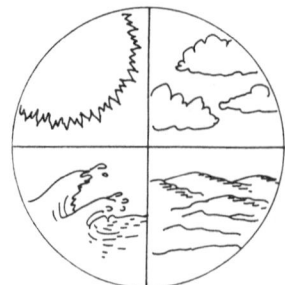

PLANTS EAT SMALL MOLECULES

COMPOSTING IS THE DECAY OF LARGE, COMPLEX MOLECULES INTO SMALL MOLECULES. SOME OF THE ENERGY GIVEN OFF IN THESE DECAY REACTIONS IS USED BY THE BACTERIA AND FUNGI IN THE PILE TO HELP THEM MAKE A LIVING. IT IS FORTUNATE THAT THE END-PRODUCT IS SMALL MOLECULES, BECAUSE THAT'S THE ONLY THING PLANTS CAN USE FOR FOOD. THAT'S BECAUSE PLANTS DON'T HAVE TEETH OR GUTS LIKE ANIMALS--THEY RELY ON SOIL BACTERIA TO DIGEST THEIR FOOD FOR THEM. THE HOLES IN THEIR ROOT CELLS (LIKE THE HOLES IN OUR GUT WALLS) ARE VERY SMALL, IN ORDER TO KEEP THINGS LIKE BACTERIA AND BACTERIAL ENZYMES OUT, SO AS A RESULT ONLY SMALL MOLECULES CAN GET IN. ESSENTIALLY, IF WE LOOK AT PLANTS AS ASSOCIATIONS OF CELLS, THEN WE CAN SAY THAT THE SMALL HOLES ARE DESIGNED TO KEEP UNINVITED CELLS FROM CRASHING THE PARTY.

HERE'S WHAT THE CROSS-SECTION OF A ROOT CELL LOOKS LIKE:

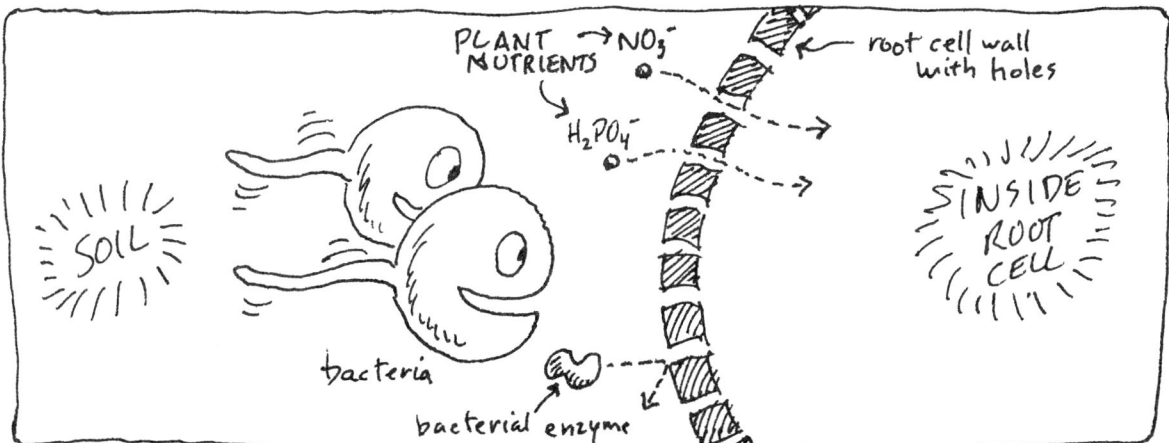

THE FACT THAT THESE PLANT NUTRIENTS ARE SMALL MOLECULES IS USEFUL TO US AS GARDENERS, SINCE FOR US HUMANS TO DETECT A SUBSTANCE BY SMELL, THE MOLECULES OF THE SUBSTANCE MUST BE SMALL AND LIGHT, SO THEY CAN BECOME A GAS EASILY AND ZIP THROUGH THE AIR INTO OUR NOSE. ONCE THEY GET INTO OUR NOSE, THEY

MUST BE SMALL ENOUGH TO INDIVIDUALLY TRIGGER SMALL GROUPS OF SMELL-CELLS IN THE LINING OF OUR NOSTRILS. THE UPSHOT IS, WE CAN TELL WHAT'S GOING ON IN A COMPOST PILE SIMPLY BY USING THE SENSITIVE "SMALL-MOLECULE DETECTION DEVICE" ON OUR FACE:

AMMONIA

BUILDING THE PILE

REMEMBER, YOU ARE ACTUALLY BUILDING A **LIVING ANIMAL**, TO BE YOUR PET. ALL ANIMALS ARE MADE UP (MAINLY) OF CELLS, NITROGEN, AND CARBON, AND THEY NEED AIR, WATER, AND WARMTH.

THE CELLS IN THIS CASE ARE BACTERIAL CELLS, AND YOU CAN GET THEM FROM TOPSOIL. SO DIG UP A WHEELBARROW FULL OF SOIL TO LAYER INTO THE PILE.

THE NITROGEN AND CARBON ARE FROM ANYTHING THAT USED TO BE PART OF A PLANT OR ANIMAL. THIS CAN INCLUDE KITCHEN SCRAPS, MANURE, STRAW, WEEDS, LAWN CLIPPINGS, COFFEE GROUNDS, ASHES, SAWDUST, LEAVES, PAPER, ETC. (THERE'S ACTUALLY A CORRECT RATIO OF CARBON AND NITROGEN--WE'LL GET TO THAT.)

DON'T GET TOO HUNG UP ON THE EXACT ORDER OF THE LAYERS--LAYERING IS JUST TO MAKE SURE NO PART OF THE PILE GETS TOO MUCH OF ANY ONE THING. THE LAYERS WILL ALL BE INTERMIXED ANYWAY WHEN THE PILE IS TURNED (IN ABOUT A WEEK).

USE YOUR IMAGINATION FOR SOURCES OF COMPOST MATERIALS. THE DUMPSTERS BEHIND PRODUCE MARKETS ARE USUALLY FULL OF VEGGIE SCRAPS THEY'RE THROWING AWAY. IF YOU KNOW SOMEONE WHO WORKS IN A RESTAURANT, HAVE THEM SAVE THE

BUILDING THE PILE

① Spread kitchen scraps or manure on the ground

② Since kitchen scraps tend to be on the wet side, add something dry and fibrous like straw, dry weeds, bark, or dry leaves, to aerate the pile.

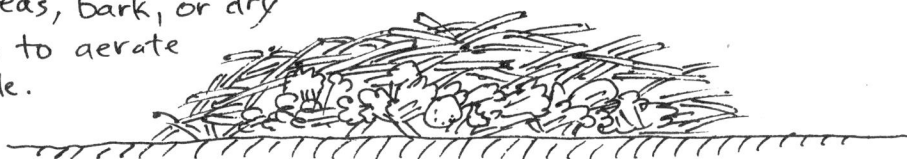

③ Throw on some topsoil, so bacteria in the soil can "innoculate" the pile. Add water.

④ Keep on layering until you run out of materials. Finish with a layer of dry stuff - weeds or straw

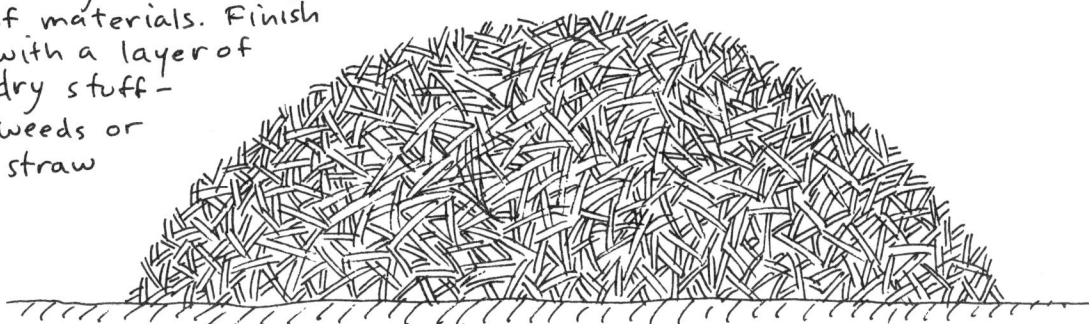

COFFEE GROUNDS. YOU CAN USUALLY GET GRASS CLIPPINGS FROM CITY EMPLOYEES WHO MOW SCHOOLYARDS AND PARKS. WEEDS ARE EVERYWHERE. CHOP UP EVERYTHING AS MUCH AS POSSIBLE TO INCREASE THE SURFACE AREA FOR THE BACTERIA TO WORK ON.

AS YOU PILE UP THE MATERIALS, ADD WATER EVERY 3 OR 4 INCHES TO GIVE THE BACTERIA SOMETHING TO DRINK AND SWIM AROUND IN. (BUT DON'T SATURATE THE PILE—— THERE MUST BE AIR POCKETS TOO.)

THE BIGGER THE PILE IS THE BETTER. IT SHOULD BE AT LEAST THREE FEET HIGH, AND FOUR FEET IN DIAMETER AT THE BASE. BIGGER THINGS HAVE LESS SURFACE AREA PER VOLUME, SO THERE'S LESS AREA FOR HEAT TO ESCAPE FROM. THAT'S WHY ALL ANIMALS IN THE ARCTIC ARE LARGE (LIKE POLAR BEARS), WHY ESKIMOS ARE PUDGY, AND WHY WATUSIS ARE SKINNY. IT ALSO HELPS IF THE PILE IS IN A NICE SUNNY PLACE (UNLESS THE WEATHER'S VERY HOT, AND THERE'S A DANGER OF THE PILE DRYING OUT). BACTERIA PRODUCE THE HEAT IN THE PILE, AND THEY NEED WARMTH (160°F) TO DO THEIR BEST. HEAT IS ALSO NEEDED TO KILL PATHOGENIC MICROBES.

WHEN YOU'RE FINISHED, PAT THE PILE ON THE BACK, SAY "NICE COMPOST PILE!" AND WAIT A FEW DAYS FOR THINGS TO START HAPPENING.

A MICROBE'S-EYE-VIEW

THE FIRST THING THAT WILL HAPPEN IN YOUR PILE IS THAT THE MANURE, WEEDS, OR KITCHEN SCRAPS (ANYTHING HIGH IN NITROGEN) WILL HAVE THEIR PROTEINS BROKEN DOWN INTO AMMONIA. LET'S TAKE A MICROSCOPIC JOURNEY INTO THE HEART OF THE JUST-COMPLETED PILE FOR A MICROBE'S-EYE-VIEW OF THE SITUATION:

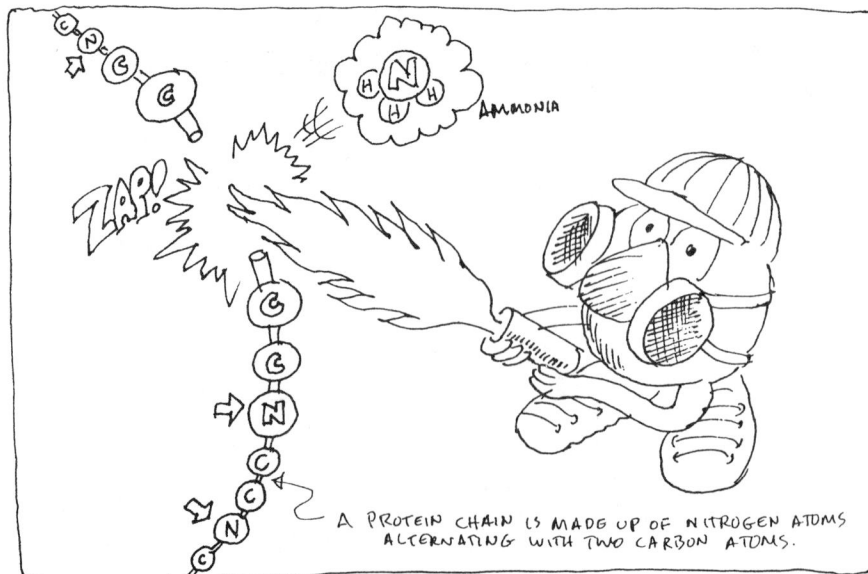

A PROTEIN CHAIN IS MADE UP OF NITROGEN ATOMS ALTERNATING WITH TWO CARBON ATOMS.

UNDER A DENSE CANOPY OF CELLULOSE FRONDS, A BACTERIAL WORKCREW IS BUSY CUTTING THROUGH A WALL OF SOLID PROTEIN, PART OF A WEED SEED OR MEAT SCRAP OR WHATEVER YOU THREW IN THE PILE. THE BACTERIA USE THEIR ENZYMES AS PORTABLE BLOW-TORCHES, BLASTING THROUGH A LEUCINE-THREONINE BOND HERE, SLASHING THROUGH A LYSINE-ARGININE BOND THERE. (LEUCINE, THREONINE, ETC. ARE AMINO ACIDS, THE BUILDING BLOCKS OF PROTEINS.) AS THE TORCHES CUT THROUGH THE DENSE TANGLE OF PROTEIN CHAINS, AMMONIA GAS COMES SPARKING OFF WHERE THE TORCHES HIT, TURNING THE PROTEIN INTO RISING BILLOWS OF PUNGENT GAS. THE BACTERIA EAT THE REMAINING CARBON FRAGMENTS, GOBBLING THEM UP LIKE TORTILLA CHIPS.

AMMONIA—A GOOD SIGN

AMMONIA GAS IS PRODUCED IN A FEW DAYS IN A WELL-MANAGED PILE, AND IT IS THE FIRST PRODUCT OF DECAY THAT CAN BE ABSORBED BY PLANTS. AMMONIA (NH_3) IS ONE SOURCE OF NITROGEN FOR PLANTS, WHICH THEY MAINLY USE TO MAKE PROTEINS AND CHLOROPHYLL. YOU SHOULD BE ABLE TO SMELL THIS AMMONIA WHEN YOU TURN THE PILE, IF EVERYTHING IS GOING RIGHT. (THE PILE SHOULD BE TURNED ONCE A WEEK TO LET IN FRESH AIR AND TO SEE HOW THINGS ARE GOING.) AS YOU TURN THE PILE, PICK OUT CLUMPS OF COMPOST AND HOLD THEM UP TO YOUR NOSE. DON'T BE BASHFUL-IT WON'T BITE!

WHAT DOES IT SMELL LIKE? YOU CAN EASILY IDENTIFY AMMONIA-IT HAS A PUNGENT, STINGY SMELL-FEELING, LIKE A HEAD MASSAGE FROM THE INSIDE. IT'S THE SAME CHEMICAL AS "HOUSEHOLD AMMONIA." IF LOTS OF FLIES SHOW UP TO CHECK OUT THE SCENE AS YOU TURN THE PILE, THAT'S ANOTHER SIGN THE DECAY PROCESS IS GOING WELL. THESE COMPOST FLIES DON'T BOTHER PEOPLE--THEY ARE MORE INTERESTED IN THE COMPOST AS A PLACE TO EAT AND LAY THEIR EGGS. THEY ARE A DIFFERENT SPECIES THAN MANURE FLIES, WHICH CAN BE A PAIN.

DON'T GET CARRIED AWAY

ACCORDING TO COMPOST SCIENTIST CLARENCE GOLUEKE OF THE UNIVERSITY OF CALIFORNIA, THE PILE SHOULD ONLY BE TURNED ONCE A WEEK, IN ORDER TO GET OXYGEN INTO THE PILE FOR THE BACTERIA TO BREATH. IF YOU TURN THE PILE ANY MORE FREQUENTLY, MUCH PRECIOUS AMMONIA WILL SIMPLY BE LOST TO THE AIR.

AN ASIDE ON SMELLS

WHY CAN WE SMELL AMMONIA SO EASILY? ALL SMELLS ARE ACTUALLY MOLECULES OF SOME SUBSTANCE WHICH IS EVAPORATING AND BECOMING A GAS. THE MOLECULES ARE BREAKING AWAY FROM THE MASS OF THAT SUBSTANCE, FLOATING THROUGH THE AIR AND GOING INTO YOUR NOSE. SMELLS ARE THE ONLY WAY OUR SENSES CAN DIRECTLY PERCEIVE THINGS THAT ARE SUB-VISIBLE, INCLUDING CHEMICAL REACTIONS, WHICH INVOLVE CHANGING ARCHITECTURAL CONFIGURATIONS TOO SMALL TO SEE EVEN WITH THE STRONGEST MICROSCOPE.

WE CAN SMELL AMMONIA BECAUSE IT IS VERY VOLATILE (MEANING IT TURNS INTO A GAS EASILY). IT IS VOLATILE MAINLY BECAUSE THE MOLECULES ARE SO SMALL.

HERE IS AN AMMONIA MOLECULE:

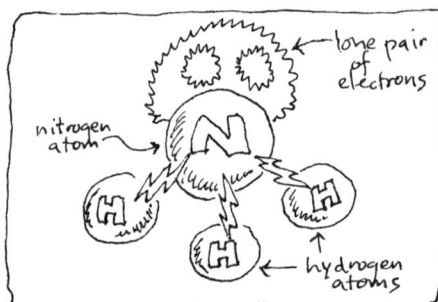

SMALL MOLECULES TURN TO GAS EASIER THAN LARGER MOLECULES BECAUSE IT TAKES MORE HEAT TO GET A MORE MASSIVE THING MOVING FAST ENOUGH TO SHOOT OFF AND BECOME A GAS. (JUST AS LARGE TRUCKS NEED BIGGER ENGINES THAN LITTLE VW BUGS.) MANY VERY LARGE MOLECULES LIKE SUGARS AND PROTEINS CAN NEVER BECOME A GAS . . . THEY EITHER BURN WHEN THE TEMPERATURE GETS HOT ENOUGH, OR CRUMBLE TO PIECES.

SO THE POINT OF ALL THIS IS: PLANTS NEED SMALL MOLECULES TO GROW, AND COINCIDENTLY WE HUMANS CAN SMELL SMALL MOLECULES, SO WE CAN TELL WHEN THE COMPOST IS PROCEEDING IN THE RIGHT DIRECTION FOR OUR PLANTS. WHAT A NIFTY ARRANGEMENT!

BAD SMELLS

IF THE PILE SMELLS BAD AS YOU TURN IT, YOU ARE DOING SOMETHING WRONG. USUALLY IT MEANS THE PILE IS "GOING ANAEROBIC." THIS MEANS THERE IS NOT ENOUGH AIR (ESPECIALLY OXYGEN) IN THE PILE. WHEN THE PILE IS ANAEROBIC, THE NORMAL AMMONIA-PRODUCING BACTERIA GO DORMANT, AND ANOTHER TYPE TAKES OVER. THESE

NEW "ANAEROBIC BACTERIA" INCLUDE CLOSTRIDIUM PUTRIFACIENS AND C. PERFRINGENS, WHICH SPLIT PROTEINS AND RELEASE H_2S (HYDROGEN SULFIDE GAS, THE FAMOUS "ROTTEN EGGS" SMELL) PLUS OTHER YECHHY-SMELLING AMINES AND MERCAPTANS.

THE REASON WE PERCEIVE ANAEROBIC COMPOST AS SMELLING "BAD" IS THAT MANY ANAEROBIC BACTERIA ARE DANGEROUS TO US (SUCH AS THE TETANUS AND BOTULISM BACTERIA, CLOSTRIDIUM TETANI AND C. BOTULINI). THOUGH EVEN THESE BAD DUDES WON'T HURT YOU UNLESS THEY ENTER AN OPEN WOUND OR YOU SWALLOW THEM (AND THEY WOULDN'T BE FOUND IN A COMPOST PILE ANYWAY), WE HAVE EVOLVED TO REACT WITH DISGUST TO **ANY** ANAEROBIC BACTERIA BEING ANYWHERE NEAR US. SO IF YOU COME ACROSS A POCKET OF ANAEROBIC ACTIVITY IN YOUR PILE, DON'T FREAK OUT--JUST BREATH THROUGH YOUR MOUTH AND THINK ABOUT ROSES.

NOT ONLY DOES ANAEROBIC COMPOST SMELL BAD, BUT THE "DENITRIFYING BACTERIA" START TO GROW AND PROSPER IN THE ABSENCE OF OXYGEN. THESE BACTERIA DON'T SMELL BAD, BUT THEY UNDO ALL THE GOOD DEEDS OF THE GOOD BACTERIA. THEY TURN NITRATE (A PLANT NUTRIENT DERIVED FROM AMMONIA) INTO N_2 GAS AND N_2O (LAUGHING GAS), WHICH ESCAPE INTO THE AIR. THIS IS A WASTE OF NITROGEN, AND THE LAUGH'S ON US.

ANOTHER SIGN OF ANAEROBIC ACTIVITY IS THE PRESENCE OF INSECT LARVAE IN THE PILE. A TYPE OF LARVA I'VE FOUND IN MANY MIS-MANAGED PILES LOOKS LIKE THIS:

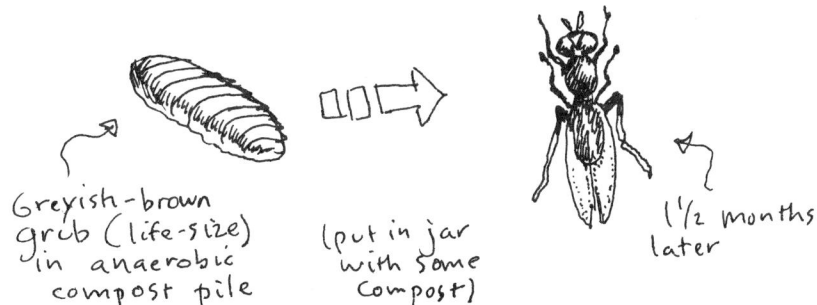

Greyish-brown grub (life-size) in anaerobic compost pile

(put in jar with some compost)

1½ months later

SO BRING OUT YOUR SMALL MOLECULE DETECTOR AND TURN IT ON OVER THE COMPOST PILE. IF YOUR COMPOST IS ANAEROBIC, THE METER WILL IMMEDIATELY JUMP OFF THE SCALE. BAD SMELLS MEAN BAD COMPOSTING PRACTICES--WHAT A NIFTY ARRANGEMENT! ANAEROBIC COMPOST TAKES LONGER TO FINISH COMPOSTING. IT BREEDS FLIES, LIKE THE ONE SHOWN ABOVE. IT DOESN'T GET HOT ENOUGH TO KILL WEED SEEDS AND PATHOGENIC ORGANISMS. IT IS FULL OF DENITRIFYING BACTERIA, WHICH WASTE NITROGEN.

CAUSES and CURES

THERE ARE MANY THINGS YOU COULD BE DOING WRONG TO MAKE THE PILE "GO ANAEROBIC." AMONG THESE ARE:

1. TOO MUCH WATER IN THE PILE. IF THE PILE IS SATURATED WITH WATER, THERE IS NO ROOM FOR AIR IN THE POCKETS BETWEEN THE STACKED MATERIALS. SPREAD THE PILE OUT TO DRY IN THE SUN, AND ADD LESS WATER NEXT TIME. IF IT'S RAINING A LOT, COVER THE PILE.

2. PILE TOO HIGH. IF YOU STACK THE PILE OVER 3 TO 4 FEET, THE PRESSURE WILL COMPACT THE BOTTOM LAYERS, AGAIN EXCLUDING AIR. IF YOU HAVE THAT MUCH STUFF TO COMPOST, MAKE TWO PILES.

3. NOT TURNING THE PILE OFTEN ENOUGH. IF THE PILE REMAINS UNTURNED FOR OVER A FEW WEEKS, THE AMMONIA-PRODUCING BACTERIA WILL USE UP ALL THE OXYGEN, AND THE ANAEROBIC BACTERIA (WHICH ARE POISONED BY OXYGEN) WILL COME OUT OF RETIREMENT AND RESUME THEIR LIFE OF CRIME. ALSO, AS THE PILE DECAYS THE BITS OF STEMS AND LEAVES WILL GET SMALLER, AND FALL INTO THE AIR POCKETS, FILLING THEM UP. SO **BE SURE TO TURN THE PILE ONCE A WEEK!**

4. KITCHEN SCRAPS NOT CHOPPED UP ENOUGH. BE SURE TO CHOP UP ALL LARGE PIECES OF FRUITS AND VEGGIES AND MEAT THAT YOU HAVE TO RECYCLE. THIS ESPECIALLY GOES FOR BIG WATERY FRUITS LIKE MELONS AND CITRUS. ALSO, WASTES WITH LOTS OF LIQUID IN THEM (LIKE SOUPS, STEWS, SPAGHETTI SAUCE, ETC.) SHOULD BE STRAINED BEFORE ADDING THEM TO THE COMPOST BUCKET. YOU CAN USE THE STRAINED LIQUID AS A DIRECT LIQUID FERTILIZER IN THE GARDEN.

LAWN CLIPPINGS CAN ALSO BE A PROBLEM, SINCE THEY TEND TO MAT TOGETHER IN THE PILE. SO WHEN YOU ADD THEM, MIX IN A LOT OF LEAVES, CHOPPED WEEDS, AND SOIL.

HEAT

THE PILE SHOULD START TO HEAT UP IN A FEW WEEKS. IF IT DOESN'T, SOMETHING IS WRONG. AS YOU TURN THE PILE, LOOK FOR WHISPS OF STEAM RISING FROM THE COMPOST IN THE INTERIOR OF THE PILE (THE OUTER LAYERS LOSE HEAT TO THE AIR TOO FAST TO HEAT UP NOTICEABLY.) THRUST YOUR HAND INTO THE PILE--IT SHOULD BE PLEASANTLY HOT. (IF IT'S TOO HOT TO TOUCH, THE PILE IS PROBABLY TOO BIG, AND THE PRESSURE IS CONTRIBUTING TO THE HEAT. THE MUNICIPAL COMPOST HEAPS IN BERKELEY, CALIFORNIA, ACTUALLY CAUGHT FIRE ONCE. THE HEAPS WERE ABOUT TEN FEET TALL AT THE TIME.)

THE HEAT IN THE PILE COMES FROM THE METABOLIC ACTIVITIES OF THE AMMONIA-PRODUCING BACTERIA. THESE BACTERIA ARE LIKE LITTLE WOOD STOVES: CARBON FRAGMENTS FROM THE PROTEINS BEING TORCHED APART ARE BURNED INSIDE THE BACTERIA, CONSUMING OXYGEN AND RELEASING CO_2 GAS. SO IF THE PILE DOESN'T HEAT

Bacteria in the pile are like little pot-belly stoves, burning up fragments of stems and other plant-parts, and releasing HEAT.

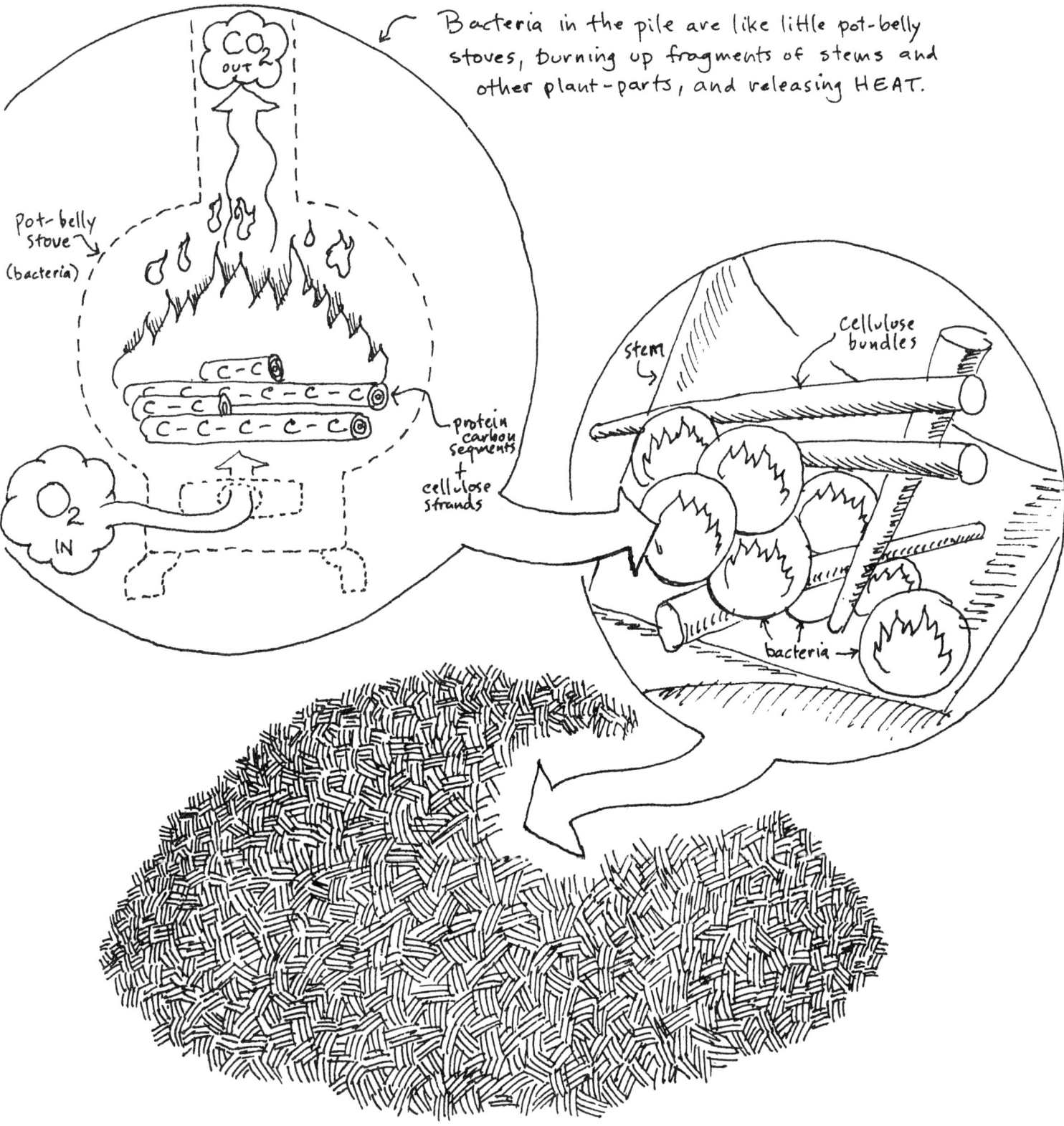

Pot-belly stove (bacteria)

CO₂ OUT

O₂ IN

C - C
C - C - C
C - C - C - C - C

protein carbon segments + cellulose strands

Stem

Cellulose bundles

bacteria →

UP, IT'S USUALLY BECAUSE IT'S ANAEROBIC: NOT ENOUGH OXYGEN TO KEEP THE LITTLE FIRES GOING. IT'S LIKE TRYING TO BURN A FIRE IN AN AIRTIGHT STOVE WITH ALL THE INLETS CLOSED.

SOME MANURES MAKE HOTTER COMPOST THAN OTHERS, BECAUSE THEY AREN'T AS COMPACTED. COW AND STEER MANURES ARE RELATIVELY COOL, SINCE THE CELLULOSE IN THE PLANTS THEY'VE BEEN EATING HAS BEEN PRE-COMPOSTED BY THE BACTERIA IN THE COW'S SECOND STOMACH, SO THE RESULTING TURD-COMPONENTS ARE SMALLER AND MORE COMPACTED. ON THE OTHER HAND, HORSE AND SHEEP MANURE STILL CONTAIN THE STRAW (CELLULOSE) RESIDUE OF THE ANIMAL'S FOOD, SO THEY ARE LESS DENSE, WITH MORE AIR POCKETS. THEY ARE KNOWN AS "HOT MANURES." THEY CAN EVEN BE DUG-IN UNDERNEATH VEGGIE BEDS TO HELP HEAT THE BEDS IN THE WINTER.

THERMOPHILIC (HEAT-LOVING) BACTERIA NOT ONLY PRODUCE THE HEAT, BUT THEY **NEED** IT (160°F OPTIMUM) TO DO THEIR BEST, SO YOU SHOULD ENCOURAGE THEM BY HELPING THEM KEEP THE PILE HOT. FIRST, MAKE SURE THE PILE IS LARGE ENOUGH. A CUBIC YARD IS A GOOD SIZE--ANY SMALLER, AND THE PILE WILL HAVE TOO MUCH SURFACE AREA PER VOLUME, SO IT WILL LOSE HEAT TO THE OUTSIDE AIR FASTER THAN THE BACTERIA CAN GENERATE IT. A LARGE PILE ALSO INSURES THAT THE OUTER LAYERS OF THE PILE WILL HELP THERMALLY-INSULATE THE INNER LAYERS. THE PILE SHOULD BE COVERED IN THE WINTER TO KEEP OFF THE COOLING WINDS. DON'T WORRY ABOUT LOSING HEAT BY TURNING THE PILE; STUDIES HAVE SHOWN THAT ONLY 10 TO 15°F IS LOST, AND THE HEAT IS REGAINED IN A FEW HOURS.

THERE IS ONE MORE POSSIBLE REASON THE PILE IS NOT HEATING UP, AND THAT IS YOU'VE PUT TOO MUCH CARBON AND NOT ENOUGH NITROGEN IN THE PILE. IF THERE'S TOO MUCH CARBON-RICH MATERIAL LIKE STRAW, A SPECIAL TYPE OF CELLULOSE-EATING BACTERIA WILL TAKE OVER. THEY DON'T GENERATE HEAT, SO THE PILE STAYS COOL. BUT YOU CAN'T BE BLAMED FOR PUTTING TOO MUCH CARBON IN THE PILE--I HAVEN'T GOTTEN TO THAT YET! SO HERE GOES . . .

THE CARBON-to-NITROGEN RATIO

BACTERIA AREN'T MAKING AMMONIA FOR PLANTS AS AN ACT OF HUMANITARIANISM (OR GERMITARIANISM, IN THIS CASE!). THEY'RE IN IT FOR THEMSELVES, LIKE EVERYONE SINCE THE "ME DECADE" OF THE 70'S. THE REASON THEY ARE TORCHING APART THE PROTEINS IN THE PILE IS TO GET AT THE CARBON IN THE PROTEINS. THEY BURN THE CARBON FOR ENERGY, AND THROW AWAY MOST OF THE PROTEIN'S NITROGEN AS AMMONIA. SO PLANTS ARE ACTUALLY SCROUNGING THE BACTERIA'S GARBAGE! (HAVE YOU EVER SCROUNGED AT THE DUMP? IT'S AMAZING THE BARGAINS YOU CAN PICK UP!)

HERE'S WHERE THE CARBON-TO-NITROGEN RATIO COMES IN. THE AMMONIA-PRODUCING BACTERIA NEED NITROGEN (TO MAKE NEW PROTEINS OF THEIR OWN, MAINLY) JUST AS PLANTS AND ANIMALS DO. THEY ALSO NEED CARBON, AGAIN FOR THE SAME REASON AS PLANTS AND ANIMALS: AS A SOURCE OF ENERGY. IT'S THE SAME OLD "BASIC FOOD GROUPS" WE ALL NEED FOR A SQUARE MEAL: YOU MUST GET YOUR PROTEIN (NITROGEN) AS YOU MUST GET YOUR CARBOHYDRATES (CARBON). HERE IS A COMMON DINNER-TIME SCENE IN THE COMPOST PILE:

USUALLY COMPOST PILES HAVE TOO MUCH CARBON, BECAUSE NITROGEN IS USUALLY HARDER TO COME BY AROUND THE HOUSE, UNLESS YOU HAVE CHICKENS OR DUCKS. IF THERE'S TOO MUCH CARBON IN THE PILE (SUCH AS OLD LEAVES OR DRIED-UP WEEDS, WITH NOT ENOUGH CHICKEN MANURE OR KITCHEN SCRAPS OR OTHER HIGH-NITROGEN MATERIALS), THE MICROBES WILL REALLY GET THE MUNCHIES FOR ALL THOSE CARBON-RICH MATERIALS, WHICH ARE THE EQUIVALENT OF TORTILLA CHIPS AND BEER FOR BACTERIA. ONE THING LEADS TO ANOTHER, AND PRETTY SOON THERE WILL BE A "BABY BOOM" OF HUNGRY BACTERIAL OFFSPRING.

THE HORDES OF BABY BACTERIA WILL BE SCREAMING FOR BREAKFAST. THEY WILL NEED LOTS OF NITROGEN, BUT THE ONLY NITROGEN LEFT WILL BE THE AMMONIA RELEASED BY THEIR PARENTS. SO THEY'LL SCARF UP ALL THIS PRECIOUS AMMONIA, LEAVING NONE FOR THE NEXT BACTERIA SPECIES IN THE SUCCESSION, AND ULTIMATELY NONE FOR THE PLANTS. (I'LL EXPLAIN ABOUT THE SUCCESSION LATER.)

IF THIS HIGH-CARBON COMPOST FULL OF NITROGEN-STARVED MANIC MICROBES IS THEN ADDED TO THE SOIL, THEY WILL GO AFTER ANY NITROGEN ALREADY IN THE SOIL. THAT'S ALSO WHY YOU SHOULD NEVER DIG SUCH HIGH-CARBON MATERIALS AS SAWDUST, OLD LEAVES, OR DRY WEEDS DIRECTLY INTO THE SOIL. BY DOING SO, YOU'D BE INTRODUCING HORDES OF RAMPAGING NITROGEN JUNKIES INTO YOUR GARDEN. IT'S AS IF, IN SOME CITY, ALL THE MEAT, DAIRY PRODUCTS, BEANS, AND BREAD SUDDENLY

DISAPPEARED FROM ALL THE MARKET SHELVES OVERNIGHT, AND THE SHELVES WERE FULL OF NOTHING BUT JAMS AND POTATO CHIPS. THERE WOULD SOON BE MASSIVE TRAFFIC JAMS OF PEOPLE INVADING THE SURROUNDING CITIES AND TOWNS, LOOKING FOR PROTEIN.

ON THE OTHER HAND, IF THERE'S TOO MUCH NITROGEN IN THE PILE (LIKE A PILE OF PURE CHICKEN MANURE WITH NO CARBONACEOUS MATTER LIKE STRAW OR OLD LEAVES), AMMONIA WILL BE PRODUCED SO FAST THAT THE NEXT GROUP OF BACTERIA, WHICH NORMALLY TURN AMMONIA INTO NITRITE, WON'T HAVE A CHANCE TO DO THEIR JOB. BEFORE THEY CAN USE THE AMMONIA IT WILL HAVE EVAPORATED INTO THE AIR, SO NITROGEN IS WASTED. IN ADDITION, CARBON-RICH MATERIALS CONTAIN LIGNIN, WHICH BECOMES HUMUS, WHICH IS IMPORTANT FOR NUTRIENT STORAGE AND BUILDING GOOD SOIL STRUCTURE WHEN THE FINISHED COMPOST IS ADDED TO THE SOIL.

THE RIGHT BALANCE

TO GIVE YOUR BACTERIA BALANCED MEALS, YOU NEED TO COMBINE MATERIALS WHICH ADD UP TO AN OVERALL 25 : 1 RATIO OF CARBON-TO-NITROGEN, OR TWENTY-FIVE TIMES AS MUCH CARBON AS NITROGEN. HERE IS A CHART WITH THE C/N RATIOS OF SOME COMMON COMPOSTING MATERIALS:

CARBON/NITROGEN RATIOS

(NUMBERS INDICATE HOW MUCH MORE CARBON THAN NITROGEN THERE IS.)

TOO MUCH NITROGEN BY ITSELF	THE RIGHT BALANCE	TOO MUCH CARBON BY ITSELF
URINE (0.8)	ALFALFA HAY (17)	OLD LEAVES (45)
BONE MEAL (3.5)	LAWN GRASS HAY (19)	PEANUT SHELLS (35)
BLOOD MEAL (3.5)	SEAWEED (19)	OAT STRAW (48)
TANKAGE (4)	COW MANURE (18)	WHEAT STRAW (150)
DRY FISH SCRAPS (5)	HORSE MANURE (25)	SAWDUST (200-500)
BEANS (5)	STEER MANURE (25)	PAPER (800)
COTTON SEEDS (5)	MOST GREEN (FRESHLY PICKED) PLANTS, INCLUDING WEEDS & FALLEN LEAVES (20-25)	
MEAT (6)		
CHICKEN MANURE (5)		
HUMAN MANURE (6-10)		
GRASS CLIPPINGS, FRESH (12)		
NON-LEGUME VEGETABLE SCRAPS (I.E. MOST KITCHEN SCRAPS) (11-19)		

M-M-M-MMM GOOD! IN THIS MENU, "STRAW" MEANS THE STEMS OF GRASSES OR WEEDS, WHILE "HAY" MEANS THE WHOLE PLANT, INCLUDING LEAVES (THAT'S WHY WHEN YOU SAY "HEY!" TO SOMEONE THEY SAY "HAY'S FOR HORSES, STRAW'S FOR COWS" . . . BECAUSE COWS HAVE THEIR FAMOUS "SECOND" STOMACH, WHICH THEY USE TO DIGEST THE CELLULOSE IN STRAW, WHILE HORSES NEED LEAVES FOR AN ADEQUATE DIET.)

AS YOU CAN SEE FROM THE CHART, THE LEAVES OF A PLANT CONTAIN MORE NITROGEN THAN THE STEMS, WHICH ARE MOSTLY COMPOSED OF HALF-DEAD STRUCTURAL ELEMENTS; STEMS ARE THE CELLULOSE (CARBON) BACKBONE OF THE PLANT. LEAVES CONTAIN CHLOROPHYLL (WHICH MAKES THEM GREEN), AND EACH CHLOROPHYLL MOLECULE HAS FOUR NITROGEN ATOMS IN A RING:

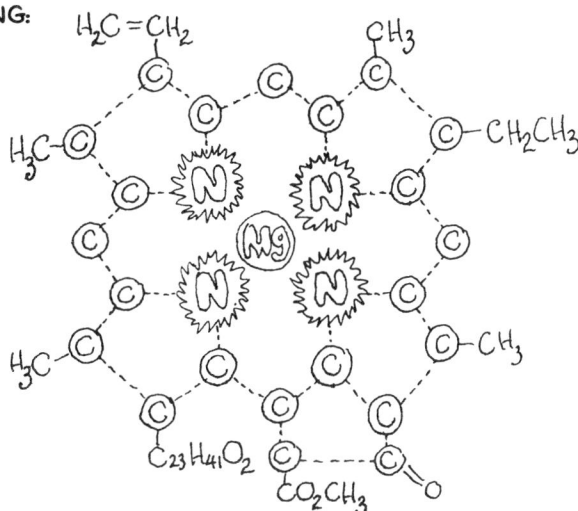

GENERALLY, YOUNG ANNUAL PLANTS (BEFORE THE FLOWER HEADS FORM) HAVE MORE NITROGEN IN THE STEMS AND LEAVES THAN MATURE PLANTS. THAT'S BECAUSE AS THE PLANT MATURES, THE CHLOROPHYLL IN THE LEAVES IS BROKEN DOWN, AND THE NITROGEN IS SENT TO THE DEVELOPING SEEDS, WHERE IT IS RECYCLED TO MAKE STORAGE PROTEINS, WHICH ARE PACKED INTO SEEDS. THE LEAVES AND STEMS TURN YELLOW, BECAUSE THEY HAVE LOST THEIR CHLOROPHYLL. SINCE NITROGEN IS USUALLY THE LIMITING FACTOR IN MOST COMPOST PILES, YOU SHOULD HARVEST YOUR WEEDS AND STICK THEM IN THE PILE BEFORE THE HEADS FORM.

MANURE IS GREAT FOR COMPOST. MANURE IS COMPOSED OF TURDS, AND TURDS ARE ACTUALLY LITTLE MINIATURE COMPOST PILES IN THEMSELVES, CONTAINING FINELY-SHREDDED PLANTS, PLUS BACTERIA AND AMMONIA. AS YOU CAN SEE FROM THE CHART, HORSE AND COW MANURES CONTAIN THE PERFECT C/N BALANCE, SO YOU CAN BUILD AN ENTIRE PILE WITH NOTHING BUT MANURE. IN MY EXPERIENCE THOUGH, YOU GET A HEALTHIER PILE WITH A VARIETY OF DIFFERENT MATERIALS. IT'S LIKE THE DIFFERENCE BETWEEN POLYCULTURE AND MONOCULTURE IN AGRICULTURE: WITH POLYCULTURE YOU HAVE A WHOLE COMPLEX ECOSYSTEM WITH DIFFERENT TYPES OF PLANTS AND INSECTS AND BACTERIA/FUNGI, SO THE WHOLE SYSTEM IS MORE STABLE, AND LESS VULNERABLE TO DISRUPTION BY UNWANTED ORGANISMS OR CHANGING ENVIRONMENTAL CONDITIONS.

CHICKEN MANURE (OR ANY OTHER BIRD MANURE, SUCH AS DUCK OR GOOSE) IS ESPECIALLY VALUABLE, SINCE IT HAS SO MUCH NITROGEN, SO IT CAN BE USED TO BALANCE CARBON-RICH THINGS LIKE OLD LEAVES OR DRIED WEEDS. SO IF YOU KEEP CHICKENS OR DUCKS IN YOUR YARD, YOU HAVE THE PERFECT COMPOST FOOD RIGHT THERE! IN FACT, YOU'VE GOT A SCALE MODEL OF THE GLOBAL NITROGEN CYCLE.

BIRD MANURE HAS SO MUCH NITROGEN BECAUSE IT INCLUDES THE BIRD'S TURDS AND URINE IN ONE CONVENIENT PACKAGE DEAL. (THEY BOTH COME OUT OF THE SAME HOLE, UNLIKE SOME MORE FAMILIAR ARRANGEMENTS.) IN THE C/N CHART, YOU'LL NOTICE URINE IS THE HIGHEST-NITROGEN THING AVAILABLE. THAT'S BECAUSE URINE CONTAINS MAINLY WATER AND UREA, AND UREA IS FULL OF NITROGEN.

DON'T WORRY ABOUT GETTING THE C/N RATIO EXACTLY RIGHT. YOU CAN PRETTY MUCH JUST WING IT. IF YOU HAVE A CERTAIN AMOUNT OF STRAW (CARBON), YOU'LL NEED AT LEAST THAT MUCH CHICKEN MANURE (OR TWICE AS MUCH KITCHEN SCRAPS) FOR NITROGEN. MOST BACKYARDS CONTAIN AN AMOUNT OF CARBON-RICH MATERIALS THAT CAN BE BALANCED BY THE KITCHEN SCRAPS OF ONE HOUSEHOLD. BUT YOU'LL PROBABLY WANT MORE COMPOST THAN THIS WILL PROVIDE, AT LEAST WHEN STARTING UP YOUR GARDEN. SO UNLESS YOU HAVE A VERY BIG YARD WITH LOTS OF EXTRA SPACE TO GROW COVER CROPS OR WEEDS, YOU'LL WANT TO BRING IN OUTSIDE MATERIALS TO ADD TO THE PILE. HORSE STABLES USUALLY GIVE MANURE AWAY. (BUT GET IT FREE WHILE YOU CAN . . . WHEN FOSSIL FUELS FOR MAKING CHEMICAL FERTILIZERS RUN OUT, THE DEMAND FOR MANURE WILL RISE, AND THE STABLES WILL START TO CHARGE.)

ALTHOUGH AMMONIA CAN BE USED DIRECTLY BY PLANTS, MOST OF IT IS CONVERTED TO ANOTHER FORM OF NITROGEN BY THE NEXT TYPE OF BACTERIA IN THE ECOLOGICAL CHAIN. THE NEW FORM OF NITROGEN IS NITRATE (NO_3), WHICH CAN ALSO BE USED BY PLANTS. NITRATE IS BETTER TO ADD TO THE SOIL THAN AMMONIA, BECAUSE IT DOESN'T EVAPORATE AS EASILY, SO LESS IS LOST TO THE AIR. SO IF YOU CAN SMELL AMMONIA IN YOUR PILE WHEN YOU TURN IT, YOU SHOULD WAIT AT LEAST A WEEK UNTIL THE AMMONIA IS CONVERTED TO NITRATE.

THIS CONVERSION IS MADE, CONVENIENTLY ENOUGH, BY TWO NEW TYPES OF BACTERIA, WHICH TAKE OVER FROM THE AMMONIA-PRODUCERS IN A TYPE OF ECOLOGICAL SUCCESSION, THE WAY TREES GRADUALLY TAKE OVER WHERE A MEADOW USED TO BE. FIRST, THE NITROSOMONAS BACTERIA TAKE OVER IN THE PILE. THEY BURN AMMONIA FOR ENERGY, AND RELEASE NITRITE (NO_2) AS A WASTE PRODUCT. THEY DIE OUT WHEN THEY USE UP ALL THE AMMONIA, AND THEY ARE REPLACED BY THE NITROBACTER AND NITROCYSTIS BACTERIA, WHICH BURN THE NITRITE FOR ENERGY AND RELEASE NITRATE AS A WASTE PRODUCT. THIS NITRATE IS THE SAME CHEMICAL FOUND IN COMMERICAL FERTILIZERS LIKE AMMONIUM NITRATE (NH_4NO_3). EXCEPT IN THIS CASE IT IS **FREE** (OR NEARLY SO, DEPENDING ON YOUR SOURCE OF PLANT WASTES OR MANURE). AND BESIDES, YOU'RE GETTING ALL THE **TRACE ELEMENTS** THE PLANT NEEDS IN EXACTLY THE RIGHT PROPORTIONS, WHICH YOU DON'T GET FROM CHEMICAL FERTILIZERS. (THAT'S ACTUALLY A COMPLEX ISSUE, AND I'LL COVER IT IN THE CHAPTER ON SOIL FERTILITY, P. 92.)

NO MATTER WHAT THE SOURCE, NITRATE IS ONE OF THE MOST IMPORTANT MOLECULES ON THE PLANET RIGHT NOW, WITH THE HUMAN POPULATION EXPLODING AS IT IS. AS THE MAJOR PLANT NUTRIENT, THE LITTLE NITRATE MOLECULE STANDS BETWEEN US AND MASS STARVATION!

HERE'S WHAT OUR LITTLE SAVIOR LOOKS LIKE. THE FIERY AURA MEANS THE ION IS NEGATIVELY CHARGED, SO IT'S ATTRACTED TO WATER... SO IF TOO MUCH WATER RUNS DOWN THROUGH THE PILE, IT WILL TAKE ALL THE NITRATE WITH IT DOWN TO THE GROUNDWATER. SO KEEP YOUR PILE COVERED WHEN IT RAINS! HELP PREVENT STARVATION!

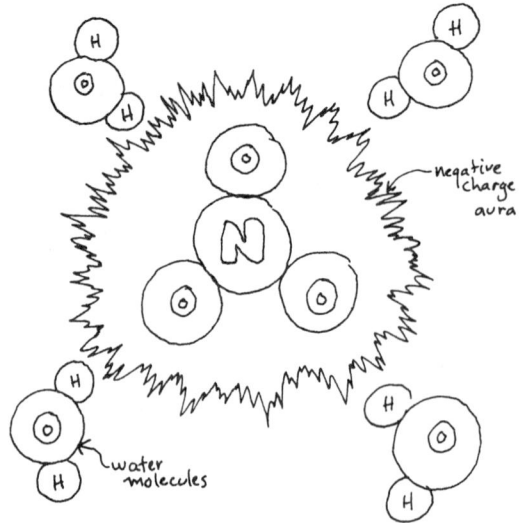

negative charge aura

water molecules

THE BIG PICTURE

COMPOST IS PART OF A LARGER PICTURE. OR, AS ONE END OF A WORM SAID TO THE OTHER END, "THIS THING IS BIGGER THAN BOTH OF US." THE WHOLE SEQUENCE OF EVENTS FROM PROTEIN TO AMMONIA TO NITRATE, AND BACK TO PROTEIN AGAIN IN THE PLANT, IS PART OF A GRAND GLOBAL RECYCLING OPERATION CALLED THE NITROGEN CYCLE. THE WHOLE EARTH IS ACTUALLY COVERED BY ONE GIANT FLAT COMPOST PILE, WITH ALL PLANTS AND ANIMALS CONTINUALLY SPRINGING OUT OF THE PILE AND BEING ABSORBED BACK INTO IT, IN GIANT CIRCULAR WAVES OF TRANSMUTATION.

A COMPOST PILE IS A MINIATURE COMPRESSED SPEEDED-UP MICROCOSM OF THE GLOBAL CYCLE. THE LITTLE BIT OF THE CYCLE IN YOUR HOUSE AND YARD MEANS YOU ARE PUTTING JUST THAT MUCH OF YOUR NITROGEN WASTES BACK INTO YOUR SOIL, INSTEAD OF DUMPING THEM ALL IN THE OCEAN LIKE MOST FOLKS IN NORTH AMERICA, WHO THEN NEED TO GET THAT LOST NITROGEN FROM SOMEWHERE ELSE.

HERE'S THE GLOBAL CYCLE, OF WHICH YOUR COMPOST PILE IS A SMALL (BUT COLLECTIVELY, VERY IMPORTANT) PART. NITROGEN IS RECYCLED CONTINUOUSLY AND ENDLESSLY, BECOMING PART OF EVERYTHING BUT KEPT BY NOTHING. ONE MINUTE IT'S IN YOU, THE NEXT MINUTE IT'S IN A SOIL FUNGUS, FIVE HOURS LATER IT'S IN A WORM'S CASTINGS, THEN TWO HOURS AFTER THAT IT'S IN THE FLOWER OF A PLANT. THE NITROGEN CYCLE IS THE BLOODSTREAM OF THE WORLD-ORGANISM. ONLY **YOU** CAN KEEP IT GOING!

THE NITROGEN CYCLE

Tree (protein (-NH₂) + chlorophyll)

Bambi (protein)

H₂S (yecchh!)

N₂O nitrous oxide (tee-hee)

N₂

NH₃

dead tree

protein(-NH₂) + chlorophyll

NO₃⁻ nitrate

Azotobacter Rhizobium etc.

Bambi manure + pee (urea)

urea bacteria

dead Bambi (sniff!) (protein —NH₂)

NH₃ ammonia

proteus vulgaris Bacillus subtilis B. cereus etc.

Pseudomonas

NO₂⁻ nitrite

nitrobacter

nitrosomonas

↑ aerobic
↓ anaerobic

clostridia

NO₂⁻ nitrite

denitrifying bacteria

SIFTING COMPOST

AFTER A FEW WEEKS, YOU CAN START SIFTING THE PILE AS YOU TURN IT, AND USE THE SIFTED COMPOST IN THE GARDEN. THE IDEA IS THAT WHATEVER IS SMALL ENOUGH TO FALL THROUGH THE HOLES IN THE SIFTER HAS DECAYED TO THE POINT WHERE IT IS FINISHED (OR ALMOST FINISHED) DECOMPOSING, SO YOU DON'T HAVE TO WAIT FOR THE WHOLE PILE TO DECOMPOSE. ("A FEW WEEKS" IS THE BARE MINIMUM AMOUNT OF TIME IT WILL TAKE. AND THAT ASSUMES YOU HAVE DONE EVERYTHING RIGHT, WHICH IS UNUSUAL.)

FIRST, BUILD YOUR SIFTER. YOU SHOULD PLAN THE DIMENSIONS OF YOUR SIFTER TO FIT THE TOP OF YOUR WHEELBARROW, SO YOU CAN SIFT DIRECTLY INTO THE BARROW AND WHEEL IT INTO THE GARDEN.

HERE IS A SIMPLE SIFTER DESIGN:

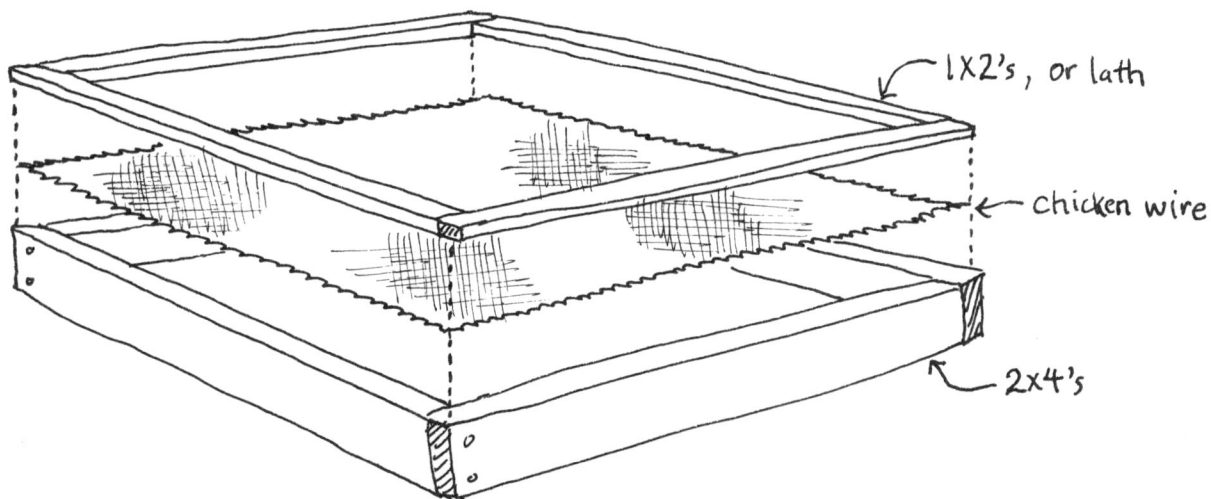

1X2's, or lath

chicken wire

2x4's

THE HOLES IN THE CHICKEN WIRE SHOULD BE 1/2" FOR SIFTING COMPOST TO BE USED FOR POTTING MIXES, MULCH IN THE GARDEN, AND FOR DIGGING INTO THE SOIL. THE HOLES SHOULD BE 1/4" FOR SIFTING SEED-BED MIXES. THAT MEANS YOU NEED TO BUILD TWO SIFTERS, UNLESS YOU CAN DEVISE SOME SNAPPY WAY TO INTERCHANGE CHICKEN WIRES.

NOW YOU'RE READY TO START SIFTING. PUT THE SIFTER ON YOUR WHEELBARROW, AND PLACE A FORK-FULL OF COMPOST ON THE SIFTER. TRY TO POSITION EVERYTHING SO WHATEVER DOESN'T FALL THROUGH THE HOLES CAN EASILY BE DUMPED ON A NEW PILE AS IT FORMS. MY ARRANGEMENT USUALLY LOOKS LIKE THIS:

NEW PILE

OLD PILE

USING GLOVES, RUB THE COMPOST INTO THE CHICKEN WIRE, TO BREAK UP THE CLUMPS. WATCH FOR VARIOUS FASCINATING INSECTS CRAWLING AROUND IN THE COMPOST. SIFTING COMPOST IS FUN--IF IT SEEMS LIKE A CHORE, YOU'RE NOT PAYING ATTENTION!

COMPOST HOUSING

MOST OF THE YEAR ON THE WEST COAST YOU DON'T NEED ANY SORT OF COMPOST BIN, UNLESS YOU ARE OFFENDED BY THE SIGHT OF AN OPEN PILE. I PERSONALLY THINK A WELL-MANAGED PILE IS BEAUTIFUL.

COMPOSTING IN THE WINTER IS ANOTHER STORY, AS IS COMPOSTING IN RAINY-SUMMER AREAS. RAIN SHOULD BE KEPT OFF THE PILE, OR IT WILL "GO ANAEROBIC." HEAT LOSS FROM THE PILE IS ANOTHER PROBLEM IN THE WINTER. THE EASIEST SOLUTION IS TO THROW A TARP OVER THE PILE, OR YOU CAN LAY PIECES OF PLYWOOD OVER IT. OR, YOU CAN GO ALL THE WAY AND BUILD A LITTLE HOUSE FOR YOUR PILE. IF YOU HAVE A GREENHOUSE, YOU CAN SIMPLY PUT THE PILE INSIDE, AND IT WILL HELP THE PLANTS GROW BY CONTRIBUTING CO_2 TO THE AIR.

COMPOST SHREDDERS

IT'S BEST TO CHOP UP LARGE COMPOSTING MATERIALS SO THE BACTERIA WILL HAVE AS MUCH SURFACE AREA AS POSSIBLE TO WORK ON. THERE ARE MANY GOOD SHREDDERS ON THE MARKET. IF YOU HAVE THE BUCKS, BUY ONE. IF NOT, YOU ALREADY HAVE A SHREDDER IN YOUR TOOL SHED . . . IT'S CALLED A "SHOVEL." IF YOU SIMPLY RUB AN ORDINARY SHOVEL ON ANY ABRASIVE SURFACE, IT WILL BE MAGICALLY TRANSFORMED INTO A COMPOST SHREDDER! YOU CAN SHARPEN IT ON ANY CEMENT PATIO OR SIDEWALK OR USE A GRINDER OR FILE.

Happy Composting!

CHAPTER TWO
PREPARING THE SOIL

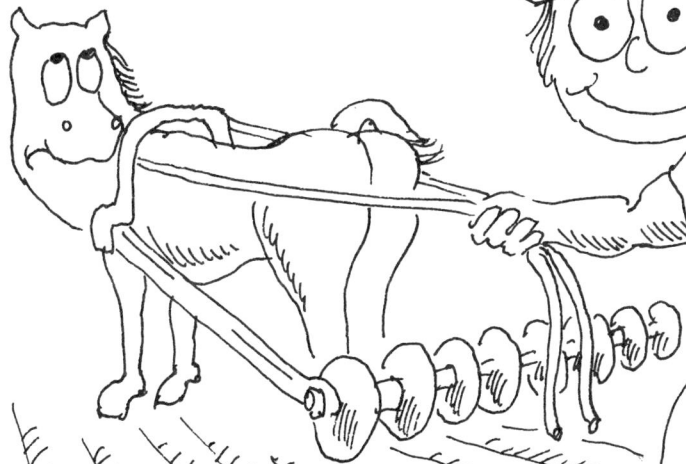

PREPARING THE SOIL

SOIL IS THE MOST IMPORTANT THING FOR PLANT GROWTH. THE SOIL IS THE GUTS, TEETH, TONGUE, AND SALIVA OF THE PLANT. IN PREPARING THE SOIL, YOU ARE ACTUALLY PREPARING PART OF THE PLANTS THEMSELVES!

WHEN WE ANIMALS BITE OFF A PIECE OF FOOD AND CHEW IT, THE ENZYMES IN OUR SALIVA START TO BREAK DOWN THE LARGE PROTEIN, CARBOHYDRATE, AND FAT MOLECULES, A PROCESS WHICH IS COMPLETED IN THE STOMACH AND INTESTINES, AIDED BY THE BACTERIA IN OUR GUTS.

PLANTS DON'T HAVE GUTS, TEETH, SALIVA, OR INTESTINAL BACTERIA. THEIR FOOD MUST BE CHEWED AND DIGESTED FOR THEM BY THE BACTERIA AND FUNGI IN THE SOIL. AND THE SOIL MUST HAVE A CERTAIN STRUCTURE AND CHEMISTRY, OR THE BACTERIA WON'T BE ABLE TO DO THEIR JOB. IT'S NO WONDER THAT SO MANY PLANT DISEASES STEM FROM SOIL PROBLEMS! SOIL PROBLEMS ARE INTESTINAL AILMENTS FOR PLANTS. WHEN WE STICK A SHOVEL INTO THE SOIL TO REMEDY A SOIL PROBLEM, WE ARE ACTUALLY SURGEONS MAKING INCISIONS WITH A SCALPEL. AS WITH ANY SURGICAL OPERATION, THIS MUST BE DONE VERY CAREFULLY.

WE ANIMALS HAVE PACKAGED A BIT OF THE SOIL TO CARRY AROUND WITH US, COMPLETE WITH BACTERIA. THAT MAKES US PORTABLE, LIKE A "BOOM BOX" TAPE PLAYER. WE ARE "AC/DC," BUT PLANTS ARE STRICTLY "AC"--THEY MUST REMAIN PLUGGED-IN TO RECEIVE THE ENERGY AND LIFE-FORCE FLOWING THROUGH THE SOIL.

ANIMALS

PLANTS

GETTING INTO IT

GO OUTSIDE. FIND A PATCH OF SOIL. SIT DOWN IN IT. (DON'T WORRY ABOUT GETTING DIRTY--WEAR OLD CLOTHES.) STICK YOUR HANDS IN THE SOIL. RUN YOUR HANDS THROUGH IT UNTIL YOU FIND A CLOD. SQUEEZE THE CLOD. FEEL THE POWDER OOZING THROUGH YOUR FINGERS. GET INTO THE SENSUAL FEELING OF IT.

NOW SQUIRT SOME WATER ON THE SOIL. RUN YOUR HANDS THROUGH THE MUD. WHAT DOES IT FEEL LIKE? IS IT SLIMY AND OOZY LIKE CLAY? OR IS IT GRITTY AND CRUMBLY LIKE SAND? RIGHT AWAY, YOU'VE ESTABLISHED SOMETHING VERY IMPORTANT ABOUT YOUR SOIL: IT'S TEXTURE.

NOW PAT THE MUD INTO A FLAT DISC, AND SET IT IN THE SUN TO DRY. REMEMBER MUDPIES? THAT'S SOIL SCIENCE, AT ITS MOST FUNDAMENTAL AND PRACTICAL LEVEL. WE ALL HAVE AN IMMENSE STORE OF SOIL SCIENCE KNOWLEDGE, FROM OUR CHILDHOOD EXPERIENCE IN MAKING MUDPIES. MUCH OF LEARNING HOW TO GARDEN IS A RE-AWAKENING OF THIS KNOWLEDGE.

GRAB A PINCH OF SOIL, AND HOLD IT UP TO THE LIGHT ABOUT FOUR INCHES FROM YOUR EYES. REALLY FOCUS IN ON IT--A SMALL MAGNIFYING GLASS HELPS.

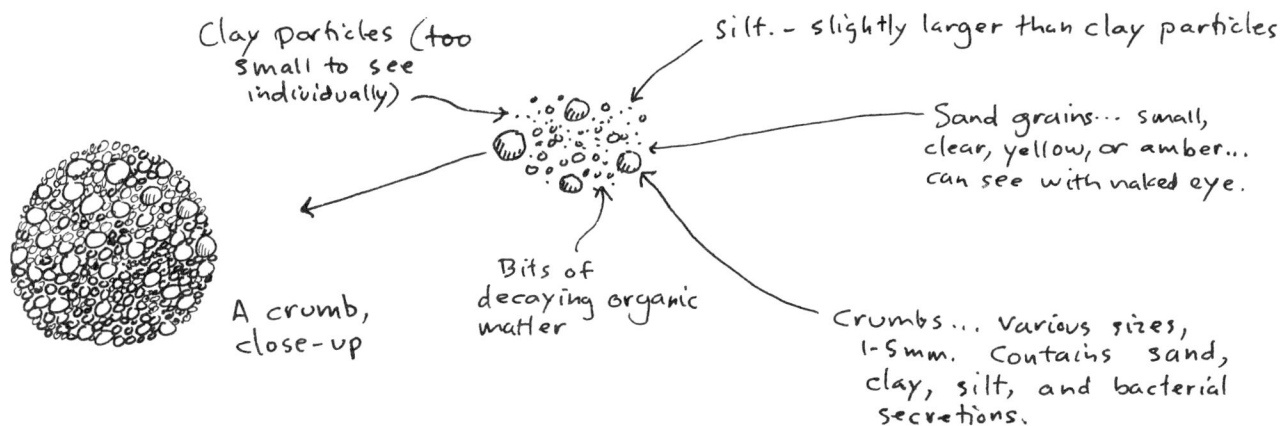

Clay particles (too small to see individually)

Silt. - slightly larger than clay particles

Sand grains... small, clear, yellow, or amber... can see with naked eye.

A crumb, close-up

Bits of decaying organic matter

Crumbs... various sizes, 1-5mm. Contains sand, clay, silt, and bacterial secretions.

IT SHOULD LOOK LIKE THE ABOVE. LARGE CRUMBS, SMALL CRUMBS, AND A FEW INDIVIDUAL SAND GRAINS. THIS IS "GOOD SOIL STRUCTURE." NOT CLODS, OR POWDER, BUT SOMEWHERE IN BETWEEN. IT'S EASY TO TELL IF YOU HAVE THIS SORT OF SOIL STRUCTURE. JUST GET DOWN ON YOUR KNEES, GRAB A LITTLE SOIL, SQUEEZE IT, AND EYEBALL IT. YOU DON'T NEED ANY OTHER ELABORATE TEST EQUIPMENT THAN THE TWO ELECTROMAGNETIC RADIATION DETECTION DEVICES MOUNTED ON YOUR FACE.

AND THAT'S SOIL STRUCTURE. TOGETHER, SOIL TEXTURE AND STRUCTURE MAKE UP 50 PERCENT OF SOIL SCIENCE. YOU ARE NOW A SOIL SCIENTIST. EASY, ISN'T IT?

NOW THAT YOU ARE A SOIL SCIENTIST, IT'S TIME TO DO SOME MORE SOPHISTICATED TESTS. THIS NEXT TEST IS SLIGHTLY HIGH-TECH, SINCE YOU'LL NEED A SHOVEL. WATER THE SOIL FIRST. THEN TRY TO THRUST YOUR SHOVEL INTO THE SOIL, WITHOUT USING YOUR FEET. IMAGINE THE SHOVEL IS A ROOT TRYING TO GET THROUGH THE SOIL. IF YOU CAN'T EASILY THRUST YOUR SHOVEL IN 6" WITH ONE HAND, THE SOIL IS **COMPACTED**, AND WILL HAVE TO BE TILLED. TO SEE WHY, WE'LL HAVE TO GET MICROSCOPIC...

GOOD SOIL IS LIKE BREAD

IN THE HIGH-TECH SHOVEL TEST THE SHOVEL SHOULD SLIP EASILY INTO THE SOIL, LIKE A KNIFE INTO FRESH-BAKED BREAD. THE ANALOGY IS NO MERE COINCIDENCE, FOR IN MANY WAYS GOOD SOIL IS LIKE BREAD:

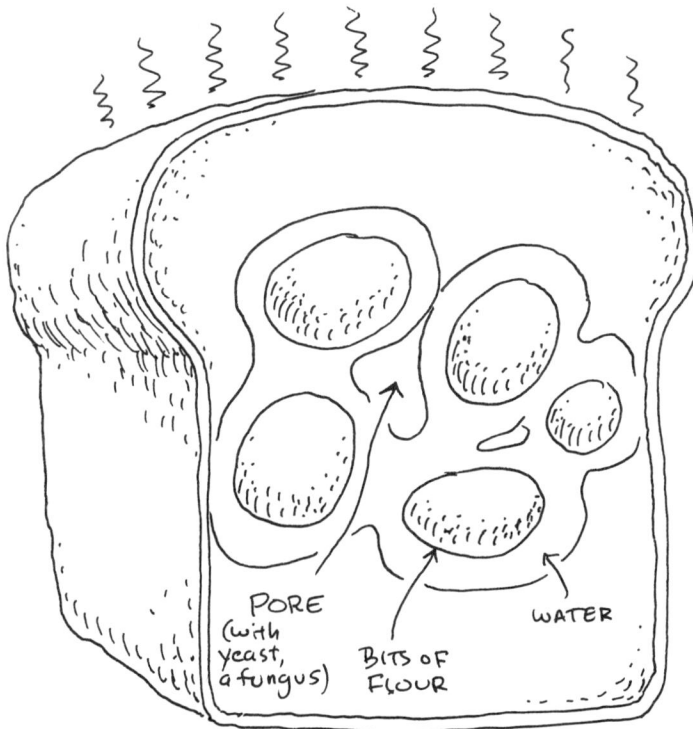

PORE (with yeast, a fungus)

BITS OF FLOUR

WATER

BREAD

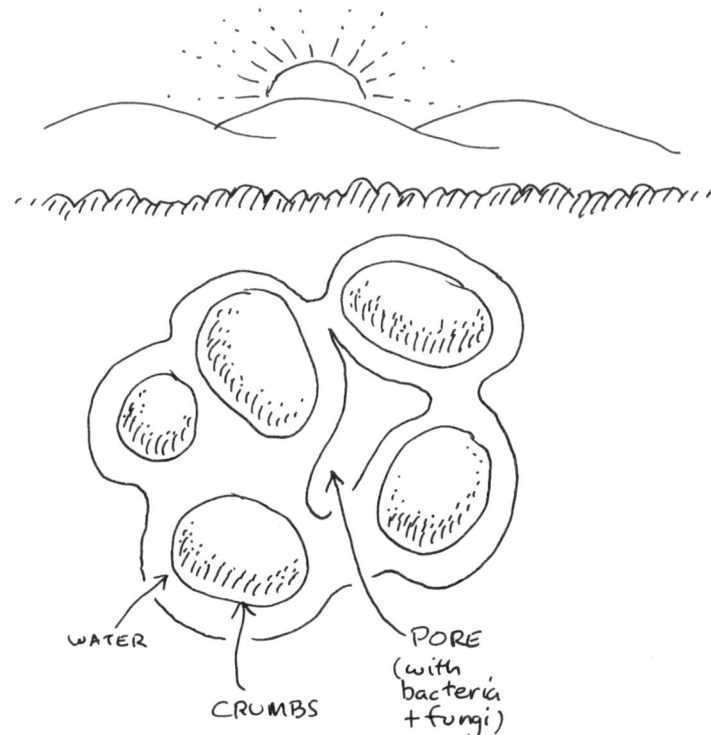

WATER

CRUMBS

PORE (with bacteria + fungi)

SOIL

BOTH SOIL AND BREAD SHOULD BE WARM, DARK BROWN, AND FRAGRANT, WITH THE SAME GRANULAR STRUCTURE. BOTH ARE ESSENTIALLY **ALIVE**, IN THAT THEY ARE FULL OF MICROORGANISMS (BACTERIA IN SOIL, YEAST IN BREAD) WHICH HELP CREATE THE POROUS STRUCTURE. BOTH CONTAIN SMALL PARTICLES AS BASIC STRUCTURAL COMPONENTS (FLOUR GRAINS IN BREAD, SAND/SILT/CLAY IN SOIL), WHICH ARE CEMENTED TOGETHER TO FORM CRUMBS WITH PORES IN BETWEEN THE CRUMBS.

SO WHILE YOU'RE AT IT, GO AHEAD AND MAKE A MUDPIE, FOR OLD TIME'S SAKE. TO AVOID JEOPARDIZING YOUR NEW STATUS AS A SOIL SCIENTIST, BE SURE NO ONE ON THE NOBEL PRIZE COMMITTEE IS WATCHING!

BACTERIA: MASTER CRUMB-MASONS

ONE OF THE ESSENTIAL PARTS OF GOOD SOIL IS THE CRUMBS, SINCE CRUMBS HELP MAINTAIN THE POROUS STRUCTURE OF THE SOIL. SOIL PORES ALLOW THE PLANT TO BREATH, AND THEY ALLOW ROOTS AND WORMS TO TRAVEL EASILY THROUGH THE SOIL. MOST IMPORTANTLY, PORES ARE HOMES FOR SOIL BACTERIA:

Organically-secreted MORTAR for all your building needs

BACTERIA ARE THE LITTLE MASONS OF THE SOIL, BUILDING MICROBE CONDOMINIUMS. ZOOMING DOWN FOR A MICROSCOPIC VIEW OF THE WORKSITE, WE SEE MILLIONS OF HARD-HATTED BACTERIAL CONSTRUCTION WORKERS SWARMING AROUND, STACKING UP SPHERICAL BRICKS MADE OF QUARTZ. THE BACTERIA SECRETE THEIR "MORTAR" THROUGH THEIR ENTIRE BODY SURFACE, ROLLING OVER THE BRICKS AND COATING THEM WITH THE STICKY SUBSTANCE. THEN THEY STACK THE MORTAR-COATED BRICKS INTO LARGE BALLS, THE SOIL CRUMBS. THE SPACES BETWEEN THE CRUMBS FORM THE SOIL PORES. FROM THE BACTERIA'S POINT OF VIEW, THE PORES ARE HUGE STONE CATHEDRALS—IMMENSE DOMED AND ARCHED STRUCTURES; A LABYRINTHINE SYSTEM OF SUBTERRANEAN CHAMBERS AND HALLS STRETCHING (FOR ALL THEY KNOW) TO INFINITY.

AS WE SAW LAST CHAPTER, THE ACTIVITIES OF BACTERIA OFTEN BENEFIT PLANTS AS WELL. AND SOIL CRUMB-PORE STRUCTURE IS NO EXCEPTION. PLANTS NEED OXYGEN TO TURN ON THEIR NUTRIENT PUMPS, AS WE CAN SEE IN THIS "ELECTRON FUNKO-GRAPH" PICTURE:

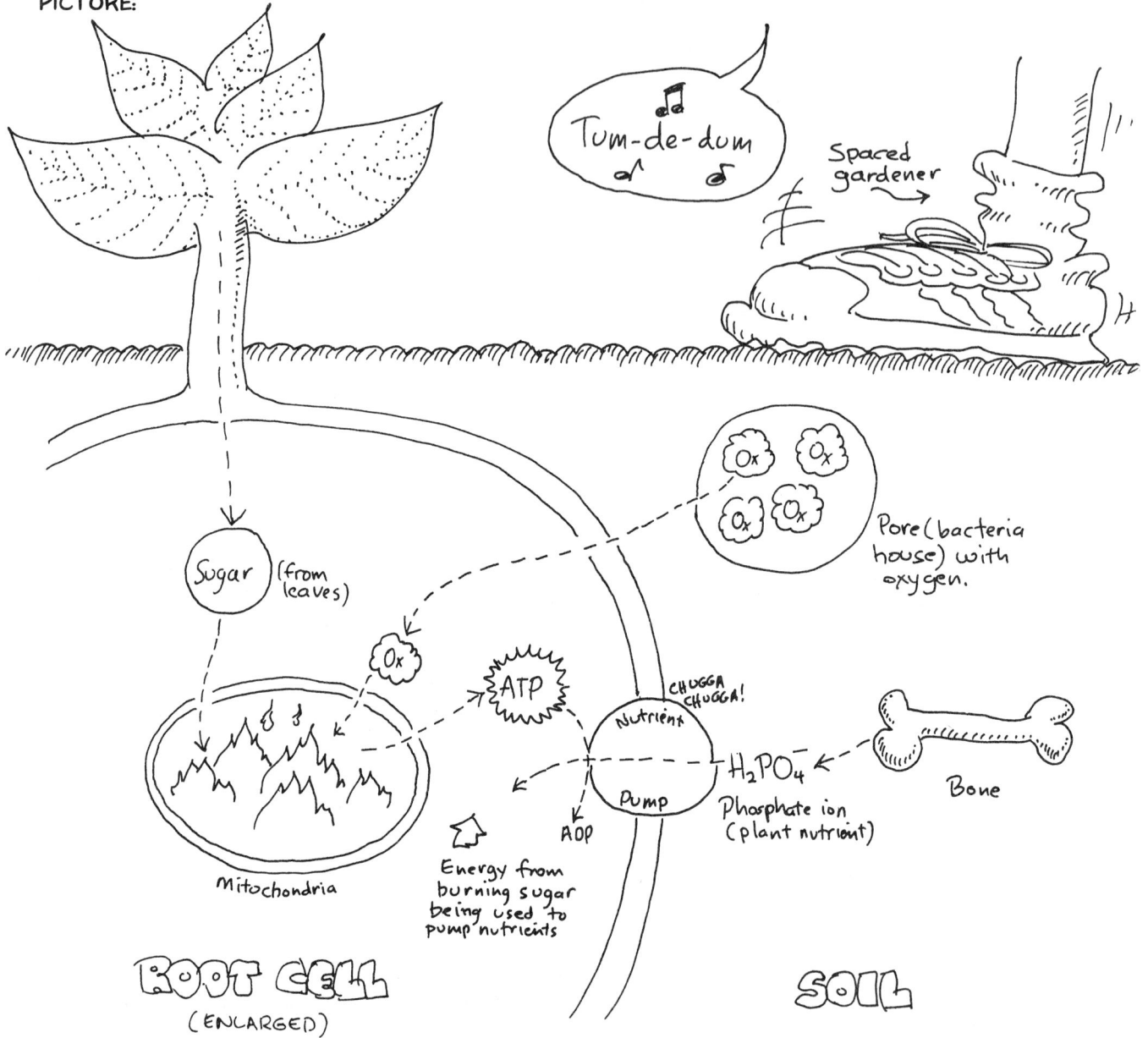

Tum-de-dum

Spaced gardener

Pore (bacteria house) with oxygen.

Sugar (from leaves)

O_x

ATP

CHUGGA CHUGGA!

Nutrient Pump

$H_2PO_4^-$

Phosphate ion (plant nutrient)

Bone

ADP

Energy from burning sugar being used to pump nutrients

Mitochondria

ROOT CELL (ENLARGED)

SOIL

"ONLY TILL IF YOUR HAVE TO," THAT'S WHAT THE SOIL BACTERIA ARE TELLING US. IF YOU TILL SOIL THAT ALREADY HAS GOOD PORE STRUCTURE, YOU'LL ACTUALLY MAKE MATTERS WORSE BY SHATTERING THE CRUMBS THE BACTERIA HAVE BUILT. THAT'S ALSO WHY WALKING ON THE SOIL (LIKE THE "SPACED GARDENER" IN THE ABOVE PICTURE) IS SUCH A NO-NO. WHEN YOU COMPACT THE SOIL, YOU CRUSH THE BACTERIA HOUSES, DRIVE OUT THE AIR, PUT OUT THE LITTLE FIRES IN THE ROOT CELLS, AND THE PLANTS DO POORLY, OR EVEN DIE.

SO IT ALL COMES DOWN TO **AIR.** "GOOD TILTH," "GOOD SOIL STRUCTURE," AND "AERATED SOIL" ALL MEAN PORES, OR AIR POCKETS. AIR IS LIFE.

EVEN THE WORD "PORE" SUGGESTS THE SOIL IS A LIVING PART OF THE PLANT, LIKE THE ALVEOLI OF OUR LUNGS, BRANCHING OUT IN EVER-INCREASING SURFACES TO RECEIVE THE LIFE-GIVING AIR.

SO IF YOU'RE PLANNING TO TILL, REMEMBER, AS BENNY BACTERIA SAYS, "DON'T BE A SHOVEL MONSTER!"

FIRE + AIR + EARTH + WATER = LIFE

SOIL TEXTURE

A SOIL'S **TEXTURE** IS ANOTHER REASON YOU MIGHT WANT TO WORK THE SOIL, USUALLY TO ADD ORGANIC MATTER (SIFTED COMPOST). "TEXTURE" REFERS TO THE AMOUNTS OF CLAY, SILT, SAND, AND HUMUS (FROM ORGANIC MATTER) IN THE SOIL. THEY MUST ALL BE THERE, IN THE RIGHT BALANCE, OR THE BACTERIA WILL HAVE TROUBLE MAKING CRUMBS, AND THE SOIL WILL HAVE TROUBLE STORING NUTRIENTS (MORE ON THAT IN THE FERTILITY AND CHEMISTRY CHAPTERS).

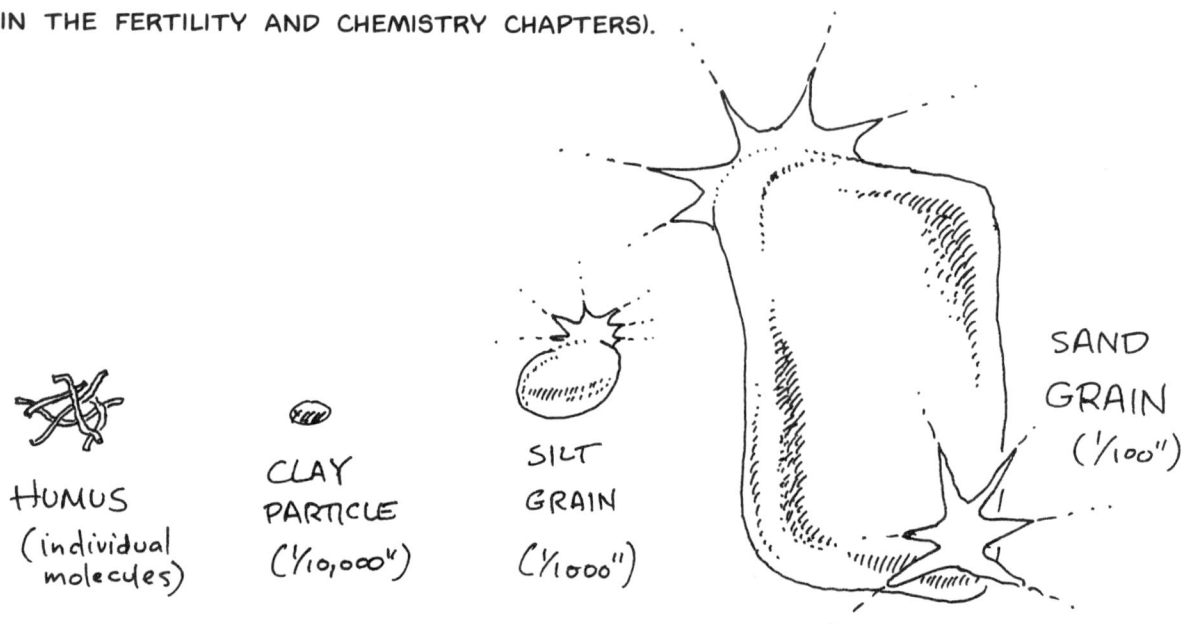

HUMUS
(individual molecules)

CLAY PARTICLE
($1/10,000$")

SILT GRAIN
($1/1000$")

SAND GRAIN
($1/100$")

THE ROLL-A-SNAKE TEST

TO FIND OUT WHAT YOUR SOIL'S TEXTURE IS LIKE, YOU GET TO PLAY IN THE DIRT AGAIN! SCOOP UP A HANDFUL OF SOIL, ADD WATER, AND ROLL A SNAKE, LIKE THIS:

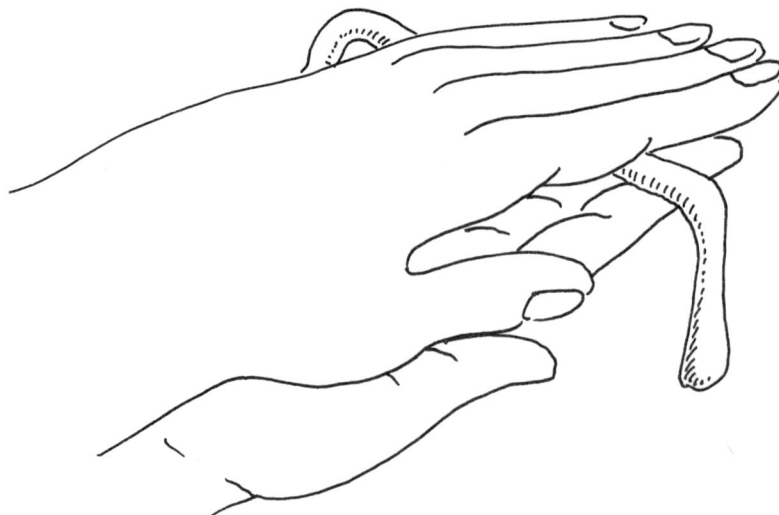

IF YOU CAN ROLL A SOIL "SNAKE" THE THICKNESS OF A PENCIL, AND THEN LIFT UP ONE END WITHOUT BREAKING THE SNAKE, IT MEANS THERE IS TOO MUCH CLAY IN THE SOIL. OR, IF YOU CAN'T ROLL A SNAKE AT ALL, IT MEANS THE SOIL IS TOO SANDY. IN EITHER CASE THE SOLUTION IS THE SAME: ORGANIC MATTER (COMPOST, PREFERABLY, OR GOOD RICH TOPSOIL) MUST BE WORKED INTO THE SOIL. ORGANIC MATTER PROVIDES THE **HUMUS** NECESSARY TO REMEDY AN EXCESS OF EITHER SAND OR CLAY.

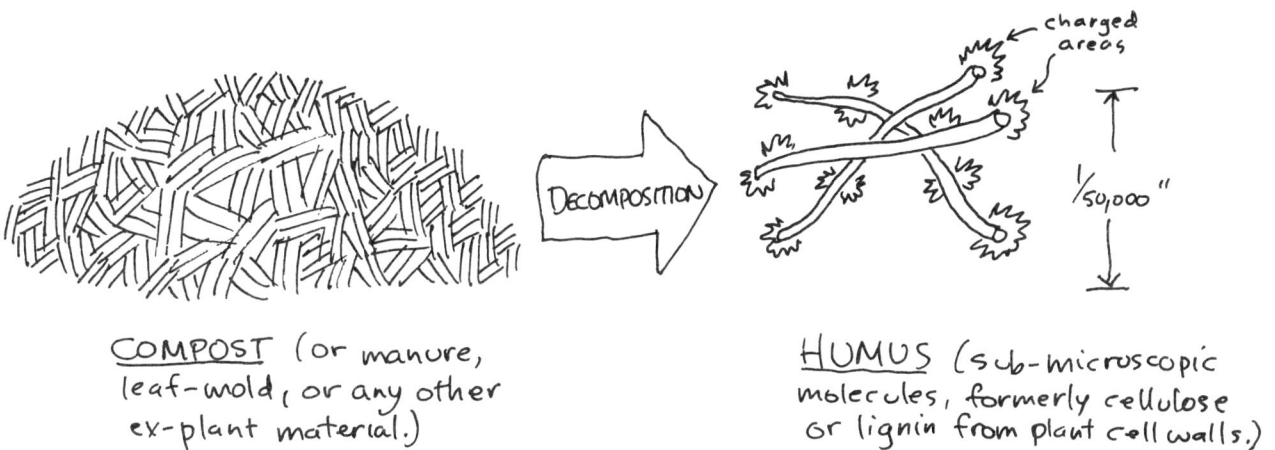

COMPOST (or manure, leaf-mold, or any other ex-plant material.)

HUMUS (sub-microscopic molecules, formerly cellulose or lignin from plant cell walls.)

HUMUS IS LIKE THE JOKER IN THE DECK, SINCE IT CAN PLAY SO MANY ROLES. IT ACTS LIKE LITTLE PIECES OF FOAM RUBBER COATED WITH SUPER-GLUE. BUT MIRACULOUSLY, IT'S A SPECIAL TYPE OF GLUE THAT ATTRACTS SAND GRAINS, BUT REPELS CLAY PARTICLES:

HUMUS CURING SANDY SOIL

HUMUS CURING CLAY SOIL

SO IT GLUES SAND GRAINS TOGETHER, HELPING THE BACTERIA BUILD THEIR CRUMBS, AND IT ALSO DISPERSES CLAY IN THE SOIL, PREVENTING CLAY-CLOD FORMATION.

HUMUS COMES FROM COMPOST, MANURE, OR ANYTHING THAT USED TO BE PART OF A PLANT. IT'S ACTUALLY STILL A PART OF THE PLANT IN EFFECT, SINCE IT IS MADE OF MODIFIED CELLULOSE AND LIGNIN MOLECULES (FROM PLANT CELL WALLS) THAT PERFORM NEW FUNCTIONS FOR THE PLANT ONCE THEY'RE IN THE SOIL (WHICH, REMEMBER, IS PART OF THE PLANT).

HUMUS ALSO HELPS STORE PLANT NUTRIENTS IN THE SOIL, SINCE ITS CHARGED, "STICKY" AREAS ATTRACT SMALL POSITIVE IONS THAT PLANTS NEED:

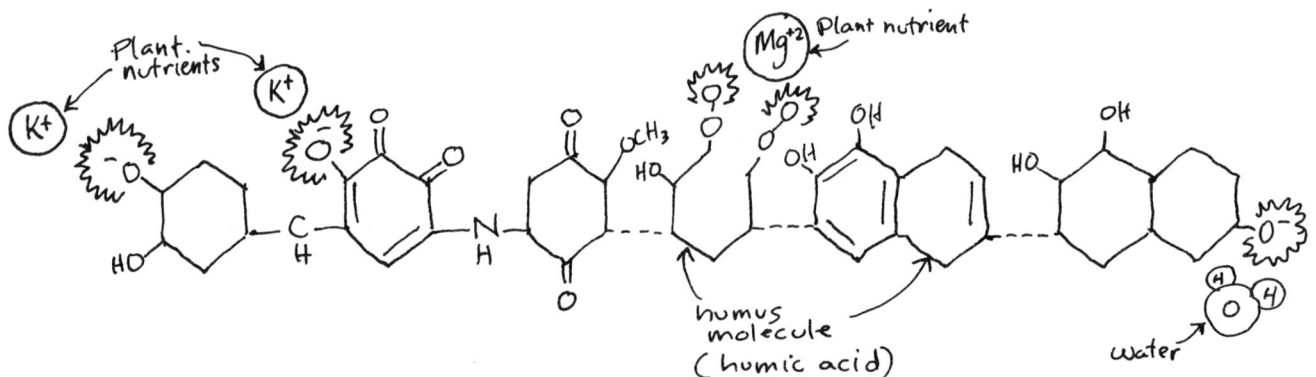

humus molecule (humic acid)

IT ALSO ATTRACTS WATER (AS SHOWN), SO IT'S IMPORTANT FOR WATER CONSERVATION. AS IF ALL THAT WEREN'T ENOUGH, HUMUS ALSO BUFFERS THE SOIL AGAINST WIDE SWINGS IN ACID/ALKALINE (PH) BALANCE. (MORE ON SOIL PH IN CHAPTER 3.)

SO HUMUS DOES EVERYTHING! IT WILL IMPROVE YOUR SOIL TEXTURE AND STRUCTURE, ITS NUTRIENT-STORAGE CAPACITY, SOIL MOISTURE RETENTION, PH BALANCE... GET SOME TODAY!

THE THIRD REASON TO WORK THE SOIL (AFTER IMPROVING SOIL STRUCTURE AND TEXTURE) IS TO ADD COMPOST TO THE SOIL AS FERTILIZER. MANY ORGANIC GARDENERS THINK COMPOST SHOULD BE DUG-IN ONLY ONCE--WHEN THE GARDEN IS FIRST ESTABLISHED. AFTER THAT, THE COMPOST SHOULD BE ADDED TO THE SURFACE AS MULCH. THIS MAKES SENSE, SINCE IF YOU KEEP ADDING COMPOST ON TOP OF THE SOIL, WHAT YOU ADD TODAY WILL END UP TWO FEET UNDER IN A FEW YEARS. SO THE SAME END RESULT AS DIGGING-IN IS ACCOMPLISHED, BUT WITHOUT THE DAMAGE TO CRUMB STRUCTURE THAT INEVITABLY OCCURS WHEN YOU DISTURB THE SOIL.

IF YOU'RE DIGGING IN THE COMPOST FOR A NEW GARDEN, YOU CAN ADD HALF-FINISHED COMPOST (OR MANURE, OR EVEN FRESH WEEDS) TWO OR THREE FEET DOWN, BUT YOU MUST USE SIFTED COMPOST IN THE TOP SOIL LEVELS, TO MAKE SURE WHAT YOU ADD IS FINISHED DECOMPOSING. BY THE TIME THE ROOTS REACH DOWN TO THE LOWER LEVELS, THE COMPOST SHOULD BE FINISHED DOWN THERE.

WHEN TO TILL?

OKAY, YOU'VE DECIDED YOU REALLY MUST DIG UP YOUR SOIL, AND YOU'VE BALANCED THE PROS AND CONS OF MESSING WITH ALL THOSE BACTERIA CONDOS. BUT WAIT A MINUTE! BEFORE YOU RUSH OUT WITH YOUR SHOVEL AND START MAKING YOUR BACKYARD LOOK LIKE THE PANAMA CANAL, MAKE SURE THE MOISTURE CONTENT OF THE SOIL IS RIGHT. IF IT'S BEEN RAINING A LOT, THE SOIL IS PROBABLY TOO WET TO WORK. IF IT'S SPRINGTIME, I KNOW YOU'RE JUST ITCHING TO GET OUT THERE AND CAVORT WITH THE BIRDS AND BEES, BUT THIS IS IMPORTANT, SO PAY ATTENTION.

TO TEST THE SOIL MOISTURE, DIG UP A SHOVELFUL OF SOIL. IT SHOULD FALL RIGHT OFF THE SHOVEL WHEN YOU BANG IT LIGHTLY ON THE GROUND. IF IT STICKS TO THE SHOVEL AT ALL, THE SOIL IS TOO WET TO BE WORKED.

WHY TOO WET? BECAUSE IF YOU COMPRESS ANY MATERIAL WHEN IT'S WET, IT DRIES HARDER AND DENSER THAN IT WAS BEFORE. WET-COMPACTION IS HOW BRICKS ARE MADE, AND HOW FELT IS MADE FROM WOOL. TRANSLATED TO THE SOIL, WET-COMPACTION MEANS YOU END UP WITH CLODS:

1. WETTING   2. EXPANSION   3. COMPRESSION   4. DRYING

THIS GOES FOR TILLING ALSO, BECAUSE IF YOU TRY TO WORK WET SOIL, YOU CAN'T HELP COMPRESSING PARTS OF IT. A SHOVEL HARDENS THE SURFACE OF EVERY BITE IT TAKES.

ON THE OTHER HAND, IT'S JUST AS BAD TO WORK THE SOIL WHEN IT'S TOO DRY, SINCE IT WILL JUST SHATTER INTO DUST. IF YOU HAVE TROUBLE GETTING YOUR SHOVEL INTO THE SOIL (USING BOTH HANDS AND ONE FOOT), IT'S TOO DRY TO WORK.

YOU MUST TILL THE SOIL WHEN IT'S NEITHER TOO WET OR TOO DRY, BUT PART-WAY IN BETWEEN. TO GET THE PROPER SOIL MOISTURE, FIRST SATURATE THE SOIL, AND THEN LET IT DRY PART-WAY. SIMPLY WATERING THE SOIL BRIEFLY WON'T WORK, BECAUSE THE WATER WILL JUST SATURATE THE TOP FEW INCHES. SO SATURATE THE SOIL AS DEEP AS YOU WANT TO TILL, BY SPRINKLING LIGHTLY FOR ABOUT AN HOUR. THE NEXT TWO PAGES EXPLAIN THE WHOLE SITUATION...

SOIL MOISTURE

SATURATION Mud

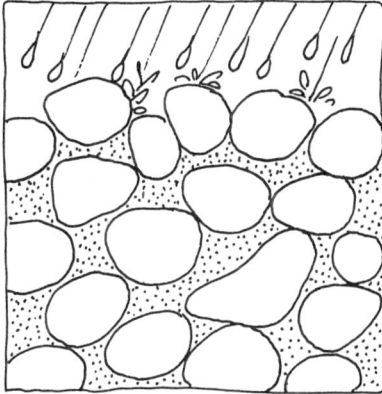

RIGHT AFTER WATER ENTERS THE SOIL, IT FILLS UP ALL THE SPACES BETWEEN THE CRUMBS. THE SOIL IS "MUDDY," AND STICKS TO THE SHOVEL. PLANTS CAN'T GROW WHEN THE SOIL IS THIS WET, BECAUSE THERE'S NO AIR FOR ROOTS TO BREATH FOR ENERGY, WHICH THEY NEED TO PUMP IN NUTRIENTS.

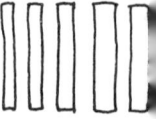

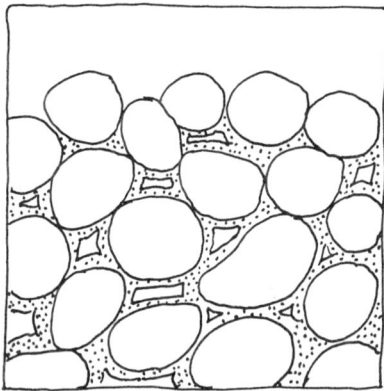

FIELD CAPACITY "Wet Soil"

WATER MOVES DOWN THROUGH THE SOIL, DRAWN BY THE EARTH'S GRAVITY. AS IT MOVES DOWNWARD, IT LEAVES THE LARGER SOIL PORES ONLY LINED WITH WATER, ENCLOSING POCKETS OF AIR. NOW THE PLANTS CAN BREATH, AND BEGIN PUMPING IN NUTRIENTS.

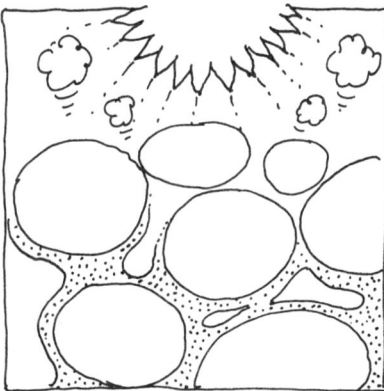

EVAPORATION & ROOT UPTAKE "Slightly Moist Soil"

THIS IS THE MAGIC TIME, WHEN EVERYTHING IS HAPPENING. WATER STARTS MOVING UPWARD IN THE SOIL, EVAPORATING FROM THE SURFACE, AND WATER DOWN BELOW COMES UP TO REPLACE IT. ALSO, WATER IS MOVING INTO THE ROOTS BY OSMOSIS. THIS IS THE RIGHT TIME FOR TILLING, PULLING WEEDS, TRANS-PLANTING SEEDLINGS, AND HARVESTING ROOT CROPS.

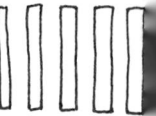

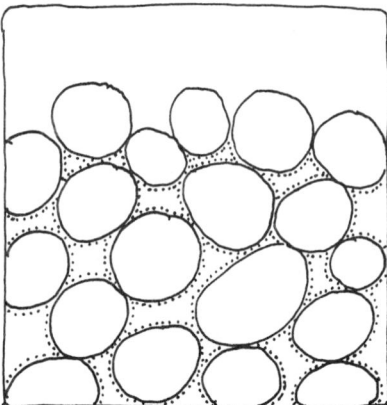

WILTING POINT "Dry Soil"

SOME WATER IS STILL IN THE SOIL, BUT ONLY IN THIN FILMS SURROUNDING THE SOIL CRUMBS. (THIS IS THE SITUATION MOST OF THE TIME IN DESERT SOIL.) MOST PLANTS WILT AT THIS POINT, SINCE WHAT LITTLE WATER THERE IS CLINGS TIGHTLY TO THE SOIL CRUMBS.

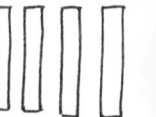

& TILLING

IF YOU TILL WHEN THE SOIL IS TOO WET, IT FORMS CHUNKS, WHICH THEN DRY TO FORM **CLODS!** AS YOU CAN SEE, THE CHUNKS ARE FORMED BY CRUMBS IN CLOSER-PACKED POSITIONS THAN THEY ARE IN THE REST OF THE SOIL.

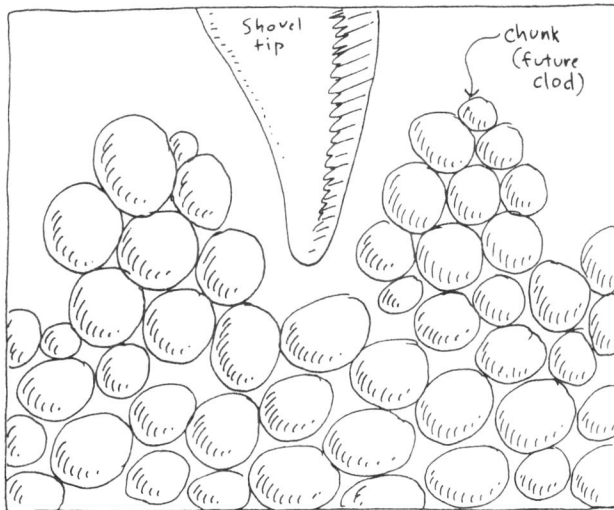

Shovel tip

chunk (future clod)

THIS IS THE RIGHT TIME TO TILL: NOT TOO WET, NOT TOO DRY.

IF YOU TILL WHEN THE SOIL IS TOO DRY, YOU TURN THE SOIL INTO POWDER-- AND WHEN THE POWDER IS WET AGAIN AND DRIED, IT REFORMS INTO **CLODS!**

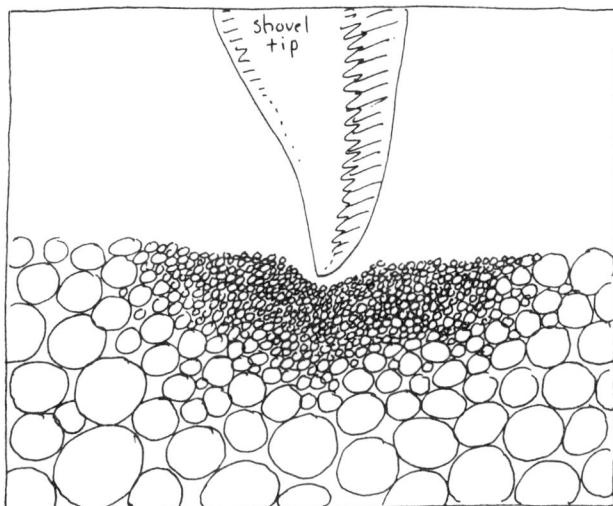

shovel tip

WHEN THE SOIL DRIES TO PARTLY-MOIST, THE SOIL PORES WILL BE LINED WITH A THIN FILM OF WATER. YOUR SHOVEL WILL GO IN EASILY AND COME OUT CLEAN. WHEN THE SOIL IS SLIGHTLY MOIST IS WHAT I CALL THE "MAGIC TIME" IN THE GARDEN. IT'S THE BEST TIME FOR MOST GARDENING ACTIVITIES: WORKING THE SOIL, HARVESTING ROOT CROPS, PULLING UP OLD PLANTS, PULLING WEEDS, AND TRANSPLANTING. IT'S ALSO WHEN PLANTS ARE ACTIVELY GROWING.

WORKING THE SOIL AT THIS SLIGHTLY-MOIST TIME IS A JOY. IF THE SOIL IS EITHER WETTER OR DRIER THAN THIS, TILLING IS VERY DIFFICULT (AND IT WILL HURT THE SOIL STRUCTURE AS WELL). SO SATURATE THE SOIL, LET IT DRY AWHILE, AND THEN TEST IT WITH A SHOVEL (THE PAIN-IN-THE-BUTT-TEST). IF YOU FIND YOURSELF SAYING "ARRGH!" A LOT, THAT MEANS THE SOIL IS EITHER TOO WET OR TOO DRY. DIGGING SOIL IS LIKE MOST EVERYTHING: IF YOU'RE DOING IT RIGHT, IT'S EASY AND FUN.

The Pain-In-The-Butt Test

FOR SMALL-SCALE OPERATIONS (INCLUDING MOST BACKYARDS), THERE'S NOTHING LIKE THE GOOD SWEATY EXERCISE, TENDER LOVING CARE, AND DIRECT GARDENER-TO-SOIL CONTACT OF HAND-TILLING.

TILLING BY HAND, YOU CAN SEE WHAT SORT OF CRITTERS ARE IN YOUR SOIL: BENEFICIAL WORMS, HARMFUL PEST LARVAE, JERUSALEM CRICKETS, SNAIL EGGS, AND THE CENTIPEDES AND MILLIPEDES––BEAUTIFUL LITTLE KINETIC SCULPTURES UNDULATING AND RIPPLING THROUGH THE SOIL CRUMBS. YOU CAN GET A DIRECT FEELING FOR THE DIFFERENT SOIL STRATA: THE HUMUS-RICH A-LAYER, THE TRANSITIONAL B-LAYER, AND THE CLAY-RICH C-LAYER, WHICH OCCUR AT VARYING DEPTHS IN DIFFERENT SOILS. BEST OF ALL, YOU CAN AVOID THE NOISY, SMELLY, INTERNAL-COMBUSTION MANIA THAT PERVADES THE LATE PETROLEUM ERA OF OUR MODERN BABYLONIAN CULTURE.

IF YOU'RE TILLING TO IMPROVE SOIL STRUCTURE, FIRST YOU'LL WANT TO LOOSEN THE SOIL AND BREAK UP THE CLODS. I USE THE "SCOOP, CHOP, AND WHAP" METHOD:

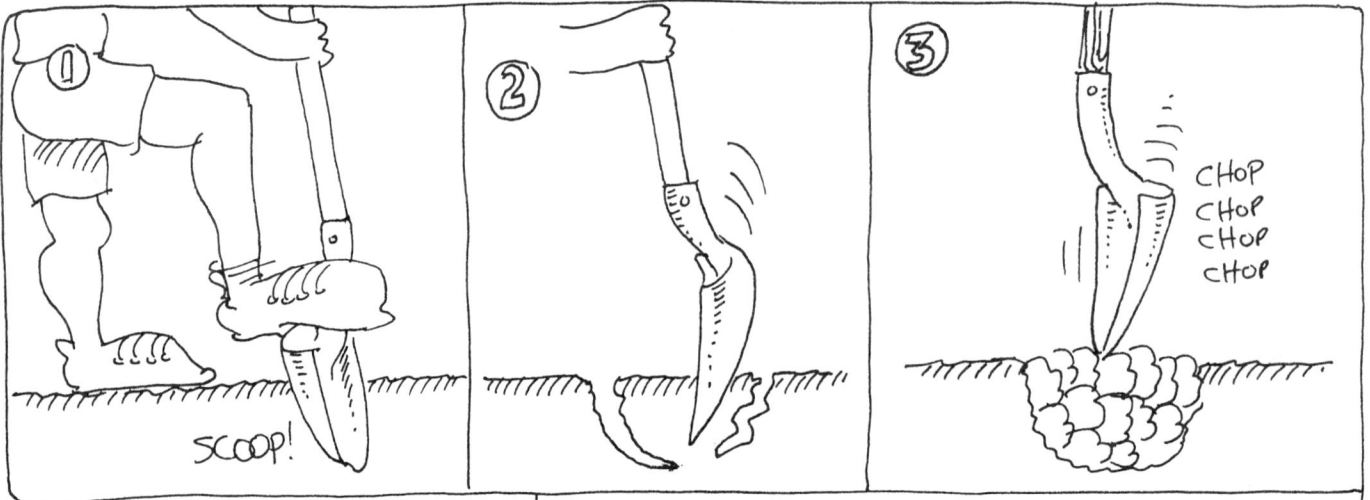

1. TAKE YOUR SHOVEL AND SCOOP A FOOT-DEEP SLIT IN THE SOIL. DO **NOT** LIFT OR TURN OVER THIS SHOVELFUL. JUST CUT A SLIT AND LIFT THE SHOVEL OUT, CREATING AN OVERHANGING CLUMP OF SOIL.

2. THEN REVERSE THE SHOVEL AND BREAK OFF THE OVERHANGING CLUMP.

3. NEXT, CHOP UP THE CLUMP INTO SMALLER CLUMPS THE SIZE OF BASEBALLS. (IF THE CHOPPING IS AT ALL DIFFICULT, THE SOIL IS EITHER TOO WET OR TOO DRY.) IF YOU'RE ADDING COMPOST OR OTHER ORGANIC MATTER, YOU CAN DO THAT NOW. PUT AT LEAST A 2-INCH LAYER OF WELL-SIFTED COMPOST ON TOP OF THE BASEBALL-CHUNKS.

4. TAKE A PITCHFORK, AND WHAP THE CLUMPS. IT'S EASIEST TO GRIP THE FORK AT THE END OF THE HANDLE AND LET IT FALL FROM EYE-LEVEL, LETTING THE WEIGHT OF THE FORK DO THE WHAPPING. KEEP IT UP UNTIL ALL THE SOIL CONSISTS OF 1–5MM CRUMBS, TO A DEPTH OF ONE FOOT (AT LEAST). ESSENTIALLY, YOU ARE MIMICKING THE ACTION OF BACTERIA IN THEIR HOUSE-BUILDING ACTIVITIES, GIVING THEM THEIR FIRST HOME IN THE SOIL. LATER THEY WILL BE ABLE TO DO THE JOB THEMSELVES, WHILE YOU SIT BACK AND WATCH THE PLANTS GROW.

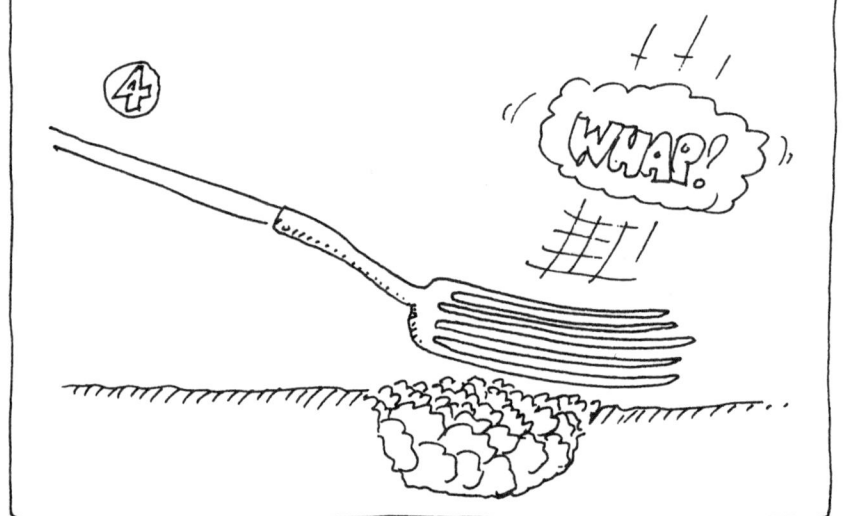

DOUBLE-DIGGING

IF YOU'RE GROWING LARGE, DEEP-ROOTED CROPS (TOMATOES, MELONS, SQUASH, BEANS, CABBAGE, ETC.), IT'S BEST TO "DOUBLE-DIG" THE SOIL THE FIRST YEAR. "DOUBLE-DIGGING," MEANS TILLING THE SUBSOIL AS WELL AS THE TOPSOIL.

DOUBLE-DIGGING IS PART OF THE "FRENCH-INTENSIVE" METHOD, DEVELOPED BY FARMERS NEAR PARIS WHO DIDN'T HAVE MUCH LAND AND WANTED TO MAKE THE MOST OF IT. INDEED, IN CONTROLLED STUDIES THE METHOD HAS BEEN SHOWN TO YIELD TWO OR THREE TIMES AS MUCH AS CONVENTIONAL METHODS. THE TERM "INTENSIVE" IS UNFORTUNATE, SINCE IT GIVES THE IMPRESSION THAT DEEP-DIGGING IS NOT REALLY NECESSARY, BUT RATHER SOMETHING THAT'S DONE BY PARTICULARLY INTENSE SORTS OF PEOPLE. ACTUALLY, IT SHOULD BE THE NORM, WITH CONVENTIONAL SHALLOW-DIGGING CALLED, PERHAPS, THE "LAZY-AMERICAN" METHOD.

HERE'S HOW IT'S DONE. START BY DIGGING A TRENCH 1-2 FEET DEEP (THE DEEPER THE BETTER). PUT THE TOPSOIL YOU REMOVE IN A PILE TO THE SIDE. LAYER ONE FOOT OF SIFTED COMPOST ON THE BOTTOM OF THE TRENCH (FIG. 1):

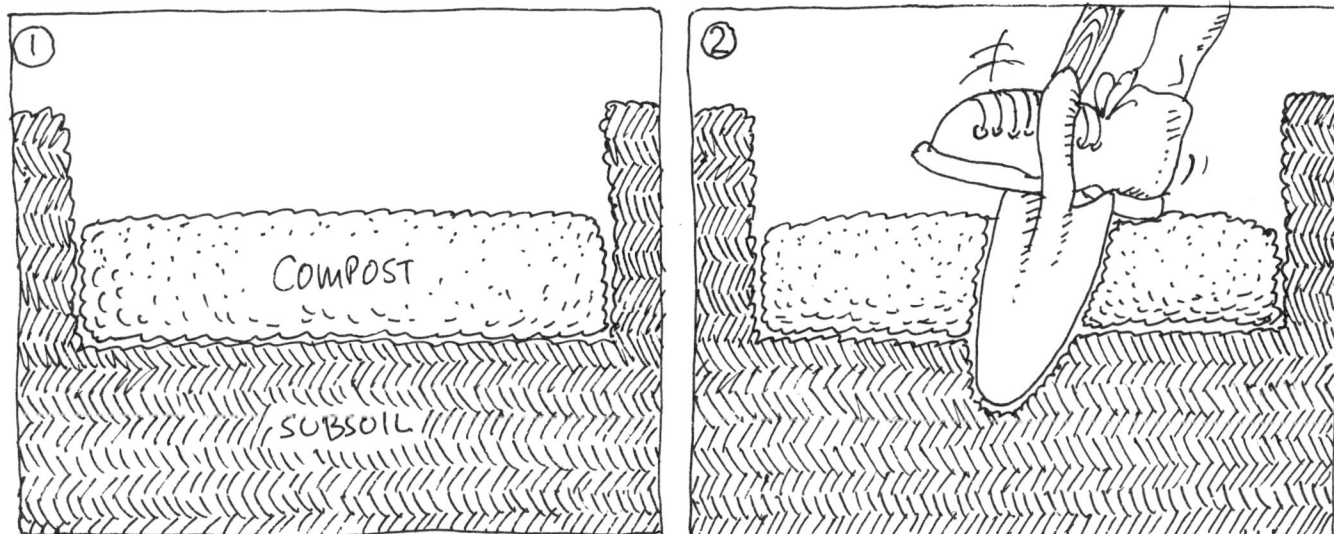

THEN PLUNGE YOUR SHOVEL THROUGH THE COMPOST INTO THE SUBSOIL BENEATH, LIFT UP (SLIGHTLY) A MIXTURE OF SUBSOIL AND COMPOST, AND FLIP IT OVER:

MIX THE COMPOST INTO THE SUBSOIL BY CHOPPING AND STIRRING WITH YOUR SHOVEL, AS IF MIXING EGGS AND FLOUR TO MAKE DOUGH (FIG. 5). THEN FILL IN THE REST OF THE HOLE, ALTERNATING SHOVELFULS OF COMPOST AND TOPSOIL (FIG. 6):

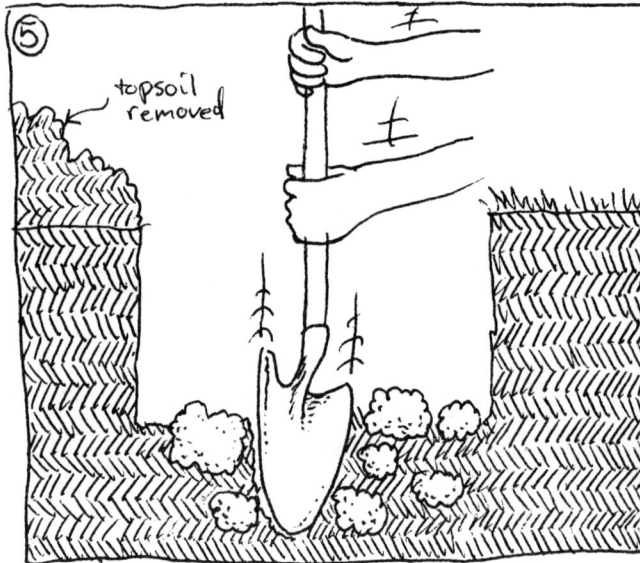

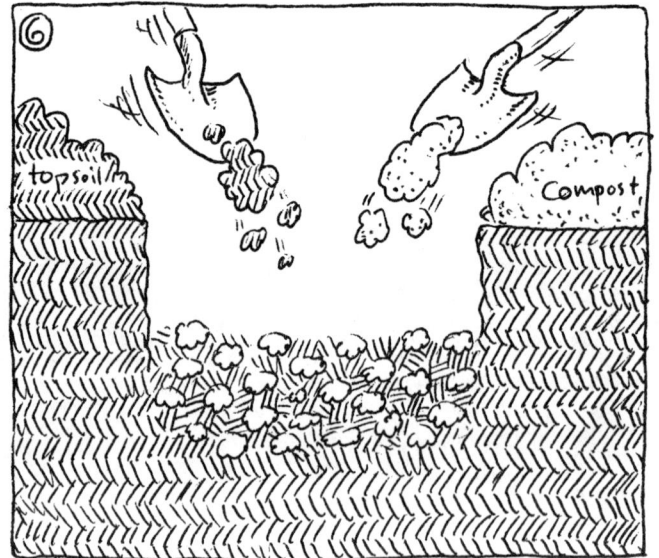

THERE'S NO EASY WAY TO DOUBLE-DIG. JUST TAKE YOUR TIME, AND DON'T EXPECT TO DO THE WHOLE GARDEN IN ONE DAY. IF MUSIC HELPS, PUT ON SOMETHING SOFTLY ENERGETIC LIKE VIVALDI OR JOHN KLEMMER, AIM THE SPEAKERS OUT THE WINDOW, AND BE PREPARED TO SWEAT A LOT.

DON'T FORGET TO MULCH!

HOWEVER YOU TILL, BE IT INTENSIVE OR LAID-BACK, BE SURE TO COVER THE SOIL WITH SOME SORT OF MULCH RIGHT AFTER TILLING, UNLESS YOU PLAN TO SOW SMALL SEEDS THERE IMMEDIATELY. FOR TEMPORARY PURPOSES, THE MULCH CAN JUST BE PIECES OF PLASTIC, CARDBOARD, OR PLYWOOD. MULCH IS NECESSARY TO RETAIN SOIL MOISTURE, KEEPING THE SOIL ALIVE AND PREVENTING THE CRUSTING OF THE SURFACE. (CHAPTER 6 CONTAINS DETAILS ON MULCHING.)

SPECIAL PROBLEMS

IF YOUR SOIL IS VERY HARD AND DRY, WATER WILL JUST RUN OFF WITHOUT PENETRATING, SO YOU CAN'T EVEN GET IT MOIST ENOUGH TO TILL. THIS IS USUALLY THE CASE IF THE SOIL HAS HAD A LOT OF FOOT OR VEHICLE TRAFFIC. (THE PROBLEM CAN BE COMPOUNDED IF THE SOIL IS VERY CLAYEY--THIS COULD MEAN THE TOPSOIL WAS STRIPPED OFF WHEN THE SITE WAS GRADED, AND THE CONTRACTOR DIDN'T BOTHER TO REPLACE IT. IN THAT CASE, YOU SHOULD BRING IN LOTS OF TOPSOIL AND RAISE THE ENTIRE SOIL SURFACE.)

TO DEAL WITH COMPACTED SOIL, YOU MUST PROCEED IN STAGES. FIRST, MULCH THE SURFACE WITH A 2-INCH LAYER OF COMPOST, MANURE, LEAVES, ETC. MULCH IMPROVES WATER PENETRATION BY HOLDING WATER ABOVE THE SOIL AND LETTING IT DRIP DOWN SLOWLY, LIKE A COFFEE POT.

WATER WITH A SPRINKLER OR SOAK-HOSE FOR A FEW HOURS, TO MOISTEN THE TOP INCH ENOUGH SO YOU CAN CUT SLITS IN THE SURFACE. IN EXTREME CASES YOU'LL NEED A PICK TO CUT THE SLITS. THERE'S NO SENSE IN GETTING MACHO ABOUT IT--JUST LIFT THE PICK UP TO EYE-LEVEL AND LET IT FALL, LIKE THIS:

IT'S EASIEST TO HOLD ONE HAND NEAR THE END OF THE PICK AS YOU LIFT, THEN LET IT SLIDE DOWN THE HANDLE AS THE PICK FALLS. YOU DON'T NEED TO SWING THE PICK! JUST LET IT FALL, AND LET THE WEIGHT OF THE PICK DO THE WORK.

ONCE YOU GET THE SLITS OPENED, THINGS WILL GO EASIER. ADD MORE MULCH, AND WATER AGAIN. YOU'LL JUST NEED A SHOVEL NOW, WHICH YOU CAN USE AS A LEVER: STICK IT IN THE SLITS MADE BY THE PICK AND ROCK IT BACKWARDS, USING THE BASE OF THE BLADE AS THE LEVER FULCRUM, LIKE THIS:

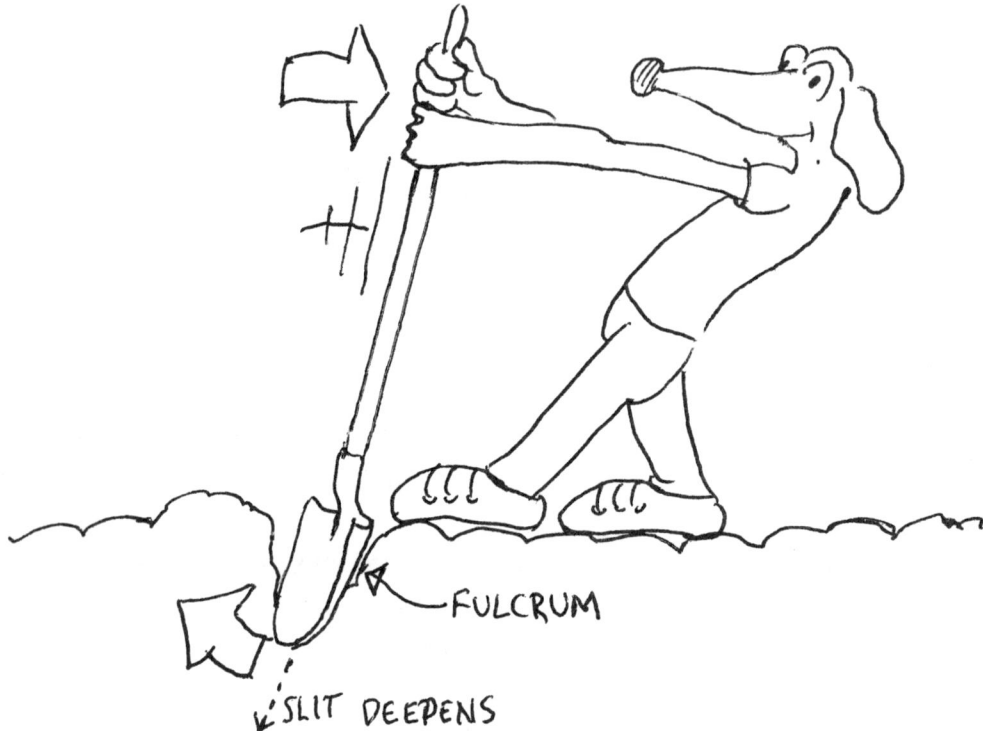

FULCRUM

SLIT DEEPENS

THEN PROCEED TO THE SCOOP, CHOP, AND WHAP METHOD, AND FINALLY YOU CAN DOUBLE-DIG THE SOIL.

LAWN DEMOLITION

IF YOU LIVE IN THE WESTERN U.S. OR OTHER DROUGHT-PRONE AREAS, ONE OF THE MOST ECOLOGICALLY-RIGHTEOUS THINGS YOU CAN DO IS DIG UP A LAWN. LAWNS (IF USED ONLY FOR ORNAMENTAL PURPOSES, AS THEY USUALLY ARE) ARE A TOTAL WASTE-- ESPECIALLY OF WATER. SOMEONE ESTIMATED IF YOU TOOK THE WATER AND FERTILIZER USED ON THE LAWNS OF CEMETARIES AND GOLF COURSES IN THE U.S., YOU COULD

GROW CROPS TO FEED THE ENTIRE COUNTRY OF INDIA (500 MILLION PEOPLE, MOST OF THEM HUNGRY). WHAT THE WORLD NEEDS IS A NEW ECO-GUERRILLA MOVEMENT. THE FIRST STEP IN THIS NEW MOVEMENT IS HOME LAWN DEMOLITION. REMEMBER, REVOLUTION STARTS IN THE HOME!

DIGGING UP A LAWN IS DIFFICULT THOUGH. IT'S HARD TO GET WATER DOWN THROUGH THE DENSE ROOT SYSTEM TO MOISTEN THE SOIL UNDERNEATH . . . IT JUST PUDDLES AND RUNS OFF. THE SOIL WILL PROBABLY BE DRIER ANYWAY THAN SOIL THAT JUST HAD ANNUAL WEEDS ON IT, SINCE THE DENSE NETWORK OF ROOTS AND LEAVES (GRASS "BLADES") IS SO EFFICIENT AT SUCKING WATER UP OUT OF THE SOIL AND EVAPORATING IT INTO THE AIR. (THAT EFFICIENCY IS ALSO WHY LAWNS ARE SUCH WATER HOGS COMPARED TO OTHER GROUNDCOVERS.)

THE FIRST STEP IN LAWN DEMOLITION IS WATERING THE LAWN THOROUGHLY, SPRINKLING FOR AT LEAST AN HOUR. THEN CUT SLITS IN THE SOD WITH A SHARP SHOVEL, ABOUT SIX INCHES DEEP IN STAGGERED ROWS. SHARPEN YOUR SHOVEL WITH A FILE IF NECESSARY. DON'T TRY TO DIG OUT ANY OF THE GRASS YET--THE POINT OF THE SLITS IS JUST TO GET WATER INTO THE ROOT AREA SO YOU CAN SEPARATE THE ROOTS FROM THE SOIL.

NOW WATER AGAIN THOROUGHLY. REALLY FLOOD THE WATER IN. THEN WAIT UNTIL THE SOIL IS DRY ENOUGH TO SHAKE LOOSE EASILY FROM THE ROOTS. IT MAY TAKE AS LITTLE AS TWO HOURS ON A SUNNY, WINDY DAY. THE SOIL WILL DRY FASTER THAN YOU EXPECT, SINCE GRASS BLADES EVAPORATE WATER INTO THE AIR SO FAST.

NOW YOU CAN PRY UP CHUNKS OF SOD. A DIGGING FORK IS BETTER THAN A SHOVEL FOR THIS, FOR THE SAME REASON IT'S EASIER TO EAT SPAGHETTI WITH A FORK THAN A SPOON. BANG THE CHUNKS AGAINST THE SIDE OF YOUR FORK TO REMOVE THE SOIL FROM THE ROOTS, BECAUSE MANY TYPES OF GRASS WILL RESPROUT FROM EVEN VERY SHORT SEGMENTS OF ROOT. BERMUDA GRASS IS ESPECIALLY NOTORIOUS FOR THIS, BUT OTHER TYPES ARE NEARLY AS BAD. ACTUALLY IT'S NOT THE ROOTS THAT ARE THE PROBLEM, BUT THE UNDERGROUND STEMS CALLED "RHIZOMES," WHICH IS HOW THESE TYPES OF GRASS REPRODUCE THEMSELVES:

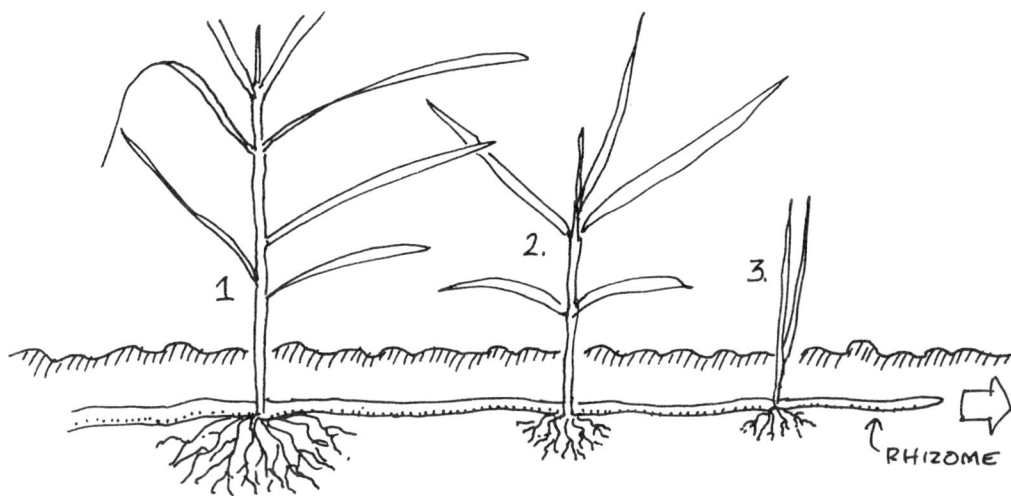

1

2.

3.

RHIZOME

THE RHIZOMES SHOULD NOT BE PUT IN THE COMPOST PILE, BECAUSE OF THE DANGER OF RESPROUTING. MAYBE IF THE SOD WAS SHREDDED VERY FINELY IT WOULD NOT RESPROUT.

SO NOW YOU'VE GOT YOUR SOIL PREPARED . . . CONGRATULATIONS! TAKE A LONG HOT SHOWER, REST YOUR ACHING BONES, AND CURL UP WITH THIS BOOK.

THE NEXT FEW CHAPTERS WILL EXPLORE IN DEPTH WHAT MAKES SOIL "FERTILE," HOW ORGANIC-RICH SOIL IS MORE FERTILE THAN INORGANIC SOIL, AND HOW TO ADJUST SUCH THINGS AS PH AND NITROGEN LEVELS. IF YOU'RE GETTING ANTSY TO GO OUT THERE AND SOW YOUR WILD CARROT SEEDS, THAT'S UNDERSTANDABLE. BUT TO FULLY MAXIMIZE YOUR PLANTS' HEALTH, YOU NEED TO KNOW AS MUCH AS POSSIBLE ABOUT WHERE THE LITTLE PLANT NUTRIENTS ARE, WHERE THEY'RE GOING, WHEN, AND HOW TO KEEP AS MANY OF THEM AS POSSIBLE AROUND FOR YOUR PLANTS TO USE. YOUR PLANTS WILL LOVE YOU FOR IT.

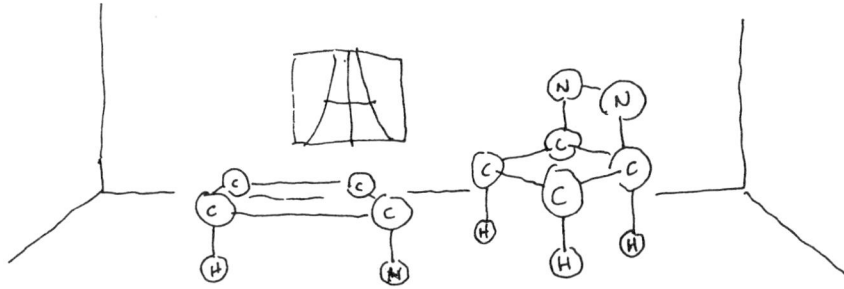

CHEMICALS ARE LIKE FURNITURE

MANY PEOPLE ARE AFRAID OF CHEMISTRY, BUT THEY SHOULDN'T BE. CHEMICALS ARE JUST LIKE LITTLE TABLES AND CHAIRS, WITH THEIR MICRO-GEOMETRY DETERMINING HOW THEY WILL FIT TOGETHER TO FORM THE "FURNITURE" OF THE LITTLE "ROOMS" WHICH ARE THE CELLS OF A PLANT, THE CELLS OF OUR BODIES, OR THE AIR/WATER POCKETS IN THE SOIL. NO ONE IS AFRAID OF TABLES AND CHAIRS, SO THERE IS NO REASON TO BE AFRAID OF CHEMISTRY, EITHER.

CHEMISTRY IS LIKE RELATIONSHIPS

CHEMICAL REACTIONS CAN ALSO BE COMPARED TO HUMAN RELATIONSHIPS. MOLECULES BEHAVE LIKE PEOPLE, PARTICULARLY IN THE WAY THEY ARE ATTRACTED AND REPELLED BY EACH OTHER. MOLECULES CAN BECOME INVOLVED IN TEMPORARY "AFFAIRS" WHICH AREN'T REALLY A PERFECT MATCH, AND WHICH BREAK UP WHEN SOMETHING BETTER COMES ALONG. THESE LITTLE SUB-MICROSCOPIC LOVE AFFAIRS ARE CONSTANTLY FORMING AND REFORMING IN THE SOIL, AND THAT'S WHAT "SOIL CHEMISTRY" IS ALL ABOUT.

CLAY: THE CASANOVA OF THE SOIL

CLAY IS ONE OF THE MAJOR STARS OF THE SOIL SOCIAL SCENE. IT'S GOT A REAL MAGNETIC PERSONALITY, AS YOU CAN SEE BY LOOKING AT THE PRIMARY UNIT OF CLAY MOLECULES, SILICON DIOXIDE (SiO_4), ON THE NEXT PAGE.

THIS LITTLE GUY JUST DRIVES PLANT NUTRIENTS AND OTHER SOIL IONS WILD WITH DESIRE. THE LIGHTNING BOLTS ARE NEGATIVELY CHARGED, WHICH ATTRACTS THE POSITIVE CHARGE OF MOST PLANT NUTRIENT IONS SWIMMING AROUND IN THE SOIL. PLANT NUTRIENT IONS HELD BY THE CLAY INCLUDE NH_4^+ (AMMONIUM), K^+ (POTASSIUM), CA^{+2} (CALCIUM), MG^{+2} (MAGNESIUM), FE^{+2} (IRON), AND MN^{+2} (MANGANESE).

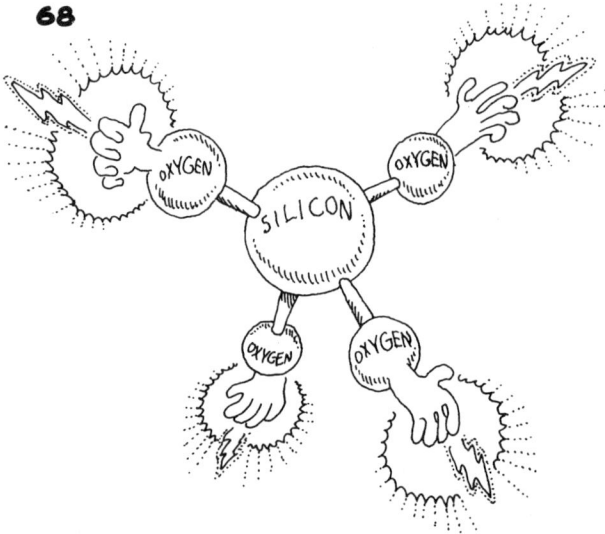

CLAY (ALONG WITH HUMUS) HOLDS THESE POSITIVE IONS SO THEY DON'T WASH OUT OF THE SOIL, AND SO THEY ARE EASILY ACCESSIBLE TO PLANTS. WHEN A PLANT WANTS ONE OF THE NUTRIENTS, ALL IT HAS TO DO IS EJECT AN ION OF ITS OWN (HYDROGEN, OR H^+), AND IT RECEIVES THE DESIRED NUTRIENT IN TRADE. PRETTY NEAT ARRANGEMENT, HUH?

AS IF THAT WEREN'T ENOUGH, CLAY ALSO HOLDS SODIUM (NA^+) AND HYDROGEN (H^+), WHICH DETERMINE THE CRITICAL ACID-BASE BALANCE OF THE SOIL. CLAY ALSO HOLDS WATER, SO THE AMOUNT OF CLAY IN YOUR SOIL HAS MAJOR IMPLICATIONS FOR WATERING DECISIONS.

IN CLAY, BILLIONS OF THOSE CHARISMATIC LITTLE SILICON OXIDE MOLECULES LINK UP TO FORM GIANT FLAT COLONIES. THESE COLONIES ARE CALLED "SHEETS," OR "LATTICES." HERE'S WHAT THEY LOOK LIKE:

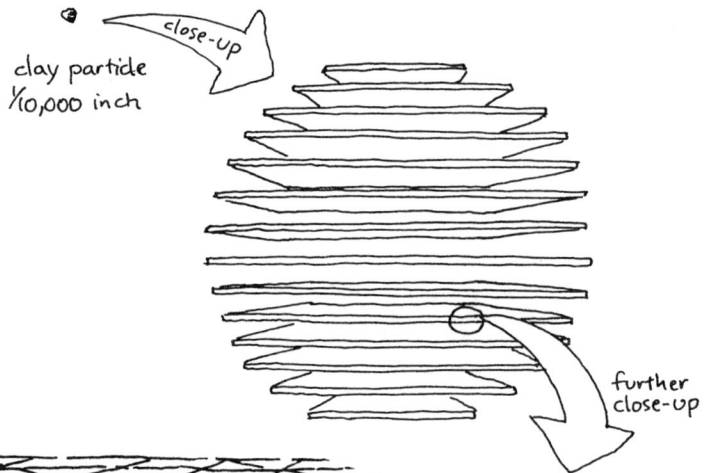

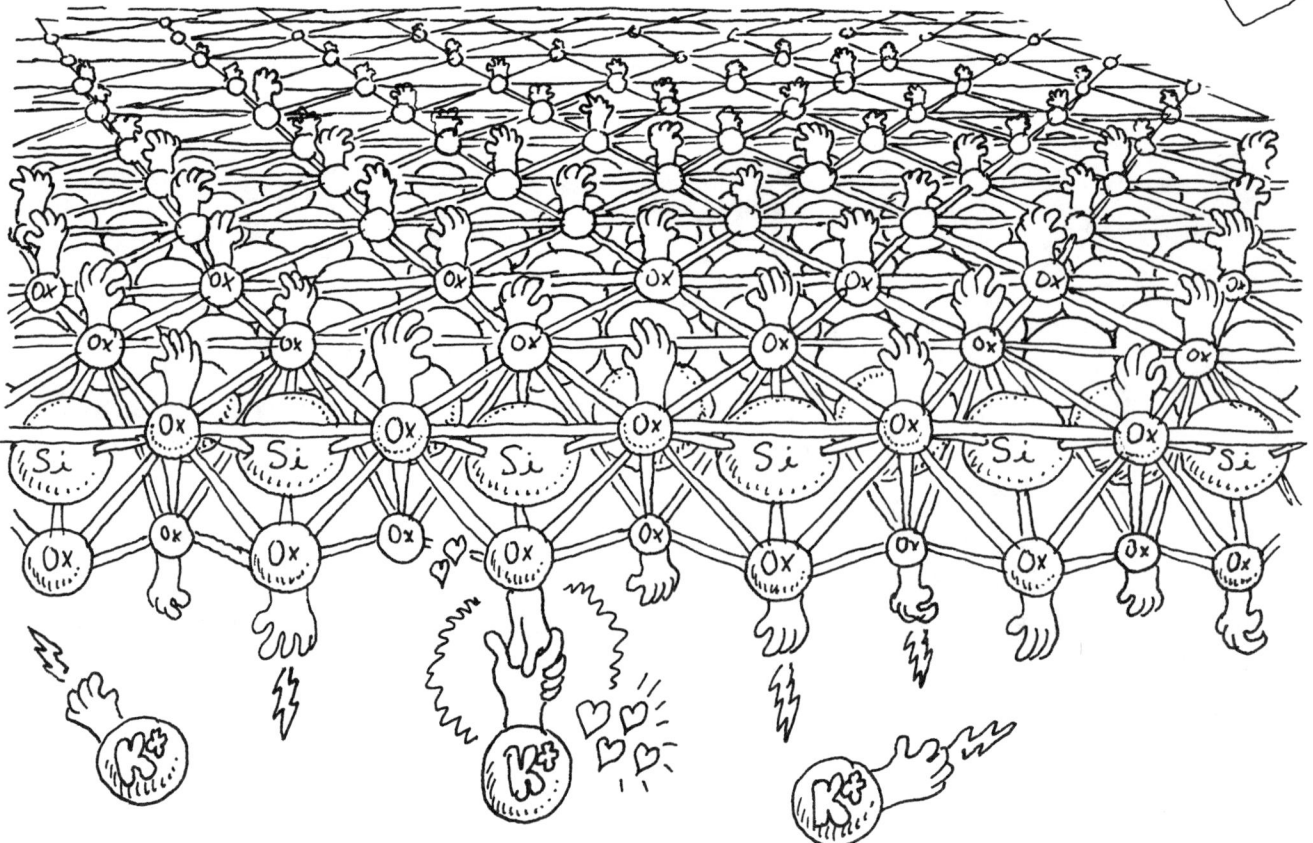

clay particle $1/10,000$ inch

close-up

further close-up

BELOW THE LATTICE, YOU CAN SEE THE PLANT NUTRIENT POTASSIUM (K^+) COMING IN BETWEEN THE SHEETS AND BONDING TO ONE OF THE OXYGENS (O) ON THE CLAY.

TURN THE PAGE FOR A PICTURE TO PUT IT ALL TOGETHER IN YOUR MIND, FROM THE MICROSCOPIC TO THE DIRECTLY SEE-ABLE, FEEL-ABLE, AND SQUEEZEABLE.

IS CLAY A COSMIC PRANK?

IT WOULD SEEM SO, IF YOU'VE EVER TRIED TO DOUBLE-DIG IN HEAVY CLAY SOIL. AT THE VERY LEAST, CLAY IS A MIXED BLESSING IN THE GARDEN. ON THE ONE HAND, IT'S NECESSARY FOR HOLDING WATER AND PLANT NUTRIENTS SO THEY ARE EASILY-ACCESSIBLE, LIKE GROCERIES ON SUPERMARKET SHELVES. ON THE OTHER HAND, TOO MUCH CLAY CAN MAKE THE SOIL HEAVY, PRESENTING A BARRIER TO ROOT GROWTH, EARTHWORM BURROWING, AND HUMAN TILLING. AND IF THE CLAY IS REALLY DENSE IN THE SOIL, IT WILL CAUSE THE SOIL TO CRACK WHEN IT DRIES. SO YOU WANT SOME CLAY, BUT NOT TOO MUCH. THE REMEDY FOR TOO MUCH CLAY IS SIMPLE: ADD ORGANIC MATTER (COMPOST, PREFERABLY). HUMUS FROM THE ORGANIC MATTER BREAKS UP THE CLAY MASSES, AND DILUTES THE OVERALL CONCENTRATION OF CLAY IN THE SOIL. AND HUMUS CAN COMPENSATE FOR A DEFICIENCY OF CLAY AS WELL, SINCE HUMUS ALSO STORES PLANT NUTRIENTS.

CLAY AND SOIL PH

THE AMOUNT OF H^+ (HYDROGEN) ATTACHED TO THE CLAY SHEETS (AND/OR HUMUS MOLECULES) DETERMINES THE PH OF THE SOIL, OR HOW ACID/ALKALINE THE SOIL IS. A LOW PH (UNDER 7.0) MEANS THERE ARE LOTS OF H^+ IONS, AND THE SOIL IS ACIDIC. A HIGH PH (OVER 7.0) MEANS THERE ARE FEW H^+ IONS, AND THE SOIL IS ALKALINE. A PH OF EXACTLY 7.0 IS "NEUTRAL;" IT MEANS THERE ARE A MODERATE NUMBER OF H^+ IONS, SO THE SOIL IS NEITHER ACID NOR ALKALINE. MOST SOIL CHEMISTRY SIMPLY INVOLVES REPLACING THESE H^+ IONS WITH VARIOUS OTHER IONS, AS WE WILL SEE.

CLAY: COSMIC PRANK OR NECESSARY EVIL?

Al · Si · Si O$_x$ Al O$_x$ Si O$_x$ O$_x$ Si O$_x$ Al O$_x$ Si Si Al

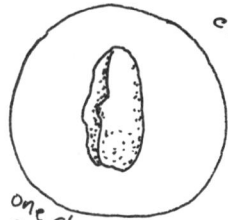

one clay particle~ magnified 10,000 times

Interior of a temperate-climate clay particle, magnified billions of times. The clay is made of "aluminum sandwiches", with silicon as the "bread." Unlike tropical clay, there is nothing holding one sandwich to the next, so water can come in between the sandwiches....

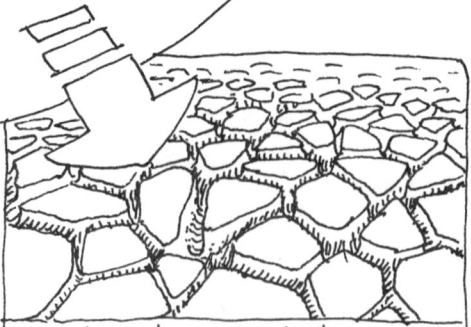

... when the water between the sandwiches evaporates, you're left with empty spaces where the water used to be. These spaces combine to form CRACKS!

PH and PLANTS

PLANTS DIFFER IN THE AMOUNT OF HYDROGEN IONS THEY LIKE TO HAVE IN THE SOIL.
THAT'S WHY YOU MAY WANT TO CHANGE THE PH WHERE CERTAIN PLANTS ARE GROWING.
HERE'S A CHART SHOWING WHICH PLANTS LIKE WHAT, AND HOW TO MAKE IT THAT WAY:

ACID-LOVERS (pH 5.5-6.0)	ALKALINE-LOVERS (pH 7-7.5)
blackberry, raspberry, blueberry, cranberry, strawberry (6.5), potato, sweet potato, peanut, radish, watermelon — hemlock, oak, pecan, yew, chrysanthemum, marigold — camelia, rhododendron, azalea, heather(Erica), madrone, manzanita, bearberry } Heath family — pine, spruce, redwood } most conifers	alfalfa, clover } most legumes — asparagus, onions, beets, spinach, brocolli, brussels sprouts, cabbage, cauliflower } cabbage family — celery, carrots, cantaloupe, cucumber, carnation, lettuce

Mulch or compost with pine needles, oak leaves, or any conifer needles/bark

Peat moss (expensive)

Lots of water

chicken/turkey manure

urine

ashes

limestone

eggshells, bones, seashells

MAKING SOIL MORE ALKALINE

LET'S SAY YOU'RE GROWING ALFALFA OR ASPARAGUS (ALKALINE-LOVERS) AND YOU WANT TO MAKE THE SOIL MORE ALKALINE. ONE WAY TO DO THIS IS BY ADDING LIMESTONE, WHICH IS CALCIUM CARBONATE (CA CO_3). ZOOMING DOWN IN BETWEEN THE CLAY SHEETS, WE CAN WATCH WHAT HAPPENS WHEN LIME IS ADDED:

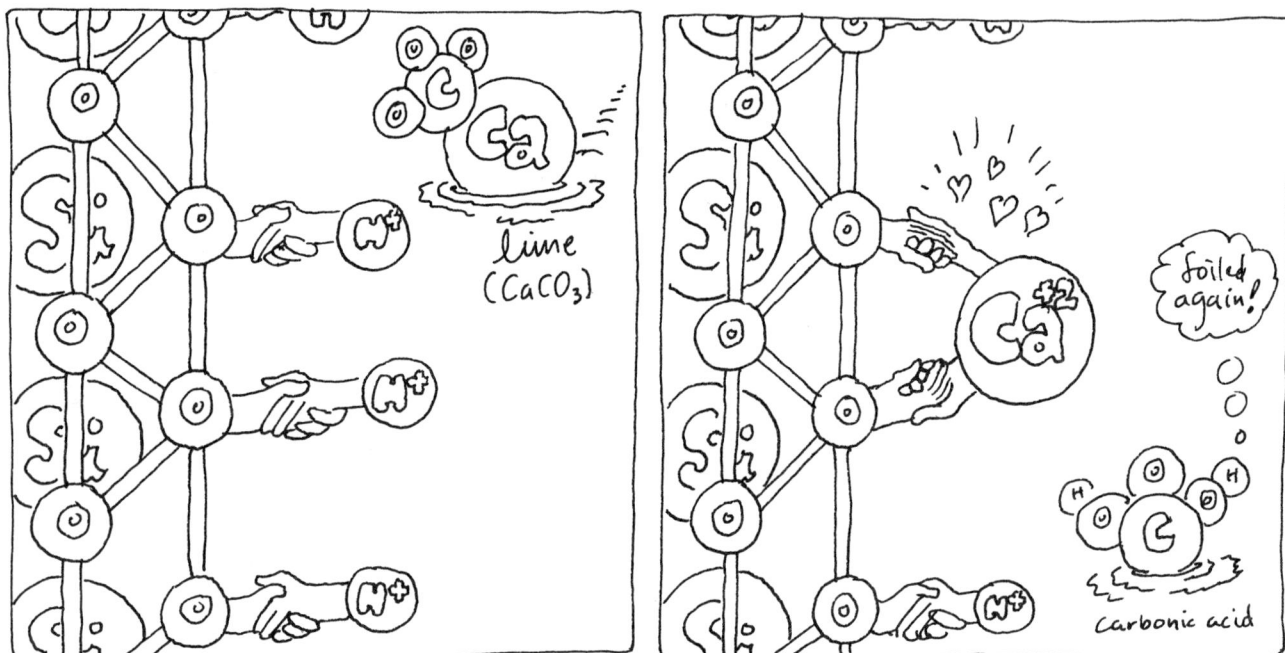

1. THIS IS WHAT ACID SOIL LOOKS LIKE. ALL THE BONDING SITES ON THE CLAY LATTICE ARE TAKEN UP BY HYDROGEN IONS. IN THE UPPER CORNER, A CALCIUM CARBONATE (LIME) MOLECULE IS FLOATING DOWN BETWEEN THE LATTICE SHEETS.

2. THE CALCIUM ION (CA^{+2}) SPLITS OFF FROM THE LIME MOLECULE AND ATTACHES TO THE LATTICE. HYDROGEN (H^+) THEN ATTACHES TO THE REMAINDER OF THE LIME MOLECULE (CO_3^{-2}), FORMING CARBONIC ACID (H_2CO_3), WHICH WASHES OUT OF THE SOIL, DOWN TO THE GROUND-WATER.

THIS TYPE OF REACTION IS CALLED BASE EXCHANGE, AND MANY OF THE OTHER REACTIONS TAKING PLACE IN THE SOIL ARE VERY SIMILAR. IN FACT, ALL THE REST OF THIS CHAPTER WILL BE VARIATIONS ON THIS THEME. CHEMISTRY'S PRETTY SIMPLE, HUH?

FOR INSTANCE, IF YOU ADD ASHES TO THE SOIL AS MULCH (OR BETTER, TO A SPECIAL ALKALINE COMPOST PILE), THEY WILL RAISE THE PH IN A WAY SIMILAR TO LIME. ASHES CONTAIN POTASH, OR POTASSIUM CARBONATE (K_2CO_3), WHICH DISSOLVES IN WATER TO FORM POTASSIUM IONS (K^+), WHICH ACT LIKE THE CALCIUM IONS IN THE PREVIOUS CARTOON, KICKING HYDROGEN IONS OUT OF THE PICTURE:

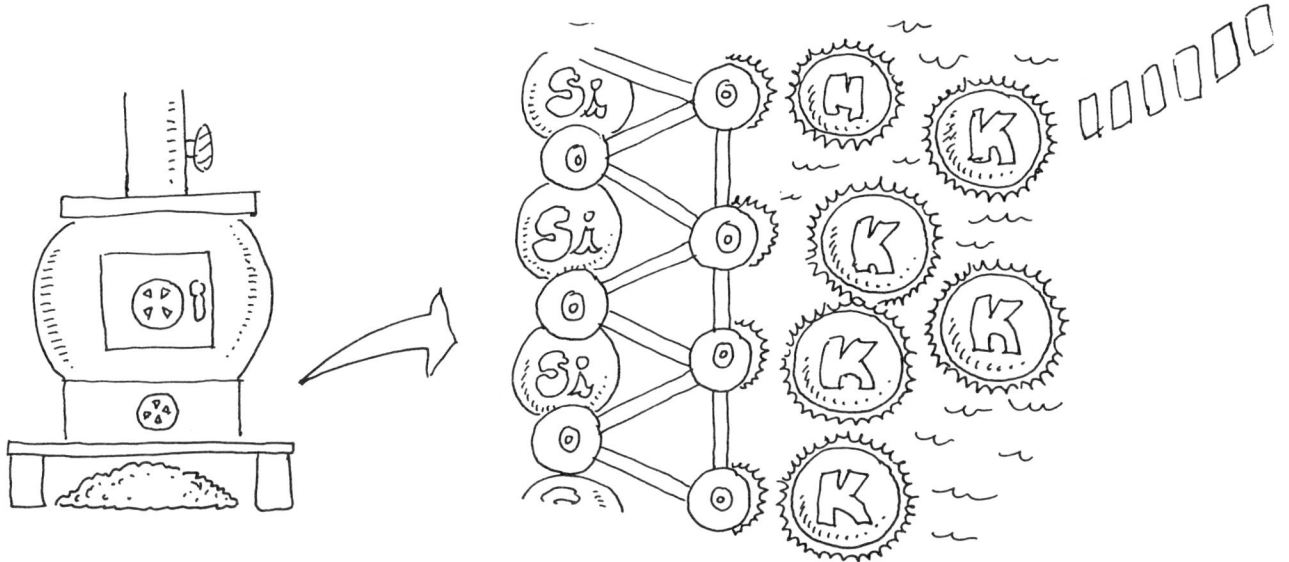

HOW MUCH LIME/ASHES/URINE?

HOW TO AVOID OVERDOING IT? SINCE YOU'RE PUTTING ALL THAT COMPOST IN YOUR SOIL, NO MATTER HOW MUCH LIME/ASHES/ETC. YOU ADD, THERE WILL BE NO DANGER OF MAKING THE SOIL TOO ALKALINE. COMPOST (OR OTHER ORGANIC MATTER) TURNS INTO HUMUS (THE SAME STUFF FROM CHAPTER TWO THAT HELPS SOIL STRUCTURE), AND HUMUS ACTS AS A BUFFER AGAINST EXCESSIVE PH'S, EITHER ACID OR ALKALINE. HUMUS IS SIMILAR CHEMICALLY TO CLAY, WITH REGIONS OF NEGATIVE CHARGE WHERE POSITIVE IONS CAN ATTACH. SO YOU CAN JUST THROW IN WHATEVER ALKALINE OR ACIDIC MATERIALS YOU HAVE AROUND THE HOUSE, AND THE HUMUS WILL SOP UP THE EXCESS:

HUMUS TO THE RESCUE

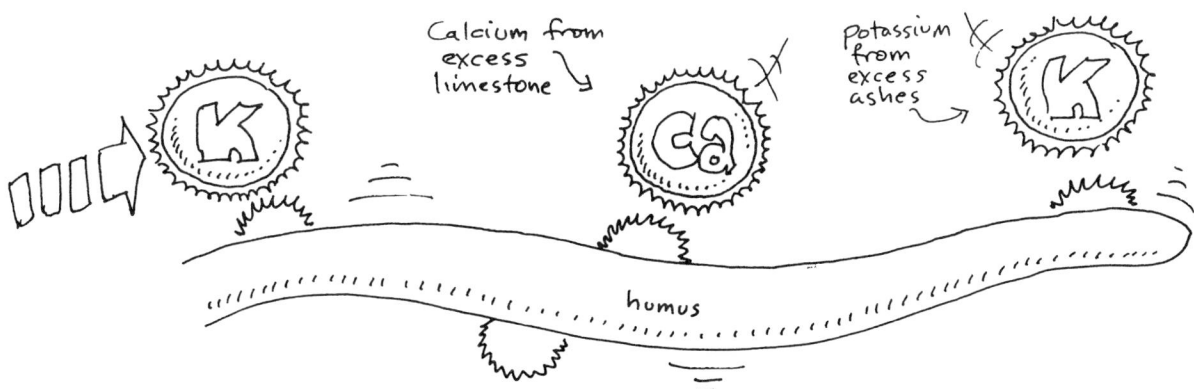

Calcium from excess limestone

Potassium from excess ashes

humus

ALTERNATIVES TO LIMESTONE

LIMESTONE IS EXPENSIVE, AND THERE ARE MATERIALS LYING AROUND THE HOUSE THAT CAN BE USED TO RAISE THE PH, AND OFTEN FERTILIZE THE SOIL AT THE SAME TIME. I ALREADY MENTIONED ONE OF THESE: ASHES. HERE ARE SOME OTHERS:

1. BONE MEAL, CRUSHED EGGSHELLS OR SEASHELLS. THESE ARE ALL ALTERNATIVE SOURCES OF LIME ($CaCO_3$). IF YOU LIVE NEAR THE OCEAN, GO TO THE BEACH, GATHER SHELLS, AND CRUSH THEM YOURSELF. DO THE SAME WITH THE SHELLS FROM EGGS YOU EAT. IF YOU EAT MEAT, GRIND UP THE BONES.

2. URINE. HUMAN URINE CONTAINS LOTS OF AMMONIA, WHICH IS ALKALINE. AMMONIA (NH_3) COMBINES WITH H^+ IN THE SOIL TO FORM NH_4^+, WHICH PLANTS CAN TAKE UP AND USE AS A NITROGEN SOURCE. THE REMOVAL OF H^+ FROM THE SOIL MAKES IT MORE ALKALINE.

3. DRY FARMING. COVER THE BEDS WITH SHEETS OF PLASTIC OR PLYWOOD TO KEEP OFF THE RAIN WHEN THE LAND IS LYING FALLOW, AND AVOID EXCESS IRRIGATION DURING THE GROWING SEASON. THIS KEEPS WATER FROM LEACHING THE Ca^{+2}, K^+, AND OTHER ALKALINE IONS OUT OF THE SOIL (H^+ CLINGS MORE TIGHTLY TO THE CLAY/HUMUS, WHICH IS WHY HEAVY RAIN OR IRRIGATION ACIDIFIES THE SOIL).

... AND THAT BRINGS US TO:

MAKING SOIL MORE ACIDIC

SUPPOSE YOU'RE GROWING BERRIES, POTATOES, RADISHES, OR SOME OTHER ACID-LOVER. YOU CAN ADD ANY ONE OF THE FOLLOWING LIST OF MATERIALS TO LOWER THE PH. ONCE AGAIN, THE MORE HUMUS YOU HAVE IN THE SOIL, THE MORE BUFFERED THE SOIL WILL BE, SO THE LESS DANGER THERE IS OF OVER-ACIDIFYING THE SOIL.

1. LOTS OF IRRIGATION. BY REALLY FLOODING THE SOIL WITH WATER, YOU CAN FLUSH ALL THE EXCESS SODIUM AND CALCIUM OUT OF THE SOIL, THUS MIMICKING THE EFFECT OF HEAVY RAINFALL. YOU SHOULD BE SURE YOUR WATER IS NOT SALTY OR SOAPY.

2. LEAVES OR NEEDLES OF ANY CONIFER. YOU CAN PREPARE A SPECIAL COMPOST OF THESE MATERIALS, ALONG WITH BIRD MANURE, OR JUST KEEP LAYING THEM ON THE SURFACE AS MULCH. YOU'LL NOTICE THAT IN NATURAL ECOSYSTEMS, THE WILD STRAWBERRIES, BLUEBERRIES, BLACKBERRIES, MADRONE, ETC. (ALL ACID-LOVERS) ARE USUALLY FOUND UNDER CONIFER TREES, NESTLED IN A NICE MULCH OF CONIFER NEEDLES. YOU CAN AND SHOULD DUPLICATE THESE CONDITIONS IN YOUR GARDEN.

3. CHICKEN, DUCK, OR GOOSE MANURE. BIRD MANURE INCLUDES THE BIRD'S URINE, WHICH CONTAINS URIC ACID INSTEAD OF UREA AS A NITROGEN-DISPOSAL MOLECULE. (ALL MAMMALS HAVE UREA.)

4. **SAWDUST**. GATHER FREE FROM LUMBER YARDS AND FURNITURE FACTORIES. BE SURE TO ADD PLENTY OF NITROGENOUS MATERIALS AT THE SAME TIME. IT WOULD BE BEST TO LET IT COMPOST FIRST IN A SPECIAL ACID-LOVER'S COMPOST PILE, TO AVOID DEPLETION OF THE SOIL'S NITROGEN.

5. **PEAT MOSS, COTTONSEED MEAL, BLOOD MEAL**. THESE ARE MORE EXPENSIVE, BUT YOU MAY FIND A GOOD DEAL ON ONE OF THEM.

PH COMPANIONS

IT'S EASIER TO APPLY THESE MATERIALS IF YOU GROUP YOUR PLANTS ACCORDING TO PH PREFERENCE. FOR INSTANCE:

brocolli + beets ~
alkaline-lovers

Potatoes + radishes ~
acid-lovers

HYPER-ACID SOIL

EVEN IF YOU'RE NOT GROWING PLANTS WHICH SPECIFICALLY LIKE ALKALINE SOIL, YOU MAY WANT TO CONSIDER ADDING SOME TYPE OF "ANTACID" TO THE SOIL. (SINCE SOIL IS SO MUCH LIKE OUR DIGESTIVE SYSTEM, "ANTACID" IS A PRETTY GOOD WORD FOR LIMING.) IF YOU LIVE ON THE EAST COAST, THE NORTHWEST, OR SOME OTHER VERY RAINY REGION, YOUR SOIL IS PROBABLY ON THE ACID SIDE, SINCE LOTS OF WATER LEACHES OUT MUCH OF THE CALCIUM, POTASSIUM, ETC., LEAVING AN EXCESS OF HYDROGEN. FARMERS ON THE EAST COAST REGULARLY LIME THEIR SOIL.

OR IF YOUR SOIL IS NEAR A SPRUCE, OAK, PINE, OR REDWOOD TREE (OR ANY CONIFER), IT'S PROBABLY ACID DUE TO THE DECOMPOSITON OF LEAVES OR NEEDLES ON THE SURFACE. THESE TREES ENJOY ACID SOIL, AND THEIR FALLEN LEAVES MAKE THE SOIL ACID.

IF YOU LIVE IN A HEAVILY-INDUSTRIALIZED OR URBAN AREA, YOUR SOIL MAY BE ACIDIC DUE TO ACID RAIN. "ACID RAIN" CONTAINS SULFURIC ACID (H_2SO_4) AND NITRIC ACID (HNO_3), BY-PRODUCTS OF FOSSIL FUEL COMBUSTION WHICH ARE WASHED OUT OF THE AIR BY THE RAIN.

IN ANY CASE, YOU'LL WANT TO ADD PLENTY OF ORGANIC MATTER TO THE SOIL TO NEUTRALIZE THE PH, AND THEN ALKALINE MATERIALS TO COUNTER THE EFFECTS OF ACIDIFICATION. IT'S POSSIBLE THAT ORGANIC MATTER ALONE WOULD DO THE TRICK . . . IF YOU HAVE ANY DOUBTS YOU CAN USUALLY HAVE YOUR SOIL TESTED FREE BY A COUNTY AGRICULTURAL EXTENSION AGENT.

ALKALINE SOIL

AS WITH OVER-ACID SOIL, OVER-ALKALINE SOIL RESULTS FROM AN EXCESS OF SOME ION CLOGGING UP THE CLAY/HUMUS BONDING SITES, SO THERE'S NO ROOM FOR PLANT-NUTRIENT IONS. IN THE CASE OF ALKALINE SOIL, THE CULPRIT IS USUALLY SODIUM (NA^+).

ALKALINE SOIL CAN OFTEN BE DIAGNOSED BY LOOKING AT THE SOIL ITSELF. IT SHOWS UP AS THIN WHITE CRUSTY PATCHES ON THE SOIL SURFACE. THESE "WHITE-CRUSTIES" ARE SODIUM CARBONATE (NA_2CO_3), A COMPOUND SIMILAR TO BAKING SODA ($NA\,HCO_3$). SODIUM CARBONATE RISES UP THROUGH THE SOIL ALONG WITH THE SOIL-WATER, AND IS LEFT BEHIND WHEN THE WATER EVAPORATES. WHITE CRUSTIES INDICATE A PH AROUND 8.5. AS THE SOIL GETS EVEN MORE ALKALINE (PH 9.5), THE CRUSTIES TURN BLACK.

BEFORE THE SOIL GETS THE CRUSTIES, YOU CAN DETECT THE ONSET OF OVER-ALKALINITY BY LOOKING AT ACID-LOVING PLANTS, WHICH ARE PRONE TO GETTING THE DISEASE KNOWN AS CHLOROSIS. CHLOROSIS IS THE RESULT OF IRON DEFICIENCY, AND ONCE AGAIN THE PROBLEM IS DUE TO SOME ION (SODIUM IN THIS CASE) CLOGGING UP THE CLAY/HUMUS, SO THE PLANT CAN'T GET SOME NUTRIENT (IRON IN THIS CASE). THE RESULT IS A YELLOWING OF THE LEAVES:

The yellow can be between the veins...

ORANGE

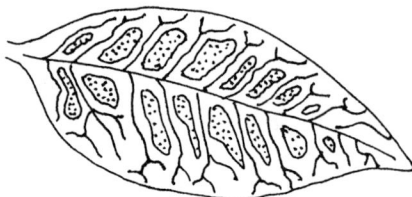

...OR, it can be in random splotches

RHODODENDRON

ALKALINE SOIL—CAUSES

I. LACK OF RAINFALL. IF YOU LIVE IN CALIFORNIA OR OTHER PARTS OF THE SOUTHWEST, THE USUAL SEMI-DROUGHT CONDITIONS MAKE ALKALINE SOIL A CONSTANT DANGER.

SODIUM CARBONATE (THE WHITE-CRUSTIE MATERIAL) IS A NORMAL PART OF ALL HEALTHY SOILS, COMING FROM THE BREAKDOWN OF MINERALS (MICA AND FELDSPAR) IN THE SOIL. THE PROBLEM HAPPENS WHEN THERE'S NOT ENOUGH RAIN TO WASH THE EXCESS SODIUM IONS DOWN AND OUT OF THE SOIL. IF SODIUM ISN'T WASHED DOWN TO THE GROUNDWATER, IT FILLS UP THE CLAY AND HUMUS, MAKING THE SOIL ALKALINE.

HERE IS A CHART RELATING RAINFALL TO ALKALINITY, TO GIVE YOU AN IDEA ABOUT THE SOIL IN YOUR AREA:

INCHES OF RAIN PER YEAR

30" AND UP	25–30"	20–25"	UNDER 20"
SOIL BECOMES ACID OVER TIME UNLESS ALKALINE MATERIALS ARE ADDED. CA^{+2}, MG^{+2}, AND NA^+ WASHED OUT OF SOIL.	SOIL USUALLY NEUTRAL AT LEAST NEAR SURFACE. CA^{+2} AND MG^{+2} MAY ACCUMULATE A FEW FEET DOWN, MAKING SOIL SLIGHTLY ALKALINE.	SOIL PH 7.5, ALKALINE ENOUGH TO BOTHER ACID-LOVERS. CA^{+2} AND MG^{+2} ACCUMULATE THROUGHOUT SOIL, WITH NA^+ A FEW FEET DOWN.	SOIL PH 8.5 AND UP. NA^+ ACCUMULATES THROUGHOUT SOIL. SOIL TOO ALKALINE FOR MOST PLANTS. WHITE CRUSTIES ON SURFACE.

(FROM SUN, SOIL, AND SURVIVAL BY KERMIT C. BERGER, 1972.)

2. HIGH WATER TABLE, POOR DRAINAGE. EVEN IF YOU'RE LIVING IN A RAIN FOREST OR YOU'RE WATERING THE HELL OUT OF THE SOIL, IT'LL GET ALKALINE IF THE WATER'S NOT DRAINING DOWN THROUGH THE SOIL TO THE GROUNDWATER. THAT'S CALLED "POOR DRAINAGE," WHICH CAN BE CAUSED BY A NUMBER OF THINGS . . . SEE CHAPTER 7 (WATERING) FOR CAUSES AND CURES.

3. SOAPY SOIL. MOST SOAPS CONTAIN SODIUM, SO POLLUTION OF THE SOIL BY SOAPY IRRIGATION WATER CAN CAUSE ALKALINITY. THIS CAN HAPPEN IF THE WATER YOU USE IS CONTAMINATED BY INDUSTRIAL WASTE, MUNICIPAL SEWAGE LEAKAGE OR DRAINAGE, OR IF YOU REUSE YOUR OWN BATH/DISH WATER ("GREYWATER") IN THE GARDEN WITHOUT TREATING IT WITH GYPSUM. (FOR A FULL DESCRIPTION OF GREYWATER TREATMENT, SEE THE EXCELLENT BOOK **THE INTREGRAL URBAN HOUSE** BY THE FARALLONES INSTITUTE.)

IF THE ALKALINITY OF YOUR SOIL IS CAUSED BY SOAP, THE SOIL STRUCTURE WILL BE A CLUE. SOAP IN THE SOIL DOES THE SAME THING AS SOAP ON YOUR HANDS: IT BREAKS UP THE SOIL AND KEEPS IT FROM FORMING AGGREGATES. THE RESULT IS A VERY FINE FLOURY SOIL WITH NO AIR SPACES, AND THE PLANT ROOTS DIE OF SUFFOCATION.

4. SALTY SOIL. MANY SALTS CONTAIN SODIUM (SUCH AS TABLE SALT, NA CL), SO SALTY SOIL CAN BECOME ALKALINE. THE CAUSES OF SALTY SOIL INCLUDE ARIDITY, POOR DRAINAGE, TERRAIN, NATURAL MINERAL FORMATIONS (COMMON IN THE SOUTHWEST), SALTY IRRIGATION WATER, AND OVER-USE OF URINE FERTILIZER. THE UPCOMING SECTION ON SALTY SOIL WILL GIVE YOU THE SYMPTOMS AND REMEDIES.

❧ ❧ ❧ ❧ ❧

IF YOUR MIND IS NOW THOROUGHLY BOGGLED BY THE MANY CAUSES OF ALKALINE SOIL, DON'T DESPAIR! JUST LOOK AT PAGE 79 TO GRAPHICALLY KEY-OUT YOUR ALKALINE SOIL PROBLEMS . . .

SALTY SOIL

"SALTS" ARE CHEMICALS COMPOSED OF TWO IONS STUCK TOGETHER, WHICH FALL APART WHEN THE SALT "DISSOLVES" IN WATER. THESE IONS CAN INCLUDE CA^{+2}, MG^{+2}, OR NA^+ (AS IN NA CL). MANY CHEMICAL FERTILIZERS ARE IN THE FORM OF SALTS, SUCH AS AMMONIUM NITRATE (NH_4NO_3). WHEN A SALT IS ADDED TO THE SOIL, THE IONS FIRST SWIM AROUND FOR A WHILE IN THE SOIL-WATER, UNTIL THEY FIND A PLACE ON THE CLAY LATTICE OR THE HUMUS. SO THEY DON'T NECESSARILY MAKE THE SOIL ALKALINE RIGHT AWAY--TO DO THAT, THEY HAVE TO REPLACE H^+ IONS ON THE LATTICE, AND THE H^+ IONS HAVE TO BE FLUSHED DOWN TO THE GROUND WATER. SO SALINE (SALTY) SOIL ISN'T NECESSARILY ALKALINE, BUT IT'S OFTEN A FIRST STEP IN THAT DIRECTION.

BUT EVEN BY SWIMMING AROUND IN THE SOIL-WATER, SALT IONS CAN HARM YOUR PLANTS. THE PLANT WILL BE UNABLE TO TAKE UP WATER EFFICIENTLY, SO THE LEAVES WILL WILT, AND OFTEN LOOK SCORCHED OR "BURNT" AROUND THE EDGES.

TO UNDERSTAND WHY THIS HAPPENS, YOU NEED TO KNOW ABOUT OSMOSIS, A TERM PEOPLE USUALLY USE TO DESCRIBE HOW THEY HOPE TO LEARN THINGS PASSIVELY, WITHOUT ANY REAL EFFORT (LIKE READING THIS FUN, EASY BOOK!) PASSIVE LEARNING IS A PRETTY GOOD ANALOGY, SINCE PLANT ROOTS DON'T SPEND ANY METABOLIC ENERGY PUMPING WATER INTO THE PLANT; WATER JUST SEEPS IN BY ITSELF BY OSMOSIS, UNLESS THE SOIL IS SALTY.

Over-use of Urine

Rock salt used to melt ice on roads

Soapy irrigation water

Near ocean (salt mist in air)

Poor tillage practices

Natural mineral deposits (e.g. Mendocino, Ca pygmy forest)

Natural mineral deposits (e.g. California deserts)

Saline Soil (Na^+ in soil water, but not attached to clay yet)

over time

20-25" of rain per year

Over-watering

Hard-pan

Valley terrain

Slightly Alkaline Soil (pH 7.5)

Boundary Layer

High water table, so sodium not washed out of soil

+ time

Under 20" of rain a year

ALKALINE SOIL (pH 8.5)

↑ CAUSES

↓ SYMPTOMS

Alkaline-loving weeds thrive

Burning of leaves

Chlorosis (iron hunger)

White crusts on soil surface

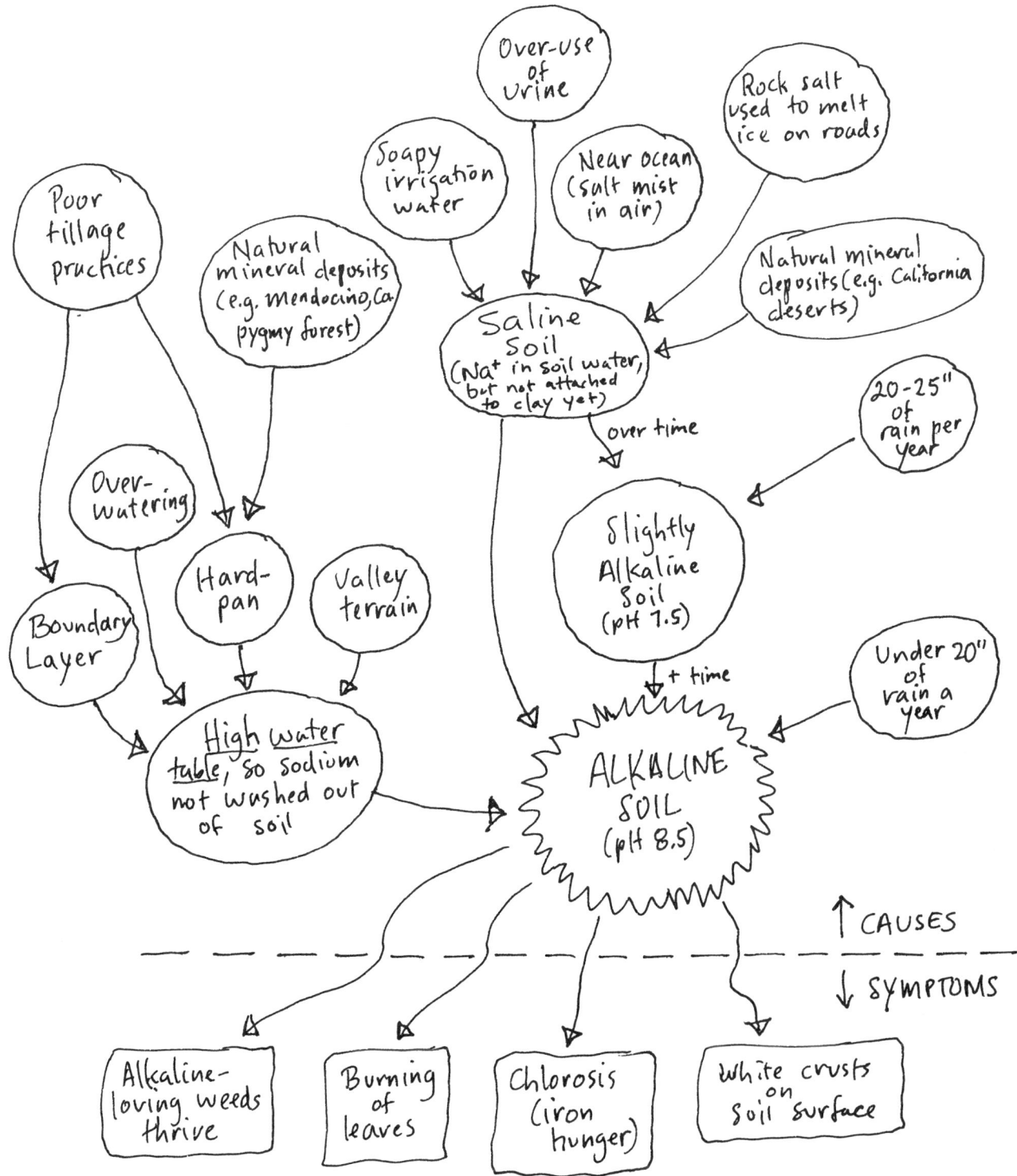

CAUSES OF ALKALINE SOIL

TO ILLUSTRATE OSMOSIS, HERE'S AN "X-RAY DIFFRACTION DRAWING" OF A PLANT ROOT CELL IN NORMAL SOIL:

THE CELL MEMBRANE (RUNNING DIAGONALLY DOWN THROUGH THE CENTER OF THE PICTURE) HAS HOLES JUST THE RIGHT SIZE AND SHAPE TO LET WATER MOLECULES GO THROUGH, AND NOTHING ELSE. EVERYTHING ELSE (SUCH AS THE PLANT NUTRIENTS K^+ AND MG^{+2} SEEN SWIMMING AROUND OUTSIDE THE CELL) MUST BE PUMPED IN BY THE CELL. SO WATER IS CONSTANTLY MOVING BACK AND FORTH AT RANDOM, INTO AND OUT OF THE CELL.

THE INTERIOR OF THE CELL HAS LESS WATER THAN THE SOIL SOLUTION OUTSIDE, SINCE THE CELL IS CRAMMED FULL OF VARIOUS SUGARS, PROTEINS, AMINO ACIDS, AND IONS. SO AS WATER MOVES RANDOMLY BACK AND FORTH, THE WATER MOLECULES ARE MORE LIKELY TO MOVE INTO THE CELL THAN OUT OF IT, SIMPLY BECAUSE THERE'S MANY MORE OUTSIDE TO BEGIN WITH. RANDOMNESS IS THE KEY: SINCE WATER IS DUMB AND DOESN'T CARE WHERE IT'S GOING, IT WILL END UP EVENLY-DISTRIBUTED INSIDE AND OUTSIDE THE CELL, JUST AS SMOKE FROM BURNING TOAST WILL EVENLY-DISTRIBUTE ITSELF THROUGHOUT A ROOM. (CLEARLY, ONCE WATER BECOMES DISTRIBUTED EVENLY INSIDE AND OUTSIDE THE CELL, NO MORE WATER WILL ENTER THE CELL, SO THE CELL MUST PUMP IN SOME SOIL IONS, SO THERE WILL AGAIN BE MORE WATER OUTSIDE THAN INSIDE. THE CELL USES K^+ (POTASSIUM) IONS FOR THIS PURPOSE, AND THAT'S THE MAIN USE FOR POTASSIUM, ONE OF THE BIG THREE PLANT NUTRIENTS, AS IN "NPK".)

IF THE SOIL IS SALTY HOWEVER, THERE WILL BE MORE WATER INSIDE THAN OUTSIDE, SO WATER WILL SEEP OUT BY OSMOSIS. WATER WON'T GET UP INTO THE LEAVES, AND THE RESULT IS SALT-BURN, A YELLOW-BROWN SCORCHED LOOK ON THE TIPS OF THE LEAVES.

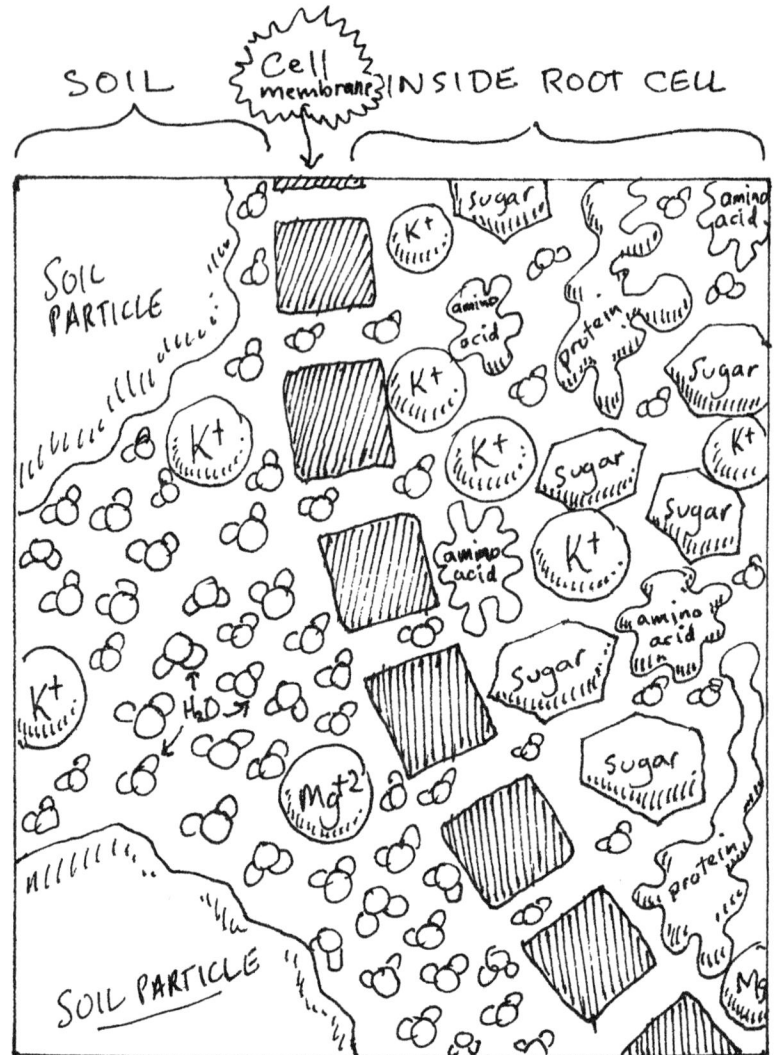

SOIL PARTICLE

FLOW OF WATER

Sugar
a.a.
Sugar
Protein

SOIL PARTICLE

↰—SALTY SOIL—————↱

SALT BURN

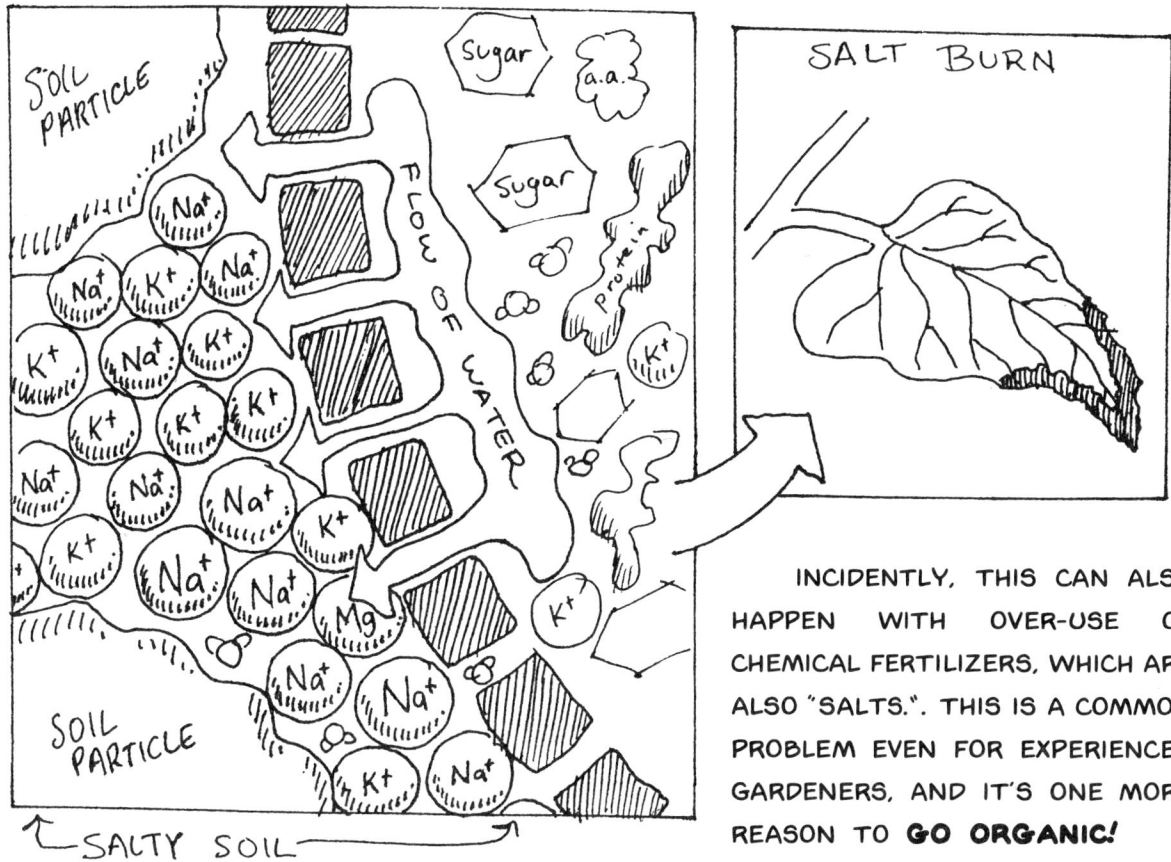

INCIDENTLY, THIS CAN ALSO HAPPEN WITH OVER-USE OF CHEMICAL FERTILIZERS, WHICH ARE ALSO "SALTS.". THIS IS A COMMON PROBLEM EVEN FOR EXPERIENCED GARDENERS, AND IT'S ONE MORE REASON TO **GO ORGANIC!**

HOW TO CURE SALTY SOIL? IT'S VERY SIMPLE--YOU JUST FLOOD THE SUCKER WITH WATER! THE DRAWING BELOW IS A SCANNING ELECTRON MICRO-HALLUCINATION OF WATER MOVING DOWN THROUGH THE SOIL. THE SALTS IN THE SOIL ARE BEING WASHED DOWN TO THE WATER TABLE (OR GROUNDWATER), THAT UNDERGROUND RIVER THAT FLOWS TO THE SEA. SO THIS METHOD WILL HELP KEEP THE OCEAN SALTY, AND THAT'LL MAKE A LOT OF FISH VERY HAPPY!

WRAP-UP and COMING ATTRACTIONS

AND THAT'S THE BASICS OF SOIL CHEMISTRY! EASY, WASN'T IT? NOW YOU'RE READY FOR THE REAL NITTY-GRITTY OF SOIL SCIENCE, WHICH ALSO INVOLVES PHYSICS, BIOLOGY, CLIMATOLOGY, ECOLOGY, AESTHETICS, MYSTICISM, MAGIC, AND (PROBABLY, IN SOME WAY) EVEN ASTRONOMY. YES, IT'S NOW TIME FOR **SOIL FERTILITY**. SO GRAB YOUR COMPOST-- WE GON' GET DOWN AND DIRTY!

BUT FIRST, BEFORE WE LEAVE CHEMISTRY, HERE'S A HANDY RECAP REFERENCE GUIDE TO ACID AND ALKALINE, AND WHAT MAKES WHAT:

ACID/ALKALINE RECAP

(MATERIALS LISTED IN ORDER OF CHEAPNESS & HEALTHINESS FOR SOIL)

THESE THINGS MAKE SOIL MORE
ACID:

(AN ACID IS SOMETHING THAT ADDS TO THE H^+ IONS IN THE SOIL.)

1. RAIN, OR LOTS OF IRRIGATION.
2. MANURE, OR ORGANIC MATTER IN GENERAL. ESP. BIRD MANURE. (MOST "ORGANIC MATTER" HAS CARBON CHAINS, WITH **HYDROGENS** STUCK ON THEM.)
3. LEAVES, OR NEEDLES, OF PINE, SPRUCE, OAK, REDWOOD, OR ANY CONIFER.
4. PEAT MOSS.
5. COTTONSEAL MEAL, BLOOD MEAL.
6. VINEGAR (ACETIC ACID--SHOULD BE ADDED TO EXPERIMENTAL COMPOST.)
7. SAWDUST (ADD NITROGEN WITH IT--COMPOST IT FIRST.)
8. GYPSUM (CALCIUM SULFATE...THE SULFATE ION (SO_4^{-2}) FROM GYPSUM GRABS H^+ IONS AND KEEPS THEM FROM LEAVING THE SOIL.
9. ACID RAIN (CONTAINS NITRIC AND SULFURIC ACID.)

THESE THINGS MAKE SOIL MORE
ALKALINE:

(AN ALKALINE SUBSTANCE IS ONE WHICH REDUCES THE NUMBER OF H^+ IONS.)

1. ARID CONDITIONS. COVER BEDS NOT IN USE WITH PLYWOOD/PLASTIC TO KEEP RAIN OFF; USE MINIMUM IRRIGATION.
2. WOOD ASHES (CONTAIN POTASH, OR K_2CO_3 ... K^+ REPLACES H^+.)
3. LIMESTONE ($CaCO_3$).
4. BONE MEAL, CRUSHED EGGSHELLS OR SEASHELLS ($CaCO_3$, PLUS PHOSPHORUS IN BONE MEAL)
5. URINE (SHOULD BE COMPOSTED)
6. AMMONIA (NH_3 ... COMBINES WITH H^+ TO FORM NH_4^+). FOR EXPERIMENTAL SPECIAL ALKALINE COMPOST.
7. BAKING SODA ($NaHCO_3$) ... SODIUM IS BAD FOR SOIL STRUCTURE.
8. SOAP (CONTAINS SODIUM).
9. LYE ($NaOH$)--PH 13.0--ABOUT AS ALKALINE AS YOU CAN GET! TOO CAUSTIC FOR HOME USE.

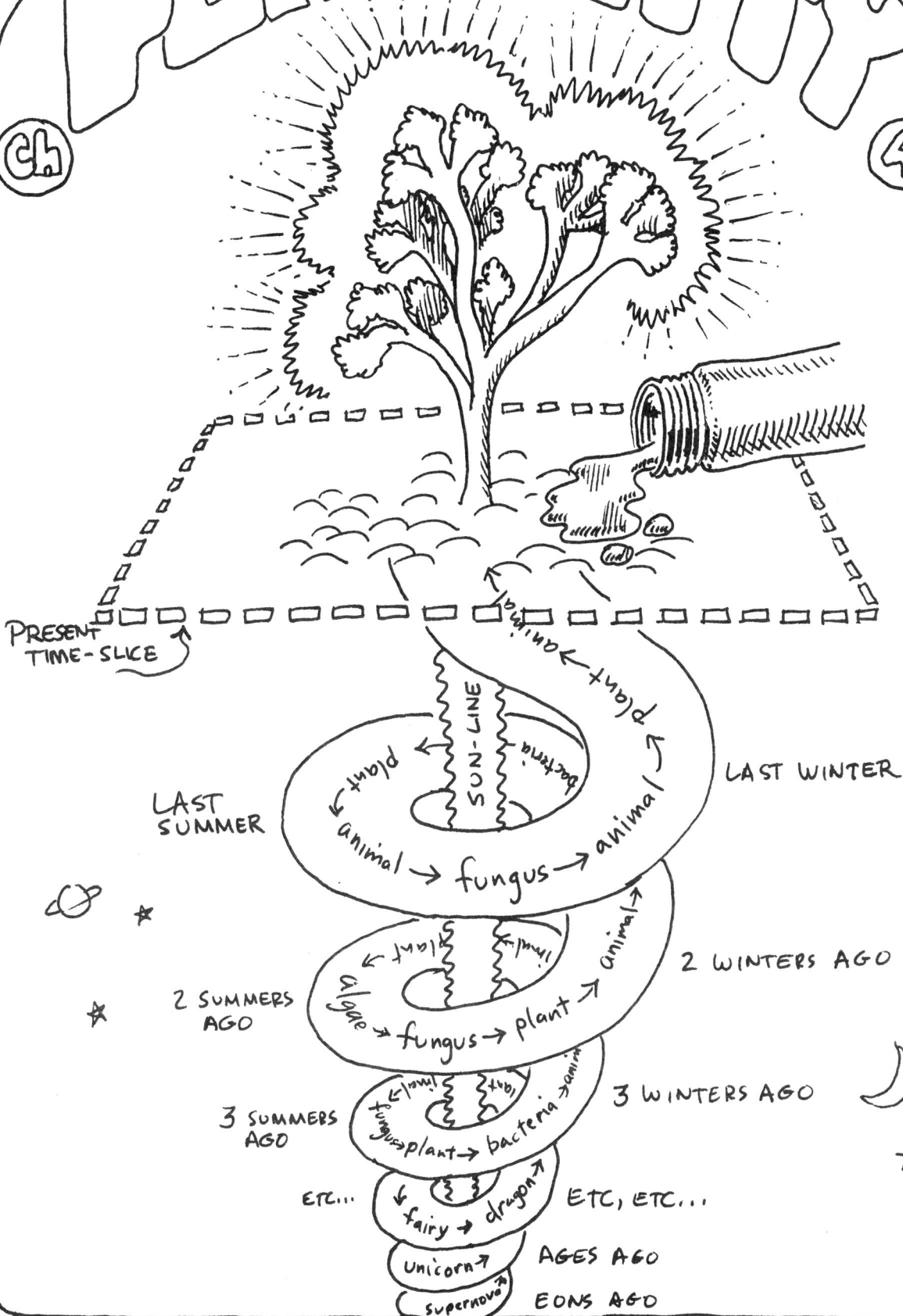

FERTILITY

Ch 4

PRESENT TIME-SLICE

SUN-LINE

plant → animal

plant ← bacteria

LAST SUMMER

animal → fungus → animal

LAST WINTER

2 SUMMERS AGO

algae → fungus → plant

plant ← animal

2 WINTERS AGO

3 SUMMERS AGO

fungus → plant → bacteria → animal

3 WINTERS AGO

ETC...

fairy → dragon

ETC, ETC...

Unicorn

AGES AGO

supernova

EONS AGO

WHY FERTILIZE?

WHY DO WE NEED TO FERTILIZE AT ALL?

AFTER ALL, NATURAL FORESTS AND GRASSLANDS DO JUST FINE WITH NOBODY RUNNING AROUND FERTILIZING THEM. SO WHY MUST WE FERTILIZE OUR GARDENS?

BECAUSE A FOREST IS A CLOSED LOOP... EVERYTHING STAYS IN THE SYSTEM:

...WHILE IN MODERN AGRICULTURE AND MOST HOME GARDENS, NUTRIENTS LEAVE THE SYSTEM:

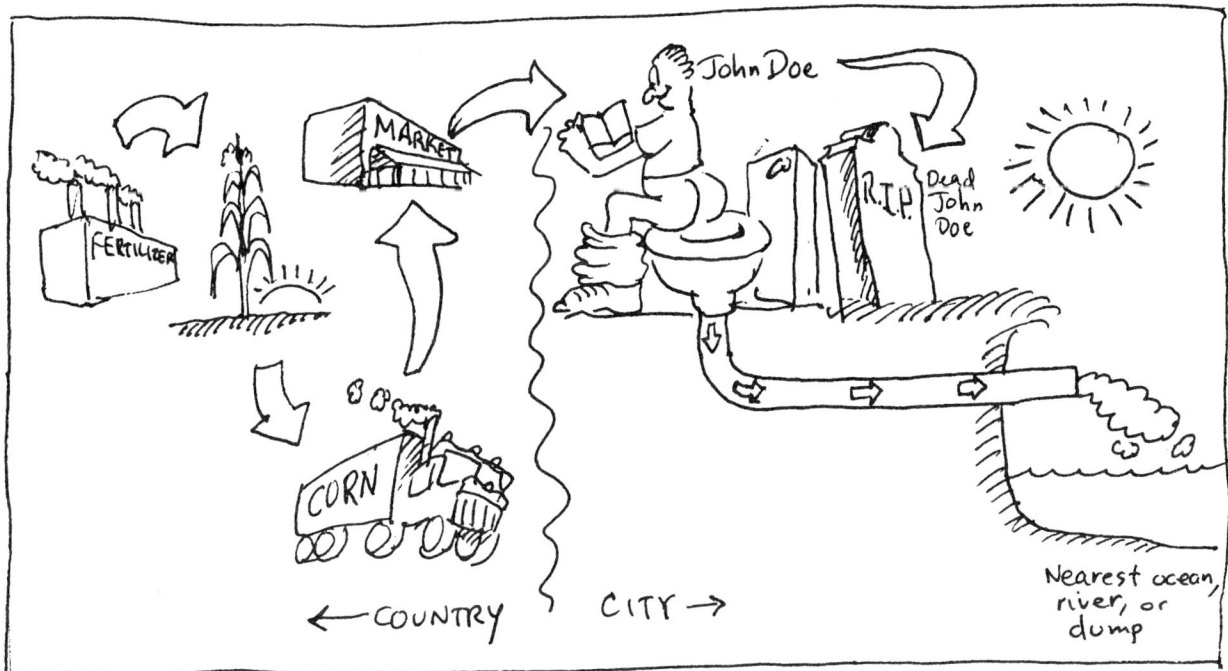

WITH EACH CARROT OR POTATO YOU PULL OUT OF THE GROUND, AND WITH EACH TOMATO YOU PICK, YOU'RE REMOVING **MATTER** FROM THE SOIL, WHERE THAT MATTER CAME FROM (EXCEPT FOR THE CARBON, WHICH CAME FROM THE AIR). THE MATTER YOU REMOVE MUST BE REPLACED. IN THIS CHAPTER I WILL DISCUSS FIVE METHODS OF REPLACING THE LOST NUTRIENTS: COMPOST, MANURE, "GREEN MANURE" (LEGUMES), HUMAN URINE, AND CROP ROTATION. ALL THESE SOURCES SHOULD BE USED IN COMBINATION, DEPENDING ON WHAT'S AVAILABLE LOCALLY--PREFERABLY FOR FREE.

USING COMPOST

REMEMBER THE COMPOST PILE WE STARTED IN CHAPTER ONE? IN TWO OR THREE WEEKS IT SHOULD BE READY TO START SIFTING AND ADDING TO THE SOIL. YOU CAN JUST BURY FRESH, UNCOMPOSTED MATERIALS (LIKE JUST-PULLED WEEDS, FRESH MANURE OR FRESH KITCHEN SCRAPS) IN THE DEEPER SOIL LAYERS 3-4 FEET DEEP) . . . BY THE TIME THE PLANT ROOTS GET THAT FAR DOWN, THE MATERIALS WILL HAVE FINISHED COMPOSTING. FOR THE UPPER LAYERS OF THE SOIL, USE FINISHED COMPOST--EITHER BY WAITING A FEW MONTHS FOR THE WHOLE PILE TO DECOMPOSE, OR BY SIFTING OUT THE FINISHED COMPOST.

COMPOST IS REALLY ALL YOU NEED TO MAINTAIN THE SOIL'S FERTILITY . . . YOU DON'T EVEN NEED MANURE, CONTRARY TO WHAT SOME ORGANIC FOLKS THINK. THE ONLY PROBLEM IS HAVING ENOUGH COMPOST . . . ENOUGH BEING ABOUT TWO FEET OF COMPOST MIXED INTO THE SOIL THE FIRST YEAR, AND ADDING ABOUT 6" AS MULCH EVERY YEAR AFTERWARDS. THIS DOESN'T MEAN YOU HAVE TO KEEP MAINTAINING HUGE PILES AFTER THE FIRST YEAR! AFTER SOIL FERTILITY AND TILTH ARE ESTABLISHED, YOU CAN PRACTICE "SHEET COMPOSTING," WHICH MEANS SIMPLY LAYING THE MATERIALS ON THE SURFACE OF THE SOIL, THE WAY NATURE DOES IT. (THERE ARE NO COMPOST PILES IN THE FOREST, ONLY A CONTINUOUSLY GROWING SURFACE LAYER OF LEAVES, TWIGS, ANIMAL DROPPINGS, ETC.) YOU'LL STILL WANT A SMALL PILE TO MAKE POTTING SOIL AND SEED-BED SOIL, SINCE ONLY AEROBIC COMPOSTING (WHICH MUST BE DONE IN A PILE TO BE EFFECTIVE) HAS THE HEAT TO PASTEURIZE THE COMPOST, KILLING DISEASE ORGANISMS WHICH AFFECT SEEDLINGS, SUCH AS DAMPING-OFF FUNGUS.

WHY COMPOST?

COMPOST IS BETTER THAN OTHER ORGANIC SOURCES SUCH AS BONE MEAL AND BLOOD MEAL. WHY?

> ... Becuz only COMPOST contains EXACTLY the right balance of nutrients your plants need! Becuz only COMPOST is made from the actual BODIES of plants and animals, while blood and bone meal are just two parts of animals only, which you must add together in (hopefully) the right proportions, since blood is deficient in phosphorus, while bones are deficient in nitrogen, and anyway, why bother with that when you can use COMPOST, which includes everything in the right balance, and is MUCH CHEAPER besides! Use COMPOST! MAKE SOME TODAY!

WITH CHEMICAL FERTILIZERS, THE PROBLEM OF GETTING THE RIGHT BALANCE IS EVEN WORSE--IT'S LIKE TRYING TO BUILD AN AIRPLANE USING ONLY PARTS FROM YOUR LOCAL HARDWARE STORE. SURE, YOU MIGHT END UP WITH SOMETHING THAT LOOKS LIKE AN AIRPLANE, BUT ODDS ARE IT WON'T FLY VERY WELL, IF AT ALL, AND IT'S NOT SOMETHING YOU'D WANT TO RISK YOUR HEALTH OVER.

NOT ONLY THAT, BUT THE CORRECT BALANCE OF NUTRIENTS IS CONSTANTLY CHANGING THROUGHOUT A PLANT'S LIFE CYCLE. PLANTS NEED A LOT OF NUTRIENTS AT FIRST, ESPECIALLY NITROGEN. THEIR NITROGEN USE TAPERS OFF GRADUALLY, SO BY THE END, WHEN THEY ARE MAKING SEEDS AND FRUIT, THEY DON'T WANT MUCH NITROGEN AROUND, AS IT INTERFERES WITH THE UPTAKE OF POTASSIUM AND PHOSPHORUS, WHICH THE PLANT NEEDS FOR FLOWERING AND FRUITING, WHILE NITROGEN IS MAINLY FOR LEAF GROWTH.

MIRACULOUSLY, ORGANIC MATTER IN THE SOIL CAUSES SOIL FERTILITY TO FLUCTUATE WITH THE SEASONS SO THERE IS ALWAYS JUST THE RIGHT BALANCE OF NUTRIENTS. HOW DOES THIS WORK? WHEN THE SUN'S HEAT WARMS THE SOIL IN THE SPRING, IT STIMULATES THE SOIL BACTERIA TO GROW AND DIVIDE. THE BACTERIA START MUNCHING ON LAST FALL'S ACCUMULATION OF ORGANIC MATTER (FALLEN LEAVES, ANIMAL DROPPINGS, ETC.), RELEASING NITROGEN INTO THE SOIL. THE NITROGEN RELEASED EXACTLY COINCIDES WITH THE PLANT'S NEEDS FOR NITROGEN:

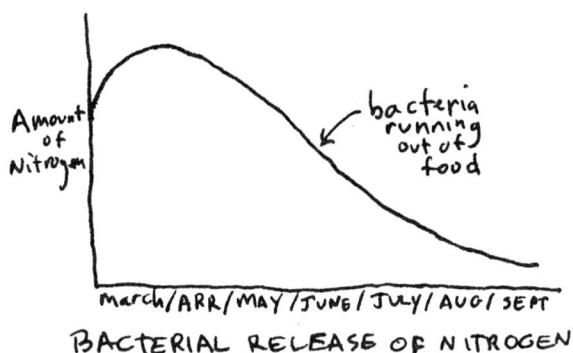

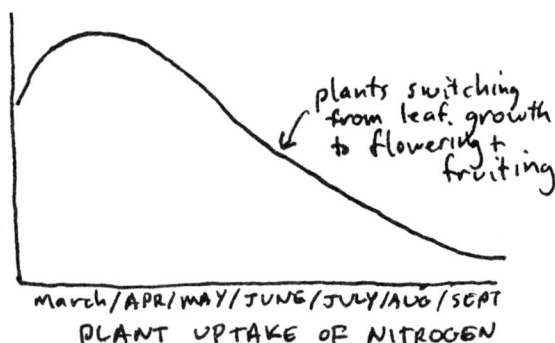

Amount of Nitrogen

bacteria running out of food

march/APR/MAY/JUNE/JULY/AUG/SEPT

BACTERIAL RELEASE OF NITROGEN

plants switching from leaf growth to flowering + fruiting

march/APR/MAY/JUNE/JULY/AUG/SEPT

PLANT UPTAKE OF NITROGEN

IF YOU DON'T LIKE GRAPHS, SEE THE NEXT PAGE FOR A CARTOON WHICH SHOWS THE PROCESS IN PICTURE FORM.

AS IF ALL THIS COSMIC RUBE GOLDBERG MACHINERY WEREN'T ENOUGH, THERE ARE THE MANY OTHER BENEFITS OF SOIL ORGANIC MATTER, AS DISCUSSED IN CHAPTER TWO: AERATION, BETTER SOIL STRUCTURE, ECOLOGICAL CONTROL OF SOIL PESTS SUCH AS NEMATODES, ETC., ETC. IT ALL ADDS UP (OR RATHER, IT ALL MULTIPLIES TOGETHER) TO THE FOLLOWING SAYING: "FEED THE SOIL, NOT THE PLANT!"

COMPOST and CARBON DIOXIDE

IN ADDITION TO PUTTING COMPOST IN THE SOIL, YOU SHOULD MULCH THE SURFACE WITH HALF-FINISHED COMPOST, OR EVEN RAW COMPOSTING MATERIALS (WAIT UNTIL YOUR VEGGIES COME UP BEFORE MULCHING!). WHEN COMPOST IS DECOMPOSING IT GIVES OFF CARBON DIOXIDE (CO_2), AND PLANTS CAN USE THE EXTRA CO_2 TO SPEED UP THEIR PHOTOSYNTHESIS. PLANTS' USE OF CO_2 IS ONE COG IN THE GREAT GLOBAL RECYCLING

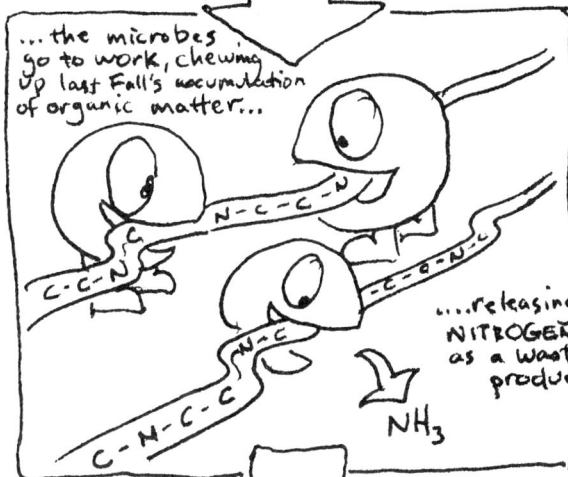

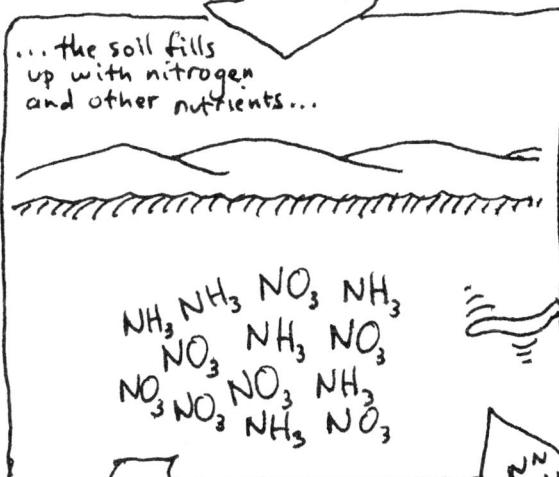

OPERATION CALLED THE CARBON CYCLE:

CO$_2$ IS HEAVIER THAN AIR, SO IT TENDS TO HANG OUT ON THE SOIL SURFACE FOR A WHILE BEFORE IT'S DISPERSED BY THE WINDS. IF YOUR GARDEN HAS WINDBREAKS, LIKE MOST BACKYARDS SURROUNDED BY BUILDINGS AND FENCES, THIS EFFECT WILL BE ENHANCED.

ANOTHER REASON TO MULCH WITH COMPOST IS TO BOOST THE SOIL FERTILITY THE FIRST YEAR. WHEN LARGE AMOUNTS OF COMPOST ARE ADDED TO A SOIL FOR THE FIRST TIME, FERTILITY CAN ACTUALLY DE-CLINE FOR A YEAR OR SO. THAT'S BECAUSE NO

MATTER HOW CAREFULLY YOU MANAGE THE COMPOST PILE, THERE WILL ALWAYS BE SMALL POCKETS OF UNDIGESTED CARBON, WHICH WILL ROB NITROGEN FROM THE SOIL AS THEY DECOMPOSE (SEE CHAPTER ONE). LAY 3-4" OF COMPOST ON THE SURFACE AT ONE-MONTH INTERVALS DURING THE GROWING SEASON, AND RUN WATER THROUGH THIS MULCH. THE RESULT IS A SORT OF "COMPOST TEA," WHICH LEACHES NITROGEN FROM THE COMPOST INTO THE SOIL. IF YOU'RE INTO TECHNOLOGY, YOU CAN BUILD A "COMPOST TEAPOT," USING A 55-GALLON DRUM:

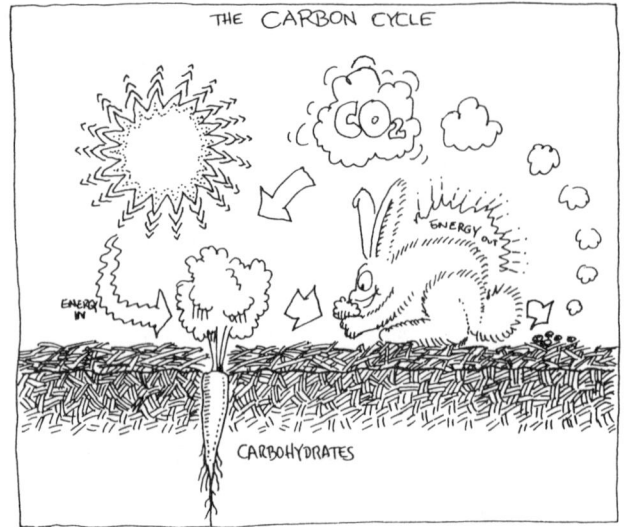

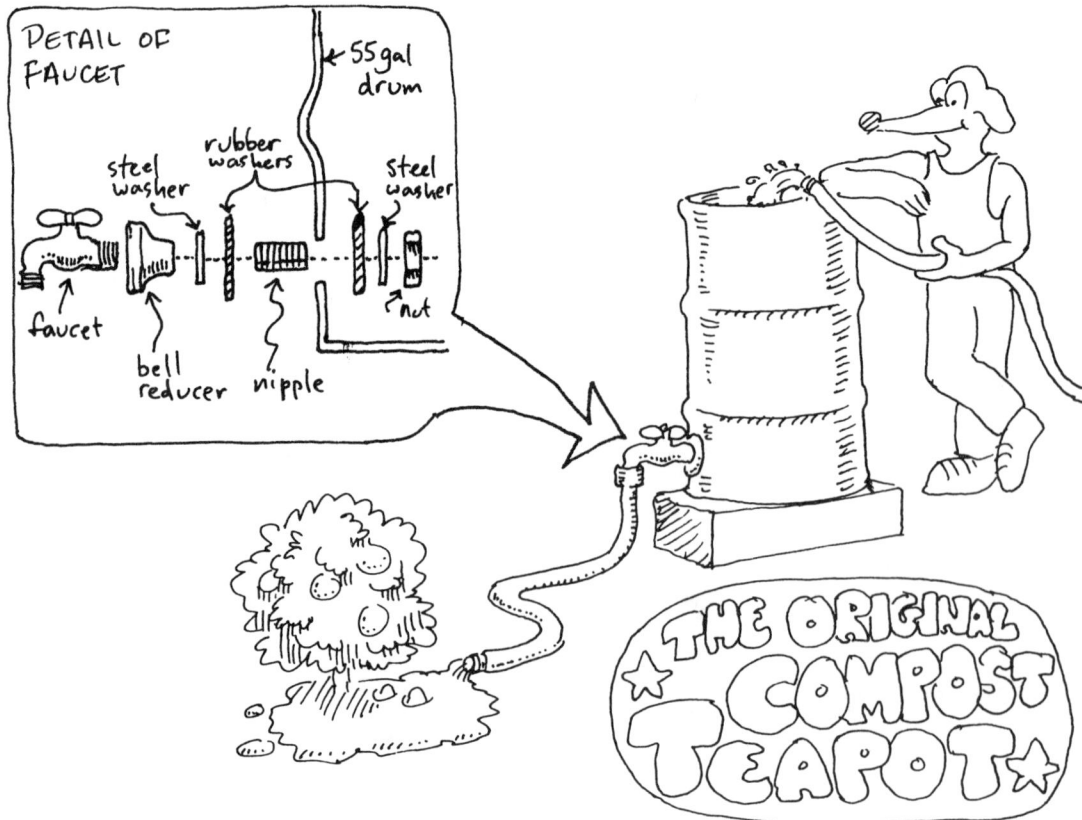

THE CARBON CYCLE

ENERGY IN

CO$_2$

ENERGY OUT

CARBOHYDRATES

DETAIL OF FAUCET

55 gal drum

steel washer

rubber washers

steel washer

faucet

bell reducer

nipple

nut

☆ THE ORIGINAL COMPOST TEAPOT ☆

THE DRUM CAN BE PAINTED BLACK TO HELP IT ABSORB HEAT FROM THE SUN. THE "SPENT" COMPOST RESIDUE CAN BE SPREAD ON THE SOIL SURFACE AS MULCH.

COMPOST TEA IS ALSO GOOD FOR PROVIDING A SHOT OF NITROGEN OR SOME OTHER NUTRIENT TO THE PLANT, A TECHNIQUE WHICH IS USEFUL IN CERTAIN SITUATIONS, SUCH AS HIGH-PHOSPHORUS TO STIMULATE FLOWERING IN SOME PLANTS (I'LL COME TO THAT LATER).

MANURE

COWS — THE REAL SOIL FERTILITY EXPERTS!

A COWPIE IS A LOT LIKE A MINIATURE COMPOST PILE: IT CONTAINS MAINLY DECAYING PIECES OF PLANTS (WHICH YOU CAN SEE IF YOU LOOK CLOSELY), BACTERIA, AND WASTE NITROGEN THE ANIMAL IS THROWING AWAY. SO YOU CAN USE MANURE MUCH AS YOU USE COMPOST: YOU CAN DIG IT INTO THE SOIL, SPREAD IT ON THE SURFACE, OR USE IT AS ONE OF YOUR COMPOSTING MATERIALS. IN FACT, MANURES USED TO BE THE MAIN METHOD OF FERTILIZATION, BEFORE THE INVENTION OF CHEMICAL FERTILIZERS.

MANURES ARE FUNKY, THERE'S NO GETTING AROUND IT. ALTHOUGH MOST MANURES SMELL BETTER THAN HUMAN MANURE, THEY STILL ARE CONSIDERED PRETTY LOW-RENT. LET'S FACE IT, "FERTILITY" IN GENERAL GETS DOWN AND DIRTY! IT'S STEAMY, SLIMY, PULSING, . . . "IT'S . . . IT'S . . . MY GOD, IT'S ALIVE!!" AND WE LIVE IN A CULTURE THAT WORSHIPS ALL THE OPPOSITE QUALITIES: STERILITY, ANISEPTICS, INFERTILITY, HARD, COLD SURFACES, INANIMATE OBJECTS, MACHINES. BUT YOU'LL GET OVER THAT, ESPECIALLY ONCE YOU SEE WHAT LIVING THINGS LIKE MANURE CAN DO FOR YOUR GARDEN.

MANURE IS GENERALLY APPLIED AT THE RATE OF 15 TONS/ACRE PER YEAR, OR ABOUT 1" THICK ON THE SOIL SURFACE. IT'S RECOMMENDED THAT YOU DON'T APPLY OVER 25 TONS PER YEAR, SINCE MANY MANURES ARE SALTY, AND THE SALTS CAN BUILD UP IN YOUR SOIL. USUALLY YOU SHOULD ALSO LAYER ON STRAW OR OTHER CROP RESIDUE. THE JAPANESE NATURAL FARMING PROPONENT MANASOBU FUKUOKA (THE ONE-STRAW REVOLUTION) JUST LEAVES THE STRAW FROM THE PREVIOUS RICE HARVEST, AND LETS DUCKS ONTO THE FIELDS. THE EFFECT IS THE SAME AS "COMPOSTING," BUT WITHOUT ALL THE WORK.

MANURE BY ITSELF IS GENERALLY CONSIDERED AN INCOMPLETE FERTILIZER, BECAUSE IT IS DEFICIENT IN PHOSPHORUS. THE "NPK" (NITROGEN-PHOSPHORUS-POTASSIUM) PERCENTAGE OF MOST MANURE IS AROUND 1-1/2-1, WHILE A BALANCED FERTILIZER WOULD BE 1-1-1. TO CORRECT THIS IMBALANCE, MOST ORGANIC FARMERS USING MANURE ADD BONE MEAL OR PHOSPHATE ROCK TO SUPPLY THE MISSING PHOSPHORUS.

MANURE IS LOW IN PHOSPHORUS BECAUSE ANIMALS HORDE THIS COMPOUND IN THEIR BONES. SO BONE MEAL IS A FITTING SUPPLEMENT TO MANURE, ALTHOUGH PHOSPHATE ROCK IS USUALLY CHEAPER. THE BEST SOLUTION IS TO SIMPLY USE MANURE AS JUST ONE COMPONENT OF A COMPOSTING PROCESS, WHETHER IN PILES OR AS MULCH OVER THE SOIL SURFACE.

GREEN MANURE

THE REAL KICKER IS, MANURE OR COMPOST AREN'T EVEN NECESSARY, AT LEAST NOT AT THE LEVEL USED SINCE ANTIQUITY, BECAUSE CERTAIN LEGUMES CAN GET ALL THE FERTILIZER THEY NEED OUT OF THIN AIR! NOT ONLY THAT, BUT THEY HELP FEED OTHER PLANTS GROWING NEARBY.

THE PLANTS THAT DO THIS ARE CALLED "GREEN MANURE," BECAUSE YOU CAN DIG THEM INTO THE SOIL (OR BURY THEM WITH MULCH), AND THE EFFECT WILL BE THE SAME AS ADDING MANURE (ACTUALLY, BETTER THAN MANURE, SINCE THEY HAVE A BALANCED NPK.) THIS MAGIC ACT IS CALLED "NITROGEN FIXATION."

HERE'S A VISION I HAD ABOUT NITROGEN FIXATION ...IT'S LIKE A GREAT HORSE'S ASS IN THE SKY, RAINING DOWN FERTILITY IN BOUNTEOUS GLORY ON THE LAND!! MANNA FROM HEAVEN; MANURE OF THE GODS. LOOKS A BIT LIKE THE BIBLICAL VISIONS OF GOD APPEARING IN THE SKY, HUH? WELL, WHY NOT? IF YOU'RE LOOKING FOR SOMETHING TO WORSHIP, DON'T WASTE YOUR TIME WITH HAIRY KRISHNA OR SWAMI SALAMI OR BABA BLAH-BLAH--THIS IS THE REAL THING!!

NITROGEN FIXATION

LET'S GET MICROSCOPIC

THERE ARE PROBLEMS WITH GROWING A GREEN MANURE PLANT IF IT'S NOT NATIVE TO YOUR LOCATION (IN OTHER WORDS, A "WEED"). THE MAIN PROBLEM IS THAT OFTEN YOU MUST INNOCULATE THE SOIL WITH A CERTAIN TYPE OF BACTERIA TO MAKE NITROGEN FIXATION HAPPEN. TO UNDERSTAND WHY, LET'S TAKE A LOOK INSIDE LEGUME ROOT CELLS TO SEE HOW THEY TAKE NITROGEN OUT OF THE AIR:

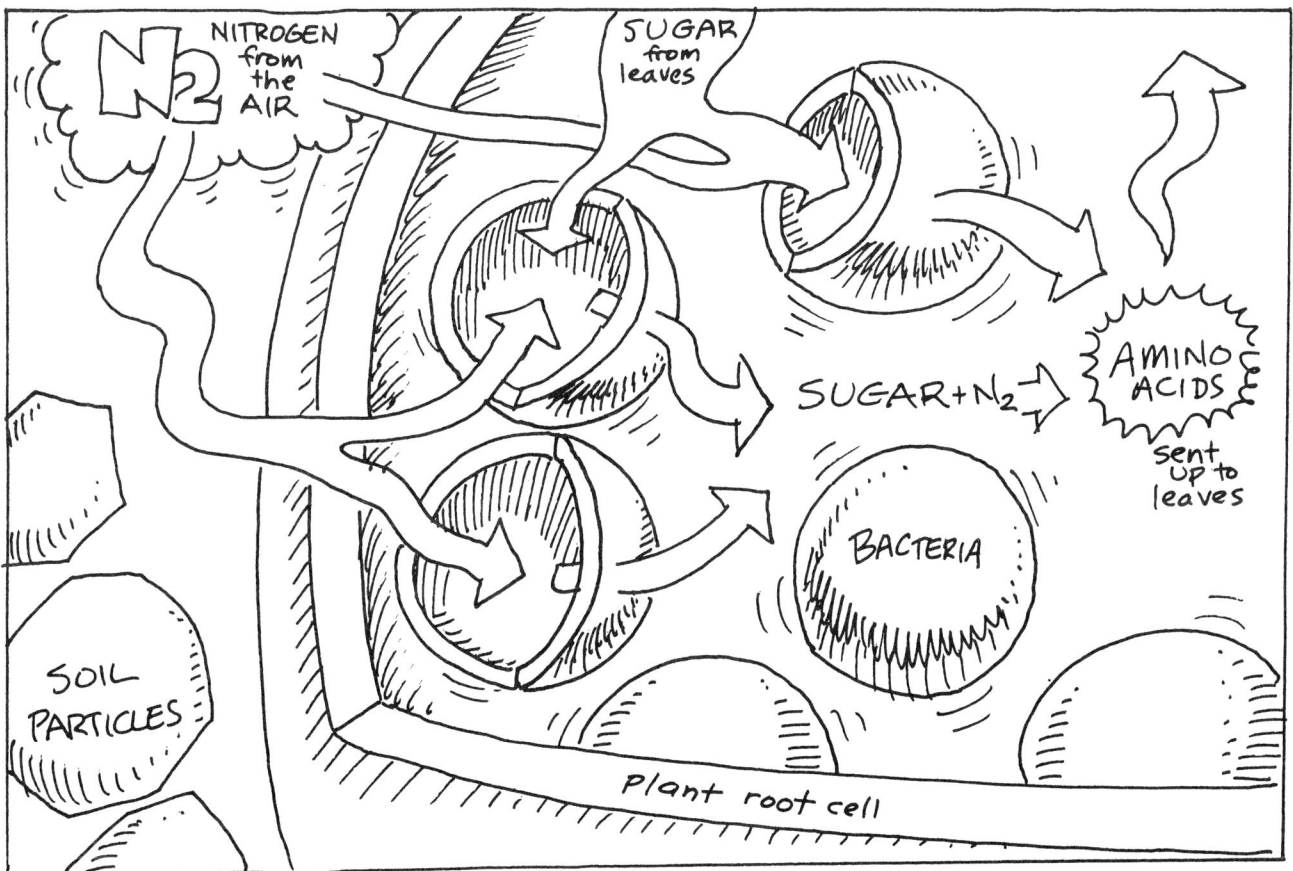

AS THE PICTURE SHOWS, THE ROOTS OF LEGUMES CONTAIN SYMBIOTIC BACTERIA WHICH ACTUALLY DO THE WORK OF GRABBING NITROGEN (N_2) OUT OF THE AIR AND INCORPORATING IT INTO ORGANIC COMPOUNDS WHICH THE PLANT CAN USE. (NITROGEN WHEN INCORPORATED INTO ORGANIC COMPOUNDS IS CALLED "FIXED" NITROGEN; HENCE THE TERM "NITROGEN FIXATION"). IN EXCHANGE FOR THIS, BACTERIA GET SUGARS FROM THE PLANT, WHICH THEY COMBINE WITH THE NITROGEN TO MAKE AMINO ACIDS, WHICH BOTH BACTERIA AND PLANT CAN USE.

THE BACTERIA ENTER THE PLANT THROUGH SPECIAL SLITS IN THE ROOT CELL WALLS:

THE BACTERIA SECRETE ENZYMES WHICH DISSOLVE THE CEMENT HOLDING TOGETHER THE CELLULOSE MICROFIBRILS (VERTICAL STRANDS IN THE PICTURE) OF THE ROOT CELLS, THUS FORMING THE SLITS. LOOKS PRETTY STAR-TREKKY, DOESN'T IT? (THE LARGE OBJECTS TO THE RIGHT AND LEFT ARE SAND GRAINS.)

THE ONLY PROBLEM IS, IT TAKES A CERTAIN SPECIES OF BACTERIA TO ENTER AND SET UP SHOP IN ANY PARTICULAR GROUP OF LEGUMES, SO YOU'LL HAVE TO INNOCULATE YOUR SOIL IF THERE HASN'T BEEN A RELATED LEGUME GROWING THERE IN THE PAST FEW YEARS, EITHER AS A WEED OR A CROP PLANT.

THESE GROUPS OF RELATED LEGUMES ARE:

1. ALFALFA GROUP. INCLUDES ALFALFA ("LUCERNE"), MOST OF THE GENUS TRIGONELLA, INCLUDING FENUGREEK (A GRECIAN LEGUME USED AS GREEN MANURE IN CALIFORNIA); MOST OF THE GENUS MELILOTUS (SWEET CLOVERS) AND THE GENUS MEDICAGO (WHICH INCLUDES ALFALFA). THE MEMBERS OF THIS GROUP ARE GENERALLY DROUGHT-TOLERANT, AND PREFER ALKALINE SOIL.

2. PEA GROUP. INCLUDES THE GENUSES PISUM (PEAS), LATHYRUS, (SWEET PEAS), VICIA (VETCH), AND LENS (INCLUDING LENTILS).

3. CLOVER GROUP. ALL CLOVERS (TRIFOLIUM GENUS) EXCEPT SWEET CLOVERS, WHICH ARE IN THE ALFALFA GROUP. CALIFORNIA IS ESPECIALLY WELL-ENDOWED WITH

CLOVERS, BOTH NATIVE AND NATURALIZED.

4. **COWPEA GROUP.** THE MOST PROMISCUOUS GROUP: INCLUDES BLACK-EYED PEAS (COWPEAS, VIGNA GENUS), MUNG BEANS, ADZUKI BEANS, TEPARY, URD, GRAM, MAT, MOTH BEANS, APARAGUS BEANS ("YARDLONG BEANS"), AND LESPEDEZA. ALSO THE SILK TREE, ALBIZIA JULIBRISSIN (A COMMON LANDSCAPING TREE).

5. **BEAN GROUP.** INCLUDES ALL BEANS EXCEPT SOY, GARBONZO, AND THE BEANS IN THE COWPEA GROUP.

6. **SOYBEAN GROUP.** INCLUDES SOYBEANS (GLYCINE MAX) AND KUDZU (GLYCINE WIGHTII).

7. **LUPINE GROUP.** INCLUDES MOST LUPINES, AND THE ORNITHOPUS GENUS.

IF THE LEGUME YOU WANT TO GROW IS IN THE SAME GROUP AS ANOTHER LEGUME THAT'S BEEN GROWING IN YOUR SOIL RECENTLY, YOU'RE IN THE MONEY. IF NOT, THE LEGUME WILL GROW, BUT IT WON'T GET "FREE" NITROGEN UNLESS YOU INNOCULATE THE SOIL WITH THE RIGHT SPECIES OF BACTERIA.

TO INNOCULATE, YOU CAN EITHER TAKE SOIL FROM THE ROOT-ZONE OF ACTIVELY-N-FIXING PLANTS IN THE SAME GROUP, AND ADD IT TO YOUR GARDEN SOIL, OR ADD A BIT OF WATER TO THE BACTERIA-LADEN SOIL AND SOAK YOUR SEEDS IN THE MUD, MAKING A SORT OF "BACTERIA TEA." OR YOU CAN BUY ALREADY-INNOCULATED SEEDS, OR BACTERIA CULTURES. ANYWAY, YOU DON'T NEED MANY BACTERIA, SINCE THE PLANT SENDS OUT CHEMICALS TO STIMULATE THE GROWTH OF THE RIGHT TYPE OF BACTERIA!!!

TO TELL WHETHER A PLANT IS ACTIVELY FIXING NITROGEN, DIG UP THE ROOTS. THERE SHOULD BE "NODULES" ON THE TAPROOT AND UPPER LATERALS, LIKE THIS:

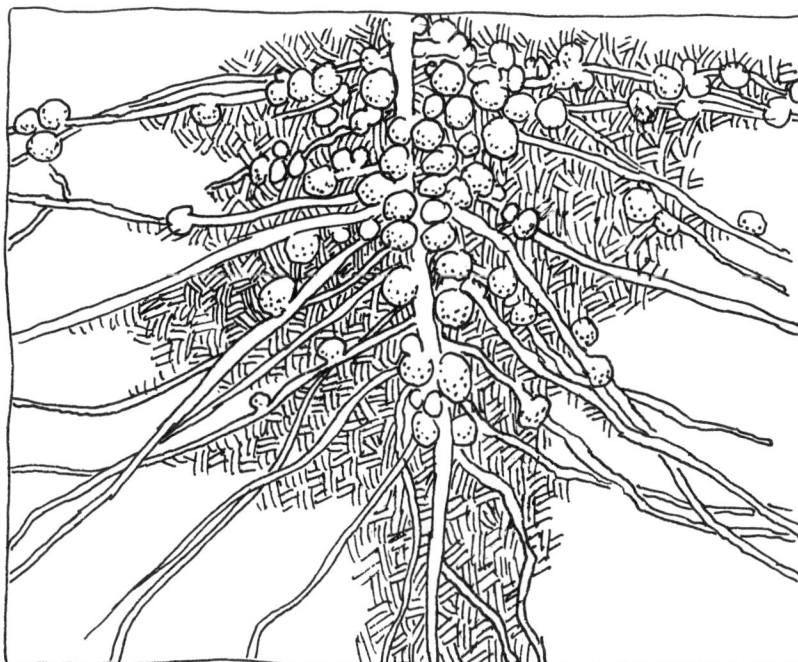

NOT ONLY THAT, BUT THE NODULES MUST BE REDDISH OR PINKISH, NOT GREEN OR WHITE. GREEN OR WHITE NODULES MEANS BACTERIA HAVE ENTERED THE ROOTS, BUT ARE NOT FIXING NITROGEN PROPERLY. RED NODULES MEANS BAC-TERIA ARE MAKING "LEG-HEMOGLOBIN," A SUBSTANCE SIMILAR TO THE HEMOGLOBIN PROTEINS IN OUR RED BLOOD

CELLS WHICH MAKE THEM RED, AND WHICH CARRY OXYGEN. SCIENTISTS THINK LEG-HEMOGLOBIN COULD CARRY NITROGEN, SIMILAR TO THE WAY HEMOGLOBIN CARRIES OXYGEN.

YOU CAN ENCOURAGE THE WEED-LEGUMES NATIVE TO YOUR AREA, OR BUY SEEDS OF PLANTS THAT WILL FIT YOUR CLIMATE. HERE'S A LIST OF GREEN MANURE PLANTS FOR DIFFERENT CLIMATES:

WARM REGIONS	**ANYWHERE**
CRIMSON CLOVER	ALFALFA
BUR CLOVER	RED CLOVER
LESPEDEZA	SWEET CLOVER
CROTALARIA	SOYBEAN
VETCH	CANADIAN FIELD PEA
AUSTRALIAN WINTER PEA	COWPEA

climbing tendril

THE AVERAGE LEGUME

TO IDENTIFY LEGUMES AMONG YOUR WEEDS, LOOK AT THE LEAF-SHAPE AND POSITION. MOST LEGUMES HAVE ROUNDISH-OBLONG LEAVES, SPACED OPPOSITE EACH OTHER ON THE STEM, OR IN A SMALL GROUP OF THREE (CLOVER) OR EIGHT (LUPINE) LEAVES. THE LEAVES ARE USUALLY DARK GREEN (BECAUSE THEY HAVE NO PROBLEM GETTING NITROGEN), AND GROWTH IS LUSH AND VIGOROUS. THE STEMS OFTEN HAVE A CLIMBING TENDRIL ON THE END. IF A PLANT LOOKS ANYTHING LIKE THE "AVERAGE LEGUME" IT PROBABLY IS ONE, AND 90 PERCENT OF ALL LEGUMES FIX NITROGEN.

NITROGEN-FIXATION WORKS BEST IF THE SOIL IS LOW IN NITROGEN. IF THE SOIL HAS PLENTY OF NITROGEN, THE PLANT (AND BACTERIA) FIGURE, "WHY BOTHER WITH GETTING NITROGEN OUT OF THE AIR, LET'S JUST LIVE OFF THE FAT OF THE LAND!" NITROGEN FIXATION EVOLVED AS A WAY FOR PLANTS TO GROW IN INFERTILE SOIL; IF THE SOIL HAS ENOUGH NITROGEN, THEY SIMPLY SHUT THE FIXATION MECHANISM OFF, TO SAVE ENERGY. LEGUMES ARE COMMON AMONG WEEDS BECAUSE WEEDS IN GENERAL ARE IMPORTANT TO THE NATURAL ECOLOGY AS "COLONIZER" OR "PIONEER" SPECIES—THEY MOVE IN WHERE NOTHING ELSE CAN GROW, OFTEN BECAUSE THE SOIL IS INFERTILE. THEN WHEN THEY DIE, THEIR BODIES FERTILIZE THE SOIL SO LARGER SHRUBS AND TREES CAN GROW. AN EXAMPLE OF THIS IS THE RED ALDER/DOUGLAS FIR SUCCESSION CYCLE ON THE WEST COAST. (ALTHOUGH ALDER IS NOT A LEGUME, IT HAS SYMBIOTIC FUNGI IN ITS ROOTS THAT FILL THE SAME FUNCTION AS BACTERIA IN LEGUMES.)

IN THE DOUGLAS FIR/RED ALDER SUCCESSION, NITROGEN LEAVES THE SYSTEM (EVAPORATES AS AMMONIA GAS) DURING THE PERIODIC FIRES THAT RAGE THROUGH MATURE DOUGLAS FIR FORESTS, BUT THE LOST NITROGEN IS REPLACED BY THE NITROGEN-FIXING FUNGI IN THE ALDER ROOTS.

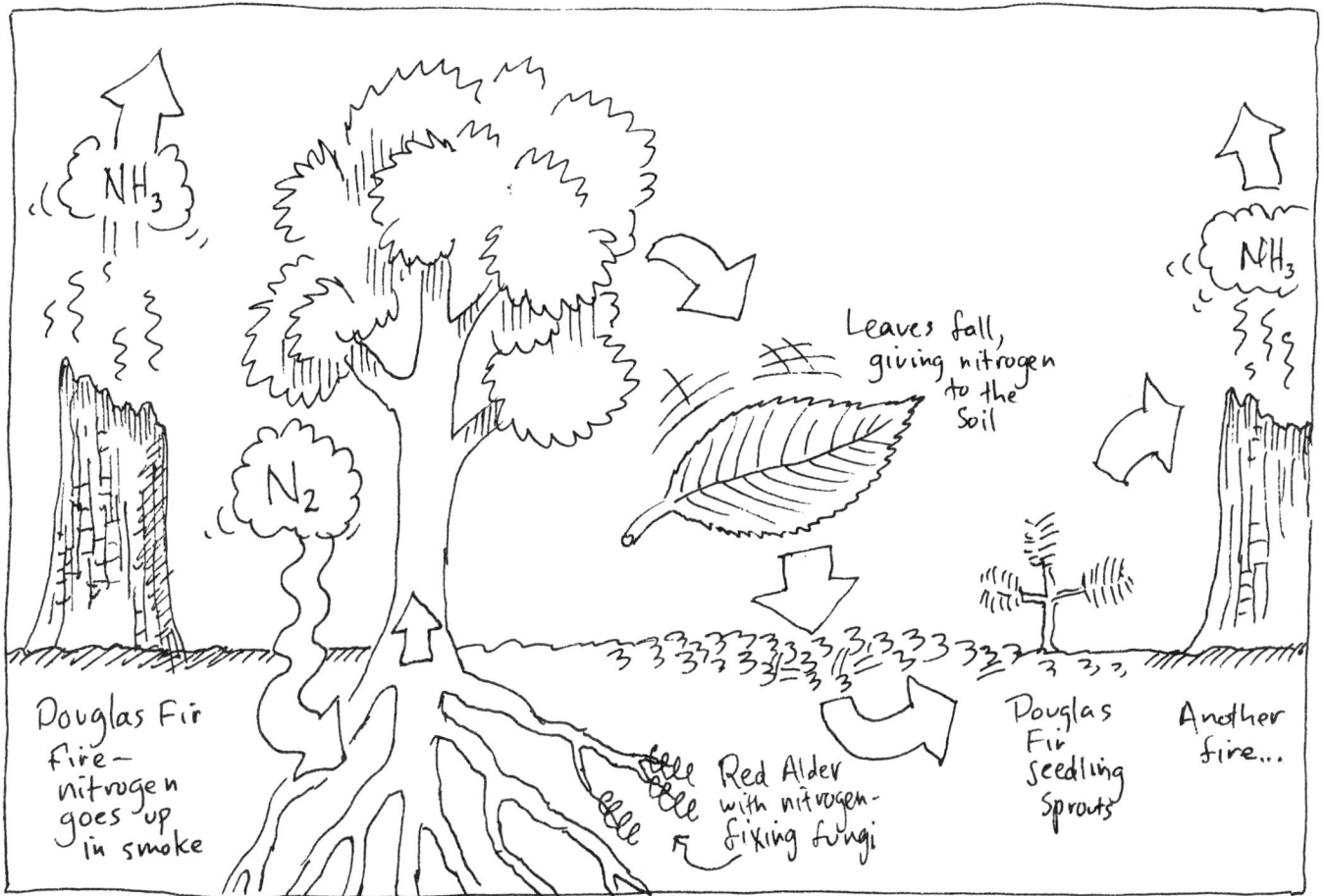

CROP ROTATION

WE CAN MIMICK THESE NATURAL CYCLES IN OUR FARMS AND GARDENS. THIS AGE-OLD PRACTICE IS CALLED "CROP ROTATION." IT IS DONE INTUITIVELY BY PRIMITIVE CULTURES, AND IT WAS REVIVED IN THE 19TH CENTURY BY MORE "ADVANCED" CULTURES AFTER "NITROGEN FIXATION" WAS DISCOVERED, ONLY TO BE ABANDONED ONCE AGAIN WITH THE ONSET OF CHEMICAL FERTILIZERS. NOW THE GREAT CULTURAL SUCCESSION CYCLE IS SWINGING AROUND AGAIN, AND IT'S TIME TO GET BACK "INTO" CROP ROTATION.

COMPARE THE TRADITIONAL CORN-CLOVER CROP ROTATION SCHEME WITH THE NATURAL FIR-ALDER SUCCESSION. IN BOTH CASES, THE NITROGEN TAKEN FROM THE SYSTEM IS REPLACED BY NITROGEN-FIXATION.

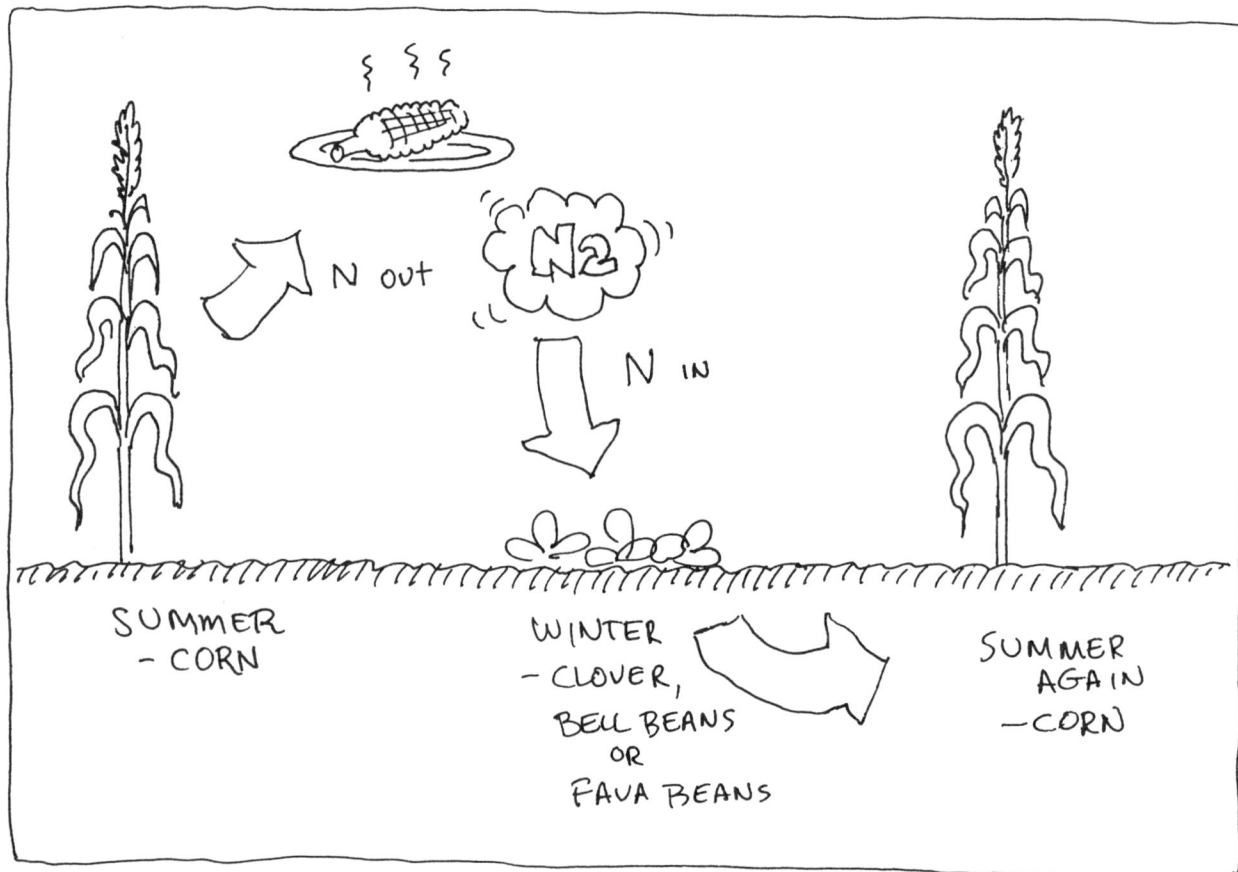

IN TRADITIONAL (19TH CENTURY) CROP ROTATION, THE CORN AND LEGUMES ARE SEPARATED IN TIME, WITH CORN IN THE SUMMER AND LEGUMES IN THE WINTER, OR WITH THE TWO ALTERNATING FROM YEAR TO YEAR. THE STATE-OF-THE-ART NOW IS TO ATTEMPT GROWING BOTH AT THE SAME TIME, WITH THE LEGUMES GROWING UNDER OR BETWEEN THE CROP PLANTS. IF THE LEGUMES HAVE SHALLOW-ENOUGH ROOTS (AS DOES CLOVER), THEY WON'T BE COMPETING WITH THE CROP PLANTS FOR WATER, OR NUTRIENTS OTHER THAN NITROGEN. THE JAPANESE FARMER MANASOBU FUKUOKA IS GROWING WHITE CLOVER SIMULTANEOUSLY WITH WHEAT, AND WITH ORANGE TREES.

THIS NEW PRACTICE IS ACTUALLY VERY SIMILAR TO THE ANCIENT "PRIMITIVE" MEXICAN SYSTEM OF INTERPLANTING CORN AND BEANS. CONTROLLED STUDIES OF THIS SYSTEM HAVE SHOWN THAT BEANS CAN SUPPLY ENOUGH NITROGEN FOR THEMSELVES, WHILE LEAVING THE OTHER NITROGEN IN THE SOIL FOR THE CORN, AND SQUASH AS WELL. IN FACT, THE CORN DOES BETTER WITH BEANS AROUND. IT'S NOT KNOWN WHY THIS SYNERGISTIC EFFECT TAKES PLACE.

THE USUAL PRACTICE IN CORN-BEAN-SQUASH POLYCULTURE IS TO PLANT THE BEAN SEEDS A FEW WEEKS AFTER THE CORN AND SQUASH ARE ALREADY ESTABLISHED. THIS INSURES BOTH THAT THE CLIMBING BEAN VINES WILL NOT STRANGLE THE YOUNG CORN PLANTS, AND THAT THE CORN WILL HAVE A CHANCE TO USE UP SOME OF THE SOIL NITROGEN, SO THE BEANS WILL HAVE THE LOW-NITROGEN CONDITIONS NECESSARY FOR EFFECTIVE NITROGEN-FIXATION.

SPECIAL FERTILIZING TECHNIQUES

LONG-DAY PLANTS ARE STIMULATED TO FLOWER BY HIGH-PHOSPHATE, LOW-NITROGEN CONDITIONS IN THE SOIL. YOU CAN CREATE THESE CONDITIONS WITH A SPECIAL HIGH-PHOSPORUS COMPOST. MAKE A SPECIAL PILE WITH ONE OR MORE OF THE FOLLOWING INGREDIENTS: PHOSPHATE ROCK, BONE MEAL, FOLIAGE OF BRIDAL BOWER (SPIREA BUMALDA), MARIGOLD, CHICKWEED (STELLARIA MEDIA), LEMON BALM (MELISSA OFFICINALE), BANANA PEELS, AND ASHES.

WHEN THIS COMPOST IS READY, YOU CAN USE IT TO STIMULATE THE FLOWERING OF LONG-DAY PLANTS, INCLUDING: DILL, OATS, PEAS, CLOVER, VETCH, CARNATION, DAISY, FOXGLOVE, SNAPDRAGON, PETUNIA, BEGONIA.

ONLY A SINGLE SHOT OF HIGH-P IS NEEDED AT THE START OF FLOWERING. YOU CAN EITHER LAY THE COMPOST ON THE SOIL SURFACE AROUND THE PLANTS AND WATER THROUGH IT, OR PUT THE COMPOST IN YOUR COMPOST TEAPOT.

SPECIAL TECHNIQUE No. 2

THERE ARE OTHER LONG-DAY PLANTS WHICH YOU NORMALLY **DON'T** WANT TO FLOWER, AND WHICH HAVE A TENDENCY TO "BOLT-TO-FLOWER" PREMATURELY IN THE LONG DAYS AND WARM WEATHER OF EARLY SUMMER. AN EXAMPLE IS LETTUCE. IF YOU GIVE THESE PLANTS A SHOT OF HIGH NITROGEN WHEN THE WEATHER TURNS WARM, YOU MAY BE ABLE TO PREVENT FLOWERING (THIS IS AN UNPROVEN, EXPERIMENTAL TECHNIQUE, SO GOOD LUCK!) YOU CAN PREPARE A SPECIAL HIGH-N COMPOST, BUT AN EASIER WAY IS TO USE YOUR OWN URINE. URINE IS GENERALLY BEST TO USE IN COMPOSTING SINCE IT IS MOSTLY NITROGEN, SO NOT A BALANCED FERTILIZER. URINE SHOULD BE DILUTED ABOUT 5-1 WHEN PUT ON FOOT-HIGH PLANTS SUCH AS LETTUCE, AND THIS SOLUTION CAN BE USED INSTEAD OF THE NORMAL IRRIGATION WATER WHEN DAYS ARE LONG, THE WEATHER IS WARM, AND THERE'S A DANGER OF BOLTING.

FERTILITY WRAP-UP
(Or What Does a Healthy Plant Look Like)

A HEALTHY PLANT GLOWS--IT JUST OOZES OUT GOOD HEALTH AND VITALITY, AS IF THE CONFINING DIMENSIONS OF ITS STEMS AND LEAVES WERE NOT ENOUGH SPACE TO CONTAIN ITS EXUBERANCE. THIS IS SOMETHING IT TAKES SOME PRACTICE TO SEE, OR RATHER FEEL . . . IT GIVES THE IMPRESSION OF AN AURA OR VIBRATING FIELD AROUND THE PLANT.

VISIONS

NOW THAT YOU GOT YOUR SOIL CLICKIN', YOU CAN START PLANNING THIS YEAR'S GARDEN (OR WINTER GARDEN, IF YOU'RE READING THIS IN THE SUMMER). NEXT CHAPTER WE GET TO SPACE OUT, FOLLOWING A SUNBEAM ON ITS JOURNEY TO EARTH. THEN, WE GET DOWN AT GROUND LEVEL AND EXPERIENCE WHAT A PLANT FEELS AT VARIOUS TIMES OF THE YEAR, IN VARIOUS LOCATIONS. WITH YOUR HEAD IN THE CLOUDS AND YOUR NOSE TO THE GROUND, YOU'LL BE READY TO RECEIVE THE VISION: YOUR NEXT GARDEN PLAN.

GARDEN PLANS

CHAPTER

5

IT ALL REVOLVES
AROUND THE SUN

WHEN YOU PLAN YOUR GARDEN, YOU GOTTA GET COSMIC. SPACE OUT FOR AWHILE, AND LOOK AT THINGS FROM THE BIG PERSPECTIVE. BECAUSE THE WHOLE SHOW BEGAN WITH THE SUN, IT CONTINUES TO DEPEND ON THE SUN FOR NEARLY EVERYTHING, AND IT WILL ALL END WITH THE SUN, WHEN OUR HARD-WORKING LITTLE STAR GETS IT UP IN THE SKY FOR THE LAST TIME AND "GOES NOVA," THE LAST HURRAH FOR THE SOLAR SYSTEM, THE SWAN SONG TO END ALL SWAN SONGS.

MEANWHILE, BEFORE THAT TIME COMES, WE'RE ALL DOWN HERE SWIMMING IN OCEANS OF LOVING WARMTH, ONE VAST ORGY OF SOLAR-POWERED RECREATION, PROCREATION, AND GOLDEN HONEY-DREAMS. AND THE WHOLE PULSING GREEN AND GOLDEN LIFE MACHINE DEPENDS ON THE SIMPLE ACT OF PLANTS GRABBING THE SUN'S RAYS, RUNNING THEM AROUND LITTLE CELLULAR GENERATORS, AND EXTRACTING THE ENERGY FOR USE IN BUILDING SUGAR MOLECULES. WITHOUT THIS CRUCIAL SUNBEAM-RECEPTION MECHANISM (CALLED PHOTOSYNTHESIS), THERE WOULD BE NO ANIMALS, NO OATMEAL, NO BASEBALL, NO SATURDAY-NIGHT FEVER. IN FACT, THE WHOLE SHOW WOULD QUICKLY GRIND TO A HALT, LIKE A MOVIE PROJECTOR WITH A PULLED PLUG.

WITH THAT HUMBLING THOUGHT IN MIND, THIS CHAPTER IS ABOUT HOW THE SUN'S POSITION IN THE SKY AFFECTS WHAT YOU PLANT, WHERE, AT WHAT TIME OF THE YEAR AND EVEN HOW YOU AS A GARDENER ARE AFFECTED BY THE SUN CYCLE, AND HOW THAT IN TURN AFFECTS WHAT YOU DO IN THE GARDEN.

SO NOW, HERE'S EVERYONE'S FAVORITE COMIC STRIP, PHOTOSYNTHESIS PHUNNIES! LET'S HAVE A BIG ROUND OF APPLAUSE FOR THAT INGENIOUS SUNBEAM-CAPTURING SYSTEM THAT MAKES IT ALL POSSIBLE!

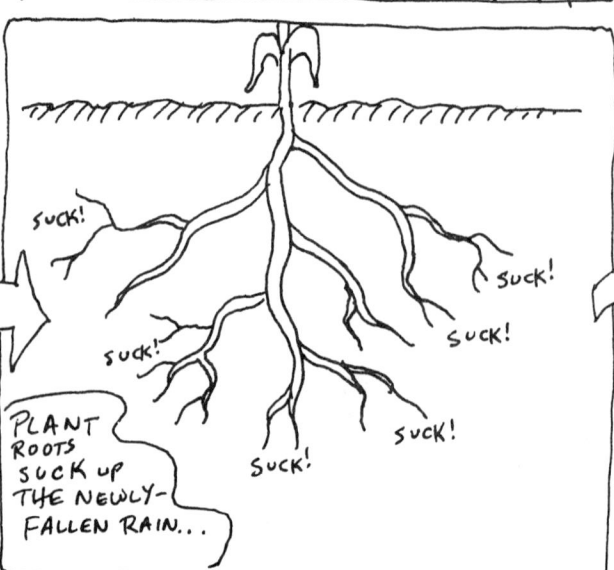

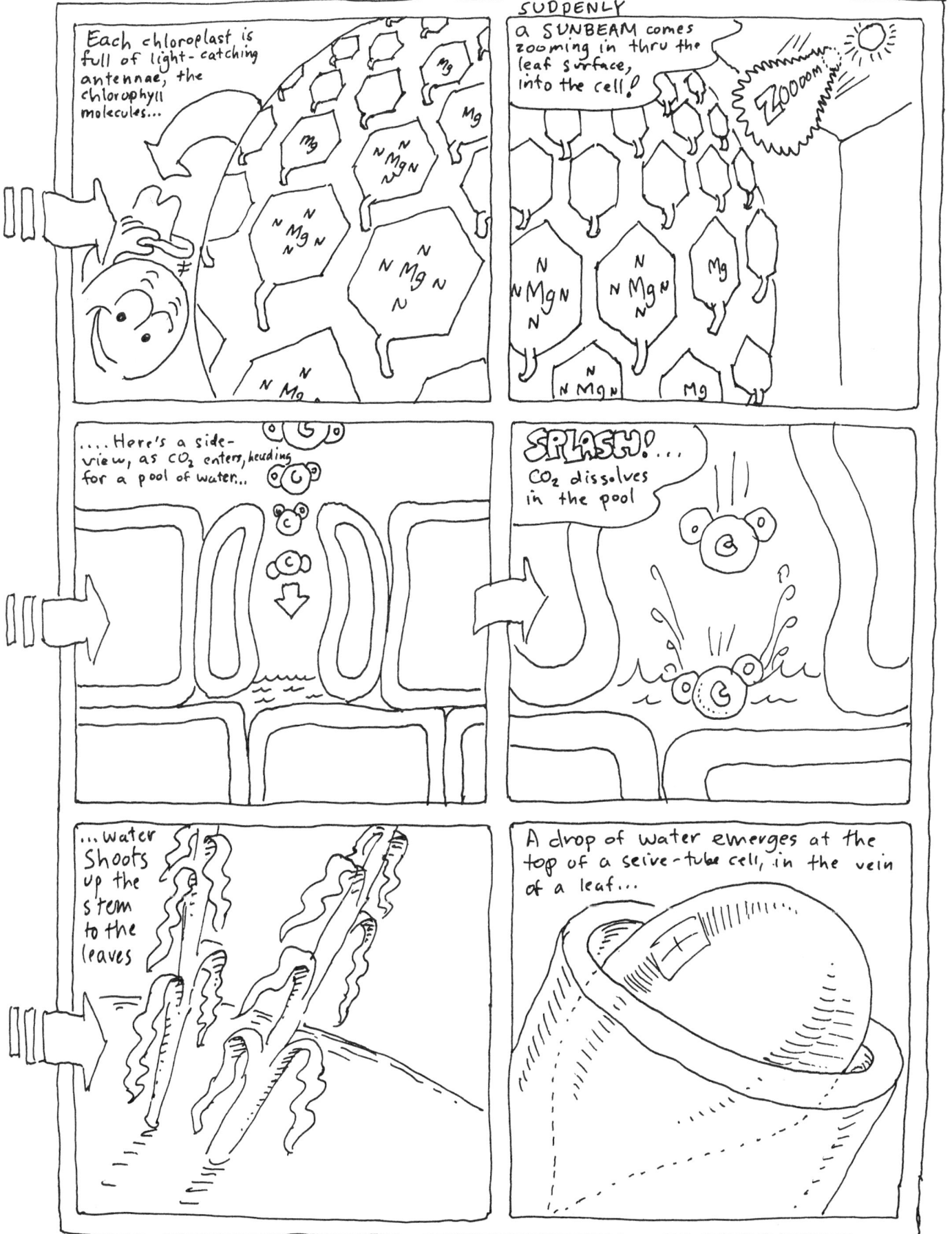

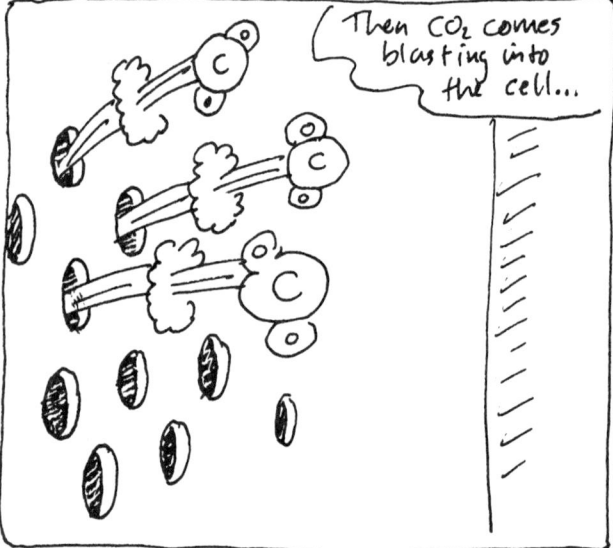

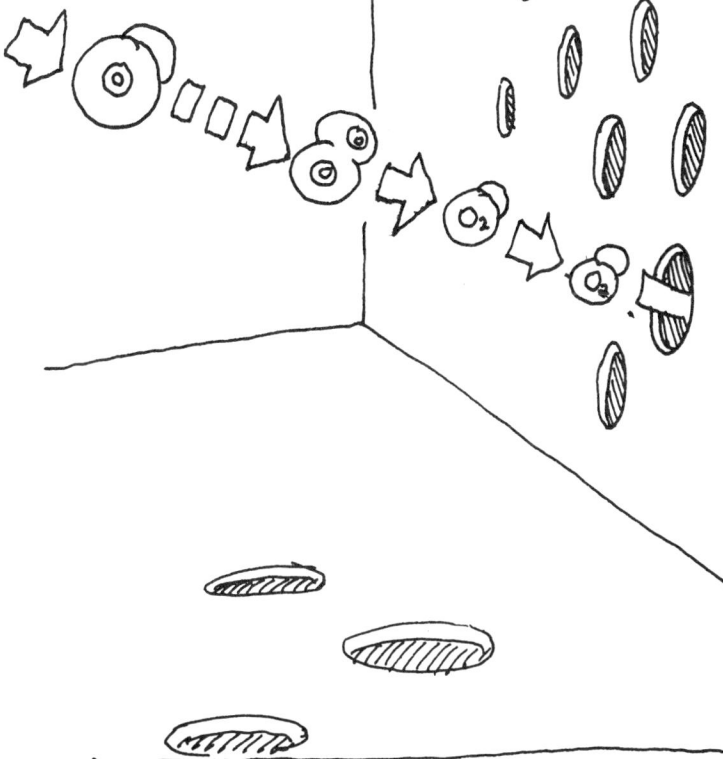

AND THAT'S PHOTOSYNTHESIS . . . THE SMALL ACT OF ENERGY-RECEPTION WHICH, MULTIPLIED BY TRILLIONS OF LEAVES THE WORLD OVER, KEEPS THE WHOLE ECO-MACHINE HUMMING. IT'S THE STATE-OF-THE-ART IN ENERGY TECHNOLOGY, MICRO-MINIATURIZED TO A SCALE THAT MAKES THE BEST EFFORTS OF THE ELECTRONICS INDUSTRY LOOK HOPELESSLY STONE-AGE.

ONCE PHOTOSYNTHESIS GETS THE BALL ROLLING, THE SUGAR MADE IN THE LEAVES GOES TO THE REST OF THE PLANT'S CELLS, WHERE IT IS USED TO MAKE CELLULOSE FOR BUILDING CELL WALLS, PROTEINS (ALONG WITH NITROGEN FROM THE SOIL), STARCH (FOR STORAGE), AND VARIOUS OTHER CHEMICALS LIKE OILS, FATS, DRUGS, TOXINS, ETC. AND SOME OF THE SUGAR IS BURNED TO MAKE A CHEMICAL CALLED ATP, WHICH THE PLANT USES FOR ENERGY TO KEEP EVERYTHING RUNNING.

THE CARBON CYCLE

IF THE PLANT IS EATEN BY AN ANIMAL, THE ANIMAL GETS THE SOLAR ENERGY STORED IN SUGAR. OR THE PLANT MAY BE BURNED IN A FIREPLACE, AND THE SUN'S ENERGY IS CONVERTED TO HEAT. IN ANY CASE, THE END RESULT IS THE LOSS OF SOME OF THE ENERGY AS HEAT, AND THE RETURN OF CARBON DIOXIDE TO THE AIR, TO BE USED AGAIN IN PHOTOSYNTHESIS. THIS WHOLE CARBON-AND-ENERGY BARTERING NETWORK IS CALLED THE CARBON CYCLE.

THE CARBON CYCLE IS (AMONG OTHER THINGS) A GRAND GLOBAL RECYCLING OPERATION, KEEPING ALL THE CARBON ATOMS (WHICH ARE RELATIVELY SCARCE, COMPARED TO SOME OTHER ELEMENTS LIKE SILICON) CONSTANTLY INVOLVED IN SOME PLANT, ANIMAL, OR BACTERIA BODY, (OR IN LONG-TERM STORAGE AS CA CO_3 (LIMESTONE), OIL, COAL, OR METHANE).

❀ ❀ ❀ ❀ ❀

SO NOW YOU KNOW HOW PLANTS GROW, AND HOW THE WHOLE ECO-MACHINE WORKS. SUNBEAMS PLUS CO_2 IN THE AIR PLUS H_2O FROM THE SOIL, AND YOU GET SUGAR, WHICH THE PLANT USES TO MAKE EVERYTHING ELSE, AND WHICH ENDS UP MAKING ALL OTHER ORGANISMS. OR, TO PUT IT IN ANCIENT GRECIAN COSMO-JARGON,

FIRE (SUN) & **AIR** (CO_2) & **EARTH** (SOIL) & **WATER** = **FLESH**

THE TRICKY PART

THE TRICKY PART IS, THE SUNBEAMS ARE COMING IN FASTER OR SLOWER, DEPENDING ON THE TIME OF DAY, THE SEASON OF THE YEAR, THE WEATHER, THE TERRAIN, AND THE LOCATION ON THE EARTH. COPING WITH THESE VARIATIONS IS A BIG PART OF WHAT GARDENING AS A SKILL IS ALL ABOUT.

NOW TURN THE PAGE FOR A PANORAMA VIEW OF THE EARTH AND HEAVENS, AND HOW THE SUN'S SHIFTING POSITION INFLUENCES PLANTING AND OTHER ACTIVITIES.

THE SEASONS

The angle of the sun changes with the seasons, and this changing angle is what coordinates the life-cycles of all Earth's co-revolving critters, from microbes to men. The angle changes fastest around the Equinoxes (March 21 + September 21), and this extra-fast changing is what signals everything to WAKE UP! in the Spring, and GATHER YOUR NUTS! in the Fall.

SUMMER

On JUNE 21, the sun is almost directly overhead at noon, so sunbeams make a direct hit on the Earth. (Also, the rays are travelling through less atmosphere.) BLAM!

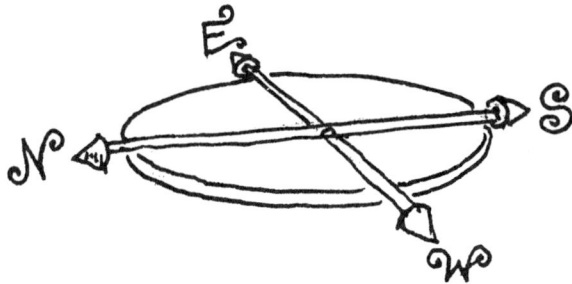

slow change

Passive solar houses are designed to let in the low winter sun, while blocking the high summer sun

One thing to avoid is plants shading each other. If you're cramped for space, have rows running East-to-West, with the tall plants (corn, sunflowers) furthest to the North, and small plants furthest South (as shown). If you have lots of space, it's better to have rows running North-South, so similar-height plants won't shade each other in the morning + afternoon.

← lettuce, onions, carrots

← tomatoes, eggplants, green peppers

← corn, sunflowers

SPRING + FALL

In mid-March and mid-September the noon sun is at an intermediate position, and the change is fastest from day to day. It is this extra-quick change (along with increasing warmth) which wakes up the world in the Spring.

Fast change

slow change

WINTER

The noon sun is at it's lowest point in the sky on Dec. 21., and the world is asleep. Sunbeams don't hit the Earth directly, but rather strike a glancing blow, so more of the energy is reflected rather than absorbed:

. . . ping!

THE SUN GEARS...

This is an alternative explanation of how the solar system works. This view makes it easier to visualize how the Sun's apparent path changes, which is more useful for our practical gardening purposes than the conventional view of the solar system as it actually operates.

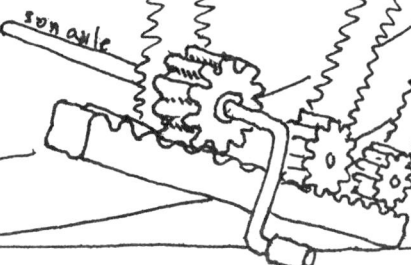

sun axle

SO NOW YOU KNOW HOW OUR GIANT NUCLEAR PLANT IN THE SKY WORKS, AND IT'S TIME TO SEE HOW THAT TRANSLATES INTO GARDEN PLANS. THE MOST IMPORTANT EFFECT IS THE LENGTHENED SHADOWS OF WINTER, CAUSED BY THE SUN BEING LOWER IN THE SKY. IF YOU'RE PLANNING A WINTER GARDEN IN AUGUST, YOU'LL WANT TO TAKE THIS INTO ACCOUNT, AND DETERMINE WHETHER THE LOW WINTER SUN WILL CLEAR OBSTACLES LIKE HOUSES, TREES, ETC., AND ALSO WHETHER YOUR PLANTS WILL SHADE EACH OTHER. THERE'S AN EASY WAY TO ESTIMATE THE SUN'S ANGLE: FACING SOUTH, HOLD YOUR FIST AT ARM'S LENGTH, THEN SET YOUR OTHER FIST ON TOP OF THE FIRST. DO THIS SIX TIMES. THEN SIGHT THROUGH YOUR TOP FIST, AND THAT'S WHERE THE SUN WILL BE AT NOON ON DECEMBER 21.

DEC. 21 SHADOW OF HOUSE

PLANTS HAVE EVOLVED TO REQUIRE DIFFERING AMOUNTS OF SUN. SOME PLANTS ARE SUN-LOVERS; THEY NEED LOTS OF SUN OVER A LONG GROWING PERIOD. YOU WANT TO PUT SUN-LOVERS IN AREAS WHICH WILL GET FULL SUN MOST OF THE DAY. IN MOST BACKYARDS THAT MEANS SMACK IN THE MIDDLE OF THE YARD, SINCE THE MORNING SUN IS USUALLY SHADED BY TREES/HOUSES TO THE EAST, WHILE LATE-AFTERNOON SUN IS SHADED BY THINGS TO THE WEST. OTHER PLANTS ARE SHADE-LOVERS; IN THE SUMMER THEY NEED SOME SHADE AT LEAST PART OF THE DAY. IN THE WINTER, YOU WANT AS MUCH SUN AS POSSIBLE FOR EVERYTHING, AND USUALLY ONLY SHADE-LOVERS WILL GROW AT ALL OUTDOORS.

SUN-LOVERS

♣ SUMMER GARDEN ♣

USUALLY GROWN ONLY IN SPRING–SUMMER. **CAN** BE GROWN IN A WINTER GREEN-HOUSE, BUT QUALITY USUALLY POOR. MAY HAVE TROUBLE IN FOGGY COASTAL AREAS IN SUMMER.

SHADE-LOVERS

♣ WINTER GARDEN ♣

CAN BE GROWN IN SUMMER, BUT MAY NEED SOME SHADE. GROWN IN WINTER WHERE WEATHER IS MILD. NEEDS FROST PROTECTION IF FROSTS OCCUR.

CROPS (LISTED IN ORDER OF NEED FOR LIGHT AND/OR HEAT.)	**ORNAMENTALS**	**CROPS** (LISTED IN ORDER OF NEED FOR SHADE IN SUMMER, AND TOLERANCE FOR WINTER COLD.)	**ORNAMENTALS**
PEANUTS	HIBISCUS	LETTUCE	ALL HOUSEPLANTS
OKRA	GARDENIA	ONION	RHODODENDRON
GRAPEFRUIT	BOUGAINVILLIA	(ABOVE ESPECIALLY NEED	CAMELIA
BELL PEPPER (SWEET)	LANTANA	COOL NIGHTS FOR SEED	AZALEA
MELONS	WATER LILY	GERMINATION)	IMPATIENS
TOMATOES	CARNATION	CELERY	FERNS
BASIL		PARSELY	MAPLE
OREGANO		CHIVES	BEGONIA
LAVENDER		MINT	FOXGLOVE
THYME		SEEDLINGS OF MOST PLANTS	PASSIONFLOWER
ROSEMARY		NEED LESS LIGHT.	IPECAC
(MOST AROMATIC HERBS)		LOQUAT	CALATHEAS
BEANS		CAULIFLOWER	ANTHURIUM
CORN		CABBAGE	
SQUASH		BROCOLLI	
HOT PEPPERS		CARROTS	
ORANGES		BEETS	
CUCUMBER (BEST WITH		KOHLRABI	
PARTIAL SHADE)		PEAS, EDIBLE POD (SNOWPEAS)	
		PEAS, INEDIBLE POD	
		STRAWBERRIES	
		POTATOES	

YOU'LL NOTICE SUN-LOVERS ARE MOSTLY FRUIT OR SEED CROPS, WHILE SHADE-LOVERS ARE GROWN MAINLY FOR THEIR LEAVES (LETTUCE, ONIONS), SHOOTS (CELERY), OR ROOTS (POTATOES, BEETS, CARROTS). (IN BOTANICAL TERMS, "FRUIT" MEANS A STRUCTURE DERIVED FROM A FLOWER, CONTAINING SEEDS. THUS, A TOMATO IS A FRUIT, AS ARE SQUASHES, CUCUMBERS, ETC.) THIS IS A GOOD RULE OF THUMB TO REMEMBER. IT'S IMPORTANT TO RECOGNISE HOWEVER, THAT SUN-LOVERS AND SHADE-LOVERS ARE NOT TWO DISTINCT GROUPS, BUT ACTUALLY A CONTINUUM, SO THE PLANTS AT THE BOTTOM OF THE "SHADE-LOVERS" LIST REALLY NEED A FAIR AMOUNT OF SUN, AND THE PLANTS AT THE BOTTOM OF THE "SUN-LOVERS" LIST ARE FAIRLY SHADE-TOLERANT. YOU COULD ATTACH THE BOTTOM OF THE SHADE-LOVERS LIST ONTO THE BOTTOM OF THE SUN-LOVERS LIST TO FORM ONE CONTINUOUS LIST.

FRUITS TAKE MORE SUN TO MATURE PARTLY BECAUSE THEY HAVE ADAPTED TO A YEARLY CYCLE OF LEAF GROWTH IN THE SPRING AND FRUITING IN THE SUMMER AS A PREPARATION FOR SEED PRODUCTION IN THE FALL, SEEDS BEING A WINTER-DORMANCY DEVICE. MANY LEAF CROPS ARE "SHADE-LOVERS" SIMPLY BECAUSE WE EAT THEM BEFORE THEY GET TO THE SUN-REQUIRING STAGE OF THEIR LIFE CYCLE. AND ROOT-CROPS ARE SHADE-LOVERS BECAUSE WE EAT THEM IN THE WINTER STAGE OF THEIR LIFE CYCLE, WHEN THEY ARE STORING SUGARS IN THEIR ROOTS TO USE THE FOLLOWING SPRING.

LOOKING AT IT FROM A LARGER ECOLOGICAL PERSPECTIVE, WE SEE THAT FRUIT CROPS ORIGINATED NEAR THE EQUATOR, WHILE LEAF, STEM, AND ROOT CROPS EVOLVED IN MOUNTAINOUS REGIONS, ALONG SEA COASTS, OR IN THE TEMPERATE ZONES. IF YOU LIVE IN A TEMPERATE ZONE, THAT MEANS YOU CAN ONLY GROW FRUIT CROPS IN THE SUMMER, SINCE THAT'S THE ONLY TIME YOU GET AS MUCH HEAT AS IN THE TROPICS. (MOST CITRUS FRUITS ARE AN EXCEPTION.)

HERE'S A MAP OF THE WORLD, SHOWING WHERE OUR COMMON GARDEN PLANTS ORIGINATED:

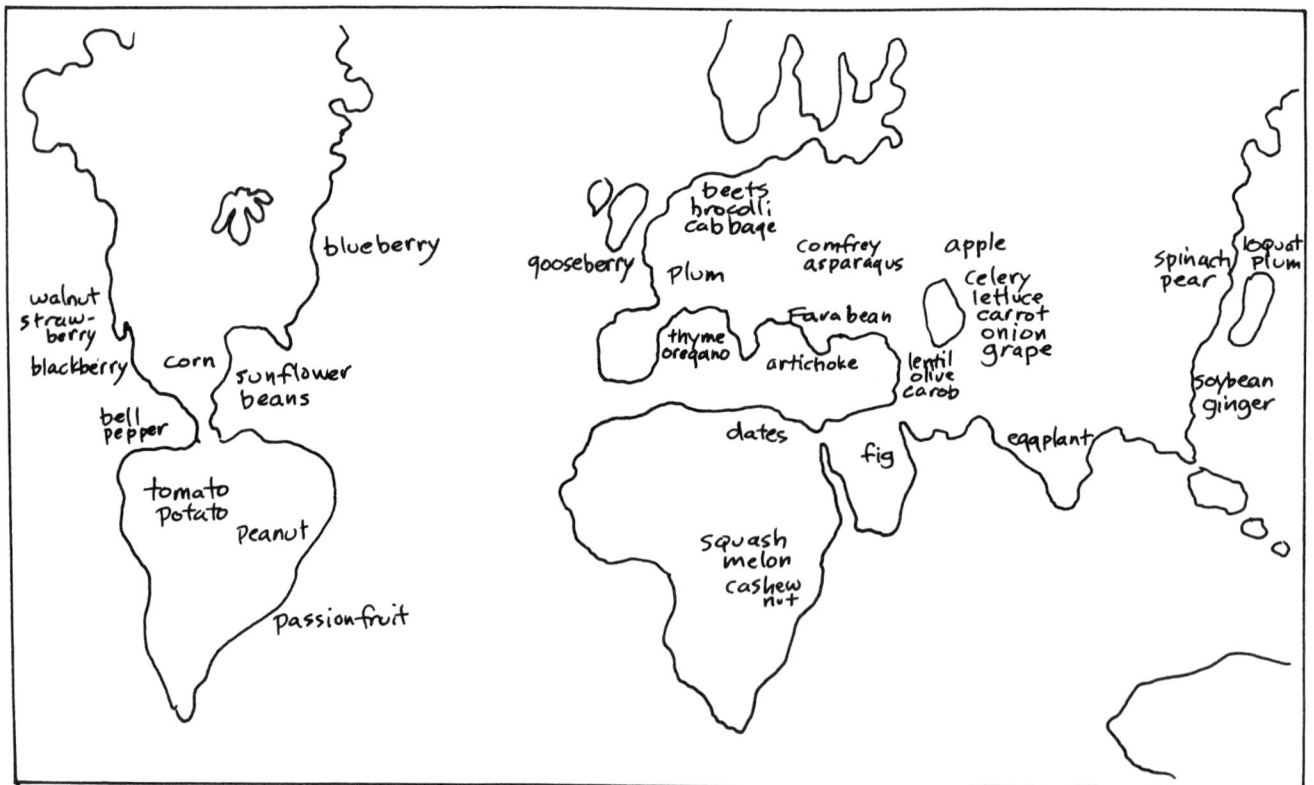

SUMMER & WINTER GARDENS

THE UPSHOT OF ALL THIS IS, SHADE-LOVERS CAN BE GROWN AS A WINTER GARDEN IN MILD-WINTER AREAS (THAT IS, WHERE THE TEMPERATURE DOESN'T GO BELOW FREEZING VERY OFTEN). IF YOU DO GET FROSTS, THEY'LL HAVE TO BE GROWN IN A GREENHOUSE. SUN-LOVERS CAN ONLY BE GROWN IN THE WINTER IF YOU HAVE A GREENHOUSE WITH SUPPLEMENTARY ELECTRIC LIGHTING, AND EVEN THEN YOU WON'T GET REALLY HEALTHY PLANTS (OR HEALTHFUL FOOD).

ON PAGE 116 IS A COMPREHENSIVE CHART SHOWING PLANTING TIMES FOR COASTAL CALIFORNIA—DATES FOR YOUR REGION WILL VARY.

AGAIN, EXACTLY WHICH PLANTS YOU CAN GROW AT WHAT TIME OF YEAR DEPENDS ON WHERE YOU LIVE. YOU SHOULD TALK TO OTHER GARDENERS AND READ GARDENING ARTICLES IN THE LOCAL PAPERS TO GET TIPS ON DEALING WITH LOCAL CONDITIONS. SHADE-TOLERANT PLANTS I CALL "WINTER GARDEN" VEGETABLES (WHICH CAN BE GROWN OUTDOORS YEAR-ROUND IN CALIFORNIA) WOULD NEED SOME TYPE OF GREENHOUSE OR OTHER FROST PROTECTION IN MOST AREAS OF THE UNITED STATES. ALSO, SPRING PLANTING DATES WOULD BE SHIFTED ONE OR TWO MONTHS LATER FOR ALL PLANTS IN MOST AREAS.

MICROCLIMATES

NOW YOU KNOW WHAT TO GROW, AND WHEN, IT'S TIME TO START THINKING ABOUT **WHERE** IN THE GARDEN TO PUT EACH PLANT. EVERY GARDEN PLOT OR FARMLAND HAS A NUMBER OF DIFFERENT "MICROCLIMATES," OR AREAS WHOSE CLIMATE DIFFERS SLIGHTLY FROM THE GENERAL OVERALL CLIMATE OF THE REGION. SOME MICROCLIMATES ARE WARMER, SOME COOLER; SOME HAVE MORE (OR LESS) SOIL MOISTURE, WIND, ETC. THESE DIFFERENCES CAN BE ABSOLUTELY CRUCIAL TO THE LIFE OF THE PLANT. FOR EXAMPLE, IF YOU LIVE IN A PLACE WITH RATHER COOL SUMMERS (SUCH AS COASTAL CALIFORNIA WITH ITS MORNING FOGS), THE ONLY WAY TO GROW A REALLY DEMANDING SUN-LOVER LIKE OKRA OR PEANUTS IS TO AUGMENT THE NATURAL HEAT BY PLANTING NEXT TO A SOUTH WALL, OR ON A SOUTH-FACING SLOPE.

SLOPES

ONE IMPORTANT MICROCLIMATE IS THE SLOPE. LUCKILY FOR US, THE EARTH IS NOT TOTALLY FLAT! THERE ARE HILLS AND DALES, AND THE VARYING SLOPES MAKE FOR LOCAL MICROCLIMATE VARIATIONS, THE TWO MOST FAMOUS BEING THE NORTH-FACING AND SOUTH-FACING SLOPES:

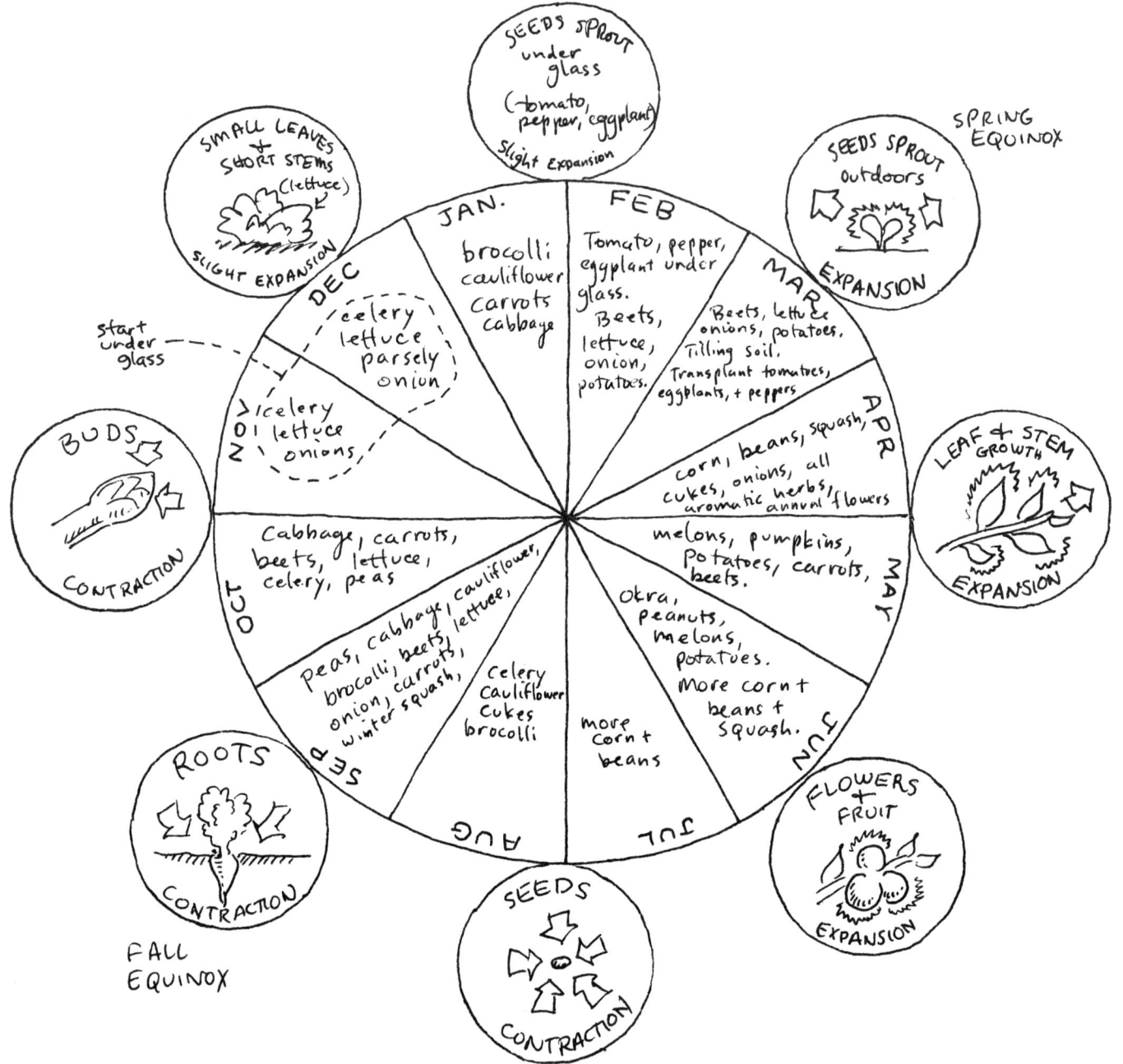

WINTER GARDEN

SUMMER GARDEN

SEEDS SPROUT under glass (tomato, pepper, eggplant) Slight Expansion

SMALL LEAVES + SHORT STEMS (lettuce) SLIGHT EXPANSION

SPRING EQUINOX

SEEDS SPROUT outdoors EXPANSION

start under glass

BUDS CONTRACTION

LEAF + STEM GROWTH EXPANSION

ROOTS CONTRACTION

FALL EQUINOX

FLOWERS + FRUIT EXPANSION

SEEDS CONTRACTION

Wheel segments:

JAN. — brocolli cauliflower carrots cabbage

FEB — Tomato, pepper, eggplant under glass. Beets, lettuce, onion, potatoes.

MAR — Beets, lettuce, onions, potatoes. Tilling soil. Transplant tomatoes, eggplants, + peppers.

APR — corn, beans, squash, cukes, onions, all aromatic herbs, annual flowers

MAY — melons, pumpkins, potatoes, carrots, beets.

JUN — Okra, peanuts, melons, potatoes. More corn + beans + squash.

JUL — More corn + beans

AUG — Celery Cauliflower Cukes brocolli

SEP — Peas, cabbage, cauliflower, beets, lettuce, brocolli, carrots, onion, winter squash,

OCT — Cabbage, carrots, beets, lettuce, celery, peas

NOV — celery lettuce onions

DEC — celery lettuce parsely onion

WINTER

CONTRACTION (seeds, roots, buds.)

PASSIVITY, RESTING (dormancy in perennial plants, hibernation in animals.)

SPRING - SUMMER

EXPANSION (leaf + stem growth, flowering + fruiting.

ACTIVITY, GROWTH (seeds sprouting, buds bursting, animals running around.)

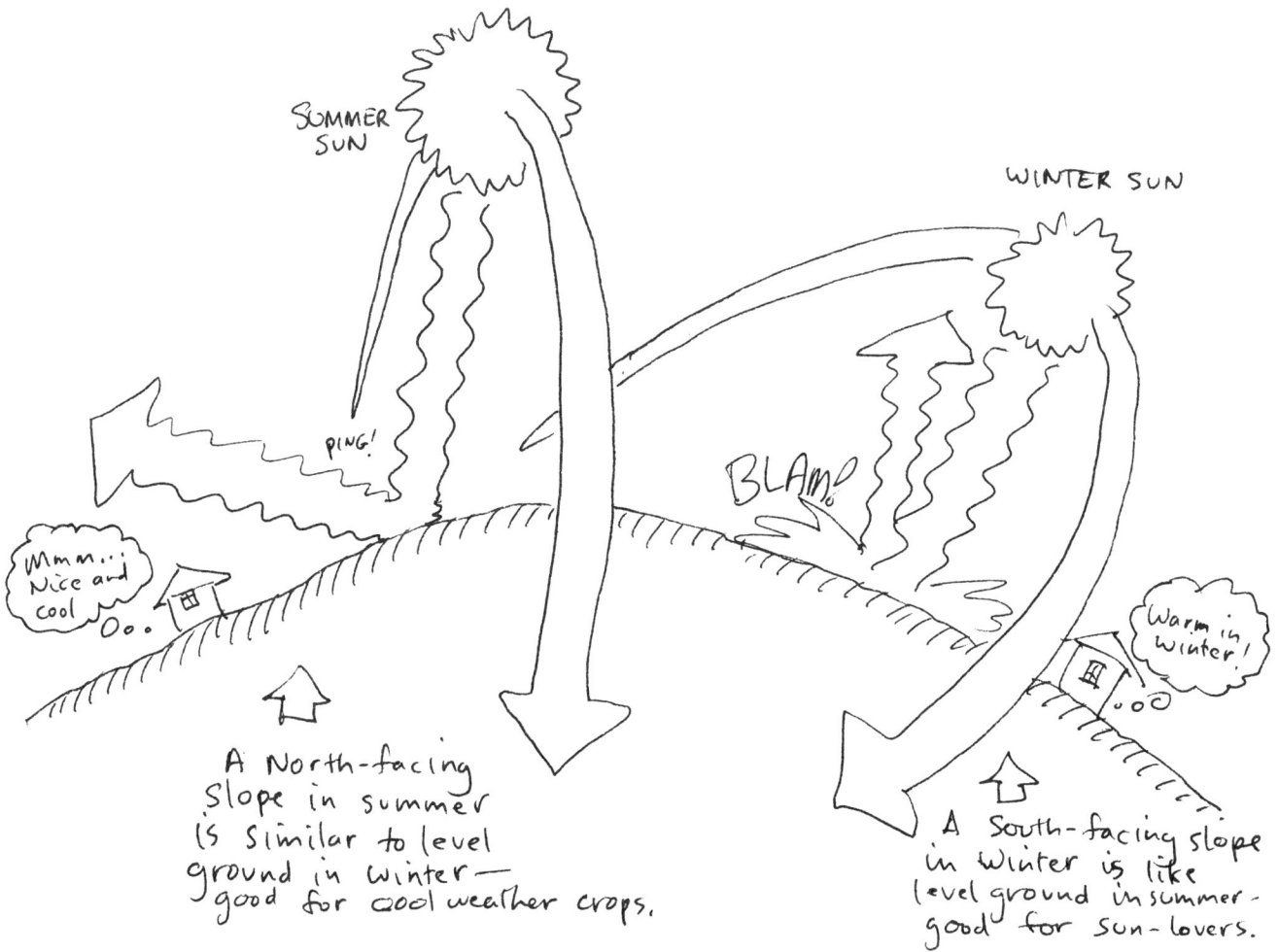

SUMMER SUN

WINTER SUN

PING!

BLAM!

Mmm... Nice and cool Oo.

Warm in winter!

A North-facing slope in summer is similar to level ground in winter— good for cool weather crops.

A South-facing slope in winter is like level ground in summer— good for sun-lovers.

HERE ARE SOME OTHER MICROCLIMATES...

Makes climate warmer

makes climate cooler

Duck or FISH pond in winter

Duck or dish pond in summer

Radiation at night of heat stored during day.

Evaporation cools surrounding air

Makes Climate Warmer

MAKES CLIMATE COOLER

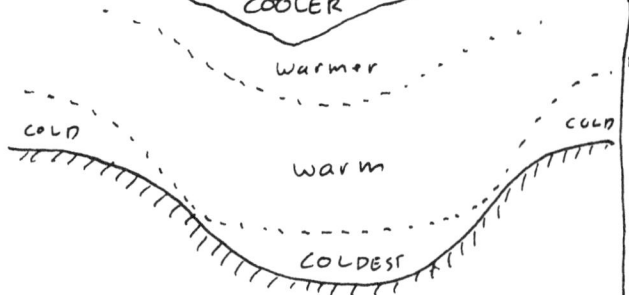

Warmer

COLD — COLD

warm

COLDEST

FROST HOLLOW, CANYON, OR ANY DIP IN THE TERRAIN

CLOCHE
(gallon jug with bottom cut off)

GREENHOUSE

COLD FRAME

WINDBREAK

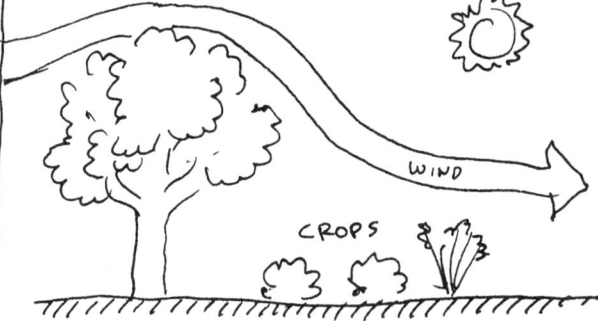

WIND

CROPS

DAPPLED SHADE

← corn

← lettuce

SOUTH WALL

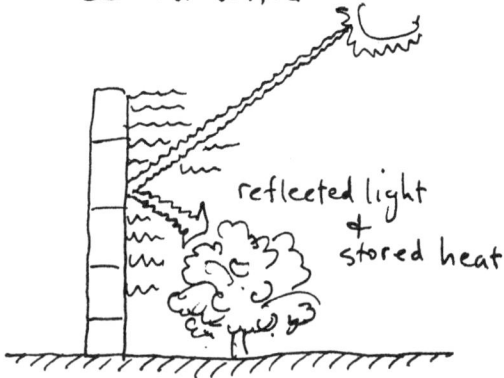

reflected light + stored heat

MORE DAPPLED SHADE

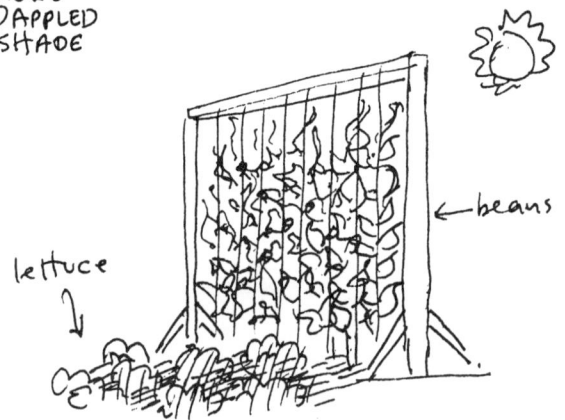

lettuce

← beans

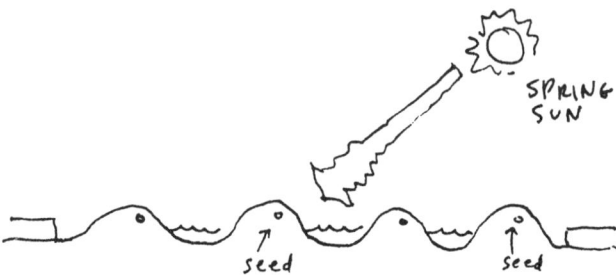

SPRING SUN

seed

seed

The traditional furrow irrigation system inadvertently creates mini-south slopes, for early germination of heat-requiring seeds.

EAST SIDE OF HOUSE OR FENCE: STRUCTURE BLOCKS AFTERNOON SUN, WHICH IS HOTTER AND MORE DAMAGING TO SHADE-LOVERS THAN THE MORNING SUN.

WEST SIDE OF HOUSE OR FENCE: ONLY SLIGHTLY COOLER OVERALL THAN IF PLANTED IN THE OPEN, SINCE THE WALL CAN REFLECT/ABSORB AFTERNOON HEAT.

HERE'S AN EXAMPLE OF A GARDEN PLAN USING A NUMBER OF DIFFERENT MICROCLIMATE FEATURES:

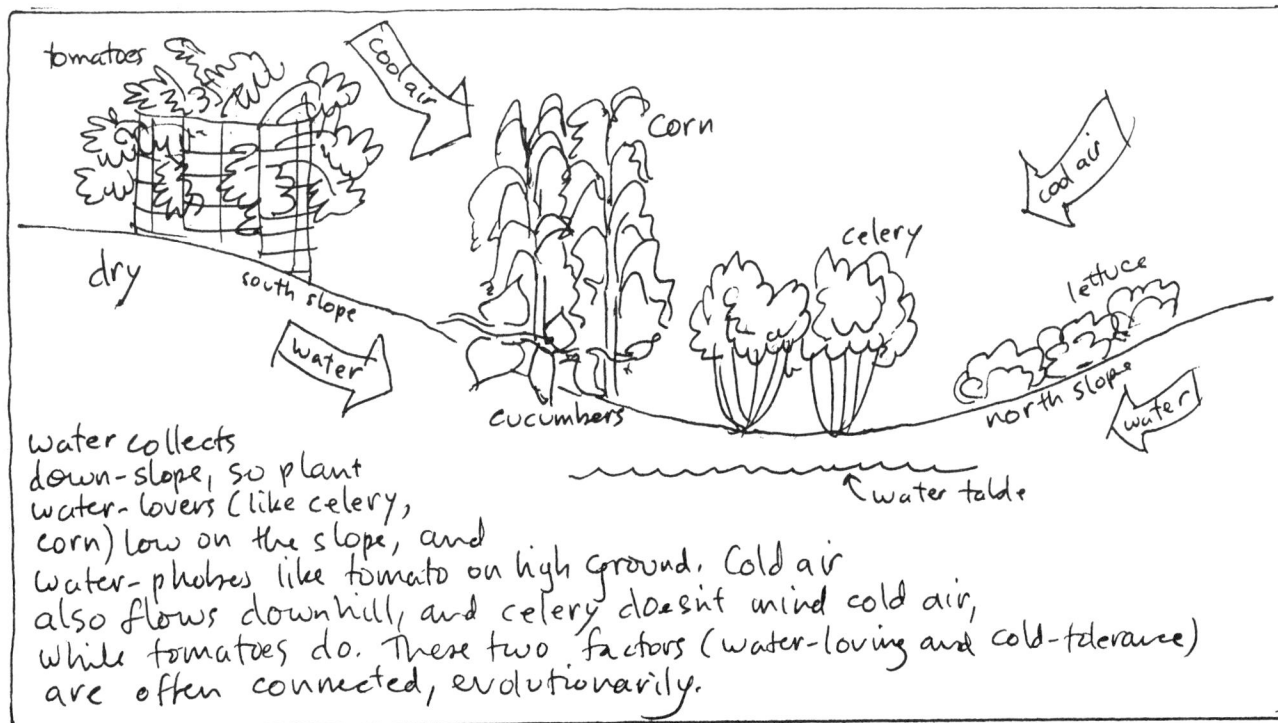

tomatoes
cool air
corn
cool air
celery
dry
south slope
lettuce
water
north slope
water
cucumbers
water table

water collects
down-slope, so plant
water-lovers (like celery,
corn) low on the slope, and
water-phobes like tomato on high ground. Cold air
also flows downhill, and celery doesn't mind cold air,
while tomatoes do. These two factors (water-loving and cold-tolerance)
are often connected, evolutionarily.

IF YOU JUST HAVE FLAT LAND TO GARDEN OR FARM ON YOU CAN USE **RAISED BEDS** TO SIMULATE A ROLLING TERRAIN. SINCE RAISED BEDS ARE A GOOD IDEA ANYWAY FOR SUCH REASONS AS SPACE-SAVING AND BETTER DRAINAGE, IT'S JUST A MATTER OF EXAGGERATING THE HEIGHT OF THE BEDS FOR MICROCLIMATE EFFECTS.

HERE'S THE CROSS SECTION OF A SUPER-RAISED BED:

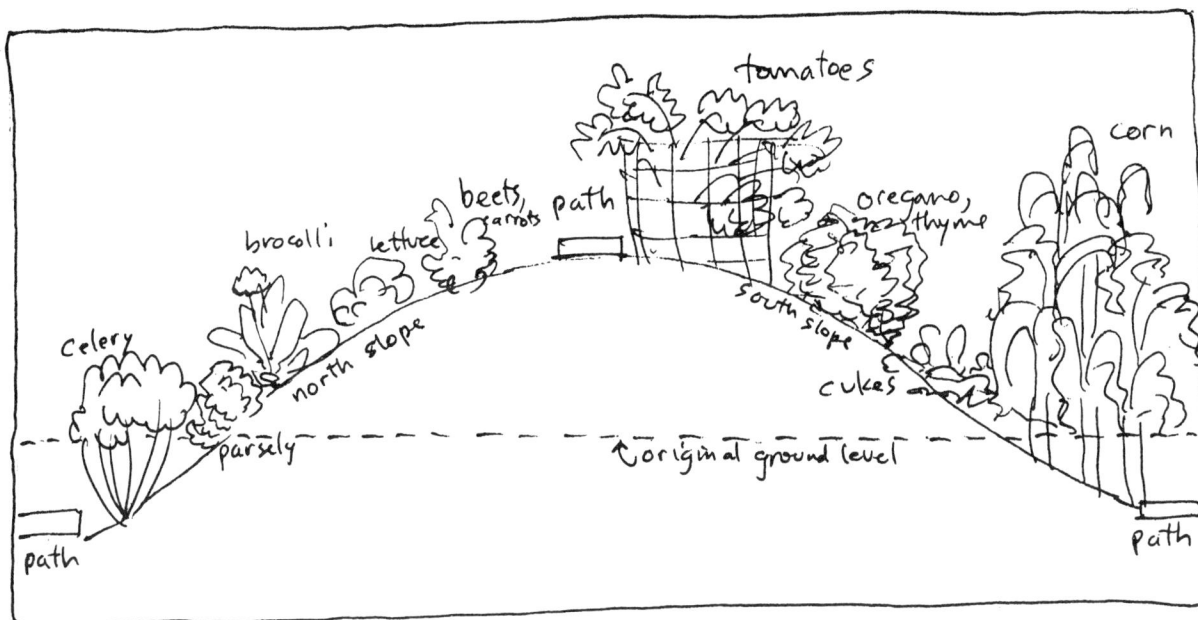

tomatoes
corn
beets, carrots
path
brocolli
lettuce
oregano, thyme
south slope
celery
north slope
cukes
parsely
original ground level
path
path

THESE SAME PLANT-SITTING PRINCIPLES ARE EMPLOYED BY NATURE, THE WORLD'S BIGGEST LANDSCAPING COMPANY. FOR INSTANCE, IN CALIFORNIA'S COASTAL MOUNTAINS, YOU'LL FIND SUCH SUN-LOVERS AS CHAPPARAL PLANTS HIGH UP ON THE SLOPES, AND COOL-AND-WET-LOVERS LIKE REDWOODS OR BAY TREES IN THE RAVINES:

IN A GARDEN SITUATION, YOU CAN IMITATE NATURAL LANDSCAPES BY MAKING YOUR GARDEN LOOK LIKE A MINIATURE SCALE-MODEL OF THE REAL THING, WITH LARGE PLANTS LIKE CORN BEING "TREES," SMALLER SHADE-TOLERANT VEGGIES LIKE CELERY AND BEETS BEING "UNDERSTORY SHRUBS," AND SMALL HERBS LIKE CHIVES AND THYME BEING GRASSES AND OTHER ANNUALS. IN THE EXAMPLE PICTURED ON THIS PAGE, THE PATH HAS BEEN COVERED WITH A PEBBLE MULCH, RESEMBLING A CREEK BED. WATER-LOVING PLANTS LIKE CELERY LINE THE BANKS OF THE "CREEK," LIKE CAT-TAILS ALONG A FULL-SCALE CREEK. ALL THE BEDS ARE MULCHED WITH ANYTHING THAT RESEMBLES SCALED-DOWN FALLEN LEAVES, SUCH AS MANURE, COMPOST, SHREDDED BARK, ETC.

THE POINT IS, SINCE THE GOAL OF ORGANIC GARDENING IN GENERAL IS TO EMULATE NATURE, YOU CAN EASILY SPOT PROBLEMS WITH YOUR GARDEN BY NOTING WHERE ITS APPEARANCE DIFFERS FROM A SCALE-MODEL NATURAL LANDSCAPE.

WITH THE CHART OF MICROCLIMATES, THE SUN-LOVER/SHADE-LOVER LIST, AND A GENERAL GOAL OF IMITATING NATURE, YOU CAN PUT EACH TYPE OF PLANT IN THE HABITAT BEST SUITED TO THAT PLANT. THE EXACT TIME OF PLANTING IS NOT SO IMPORTANT AS WHERE IN THE GARDEN THE PLANT GOES, AND WHAT OTHER MICROCLIMATE FEATURES YOU CAN USE. SO START BY DRAWING AN AERIAL VIEW OF YOUR GARDEN PLOT, INCLUDING SURROUNDING STRUCTURES SUCH AS BUILDINGS, FENCES, TREES, ETC. NOTE WHERE SHADE WILL FALL AT DIFFERENT TIMES OF THE YEAR, WHERE SOIL MOISTURE IS LIKELY TO ACCUMULATE, WHERE PREVAILING WINDS WILL BE COMING FROM, ETC. PICK PLANTS TO FIT YOUR HABITATS, THEN SOW YOUR SEEDS AND CROSS YOUR FINGERS.

SUNFLOWERS

PATH →

CELERY

← PATH →
w/
pebble
mulch

CELERY

PEPPER

MISTAKES—THE BEST TEACHER

THERE IS NO SUBSTITUTE FOR MAKING MISTAKES. SINCE EVERY GARDEN SITE IS DIFFERENT, THERE IS NO WAY ANY BOOK OR PERSON CAN TELL YOU WHAT WILL GROW, OR WHEN, IN YOUR GARDEN. THE ONLY THING TO DO IS TRY AND FAIL, AND IN YOUR BUMBLING AROUND YOU'LL EVENTUALLY END UP WITH SOME IDEA OF WHERE TO PLANT WHAT.

ABOVE ALL, LEARN FROM YOUR MISTAKES. DON'T JUST HANG YOUR HEAD AND THINK, "OH WELL, I JUST DON'T HAVE A GREEN THUMB." IF YOU CAN STAY ALERT AND AWARE, ESPECIALLY WHEN THINGS GO WRONG, YOU'LL LEARN AS MUCH OR MORE THAN IF THINGS GO RIGHT.

WITH THAT IN MIND, ON PAGE 122 IS A BOO-BOO CHART TO DIAGNOSE POSSIBLE PLANT-SITTING MISTAKES. (OF COURSE, IT HELPS IF YOU'VE FAITHFULLY FOLLOWED ALL THE ADVICE FROM THE FIRST FOUR CHAPTERS, SO YOU CAN RULE OUT SOIL CONDITIONS AS A POSSIBLE CAUSE OF THE PLANT'S DEMISE OR GENERAL MALAISE.)

COMPANION PLANTING
(FINE-TUNING YOUR GARDEN)

COMPANION PLANTING IS THE LEADING EDGE OF ECOLOGICAL GARDENING AND FARMING. ALTHOUGH HEAT AND LIGHT REQUIREMENTS ARE MORE IMPORTANT FOR THE HEALTH OF ANY INDIVIDUAL PLANT, THERE ARE SYNERGISTIC BENEFITS TO BE GAINED BY GROWING CERTAIN PLANTS NEXT TO EACH OTHER, AND AVOIDING OTHER COMBINATIONS. THE ACTUAL REASONS BEHIND MOST COMPANION PLANTING ARE POORLY UNDERSTOOD, AND ARE BASED MAINLY ON OBSERVATION DOWN THROUGH THE AGES.

ONE COMBINATION THAT IS UNDERSTOOD TO SOME DEGREE IS THE CORN-BEAN-SQUASH POLYCULTURE. CORN IS A HEAVY NITROGEN–FEEDER, WHICH NORMALLY RESENTS MOST OTHER PLANTS GROWING NEARBY. BUT BEANS HAVE SYMBIOTIC BACTERIA IN THEIR ROOTS WHICH GRAB NITROGEN OUT OF THE AIR AND SEND IT UP INTO THE BEAN PLANT, SO CORN AND BEANS CAN LIVE TOGETHER AMICABLY WITHOUT COMPETING FOR NITROGEN. BOTH GAIN FROM THE ASSOCIATION, SINCE ANY MIXED GROUPING OF PLANTS (CALLED POLYCULTURE) CONFUSES INSECT PESTS, MAKING IT HARDER FOR THEM TO FIND THEIR PREFERRED MEAL. (SEE CHAPTER 8 FOR A FULL DESCRIPTION OF THIS EFFECT.) THE CORN PLANTS ALSO PROVIDE CLIMBING STRUCTURES FOR THE BEANS, AND THE SQUASHES HELP OUT BY SHADING THE SOIL WITH THEIR BROAD LEAVES, FORMING A "LIVING MULCH" WHICH SLOWS THE EVAPORATION OF SOIL WATER.

ALL THE MAIN "SALAD VEGETABLES" (LETTUCE, ONION, CELERY, AND CARROT) ARE KNOWN AS COMPANION PLANTS, A FACT WHICH MAKES HARVESTING EASIER——IF YOU'RE PREPARING A SALAD, YOU JUST HAVE TO GO TO ONE PLACE IN THE GARDEN! LIKEWISE, BASIL AND TOMATO ARE KNOWN AS COMPANIONS, AND THEY ALSO TASTE GOOD TOGETHER.

TOO MUCH SUN

1. SUN-SCALDING. ENTIRE LEAF TURNS YELLOW IN SPLOTCHES, THEN BROWN.

DIFFERENT THAN SALT-BURN (P. 88) IN WHICH THE LEAF-**TIPS** TURN BROWN FIRST.

DIFFERENT THAN NITROGEN-DEFICIENCY, IN WHICH THE LEAF JUST TURNS YELLOW, BUT NOT BROWN.

2. LEAVES TURN RED——TO BLOCK EXCESS LIGHT ABSORPTION WHEN THE PLANT IS UNDER WATER STRESS, CHLOROPHYLL IS DEGRADED, LEAVING ANOTHER PIGMENT, "ANTHOCYANIN," WHICH IS RED.

IT'S SORT OF LIKE THE LEAVES GETTING A TAN.

3. WILTING. LOOKS IDENTICAL TO WILTING FROM WATER STRESS. IT'S A PROTECTIVE RESPONSE BY PLANT——EXPOSES LESS LEAF AREA TO SUNLIGHT. SOME MID-DAY WILTING IS NORMAL IN SUCH PLANTS AS CORN AND SQUASHES.

4. PREMATURE BOLTING-TO-SEED OF LONG-DAY PLANTS (ESP. LETTUCE AND CABBAGE-FAMILY PLANTS) IN SUMMER.

TOO LITTLE SUN

1. ETIOLATION. THE PLANT STEM ELONGATES ABNORMALLY AS THE PLANT SEARCHES FOR SUNLIGHT, WHICH IT KNOWS "MUST BE UP THERE SOMEWHERE!"

HERE'S WHAT IT LOOKS LIKE IN TOMATO PLANTS:

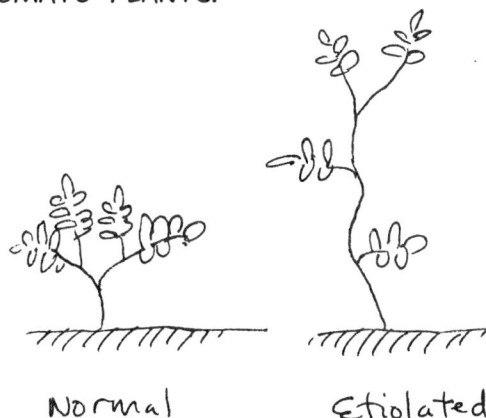

Normal   Etiolated

2. SLOW GROWTH. THIS CAN BE HARD TO DISTINGUISH FROM SLOW GROWTH DUE TO SOIL NUTRIENT DEFICIENCIES.

HOWEVER, IF YOU FERTILIZE COPIOUSLY WITH COMPOST OR MANURE, YOU KNOW THAT VARIABLE IS COVERED, SO YOU CAN SUSPECT THE PROBLEM IS DUE TO INSUFFICIENT SUN.

THE BOTTOM LINE

ALTHOUGH COMPANION PLANTING CAN MAXIMIZE THE HEALTH OF YOUR GARDEN, FIRST PRIORITY SHOULD ALWAYS BE GIVEN TO MEETING THE SUN OR SHADE NEEDS OF YOUR PLANTS. PLANTS **CAN** GROW AND PROSPER IN TOTAL ISOLATION FROM EACH OTHER, BUT IF THE SUN/SHADE NEEDS AREN'T MET THE PLANTS WILL SURELY DO POORLY, NO MATTER HOW MANY OF ITS COMPANIONS ARE AROUND, CHEERING IT ON.

AND THAT BRINGS US BACK TO THE CENTRAL THEME OF THIS CHAPTER: **IT ALL REVOLVES AROUND THE SUN!**

ALL RIGHT, HERE'S THAT SEXY STUFF YOU'VE ALL BEEN WAITING FOR! STAMENS AND PISTILS AND BIRDS AND BEES AND SOWING YOUR WILD OATS, NOT TO MENTION CARROTS AND PEAS. THIS CHAPTER IS A NO-HOLDS-BARRED EXPOSÉ OF THE SEAMY UNDERWORLD OF PLANT PROPAGATION, A WORLD OF MOONLIGHT POLLEN TRYSTS AND UNBRIDLED CROSS-FERTILIZING PASSION.

THE GREAT THING ABOUT GARDENING IS THAT THE TRICKIEST PART OF PLANT PROPAGATION (FERTILIZATION) IS DONE **FOR** US, BY THOSE ACE GARDENERS-IN-THE-SKY, HONEYBEES AND SYRPHID FLIES. (THAT'S WHAT'S HAPPENING ON THE TITLE PAGE TO THIS CHAPTER.) IMAGINE IF WE HAD TO GO AROUND TO EACH FLOWER WITH A LITTLE BRUSH AND UNITE POLLEN WITH EGG!

TO SEE WHERE FERTILIZATION FITS INTO THE OVERALL SCHEME OF THINGS, HERE'S A PICTURE OF A PLANT'S LIFE CYCLE:

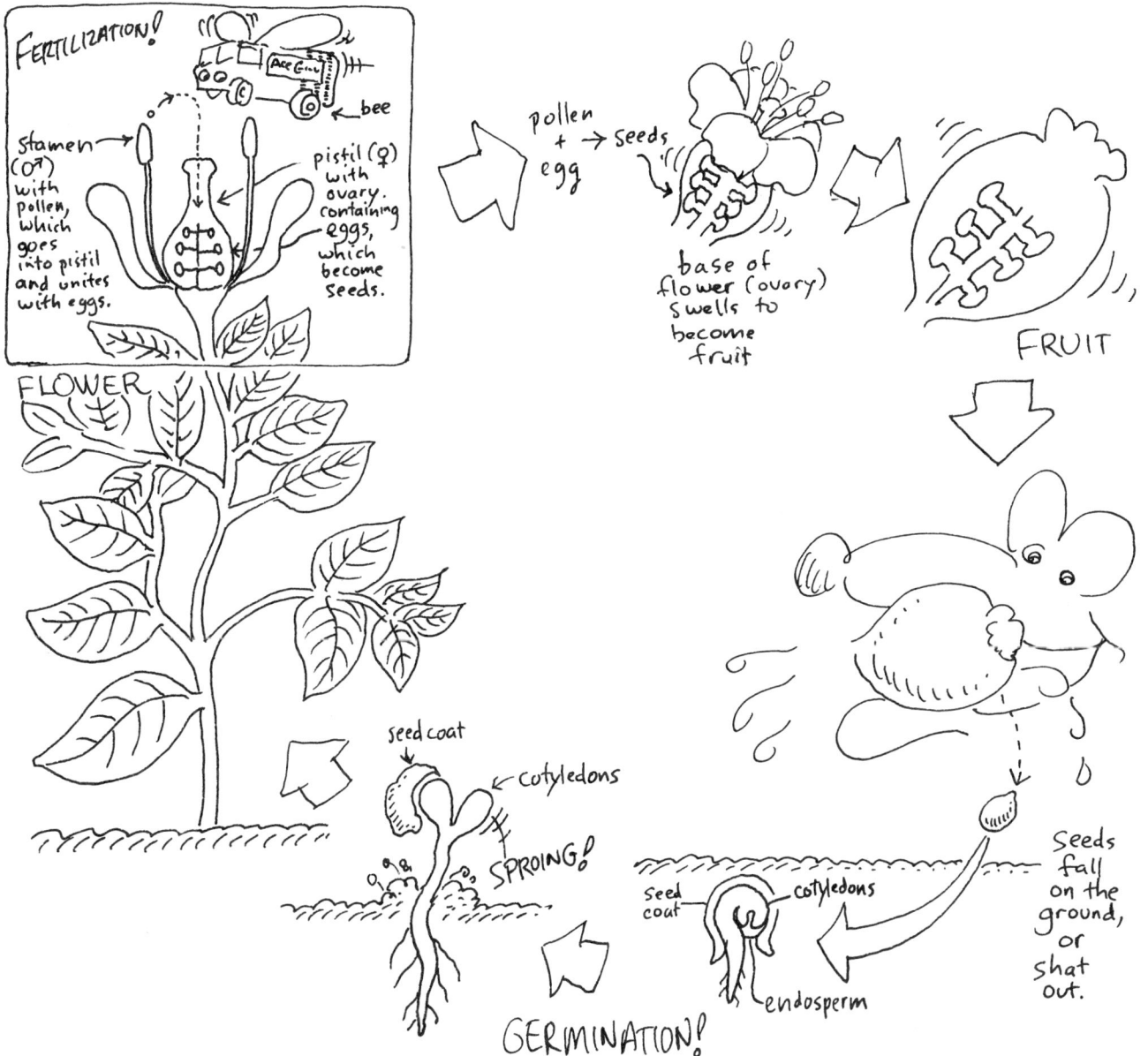

A FEW THINGS ARE NOTEWORTHY ABOUT THIS DIAGRAM. ONE IS THAT ANIMALS-EATING-PLANTS IS AN ESSENTIAL PART OF THE CYCLE. IF PLANTS ARE SENTIENT, THEY SURELY MUST LOOK FORWARD TO BEING EATEN . . . IN FACT, TO BE EATEN ALIVE WOULD BE THE CROWNING GLORY OF A PLANT'S LIFE.

A SECOND THING THAT STANDS OUT IS THE NEARLY-SEXUAL RELATIONSHIP BETWEEN PLANTS AND POLLINATING INSECTS. INSECTS ARE SORT OF LIKE A COMPUTER DATING SERVICE, BRINGING TOGETHER THE MALE PART OF ONE FLOWER WITH THE FEMALE PART OF ANOTHER. THE VALUE OF SEX ISN'T JUST FOR MIDNIGHT GROPINGS AND PAJAMA DRAMAS! IT'S A WAY MOST ORGANISMS HAVE OF EXCHANGING GENES FOR NEW GENETIC COMBINATIONS, FROM WHICH ULTIMATELY COME NEW SPECIES. WITHOUT SEX, THERE WOULD BE NO EVOLUTION. AND WITHOUT POLLINATING INSECTS, PLANT SEX WOULD BE IMPOSSIBLE, SINCE PLANTS ARE IMMOBILE, NOT HAVING WHEELS TO GO CRUISING WHEN SATURDAY NIGHT FEVER HITS. (SOME PLANTS ARE WIND-POLLINATED, BUT THE USE OF INSECT GO-BETWEENS IS THE NORM.) OUR DEPENDENCE ON POLLINATING INSECTS IS ONE REASON THE USE OF PESTICIDES MUST END, IF LIFE ON EARTH IS TO SURVIVE. (SEE CHAPTER 8 FOR DETAILS.)

THE THIRD THING TO RECOGNIZE IS THE PHYSICAL AND GENETIC CONTINUITY MAINTAINED BETWEEN ALL PHASES OF THE PLANT LIFE CYCLE. IT'S SENSELESS TO SPEAK OF PLANTS BEING "BORN" OR "DYING;" EVERYTHING THE PLANT DOES IS JUST A PRE-PROGRAMMED SHIFTING OF ENERGY AND RESOURCES FROM ONE FORM TO ANOTHER. THE EASTERN MYSTICS SAY, "THERE IS NO DEATH, ONLY TRANSFORMATION." WHEN AN ANNUAL PLANT SHRIVELS AND TURNS YELLOW IN THE FALL IT IS NOT DYING, BUT MERELY CHANGING FORM; WITHDRAWING AND CONTRACTING ITS RESOURCES AND PACKING THEM IN THE SEEDS, WHICH ARE "MOBILE UNITS" THE PLANT USES TO SPREAD ITSELF OVER THE PLANET.

WHAT IS A SEED?

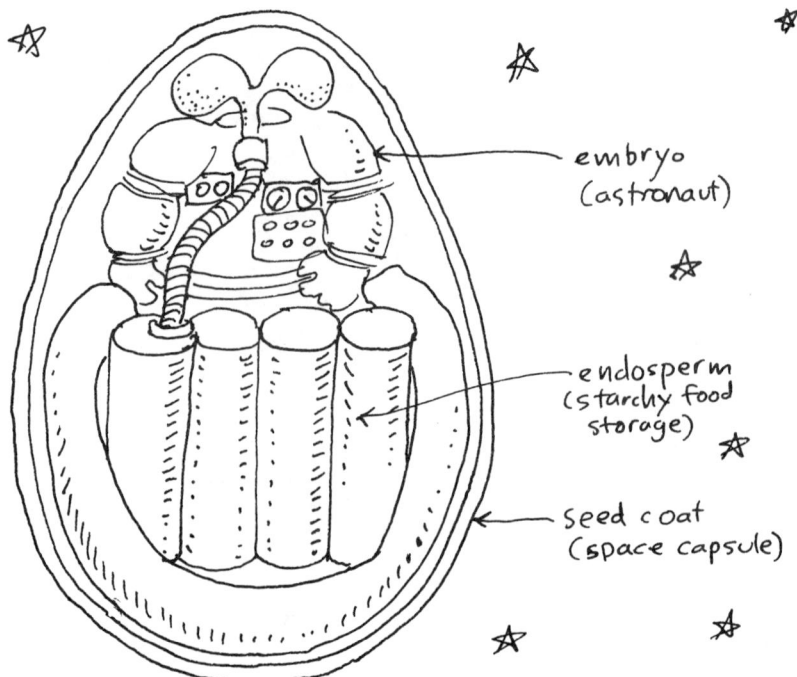

embryo (astronaut)

endosperm (starchy food storage)

seed coat (space capsule)

A SEED IS A SPACE SHIP.

THE SPACE SHIP CONTAINS A TINY ASTRONAUT (THE EMBRYO), AND ALL THE STORED FOOD RESERVES AND ROCKET FUEL (PROTEINS, OILS, STARCH) THE ASTRONAUT WILL NEED DURING HIS LONG JOURNEY THROUGH THE COLD DARK OUTER LIMITS OF EARTHLY WINTER.

WINTER IS LIKE BEING IN OUTER SPACE . . . IN WINTER, WE ARE **FACING** OUTER SPACE, SO FOR ALL PRACTICAL INTENTS AND PURPOSES, WE **ARE** IN OUTER SPACE.

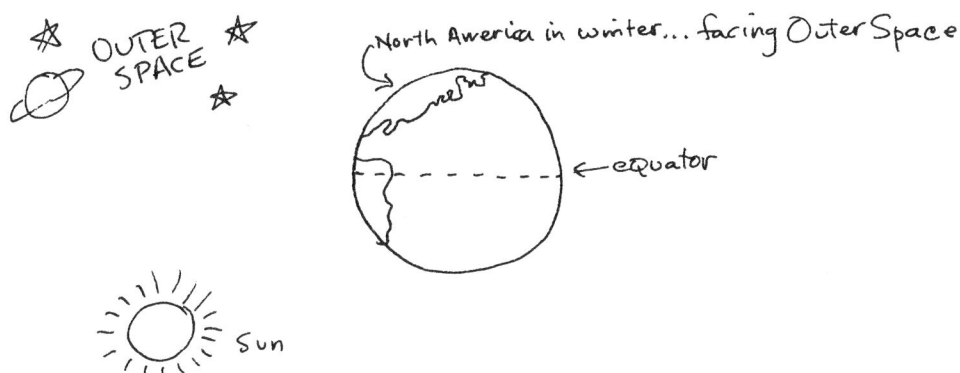

OUTER SPACE

North America in winter... facing Outer Space

←equator

Sun

THE ASTRONAUT IS IN A SORT OF SUSPENDED ANIMATION, LIKE A HIBERNATING BEAR IN A CAVE. HE IS USING HIS STORED FOOD RESERVES VERY SLOWLY, SO HE HAS ENOUGH FOR A FOUR OR FIVE YEAR TRIP, SOMETIMES EVEN LONGER. HE IS OFTEN ACTUALLY FROZEN IN A CRYOGENIC STATE FOR EVEN BETTER CONSERVATION OF HIS RESERVES, WAITING FOR THE WARMTH OF THE TARGET SUN TO WAKE HIM FROM HIS INTERSTELLAR SLUMBERS.

THE SPACE CAPSULE IS DESIGNED "TO BOLDLY GO WHERE NO SEED HAS GONE BEFORE." EVERY SPRING IS LIKE A NEW PLANET TO ANNUAL PLANTS; A STRANGE NEW WORLD FAR FROM THE LAND OF ITS PARENTS. THE SHIP IS BUILT TO TAKE ITS SLEEPING PASSENGER NOT ONLY AWAY FROM HIS (OR HER), PARENTS, BUT HOPEFULLY (USUALLY) AWAY FROM ALL OTHER PLANTS. SOMETIMES THIS IS DONE WITH WINGS (MAPLE), SOMETIMES WITH BURRS (BURR CLOVER), SOMETIMES WITH AN OUTER COATING OF YUMMY MATERIAL, CAUSING HUGE CRUISING SPACE MONSTERS TO GOBBLE UP THE SHIP AND SHIT IT OUT LIGHT-YEARS FROM ITS ORIGINAL LOCATION (THIS BEING A SORT OF HYPERSPACE SHUTTLE). THIS DISPERSAL STRATEGY WAS THOUGHT UP BY THE MASTER PLANNERS AT DNA CENTRAL AS ONE WAY TO SURVIVE IN A COMPETITIVE, DOG-EAT-DOG GALAXY.

WHEN THE ASTRONAUT LANDS AND WAKES UP, HE RECEIVES TAPED INSTRUCTIONS (THE DNA TAPES) TO LEAVE HIS CAPSULE AND BEGIN GATHERING MATERIALS AND FOODSTUFFS FROM THE "NEW PLANET," IN ORDER TO COLONIZE THE NEW WORLD BY EXPANDING OUTWARD FROM HIS LANDING PLACE, REBUILDING HIS SHAPE AND FORM TO A NEAR-EXACT REPLICA OF HIS FORMER SELF.

So where do we gardeners fit into this BOTANICAL STAR—TREK?

GETTING SEEDS TO GERMINATE CAN BE DIFFICULT EVEN FOR EXPERIENCED GARDENERS, SO DON'T DESPAIR IF YOU DON'T GET THE HANG OF IT RIGHT AWAY. THE MOST VULNERABLE PERIOD OF ANY PLANT'S ENTIRE LIFE CYCLE, EVEN IN NATURE, IS THE TRANSITION FROM SEED TO SEEDLING. EVERYTHING MUST BE JUST RIGHT: SOIL MOISTURE, TEMPERATURE, FERTILITY, BURIAL DEPTH, EVEN DAY LENGTH SOMETIMES. MOST SEEDS IN NATURE DON'T SURVIVE——A MAPLE TREE MAY PUT OUT BILLIONS OF SEEDS, AND ONLY HAVE 2 TO 5 OF THOSE SEEDS SPROUT IN ITS ENTIRE LIFE. FOR MOST SEEDS, AT LEAST ONE OF THE REQUIRED FACTORS IS MISSING, AND THAT'S WHY PLANTS PUT OUT SO MANY SEEDS: SO THERE WILL BE AT LEAST A FEW THAT MAKE IT. AS A GARDENER, YOU'RE TRYING TO MAKE MOST OF YOUR SEEDS SURVIVE, NOT JUST A LUCKY FEW. SO YOU MUST GIVE THEM JUST THE RIGHT AMOUNT OF EVERYTHING——AND THAT'S NOT EASY.

WHILE STARTING PLANTS FROM SEED IS THE MOST DIFFICULT PART OF GARDENING, IT IS ALSO THE MOST THRILLING: TO THINK THAT YOU CAN START WITH A COLD, HARD, DRY LITTLE BIT OF NEARLY-NOTHING, AND END UP WITH AN HERB PLANT, A BUSH, OR EVEN A TREE! THIS IS THE SINGLE MOST AMAZING THING ABOUT PLANTS (ASIDE FROM THE FACT THAT THEY EXIST AT ALL): THAT SUCH A SMALL BIT OF BARELY-LIVING TISSUE CAN NOT ONLY DIRECT THE UPTAKE OF ENOUGH NUTRIENTS TO MAKE A SELF-BUILDING STRUCTURE HIGH IN THE AIR, BUT THAT IT CAN ALSO TELL WHICH OF THESE NUTRIENTS (THE SUPPLY BEING THE SAME FOR ALL PLANTS) SHOULD GO WHERE TO FORM WHICH **CERTAIN TYPE** OF LEAVES, FLOWERS, AND FRUIT, AND THAT IT CAN END UP AT JUST THE RIGHT TIME A FEW MONTHS LATER WITH IDENTICAL COPIES OF WHAT IT STARTED OUT WITH: NEXT YEAR'S SEED!

THE SPROUTING MEDIUM

NORMALLY YOU CAN START SEEDS IN PURE FINE-SIFTED COMPOST, EITHER ADDED ON TOP OF THE GARDEN BED, OR IN SMALL CONTAINERS. WHY COMPOST? BECAUSE THAT'S WHERE SEEDS SPROUT IN NATURE. LOOK AT A FOREST FLOOR, OR THE SOIL IN A LUSH MEADOW. WHAT'S ON THE GROUND? IT'S COMPOST, PURE AND SIMPLE (AND COMPLEX). DECAYING LEAVES, TWIGS, STEMS, OLD FLOWER PETALS, VARIOUS MANURES, LITTLE BIRD AND RODENT BONES, DEAD BUGS. SEEDS JUST LOVE TO SPROUT IN COMPOST: IT'S LIKE WAKING UP IN THE MORNING IN A NICE SOFT BED UNDER WARM COVERS . . . STRETCHING,

TURNING, GRADUALLY OPENING YOUR EYES, THROWING BACK THE COVERS ONE BY ONE AS THE SUN'S WARMTH HEATS YOU UP, THEN SUDDENLY **JUMPING** OUT OF BED, AND HEADING INTO THE KITCHEN FOR BREAKFAST. IT'S ALL THERE IN THE COMPOST: THE AIRY STRETCH-ABILITY, THE WARM SOFT COVERS THE SEEDLING CAN PEEL OFF EASILY, THEN THROW BACK SUDDENLY WHEN IT SPROUTS, AND FINALLY BREAKFAST, IN THE FORM OF NUTRIENTS IN THE COMPOST. COMPOST ALSO PROTECTS AGAINST SEEDLING DISEASES (MORE ON THAT LATER).

DIRECT SOWING

MANY TIMES IT'S BETTER TO SOW SEEDS DIRECTLY IN THE GARDEN BEDS, RATHER THAN STARTING THEM IN CONTAINERS AND TRANSPLANTING. THIS IS ESPECIALLY TRUE FOR CARROTS, MELONS, SQUASHES, CUKES, CORN, BEANS, AND PEAS, ALL OF WHICH REALLY HATE BEING TRANSPLANTED. PLANTS THAT **PREFER** DIRECT-SOWING, BUT WHICH **CAN** BE TRANSPLANTED, INCLUDE NASTURTIUMS, MORNING GLORIES, OKRA, SUNFLOWERS, BALSAM, AND LARKSPUR.

IF YOU ALREADY HAVE THE SOIL PROPERLY CULTIVATED AND COMPOST-FERTILIZIED (CHAPT. 2-4), SOWING THE SEED WILL BE EASY. FIRST, MAKE SURE THE TOP 3-4 INCHES IS LOOSE AND FREE OF CLODS. RAKE GENTLY, AND WHAP ANY CLODS WITH THE BACK OF A PITCHFORK. THIS SHOULD BE DONE WHEN THE SOIL IS SLIGHTLY MOIST (THE "MAGIC TIME," SECTION ON PAGE 54). AS YOU DO THIS, ADD AT LEAST 2" OF FINELY SIFTED COMPOST. (IF YOU HAVE BEEN GARDENING ORGANICALLY AT THE SAME LOCATION FOR OVER A YEAR OR SO, YOU DON'T NEED TO ADD COMPOST FOR SEED-SOWING.)

SMALL SEEDS—"r-selection"

IF THE SEEDS ARE VERY SMALL (LETTUCE, CARROTS, RADISHES), SCATTER THEM ON THE SURFACE OF THE PREPARED BED, AND COVER WITH ABOUT 1/4" OF FINE-SIFTED COMPOST, LIKE THIS:

ONCE YOU GET SOME EXPERIENCE, YOU CAN SIMPLY WHAP THE SEEDS INTO THE SOIL WITH THE BACK OF A PITCHFORK.

SMALL SEEDS SHOULD BE SOWN RATHER THICKLY, ABOUT 5-6 SEEDS PER SQUARE INCH. SMALL-SEEDED PLANTS MAKE MORE SEEDS THAN LARGE-SEEDED PLANTS, AND THESE SMALL SEEDS ARE DESIGNED TO GROW UP IN THICK BUNCHES WITH THEIR BROTHERS AND SISTERS. GROWING CLOSE TOGETHER HELPS SUPPORT THE FRAGILE YOUNG STEMS, AND GIVES A "LIVING MULCH" EFFECT, SHADING THE SOIL UNDER THE SEEDLINGS. AS THE SEEDLINGS GROW, THE FASTER-GROWERS WILL SHADE OUT THE SLOW POKES, RESULTING IN AN AUTOMATIC THINNING PROCESS. MANY OF THE SMALL SEEDS WON'T SPROUT AT ALL, SINCE SMALL SEEDS HAVE FEWER FEED RESERVES THAN LARGE SEEDS, AND THEY WILL HAVE USED UP ALL THEIR CAMPBELL'S SOUP DURING THE LONG INTERSTELLAR TRIP THROUGH WINTER.

MAKING A LARGE NUMBER OF SMALL SEEDS IS A GENERAL PHENOMENON IN BIOLOGY CALLED "R-SELECTION," WHICH IS A REPRODUCTIVE STRATEGY MANY ORGANISMS USE, ESPECIALLY COLONIZING SPECIES INTERESTED IN RAPID DISPERSAL. R-SELECTION SPECIES PRODUCE LOTS OF OFFSPRING BUT PUT VERY LITTLE ENERGY INTO EACH ONE, SO FEW OF THE OFFSPRING SURVIVE--SORT OF A SHOTGUN EFFECT.

LARGE SEEDS—"k-selection"

WITH LARGE SEEDS (CORN, MELON, SQUASH, CUCUMBER, SUNFLOWER, BEANS, PEAS, ETC.) YOU CAN SIMPLY POKE A HOLE IN THE SOIL SURFACE AND DROP THE SEEDS IN:

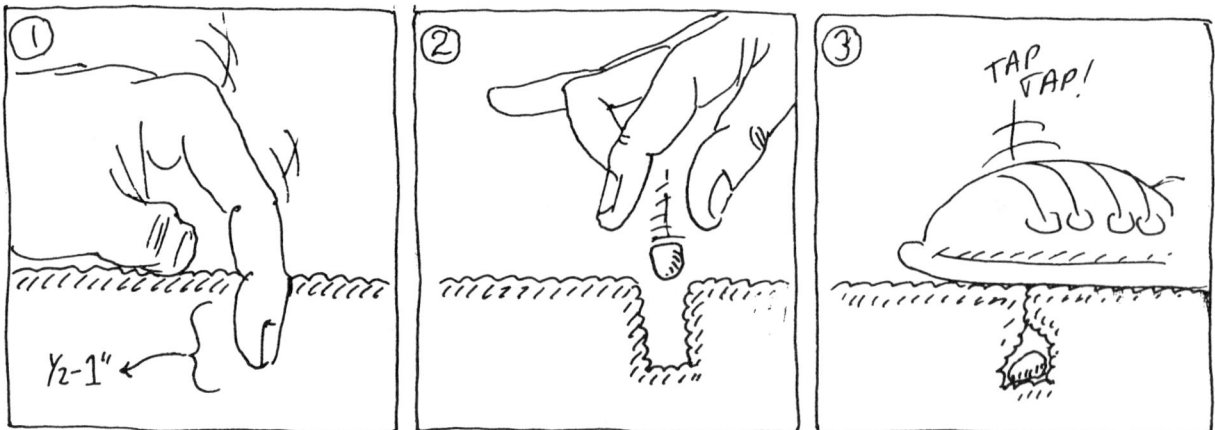

MOST LARGE SEEDS WILL SPROUT AND GROW WELL, SINCE THESE PLANTS EMPLOY THE "K-SELECTION" STRATEGY: THEY PRODUCE ONLY A FEW OFFSPRING, BUT GIVE THEM LOTS OF ENERGY AND FOOD RESERVES--SORT OF LIKE "PUTTING ALL YOUR EGGS IN ONE BASKET." (HUMANS ARE AN EXAMPLE OF ANOTHER ORGANISM USING THIS STRATEGY. MOST INSECTS, ON THE OTHER HAND, ARE "R-SELECTORS"--A FACTOR WE ENCOUNTER

AGAIN IN CHAPTER EIGHT, PEST CONTROL.) EVEN SO, YOU'LL STILL WANT TO SOW 2 OR 3 SEEDS PER FUTURE PLANT, JUST TO MAKE SURE AT LEAST ONE COMES UP AND GROWS TO ADOLESCENCE WITHOUT BEING GOBBLED UP IN ONE FELL SWOOP BY A BIRD OR OTHER SEEDLING—LOVER.

RULE OF THUMB: SEEDS SHOULD BE COVERED BY AS MUCH COMPOST AS THE DIAMETER OF THE SEED.

AFTER THE SEEDS ARE BURIED, GIVE THE SOIL LITTLE TAPS WITH YOUR FOOT. FIRMING THE SOIL IS NECESSARY TO RECREATE A NATURAL—LIKE SOIL TEXTURE.

BUT DON'T STAMP HARD! JUST LITTLE TAPS WILL DO IT, OR GENTLE PATS WITH YOUR HANDS.

. . . ANY HARDER THAN A LIGHT TAP, AND THE SOIL WILL FORM A THIN, HARD CRUST IN THE SUN, AND THAT'LL BE HARD FOR THE SEEDLING TO PENETRATE.

IN FACT, IT'S BEST WITH LARGE SEEDS TO HAVE A LIGHT MULCH ON THE SURFACE TO HELP PREVENT CRUSTING.

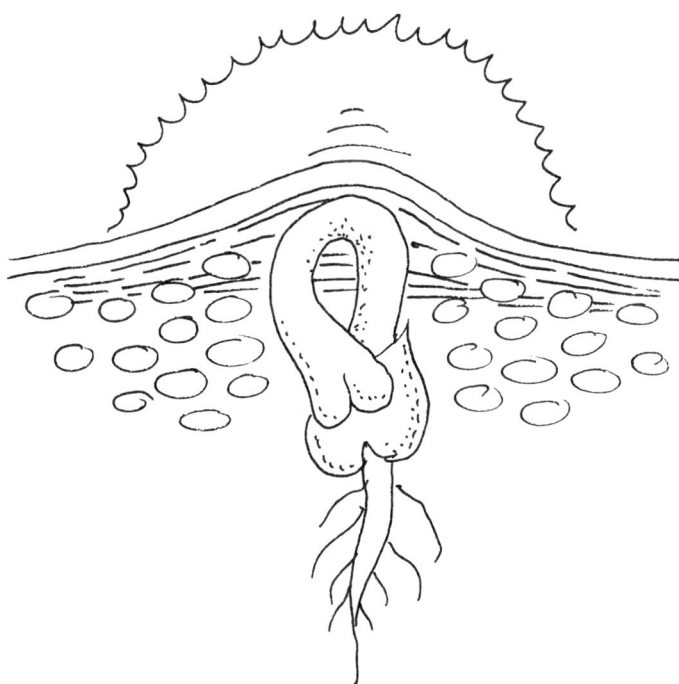

SEEDING A LAWN OR COVER CROP INVOLVES SPECIAL TECHNIQUES:

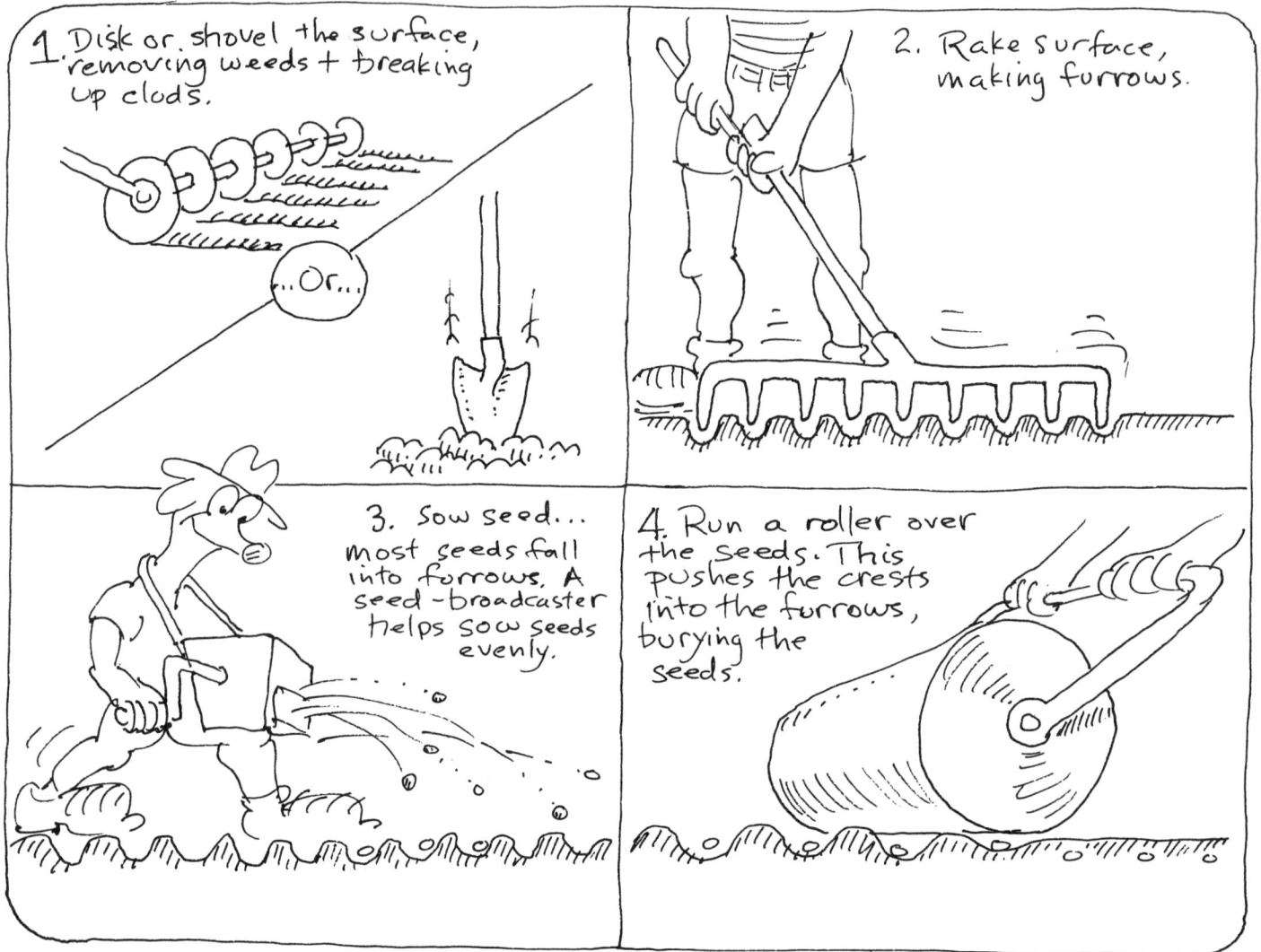

1. Disk or shovel the surface, removing weeds + breaking up clods.

...Or...

2. Rake surface, making furrows.

3. Sow seed... most seeds fall into furrows. A seed-broadcaster helps sow seeds evenly.

4. Run a roller over the seeds. This pushes the crests into the furrows, burying the seeds.

SEED SPACING

LARGE SEEDS SHOULD BE SPACED ACCORDING TO HOW WIDE THE PLANTS WILL BE, SO THEIR LEAVES WILL BARELY TOUCH WHEN THE PLANTS ARE FULLY GROWN. THEY SHOULD BE ARRANGED IN A TRIANGULAR PATTERN, AS SHOWN ON THE TOP OF 135. THIS SORT OF "FRENCH INTENSIVE" PATTERN PACKS THE PLANTS TOGETHER AS CLOSELY AS POSSIBLE. CLOSE-PACKING IS IMPORTANT FOR EFFICIENT USE OF SPACE, AND FOR A "LIVING MULCH" EFFECT (THE LEAVES SHADE THE SOIL SO THERE'S LESS SOIL-WATER EVAPORATION).

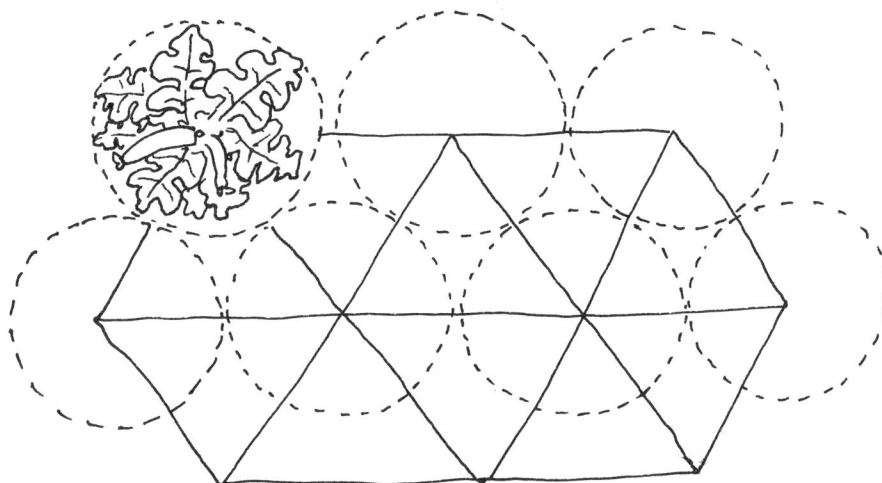

MANY ORCHARDS ARE PLANTED IN THIS PATTERN, AND IT GIVES THEM A PRETTY
KINETIC-SCULPTURE EFFECT DRIVING PAST IN A CAR, AS THE VARIOUS NODAL LINES
PHASE-SHIFT IN AND OUT OF ALIGNMENT WITH YOUR EYES. YOU'LL NOTICE THIS IS ALSO A
MACRO-VERSION OF THE CLAY CRYSTAL LATTICE (P. 68).

IF YOU WANT TO GET **REAL** FANCY YOU CAN INTERPLANT WIDE PLANTS WITH
NARROWER PLANTS, WITH THE NARROW ONES NESTLED INTO THE HOLES BETWEEN THE
WIDE ONES:

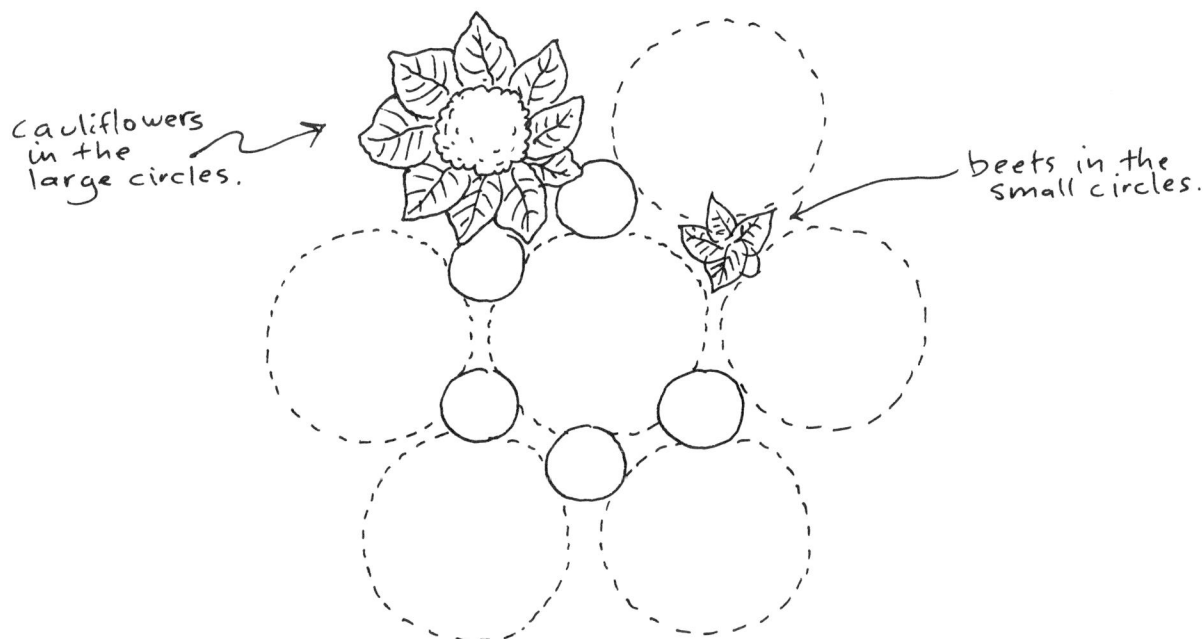

cauliflowers
in the
large circles.

beets in the
small circles.

IN THIS EXAMPLE, IT WOULD BE BETTER TO START BOTH THE BEETS AND THE
CAULIFLOWER IN SMALL CONTAINERS, AND TRANSPLANT THEM LATER INTO THE GARDEN.
THAT'S BECAUSE BOTH PLANTS ARE SLOW GROWERS THAT NEED LOTS OF INTENSIVE CARE
AS SEEDLINGS, AND DON'T MIND BEING TRANSPLANTED. WE'LL GET TO THAT NOW . . .

WHEN TO START SEEDS IN CONTAINERS

SEEDS SHOULD BE STARTED IN CONTAINERS IF THEY ARE SLOW TO SPROUT AND GROW, OR IF YOU WANT TO START THEM ON TABLES TO PROTECT THEM FROM PESTS, OR IF YOU WANT TO START THEM IN A COLD FRAME OR GREENHOUSE.

SEEDS WHICH SPROUT OR GROW SLOWLY ARE TOMATO, PEPPER, EGGPLANT, CABBAGE FAMILY (CABBAGE, BROCOLLI, CAULIFLOWER, KALE, KHOLRABI, BRUSSELS SPROUTS), CELERY, BEETS, LETTUCE, ONION, PARSELY, AND MOST HERBS. THESE PLANTS NEED INTENSIVE CARE AS SEEDLINGS--FREQUENT WATERING, PROTECTION FROM FASTER-GROWING WEEDS, PEST CONTROL, ETC. SO IT'S MUCH EASIER TO START THEM UP ON A TABLE WHERE IT'S EASY TO SEE AND CARE FOR THEM. ALSO IF THEY'RE ON A TABLE, GROUND-CRAWLING PESTS LIKE SNAILS, SLUGS, AND EARWIGS WILL HAVE TROUBLE GETTING TO THEM.

ANOTHER REASON TO START SEEDS IN CONTAINERS IS WHEN YOU'RE STARTING THEM UNDER GLASS, EITHER IN THE HOUSE IN A SOUTH-FACING WINDOW, OR IN A GREENHOUSE OR COLD-FRAME. THIS METHOD IS USED WITH CERTAIN SLOW-GROWING, HEAT-LOVING VEGGIES LIKE PEPPERS, EGGPLANTS, TOMATOES, AND BASIL (MOST HERBS). YOU CAN START THESE AS EARLY AS JANUARY, TO BE TRANSPLANTED INTO THE GARDEN BY LATE MARCH.

STARTING SEEDS IN FLATS

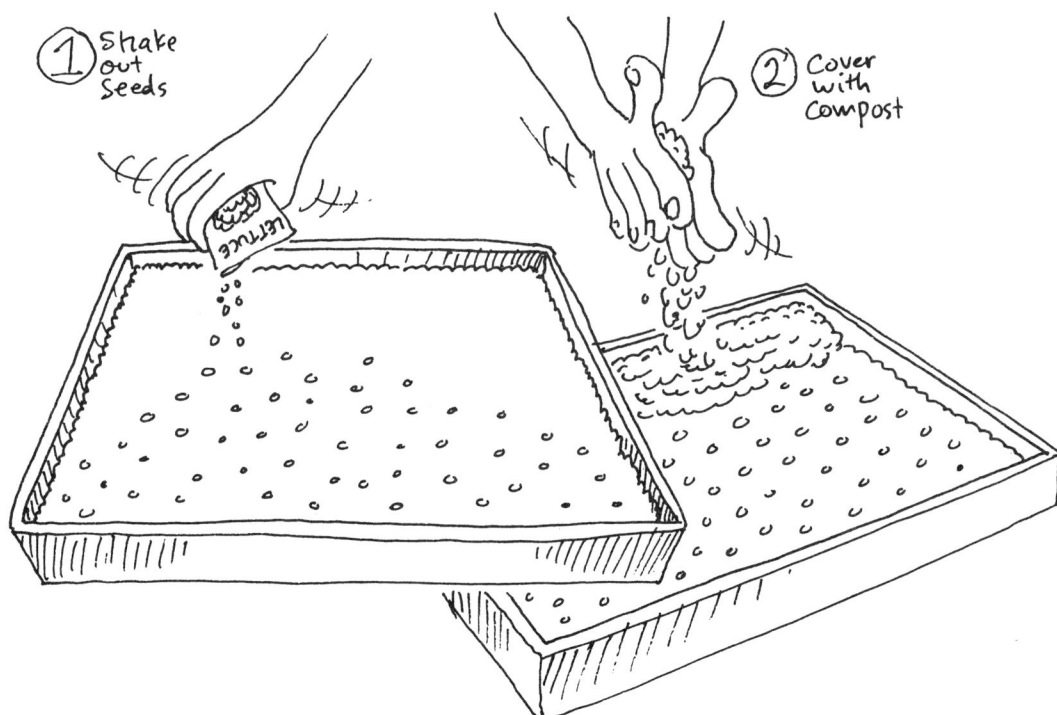

① Shake out seeds

② Cover with compost

THE CONTAINERS USED IN STARTING SEEDS ARE CALLED "FLATS," BECAUSE THEY ARE SHALLOW. YOU CAN USUALLY GET USED FLATS OR "SIX PACKS" FREE FROM NURSURIES. OR YOU CAN USE EGG CARTONS, ALTHOUGH THEY TEND TO BE UNWIELDY AND UNSTABLE WHEN FULL OF WET SEEDLING MIX.

SEEDING MIX

1/3 SAND, OR SANDY SOIL + 2 1/3 SIFTED COMPOST

= SEEDING/POTTING MIX

TO MAKE SEEDING MIX, START WITH SIFTED COMPOST (WHAT ELSE?), AND MIX IN SOME SIFTED SANDY TOPSOIL, OR SAND (**NOT** BEACH SAND). A GOOD RATIO IS ABOUT 1/3 SAND TO 2/3 COMPOST. THE SAND IS NECESSARY BECAUSE IT IMPROVES THE DRAINAGE (ALWAYS A PROBLEM IN CONTAINERS), AND BECAUSE COMPOST IS USUALLY TOO RICH TO USE "UNCUT." WHY? BECAUSE SEEDS GERMINATE BY TAKING UP WATER BY OSMOSIS. OSMOSIS IS THE MOVEMENT OF WATER FROM AN AREA OF FEW DISSOLVED MOLECULES (LIKE THE SOIL) TO AN AREA WITH MORE DISSOLVED MOLECULES (LIKE A SEED). IF YOUR COMPOST (OR A SMALL POCKET OF IT) IS ESPECIALLY RICH IN NUTRIENT-MOLECULES, IT COULD PREVENT THE SEED'S WATER UPTAKE. SO BE ON THE SAFE SIDE AND ADD SOME SAND.

SUN NEEDS OF SEEDLINGS

BEFORE SPROUTING, IT'S BEST TO KEEP SEEDS IN THE SHADE, TO SLOW EVAPORATION. (AN EXCEPTION IS DURING COOL WEATHER, WHEN MANY SEEDS NEED ALL THE HEAT THEY CAN GET). AFTER SPROUTING, ALL VEGETABLE AND HERB SEEDS SHOULD GET FULL SUN, WITH TWO EXCEPTIONS. IN THE SUMMER, OR WHENEVER IT GETS REALLY WARM, LETTUCE AND ONIONS MUST GET EITHER PARTIAL SHADE ALL DAY LONG (THE BEST), OR FULL SHADE MOST OF THE DAY. UNDER A TREE IS IDEAL, FOR A DAPPLED SUN-SPOT EFFECT. IF IT'S REALLY SCORCHING OUTSIDE, YOU MAY HAVE TO BRING THEM INDOORS.

WATER NEEDS

ALL SEEDS AND SEEDLINGS MUST BE WATERED DAILY UNTIL THEY ARE READY TO TRANSPLANT. WATER MORE OFTEN IF DAYS ARE HOT, DRY, OR WINDY; WATER LESS IF THE SOIL REMAINS WET, OR IF ALGAE STARTS TO GROW ON THE SURFACE. ALGAE LOOKS LIKE A LAYER OF GREEN FUZZ, AND IT MEANS YOU'VE GOT AN AQUATIC ENVIRONMENT. (OFTEN A LAYER OF BLACK SCUM WILL FORM, AND THIS AGAIN MEANS TOO MUCH WATER.)

WATER IN THE MORNING RATHER THAN THE EVENING. IF YOU WATER IN THE EVENING, THE SOIL WILL BE COLD AT NIGHT, SINCE WATER CONDUCTS HEAT FASTER THAN DRY SOIL. MANY SEEDS WON'T EVEN SPROUT IN THE SPRING UNTIL THE SOIL TEMPERATURE IS HIGH ENOUGH; WATERING IN THE MORNING HELPS KEEP THE SOIL WARM ENOUGH FOR SPROUTING.

IT'S BETTER TO OVERWATER SPROUTING SEEDS THAN TO UNDERWATER THEM. IF YOU MISS A SINGLE DAY THE SEEDS CAN DIE, ESPECIALLY IF THEY'RE SPROUTED HALFWAY, AND THEN DRY OUT. THIS IS SOMETHING TO THINK ABOUT IF YOU'RE PLANNING A TRIP SOME-WHERE, EVEN FOR THE WEEKEND.

USE A SPRINKLER THAT MAKES FINE DROPLETS--THE IDEA IS TO TRY AND DUPLICATE THE EFFECT OF A LIGHT SPRING RAIN. OR, YOU CAN STICK YOUR THUMB OVER THE END OF THE HOSE.

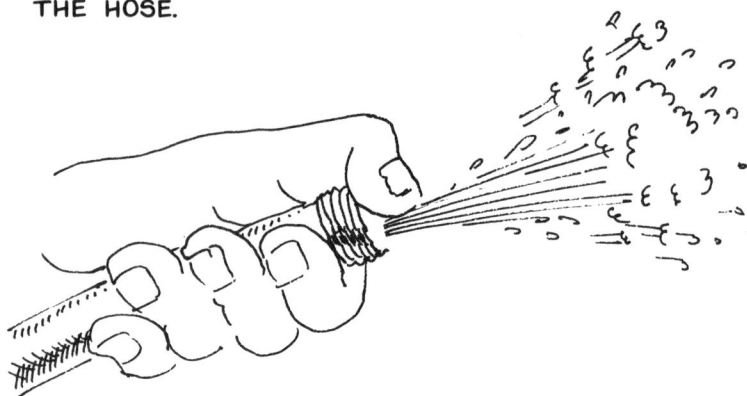

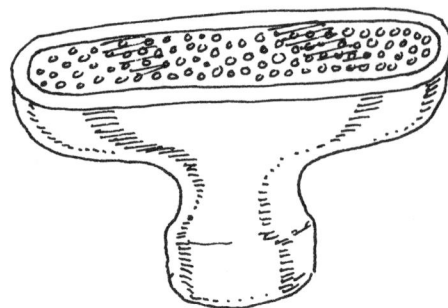

SOME SEEDS NEED MORE FREQUENT SPRINKLING THAN OTHERS, BOTH BEFORE AND AFTER SPROUTING. BEANS, PEAS, LETTUCE, CELERY, AND BEETS BENEFIT FROM TWO WATERINGS PER DAY WHEN VERY YOUNG. CELERY NEEDS THE MOST WATER: THE SEEDING MIX SHOULD BE CONSTANTLY WATERLOGGED FOR BEST GERMINATION, ALTHOUGH TWICE-A-DAY WATERING IS OKAY. ADD EXTRA SAND TO THE MIX FOR BETTER DRAINAGE, AND KEEP IN THE SHADE UNTIL THE SEEDS SPROUT. ON THE OTHER HAND, SPINACH NEEDS SOME DRYNESS—THE MIX SHOULD BE ALLOWED TO DRY SLIGHTLY BETWEEN WATERINGS.

SELF-SEEDING

SELF-SEEDING IS THE STATE-OF-THE-ART IN NATURAL, DO-NOTHING GARDENING, A LA FUKUOKA: LETTING A FEW OF YOUR PLANTS GO TO SEED AND PROPAGATE THEMSELVES. THE PLANTS WHICH RESULT ARE CALLED "VOLUNTEERS." VOLUNTEERS ARE USUALLY HARDIER AND GROW HEALTHIER THAN HUMAN-SOWN PLANTS, SINCE THE SEEDS WHICH SPROUT ON THEIR OWN ARE THE ONES BEST-SUITED GENETICALLY FOR THE PARTICULAR MICROCLIMATE WHERE THEY SPROUTED. AND SINCE THEY CHOSE THEIR OWN TIME TO SPROUT, THEY SPROUTED AT THE BEST TIME FOR **THEM**, NOT WHEN **YOU** THOUGHT (MAYBE WRONGLY) WOULD BE THE BEST TIME. OVER TIME (3-4 YEARS), YOU CAN ACTUALLY END UP WITH NEW GENETIC STRAINS THAT ARE BEST-SUITED FOR YOUR GARDEN. OF COURSE, YOU MUST USE NON-HYBRID SEEDS TO START WITH, BECAUSE HYBRID SEEDS WON'T BREED TRUE, OR EVEN SPROUT SOMETIMES.

MANY PLANTS "BOLT" WHEN THEY GO TO SEED, MEANING THEY SHOOT THEIR CENTRAL STALK WAY UP ABOVE THE GROUND, AND THEN OFTEN DROOP OVER, LIKE THIS CHARD PLANT:

ONIONS, BEETS, AND CELERY ALSO DO THIS. IF THIS HAPPENS, DON'T TRY TO SUPPORT THE PLANT. DROOPING ALONG THE GROUND IS AN EVOLVED SEED-DISPERSAL METHOD. IF THE PLANT STOOD STRAIGHT UP, MOST OF THE SEEDS WOULD FALL RIGHT AROUND THE BASE OF THE PLANT, WHERE THE OLD STALK AND ROOTS WOULD GET IN THE WAY OF THE NEW GENERATION, AND WHERE THE MOST-PREFERRED NUTRIENTS WOULD HAVE BEEN TEMPORARILY DEPLETED.

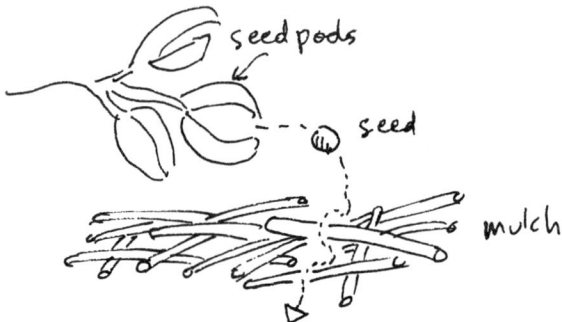

A LAYER OF COMPOST-MULCH ON THE SURFACE IS VITAL FOR SELF-SEEDING. IF A SEED FALLS ON BARE HARD SOIL, IT WILL JUST SIT THERE ON THE HOT DRY SURFACE, AND NEVER STAY WET LONG ENOUGH TO GERMINATE. BUT IF THERE'S A THICK MULCH ON THE SURFACE, THE SEED WILL FALL BETWEEN PIECES OF STRAW, STEMS, OR WHATEVER, BURYING ITSELF IN THE COOL DARK MOIST RECESSES OF THE MULCH, WHERE FALLING WATER DROPS CAN COMPLETE THE JOB OF TUCKING THE SEEDS IN.

seed pods

seed

mulch

DAMPING-OFF DISEASE

DAMPING-OFF IS A FUNGUS DISEASE OF SEEDLINGS, WHICH HAPPENS LIKE THIS.

DAMPING OFF is a fungus disease of seedlings, in which the young seedling is doing fine at first, then suddenly topples over. It's especially a problem with cabbage-family plants. It affects only seeds and very young (2-3 weeks) plants, since after that age the stem hardens so the fungus can't enter the tissue.

oh boy - Big mac!

spore capsules

mycelium

hyphal tips

Seedling

① Here is the fungus creeping along the soil surface, stalking the unsuspecting seedling...

② The fungus porks out on the seedling stem...

MUNCH MUNCH

③ The seedling falls over & dies.

TIMBERRRRR!

CRASH!

TO PREVENT THIS DREADED DISEASE, ALWAYS USE COMPOST YOU'VE MADE YOURSELF, FOLLOWING THE AEROBIC METHODS DESCRIBED IN CHAPTER ONE. PROPERLY MADE COMPOST CONTAINS BENEFICIAL FUNGI WHICH ARE ABLE TO OUT-COMPETE DAMPING-OFF FUNGI, SINCE THEY GOBBLE UP NUTRIENTS FASTER. INORGANIC GARDENERS ARE FORCED TO STERILIZE THEIR SEEDLING MIX, EITHER BY HEAT OR WITH CARCINOGENIC FUNGICIDES, SINCE DISEASE FUNGI HAVE A FREE REIGN WHEN THERE ARE NO BENEFICIAL FUNGI AROUND.

IF YOU'RE JUST STARTING A GARDEN AND DON'T YET HAVE A SUPPLY OF COMPOST, THERE ARE CULTURAL CONTROLS YOU CAN USE THAT WILL HELP PREVENT SERIOUS EPIDEMICS OF DAMPING-OFF:

1. FIRST, MULCH AROUND THE SEEDLINGS WITH COURSE SAND, SO THE FUNGUS CAN'T CRAWL ALONG THE SURFACE (FUNGI NEED TO BE IN CONTACT WITH EITHER SOIL OR PLANT TISSUE TO SURVIVE.)

2. EXCESS MOISTURE FAVORS MOST TYPES OF FUNGUS. SO WATER THE BARE MINIMUM, AND IMPROVE DRAINAGE BY ADDING EXTRA SAND TO THE SEEDLING MIX, SO WATER DOESN'T STICK AROUND IN THE MIX. ALSO BE SURE TO WATER ONLY IN THE MORNING WHEN THE SUN IS SHINING, SO THERE'S RAPID EVAPORATION OF SURFACE MOISTURE. IF THIS ALL SEEMS LIKE A BIG HASSLE, GOOD! MAYBE IT'LL GET YOU IN GEAR TO START CRANKIN' ON THE COMPOST!

142

TRANSPLANTING

NOW IT'S A FEW WEEKS TO A MONTH LATER, AND THE SEEDLINGS YOU STARTED IN FLATS OR SIX-PACKS ARE TALLER THAN THE DEPTH OF THE CONTAINER (A NO-NO), AND THEY'RE PROBABLY ON THE VERGE OF BEING ROOTBOUND, ALL BECAUSE YOU'VE BEEN SPACING OUT THE TRANSPLANTING. IT'S OKAY, DON'T FEEL GUILTY, JUST **TRANSPLANT** THEM NOW! YOU COULD HAVE PROBABLY DONE IT EVEN BEFORE THEY GOT TOO TALL; THE MINIMUM TRANSPLANTING AGE IS WHEN A SEEDLING HAS 4 OR 5 "TRUE" LEAVES, NOT COUNTING THE COTYLEDONS:

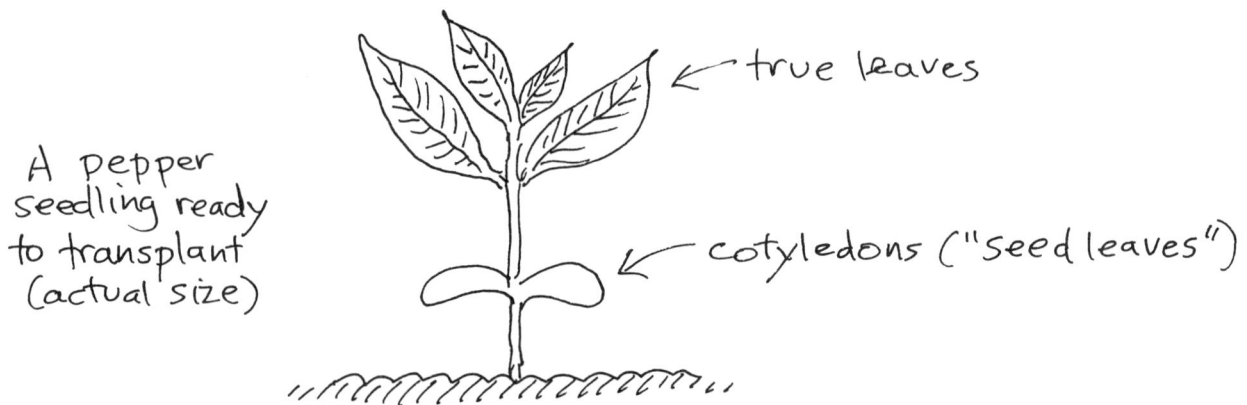

A pepper seedling ready to transplant (actual size)

← true leaves

← cotyledons ("seed leaves")

TRANSPLANTING INTO POTS

NOW YOU HAVE TWO CHOICES: YOU CAN TRANSPLANT THE LITTLE TYKE INTO A POT, OR DIRECTLY INTO THE GARDEN. MOST THINGS (LETTUCE, ONIONS, BEETS, CABBAGE-FAMILY PLANTS, FLOWERS, EGGPLANTS, ETC.) CAN GO DIRECTLY INTO THE GARDEN. ONLY EXTREMELY SLOW-GROWING SEEDLINGS (TOMATO, PEPPER, MOST HERBS, SHRUBS, AND TREES) NEED BE TRANSPLANTED INTO POTS, SO YOU CAN PROTECT THESE MELLOW SLOW POKES FROM RAMPANT YUPPIE WEEDS AND MARAUDING REDNECK INSECTS. ADVANCED GARDENERS TRY TO DISPENSE WITH POTS AS MUCH AS POSSIBLE, BECAUSE IN GENERAL POTS AREN'T AS GOOD AS A GARDEN BED. FIRST OFF THEY'RE A HASSLE, AND BESIDES EVERY TIME A PLANT IS TRANSPLANTED THE ROOTS ARE BOUND TO GET DAMAGED A LITTLE. ALSO, THE SIDES AND BOTTOM OF THE POT ARE LIKE A HARD-PAN AROUND THE PLANT--A RESISTANCE TO WATER DRAINAGE AND ROOT GROWTH. IT MAKES MOST PLANTS CLAUSTROPHOBIC JUST THINKING ABOUT IT.

TO MINIMIZE THE "HARD-PAN" EFFECT, START BY MAKING SURE THERE ARE LARGE HOLES IN THE BOTTOM AND LOWER SIDES OF THE POT. THEN LINE THE BOTTOM OF THE POT WITH A DRAINAGE LAYER OF COARSE MATERIAL--SUCH AS STRAW, WEEDS, LEAVES, OR HALF-FINISHED COMPOST--SO THE POTTING MIX WON'T CLOG UP THE HOLES. FOR A MORE PERMANENT PLANTING (LIKE A HOUSEPLANT OR WINDOW BOX) YOU CAN USE GRAVEL, WOOD CHIPS, BARK, ETC. FOR THE DRAINAGE LAYER.

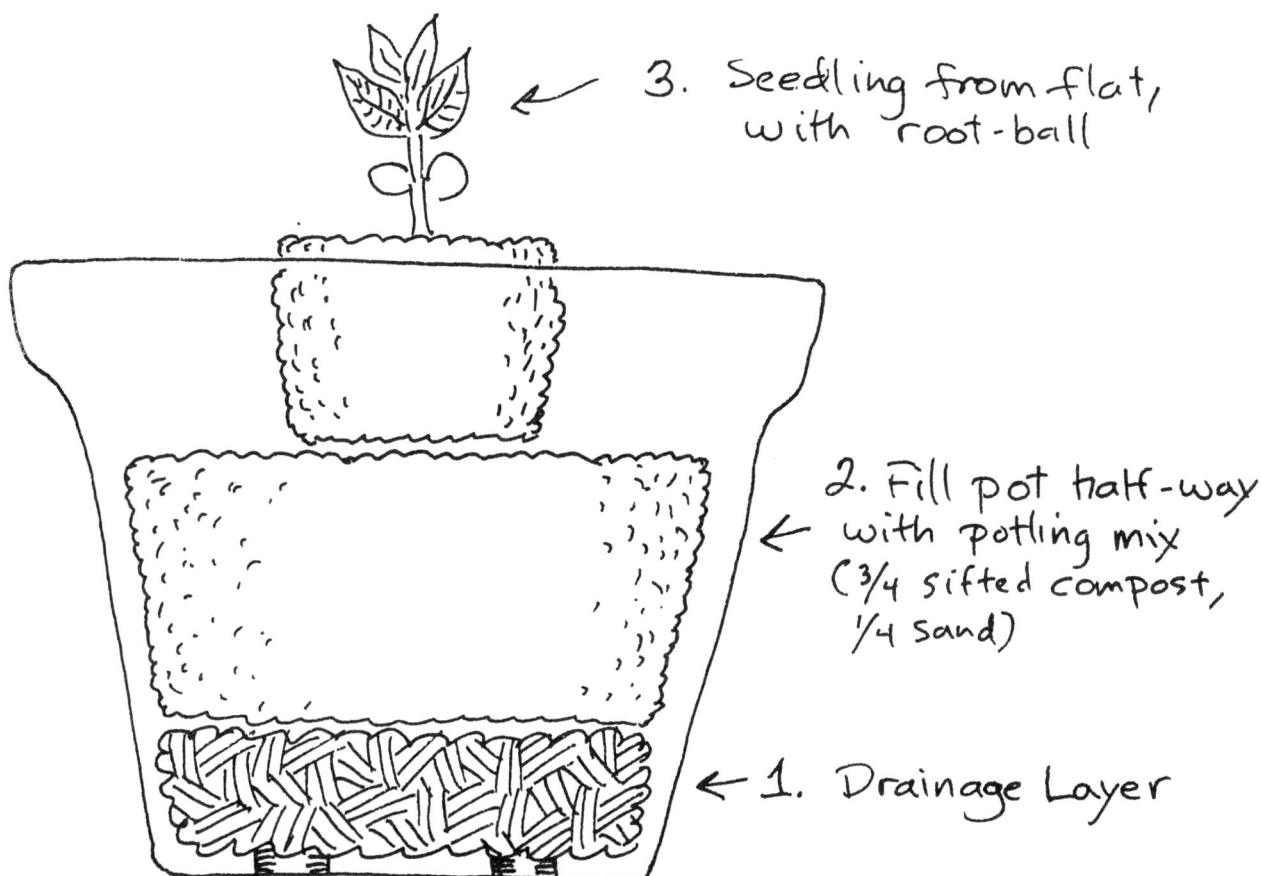

3. Seedling from flat, with root-ball

2. Fill pot half-way with potting mix (3/4 sifted compost, 1/4 sand)

1. Drainage Layer

THEN FILL THE POT PART-WAY WITH 3/4 SIFTED COMPOST AND 1/4 SAND OR SANDY SOIL (THE EXACT RATIOS AREN'T IMPORTANT--THE IDEA IS TO HAVE A FERTILE, WELL-DRAINING MEDIUM).

ONCE YOU HAVE THE POT READY, BRING THE FLAT FULL OF SEEDLINGS OVER AND PREPARE FOR THE FINAL TRANSPLANTING COUNTDOWN. FIRST, THE SEEDLING MIX IN THE FLAT SHOULD BE PARTLY MOIST, AS IN THE "MAGIC TIME" FROM CHAPTER TWO. IF IT'S TOO WET, YOU'LL CREATE CLODS BY HANDLING IT. IF IT'S TOO DRY, THE MIX WILL ALL FALL OFF THE ROOTS AS YOU TRANSFER THE SEEDLING, TEARING OFF SOME ROOT-ENDS IN THE PROCESS. EITHER WAY, A BIG BUMMER.

SINCE THE SEEDLINGS IN A FLAT AREN'T SEPARATED INTO NEAT COMPARTMENTS AS WITH A SIX-PACK, YOU HAVE TO SEPARATE THEM YOURSELF. AN ORDINARY DINING FORK OR SPOON IS EXCELLENT FOR THIS--JUST STEAL ONE FROM THE KITCHEN WHEN NO ONE'S LOOKING. MOST SEEDLINGS LIKE TO HAVE A "ROOT-BALL" OF SEEDING MIX LEFT AROUND THEIR ROOTS AS THEY'RE BEING TRANSPLANTED. SO LIFT UP THE SEEDLING WITH ROOT-BALL INTACT, PLUNK IT DOWN IN THE MIDDLE OF THE POT, AND FILL UP THE REST OF THE POT WITH POTTING MIX. TAMP DOWN THE MIX TO SQUEEZE OUT EXCESS AIR SPACE, AND WATER IMMEDIATELY.

(1.) MULCH
up to first leaves with half-finished compost, manure, leaves, grass clippings, weeds, etc.

(2.) WATER

AND ABOVE ALL, **MULCH** AROUND THE SEEDLING AS SOON AS POSSIBLE: MULCH HELPS PREVENT WATER LOSS FROM THE POTTING MIX, AND A LOT ELSE BESIDES.

USE DIFFERENT MATERIALS FOR MULCH, DEPENDING ON THE SIZE OF THE PLANT. FOR TINY SEEDLINGS YOU WANT A FINE-CHOPPED MULCH, LIKE SHREDDED WEEDS, HALF-DONE COMPOST, SMALL LEAVES, COFFEE GROUNDS, GRASS CLIPPINGS, ETC. LOOK AROUND AND SEE WHAT'S AVAILABLE. AS THE PLANTS GET LARGER YOU CAN USE WHOLE WEEDS, LARGE LEAVES, STRAW, MANURE, ETC. (AFTER THE PLANTS ARE IN THE GARDEN).

. . . AND NOW, A WORD FROM OUR SPONSOR--

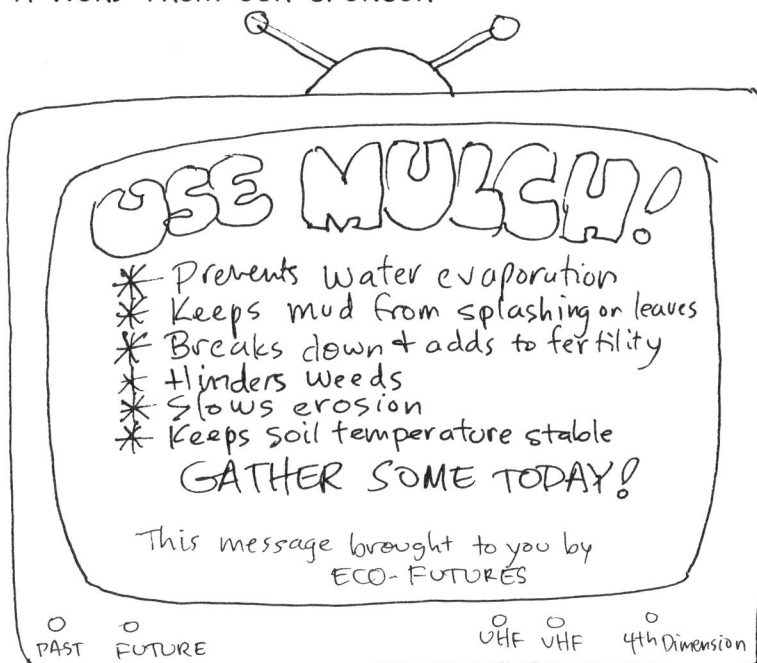

USE MULCH!
* Prevents water evaporation
* Keeps mud from splashing on leaves
* Breaks down + adds to fertility
* Hinders weeds
* Slows erosion
* Keeps soil temperature stable
GATHER SOME TODAY!

This message brought to you by
ECO-FUTURES

PAST   FUTURE   UHF UHF 4th Dimension

SEEDLINGS ESPECIALLY APPRECIATE MULCH, SINCE WITHOUT MULCH THE SOIL SURFACE EXPANDS AND CONTRACTS AS IT ABSORBS WATER AND DRIES OUT, AND AS IT CONTRACTS IT SQUEEZES THE TENDER YOUNG STEMS, PREVENTING THEIR OUTWARD GROWTH AND LITERALLY CHOKING THEM--CONSTRICTING THE PHLOEM AND XYLEM VESSELS WHICH CONDUCT WATER AND NUTRIENTS BETWEEN THE SOIL AND THE LEAVES.

IDEALLY SEEDLINGS SHOULD HAVE MULCH AROUND THEM FROM THE INSTANT THEY EMERGE FROM THE SOIL OR SEEDLING MIX. LARGE SEEDS ARE NO PROBLEM--THEY CAN COME UP THROUGH A LIGHT MULCH OF MANURE OR SMALL LEAVES, AND BE MULCHED FROM BIRTH. SMALL SEEDS ARE A DIFFERENT STORY . . . THEY CAN'T COME UP THROUGH EVEN A THIN MULCH. THIS PROBLEM IS PARTLY OVERCOME BY MAKING SURE THE SOIL HAS PLENTY OF COMPOST, WHICH ACTS AS A SORT OF "INTERNAL MULCH" TO PREVENT STEM CONSTRICTION, AT LEAST. AND SINCE SMALL SEEDS ARE USUALLY SOWN RATHER THICKLY, THE SEEDLINGS THEMSELVES FORM A "LIVING MULCH" BY SHADING OUT THE SOIL UNDERNEATH. (FOR MORE MULCHING LORE, TUNE IN TO CHAPTER SEVEN, ON WATERING.)

TRANSPLANTING into the garden

THE KEY TO TRANSPLANTING INTO THE GARDEN (OR "PLANTING OUT") IS TO **VISUALIZE** THE FULL-GROWN ADULT PLANT WHERE YOU ARE PLACING THE SEEDLING. THIS WILL HELP YOU JUDGE WHAT THE FINAL ECOLOGY WILL LOOK LIKE--THE SPACING OF THE PLANTS, POTENTIAL COMPETITIONS OR COOPERATIONS, ETC.

WITH A LITTLE EXPERIENCE (PLUS KNOWLEDGE OF WHAT FULL-GROWN PLANTS **LOOK** LIKE!), YOU SHOULD BE ABLE TO PRODUCE A THREE-DIMENSIONAL HOLOGRAPHIC IMAGE. THESE VISIONS ARE SOMETIMES CALLED "EIDETIC IMAGES." MANY PEOPLE CAN PRODUCE THEM WHEN THEY'RE ABOUT TO FALL ASLEEP, AND IT ONLY TAKES A BIT OF PRACTICE AND CONCENTRATION TO DO IT WIDE AWAKE IN BROAD DAYLIGHT. EXPERIENCE IN DRAWING HELPS, SINCE ONE WAY OF DRAWING INVOLVES FIRST "SEEING" THE COMPLETE PICTURE FOR A SPLIT SECOND IN YOUR MIND'S EYE, THEN SIMPLY COPYING WHAT YOU SEE.

FROM FLAT TO GARDEN

IN SOME CASES YOU WANT TO GO DIRECTLY FROM FLATS TO THE GARDEN, AND ELIMINATE THE MIDDLEMAN, OR POT. THERE ARE MANY PLANTS WHICH START OFF SLOW (SO ARE STARTED IN FLATS), BUT ONCE THEY GET A FEW INCHES HIGH THEY REALLY START TO TAKE OFF (SO THEY DON'T NEED POTS, WHICH ARE SORT OF A "HALFWAY HOUSE" BETWEEN FLAT AND GARDEN). AMONG THESE PLANTS ARE LETTUCE, ONION, BEETS, CELERY, AND THE CABBAGE FAMILY.

BY FORTUNATE COINCIDENCE, MOST OF THESE PLANTS CAN ALSO BE TRANSPLANTED "BARE-ROOT," MEANING THEY DON'T NEED A ROOTBALL. THAT MEANS YOU CAN SOW THEM AS THICKLY AS YOU WANT IN THE FLAT FOR A "LIVING MULCH" EFFECT, AND THEN EASILY SEPARATE THE ROOTS FROM EACH OTHER WHEN YOU PLANT THEM OUT.

WHEN YOU TRANSPLANT BARE-ROOT SEEDLINGS, MAKE SURE THE SEEDLING MIX IN THE FLAT IS FAIRLY DRY, SO WHEN YOU SEPARATE THE SEEDLINGS, THE MIX WILL FALL EASILY OFF THE ROOTS. TAKE THE FLAT TO THE GARDEN BED. CLEAR AWAY THE MULCH, POKE HOLES WITH YOUR FINGER, PLUNK THE SEEDLINGS IN, RE-MULCH AROUND THE PLANTS, AND WATER. HERE'S THE WHOLE OPERATION IN PICTURES:

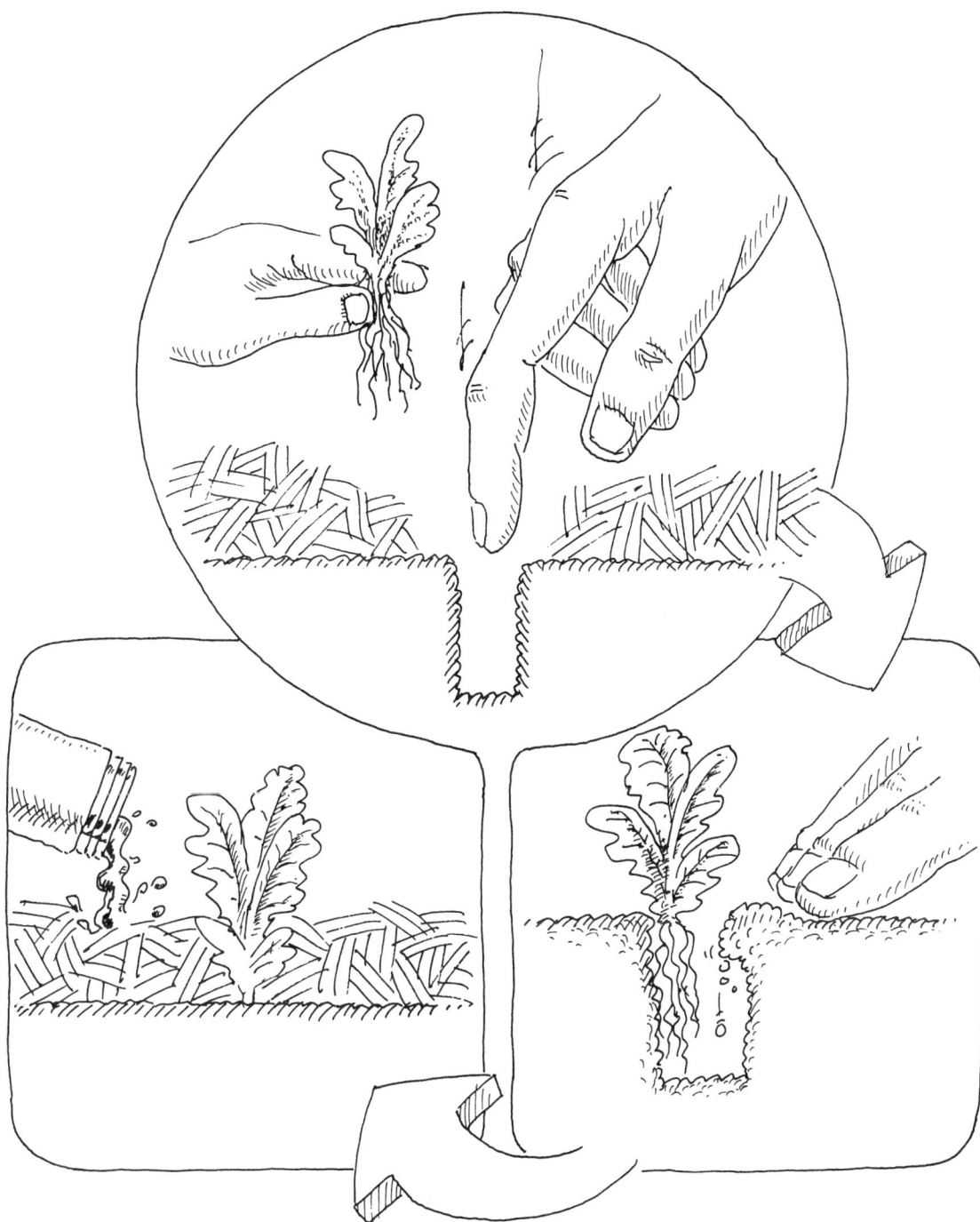

SEEDLING BEDS

IF YOU HAVE MORE SEEDLINGS TO PLANT OUT THAN YOUR CURRENT AVAILABLE BED SPACE ALLOWS, YOU CAN PUT THEM IN "SEEDLING BEDS," SPACE THEM CLOSER THAN NORMAL, AND THEN TRANSPLANT SOME OF THEM TO OTHER BEDS WHEN THEY START TO CROWD EACH OTHER (HOPEFULLY BY THEN YOU'LL HAVE MORE SPACE OPENING UP):

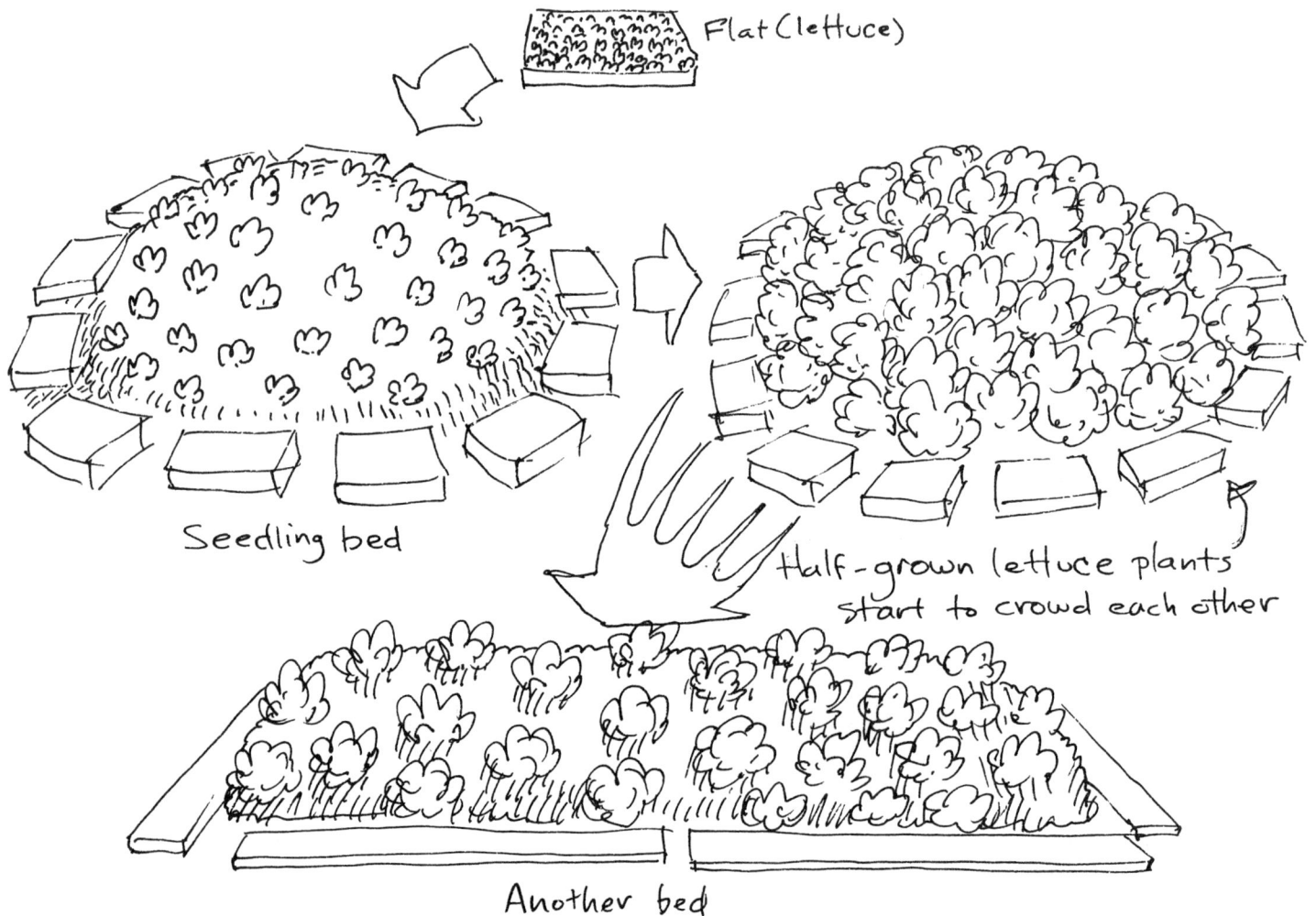

Flat (lettuce)

Seedling bed

Half-grown lettuce plants start to crowd each other

Another bed

FROM FLAT TO GARDEN

FROM POT TO GARDEN

FIRST, THE SOIL IN THE POT MUST BE MEDIUM-MOIST--THE SAME SOIL MOISTURE AS FOR TILLING, SOWING SEED, HARVESTING ROOT CROPS, ETC. . . . REMEMBER THE "MAGIC TIME" FROM CHAPTER TWO. USUALLY THIS MEANS NOT WATERING THE PLANT FOR A DAY OR TWO BEFORE TRANSPLANTING. OR, IF IT'S RAINING, PUT THE PLANT IN A GREENHOUSE OR UNDER AN AWNING ON THE PORCH, OR INDOORS. SIMILARLY, THE GARDEN BED YOU'RE TRANSPLANTING INTO MUST BE MEDIUM-MOIST . . . IF IT'S RAINING, COVER THE BED WITH A SHEET OF PLYWOOD, OR PIECES OF PLASTIC, CARDBOARD, OR WHATEVER. TRANSPLANT IN THE LATE AFTERNOON OR EVENING, SO THE DISRUPTED AND TORN ROOTS WON'T HAVE TO WORK HARD REPLACING MOISTURE TRANSPIRED FROM THE LEAVES IN THE SUN. (IF IT'S OVERCAST, YOU CAN TRANSPLANT ALL DAY.)

THE ROOT BALL IS USUALLY STUCK TO THE INSIDE OF THE POT, SO IT MUST BE UNSTUCK. STEAL A KNIFE FROM THE KITCHEN, AND STICK IT DOWN ALL AROUND THE SIDES OF THE POT. THEN GIVE THE SIDES OF THE POT A GOOD HEALTHY WHACK. DON'T BE AFRAID OF HURTING THE PLANT--REALLY SMACK THE SUCKER.

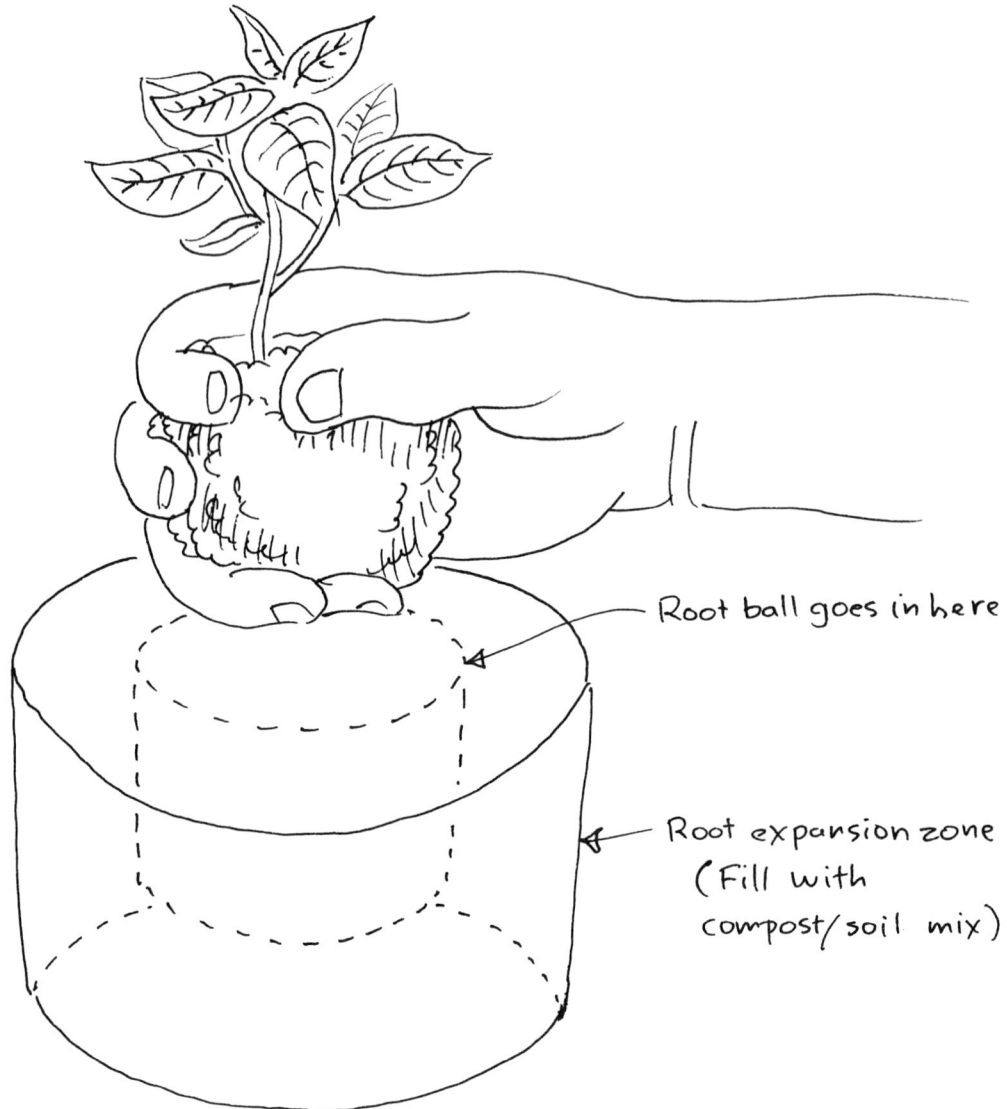

Root ball goes in here

Root expansion zone
(Fill with
compost/soil mix)

NOW YOU'VE GOT THE PLANT OUT OF THE POT, AND THE ROOT BALL IS STILL INTACT (MORE OR LESS) . . . SO FAR, SO GOOD. YOU SHOULD ALREADY HAVE A HOLE READY IN THE BED AT THE SPOT YOU'VE "VISUALIZED" THE FULLY-GROWN PLANT.

THE NEW HOLE SHOULD BE AT LEAST TWICE AS WIDE AND DEEP AS THE ROOT BALL, SO YOU CAN FILL THE EXCESS SPACE WITH A MIXTURE OF SIFTED COMPOST AND TOPSOIL. THIS ROOT EXPANSION ZONE MUST BE SLIGHTLY LESS POROUS THAN THE POTTING MIX, SO THERE'S A GRADUAL TRANSITION FROM POTTING MIX TO TOPSOIL. IF INSTEAD THERE'S AN ABRUPT CHANGE (CALLED A "BOUNDARY LAYER"), THE ROOTS AND WATER WILL GO STRAIGHT DOWN, RATHER THAN SPREAD OUT THROUGH THE SOIL.

IN SOME CASES (SUCH AS LETTUCE AND CABBAGE-FAMILY PLANTS) IT'S SOMETIMES A GOOD IDEA TO PUT AN OVERTURNED POT OR CARDBOARD BOX OVER THE NEWLY-TRANS-PLANTED PLANT, ESPECIALLY IF THE WEATHER IS VERY HOT.

IF YOU ARE JUST BEGINNING YOUR GARDEN, IT'S A GOOD IDEA TO ADD FISH EMULSION FERTILIZER, COMPOST TEA, OR MANURE TEA ONCE A MONTH. FIRST-YEAR ORGANIC SOIL INCLUDES MUCH PARTIALLY-DIGESTED MATTER (BITS OF STRAW, ETC.) WHICH PUTS A NITROGEN DEMAND ON THE SOIL AS THE BACTERIA LABOR TO EAT UP THIS MATERIAL. SEE CHAPTER FOUR FOR A FULL DESCRIPTION OF THESE SUPPLEMENTARY FERTILIZING METHODS.

THE MONTHS GO BY . . . THE PLANTS EXTEND THEIR LEAFY SPLENDOR TOWARD THE HEAVENS . . . MEANWHILE, BACK AT THE RANCH, GARDENERS STRAP ON PRUNING SHEARS IN LEATHER HOLSTERS, LOOKING EXCEEDINGLY MACHO. THEY ADVANCE TOWARD THE UNSUSPECTING FOLIAGE, SHEARS IN HAND . . .

PRUNING—
directing the flow of life!

PRUNING WAS INVENTED BY DEER AND OTHER BROWSING ANIMALS. IT HAS BEEN DISCOVERED IN MANY NATURAL ECOSYSTEMS THAT MODERATE BROWSING RESULTS IN GREATER NET LEAF GROWTH, SINCE IT CAUSES BUDS ON THE STEM TO SPROUT. ANIMAL SALIVA IS THOUGHT TO CONTAIN SUBSTANCES WHICH MIMICK PLANT HORMONES, THUS STIMULATING CELL DIVISION AND GROWTH OF THE NEW SHOOTS. (ROSENTHAL, JAMES; **HERBIVORES**, 1982, P. 279.

REMOVING APICAL DOMINANCE

ANYTIME YOU REMOVE THE END OF A SHOOT, WHETHER THE "LEADER" OR A "LATERAL," IT CAUSES THE BUDS FURTHER DOWN ON THE SHOOT OR STEM TO SPROUT, AND PRODUCE NEW LEAFY GROWTH:

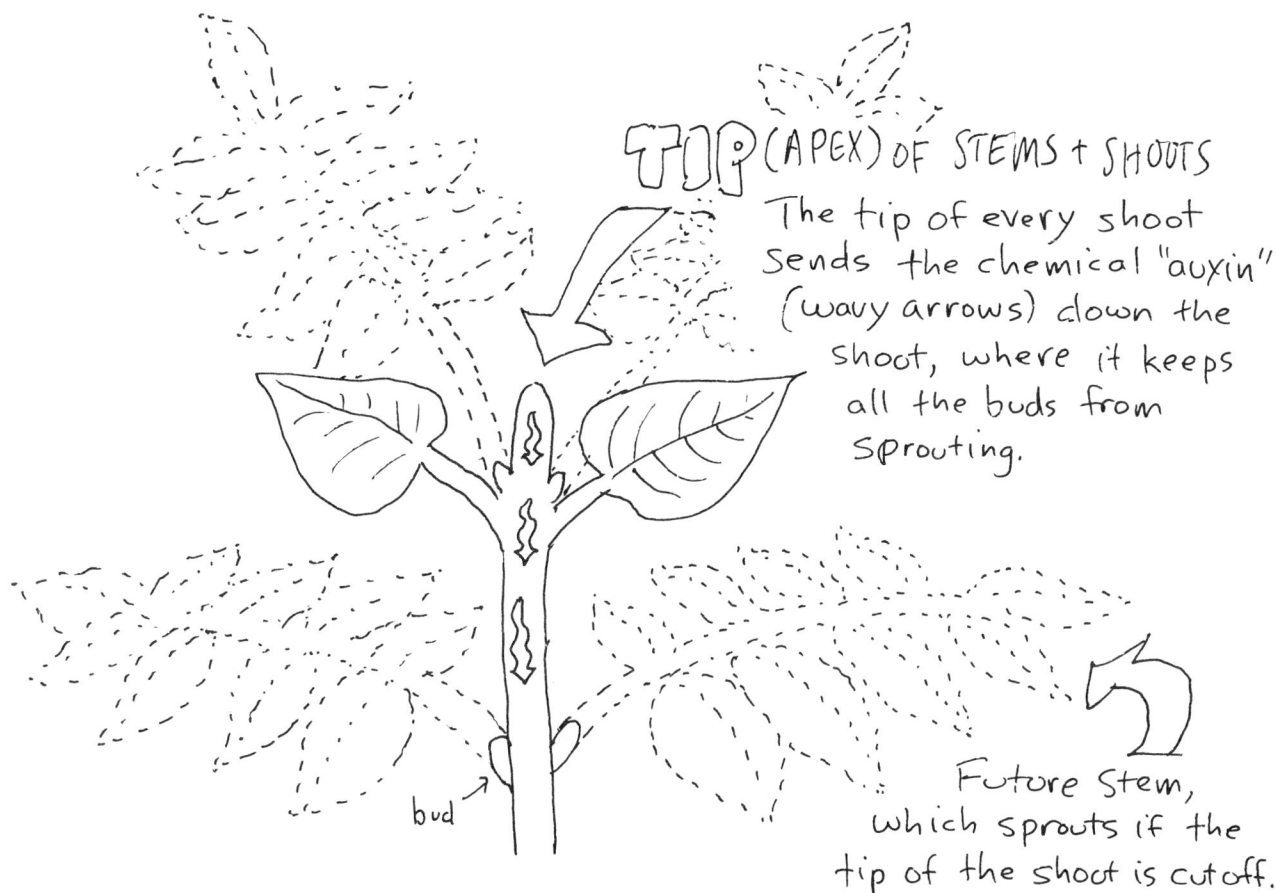

TIP (APEX) OF STEMS + SHOOTS
The tip of every shoot sends the chemical "auxin" (wavy arrows) down the shoot, where it keeps all the buds from sprouting.

bud

Future stem, which sprouts if the tip of the shoot is cut off.

THE END OF EVERY STEM (CALLED THE TIP, OR "APEX") PRODUCES A CHEMICAL (AUXIN) THAT DIFFUSES DOWN THE STEM, PREVENTING THE BUDS ON THE STEM FROM SPROUTING NEW STEMS. THIS IS CALLED "APICAL DOMINANCE." IN THIS WAY, THE PLANT CAN GET ITS LEAVES UP AS HIGH AS THE COMPETING PLANTS AROUND IT, AND IT HAS RESERVE BUDS TO USE IN CASE AN ANIMAL EATS THE TOP OFF.

HOWEVER, IF YOU AS A GARDENER KNOW THE PLANT IS IN NO DANGER OF COMPETITION FROM OTHERS (SINCE YOU HAVE BEEN SO CLEVER AT PLANNING THE GARDEN AND USING "VISUALIZATION"), YOU CAN HELP THE PLANT PRODUCE MORE LEAFAGE (AND,

MORE IMPORTANTLY FOR CERTAIN LANDSCAPING PLANTS, MORE FLOWERS) BY CLIPPING
OFF THE ENDS OF THE STEMS, LIKE THIS:

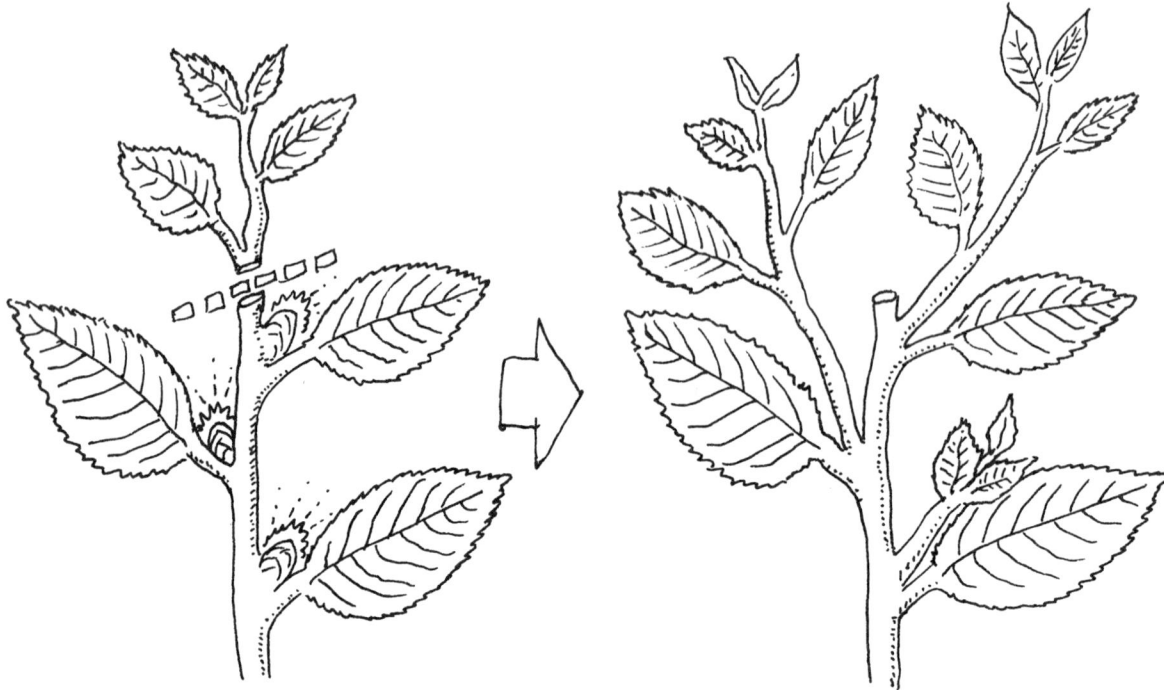

THIS USUALLY MEANS MORE FLOWERS AS WELL AS LEAVES, SINCE FLOWERS USUALLY
APPEAR EITHER AT THE ENDS OF THE STEMS, OR IN THE CROTCHES BETWEEN STEM AND
LEAF. SO MORE STEMS MEANS MORE FLOWERS. THIS HAS OBVIOUS ADVANTAGES IF YOU'RE
GROWING A PLANT MAINLY FOR ITS FLOWERS, AS WITH FUSCIAS, ROSES, OR HYDRANGEAS.
IT'S NOT RECOMMENDED IF YOU'RE GROWING FOR FRUIT, SINCE SO MUCH ENERGY GOES
INTO MAKING FRUIT THAT IF A PLANT TRIES TO MAKE TOO MANY FRUITS, ITS ENDS UP
SPREADING ITSELF TOO THIN.

WHEN CUTTING THE TIP OFF A STEM, MAKE YOUR CUT JUST ABOVE A BUD, WHETHER
THE BUD IS IN THE CROTCH WHERE A LEAF MEETS THE STEM, OR ON THE SIDE OF THE
STEM. (SEE PICTURE, ABOVE.)

INCIDENTLY, THE SAME PRIN-
CIPLE IS OPERATING WHEN YOU
SLICE UP A POTATO TO PLANT IN
THE SOIL. IF YOU DON'T SLICE IT
UP, ONLY THE END SPROUTS,
SINCE IT IS THE "APEX" OF THE
POTATO, WHICH IS ACTUALLY AN
UNDERGROUND STEM, COMPLETE
WITH BUDS AND EVERYTHING.

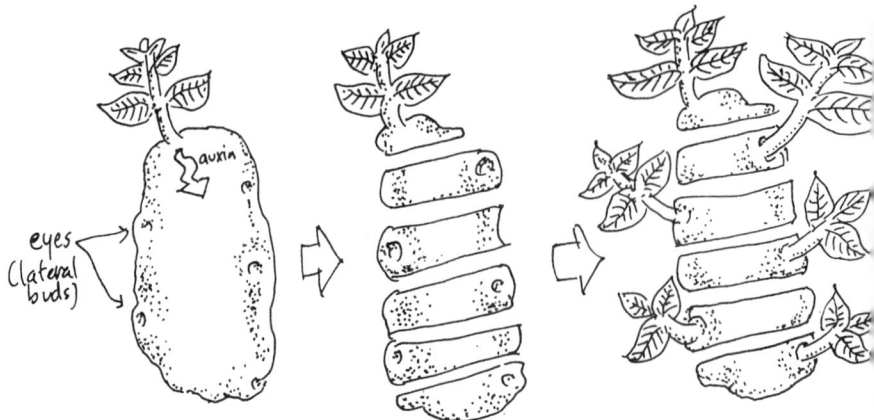

ALL PROPAGATION FROM STEM CUTTINGS ("SLIPS") IS BASED ON THE SAME PRINCIPLE: SEPARATE THE APEX FROM THE STEM, AND YOU CAUSE THE STEM BUDS TO SPROUT. THIS IS A COMMON WAY TO PROPAGATE SUCH PLANTS AS ICE PLANT, IVY, STRAWBERRIES, AND MANY HOUSEPLANTS SUCH AS WANDERING JEW:

OR, WHEN YOU HARVEST THE CENTRAL STALK OF BROCOLLI, IT CAUSES SECONDARY STALKS TO DEVELOP, AGAIN BECAUSE YOU HAVE REMOVED THE APICAL DOMINANCE:

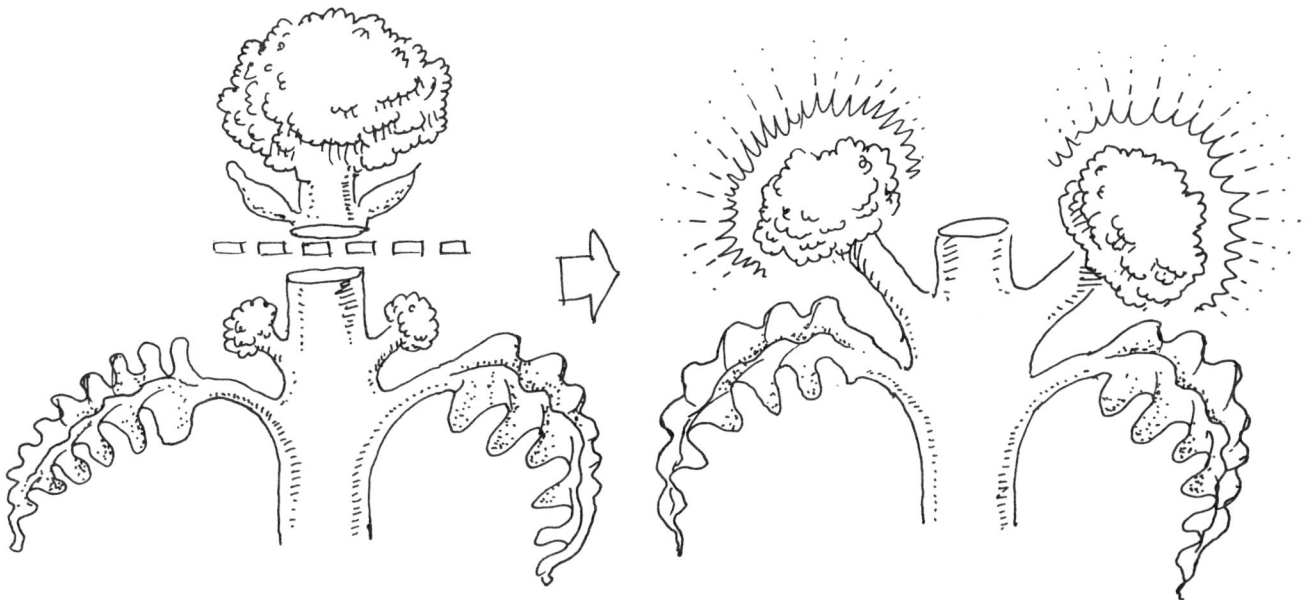

HARVESTING LOWER LEAVES

THE WAY TO GET THE GREATEST TOTAL YIELD (AND FRESHEST PRODUCE) FROM MANY LEAF-CROPS LIKE LETTUCE, SPINACH, CELERY, CHARD, BASIL, AND MOST HERBS, IS BY EATING THE LOWER (OLDER) LEAVES AS NEW LEAVES DEVELOP, RATHER THAN WAITING FOR THE WHOLE PLANT TO MATURE. THE RESULT IS A FLOW OF ENERGY UP THE PLANT.

HERE'S A SCHEMATIC CROSS-SECTION OF A LETTUCE PLANT TO ILLUSTRATE WHAT'S GOING ON:

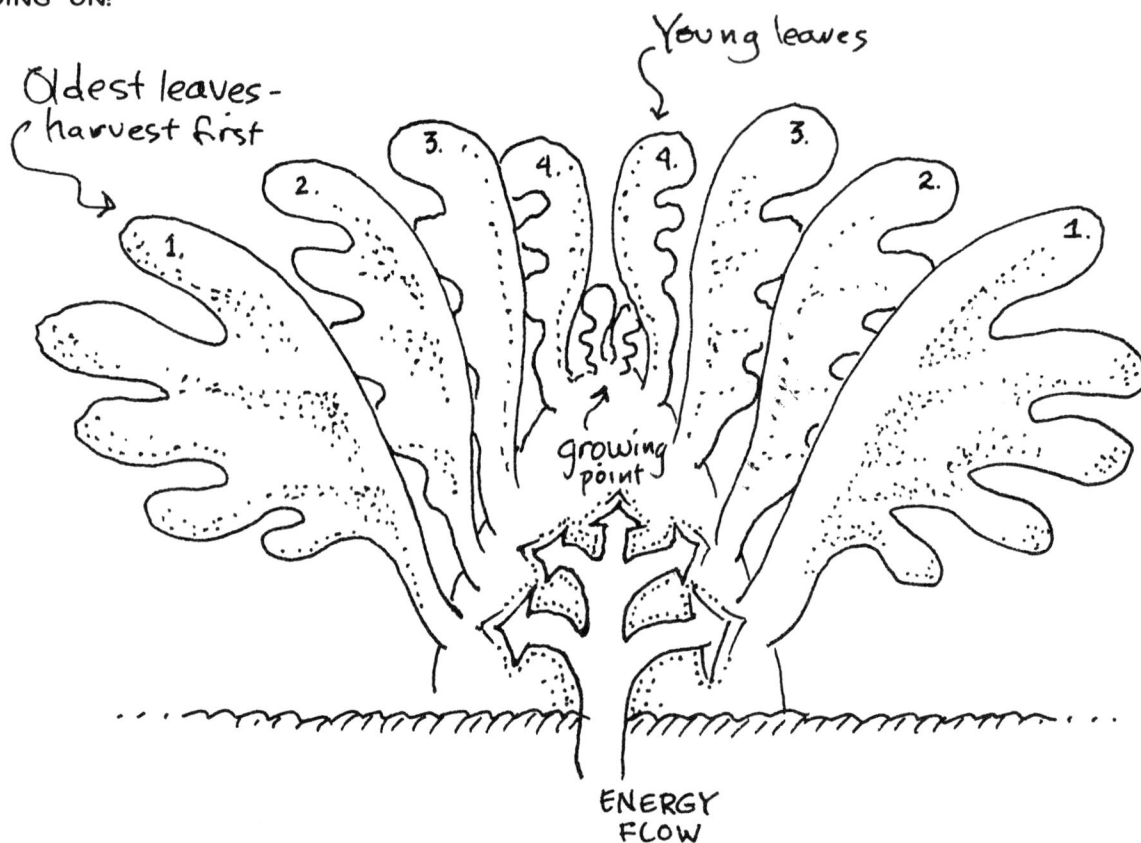

Young leaves

Oldest leaves - harvest first

3. 4. 4. 3.
2. 2.
1. 1.

growing point

ENERGY FLOW

REMOVING OLD GROWTH

THIS SECTION IS ABOUT PERENNIALS, SINCE ANNUALS NEVER GET OLD—THEY JUST TURN INTO SEEDS. YOUNG GROWTH ON PERENNIALS IS USUALLY MORE EFFICIENT AT ENERGY-USE, MORE PRODUCTIVE IN TERMS OF PHOTOSYNTHESIS, FLOWERING, AND FRUITING, MORE RESISTANT TO DISEASE, AND BETTER-LOOKING. OLDER WOOD ON FRUIT AND NUT TREES (EXCEPT APPLE AND PEAR) GENERALLY PRODUCES LESS FRUIT/NUTS. ALTHOUGH MOST PLANTS IN NATURE HAVE MECHANISMS FOR REMOVING OLD GROWTH, YOU CAN HELP THE PROCESS ALONG BY "REMOVING THE DEAD WOOD FROM THE ORGANIZATION," THUS ALLOWING THE PLANT'S ENERGY TO GO TO THE YOUNG GROWTH.

HOW TO TELL DEAD WOOD: SCRAPE THE BARK WITH A KNIFE. IF THERE IS A GREEN LAYER ABOUT 1/16" UNDER THE SURFACE, THE BRANCH IS ALIVE. THE GREEN LAYER IS THE **CAMBIUM**, A RAPIDLY-DIVIDING TISSUE GIVING RISE TO NEW PLANT CELLS. BUT IF THE WOOD IS ALL BROWN OR GRAY UNDER THE BARK, OR IF IT YELLS, "THESE KIDS TODAY HAVE NO SENSE OF PROPORTION," THEN IT'S DEAD WOOD--CUT IT OUT.

WHEN CUTTING OFF A BRANCH, BE SURE TO MAKE THE CUT FLUSH WITH THE BRANCH IT'S COMING OUT OF. IF YOU LEAVE A STUMP, DISEASE ORGANISMS CAN BREED IN THE DEAD WOOD. THE OLD RULE OF THUMB IS: "DON'T LEAVE A STUMP YOU CAN HANG YOUR HAT ON."

EVEN IF THE BRANCH OR SHOOT IS NOT DEAD, IN MANY CASES IT SHOULD BE CUT OFF IF IT'S OLD, EVEN IF IT LOOKS HEALTHY. THIS IS ESPECIALLY TRUE OF PLANTS THAT SEND UP SHOOTS FROM THE CROWN (AT GROUND LEVEL), RATHER THAN MERELY ADDING NEW SHOOTS ON THE ENDS OF EXISTING BRANCHES. CROWN-SHOOTERS INCLUDE ROSES, ASPARAGUS, AND MOST BERRIES. NEW SHOOTS ON THESE PLANTS ARE USUALLY GREEN ON THE SURFACE, WHILE OLDER SHOOTS ARE BROWNISH. THE COMMON TECHNIQUE FOR THESE PLANTS IS TO CUT THE OLDER SHOOTS DOWN TO GROUND LEVEL, LEAVING FOUR OR FIVE YOUNG GREEN SHOOTS.

CROWN SPROUTING—
the extreme case of "removing old growth"

IN SOME CASES YOU CAN REMOVE THE ENTIRE ABOVE-GROUND PART OF THE PLANT IN THE WINTER, AND IT WILL RESPROUT IN THE SPRING. IN FACT, THIS IS CONSIDERED A GOOD PRACTICE FOR SUCH PLANTS AS BLACKBERRIES, WHICH PRODUCE ESPECIALLY LARGE AND DELICIOUS FRUIT AFTER THEY'VE BEEN CUT DOWN TO THE GROUND. IT'S AS IF THE PLANT FREAKS OUT, THINKING "WOW, I BETTER REPRODUCE FAST AND GET THE HECK OUTA HERE! AND I BETTER MAKE MY FRUIT **EXTRA** YUMMY AND LUSCIOUS TO MAKE SURE SOME ANIMAL EATS IT AND TAKES MY SEED FAR AWAY . . . HOPEFULLY A MIGRATING BIRD WITH CONSTIPATION!"

CROWN-SPROUTING ALSO HAPPENS WITH MANY COMMON PERENNIAL PASTURE PLANTS. . . . WHEN GRAZED TO THE GROUND BY A PASSING FOUR-LEGGED

MEAT FACTORY, THEY CONVENIENTLY RESPROUT. WHEN THESE PLANTS SHOW UP IN OUR GARDEN WE CALL THEM "WEEDS," SAYING "BE SURE TO GET THE ROOTS, OR THEY'LL JUST RESPROUT!" AND THAT BRINGS US TO . . .

HARVESTING WEEDS

WEEDS ARE GOOD FOR THE GARDEN. THEY ARE A FORM OF GREEN MANURE, AND THEY SHOULD BE CONSIDERED ONE OF YOUR CROPS. WEEDS ARE "PIONEER" SPECIES IN NATURAL ECOLOGIES; THEY CAN BREAK APART THE COMPLEXES OF MINERALS THAT IMPRISON NUTRIENTS IN THE SOIL, AND THEY HAVE ESPECIALLY EFFICIENT WAYS TO CAPTURE NUTRIENTS AND PUMP THEM INTO THEIR ROOTS. (FOR INSTANCE, BRACKEN FERN IS A REAL WHIZ AT PICKING UP POTASSIUM IONS (K^+). THAT'S WHY IT'S ALWAYS THE FIRST THING TO SPROUT AFTER A FIRE IN THE CALIFORNIA COASTAL MOUNTAINS.) WHEN YOU PULL YOUR WEEDS UP AND PILE THEM ON THE SURFACE AS MULCH (OR COMPOST THEM), YOU ARE MAKING THESE NUTRIENTS AVAILABLE FOR YOUR VEGETABLES. (ONE OF THE BEST USES FOR WEEDS IS AS A SUPER-CONVENIENT SOURCE OF MULCH . . . JUST PULL UP THE WEED AND LAY IT UNDER THE NEAREST VEGETABLE PLANT.)

SAVE THE WEEDS!

MOST WEEDS DON'T HAVE TO BE PULLED AT ALL. WEEDS ARE BEAUTIFUL AND USEFUL--THEY'RE EVERY BIT AS ATTRACTIVE AND INTERESTING TO WATCH AS OUR CULTIVATED PLANTS. IT'S ONLY OUR UPTIGHT CULTURE THAT MAKES US THINK ALL "WEEDS" SHOULD BE IMMEDIATELY DESTROYED. (ALSO, OF COURSE, WEEDS HAVE NO SNOB VALUE--THEY ARE THE EASIEST PLANTS OF ALL TO GROW!)

WEEDS SHOULD ONLY BE PULLED (OR TOPPED) IF THEY ARE SHADING OUT A VEGETABLE PLANT, OR IF THEY ARE NEEDED FOR MULCHING OR COMPOSTING. WEEDS WON'T SERIOUSLY COMPETE WITH THE VEGGIES FOR NUTRIENTS--SO LONG AS YOU KEEP UP THE SOIL FERTILITY WITH REGULAR ADDITIONS OF COMPOST, THERE'LL BE ENOUGH FOR EVERYONE. AND BESIDES, IF YOU'RE REGULARLY ADDING COMPOST OR OTHER MULCH, MOST WEEDS RIGHT AROUND THE VEGGIES WILL BE BURIED BEFORE THEY GET TOO LARGE. THOSE THAT DO GET IN THE WAY CAN BE GENTLY PLUCKED OUT AND ADDED TO THE MULCH WHERE THEY WERE GROWING. OTHER WEEDS NOT IN THE WAY WILL SHADE THE SOIL, ACTING AS A "LIVING MULCH."

MANY WEEDS SHOULD BE ACTIVELY CULTIVATED AND CARED FOR. ONE OF THESE IS SOW THISTLE (SONCHUS OLERACEUS). SOW THISTLE ATTRACTS BIRDS LIKE FINCHES AND WARBLERS, WHO EAT THE SEEDS, AND THEY ALSO EAT HARMFUL INSECTS IN THE GARDEN.

SOW
THISTLE

STINGING NETTLE (URTICA DIOTICA) AND HORSETAIL FERN (EQUISETUM ARVENSE) REPORTEDLY AID IN DISEASE PREVENTION. WHEN THESE PLANTS ARE ADDED TO SURFACE MULCH OR COMPOST, THEY DISCOURAGE THE GROWTH OF FUNGI LIKE DAMPING—OFF (MENTIONED EARLIER THIS CHAPTER), VERTICILLIUM, AND FUSARIUM, LIKE THIS . . . .

OTHER USEFUL WEEDS

ANY MEMBER OF THE COMPOSITAE FAMILY (DAISY, DANDELION, SUNFLOWER, ETC.) OR UMBELLIFERAE (YARROW, DILL, ANISE, FENNEL, CARROT, ETC.) ATTRACTS BENEFICIAL INSECT PREDATORS. MANY OTHER WEEDS ARE WILD RELATIVES OF OUR CROP PLANTS, SO THEY CAN BE USED AS "TRAP PLANTS" WHICH ATTRACT INSECT PESTS. (MORE ON THESE USES OF PLANTS IN CHAPTER EIGHT.)

WEED HARVESTING TIPS

WEEDS SHOULD BE HARVESTED FOR MULCH OR COMPOST WHEN THEY ARE STILL YOUNG AND GREEN, SINCE AS A WEED GROWS OLD AND YELLOW, IT SENDS MOST OF ITS NITROGEN AND OTHER NUTRIENTS INTO THE SEEDS, WHERE THEY'RE HARDER TO GET AT FOR COMPOSTING BACTERIA. YOU SHOULD PULL THEM UP BY THE ROOTS, SINCE ROOTS LEFT IN THE SOIL ARE MOSTLY **CARBON**, SO SOIL BACTERIA WILL NEED MUCH OF THE SOIL'S **NITROGEN** TO DIGEST THEM. (AN EXCEPTION TO THIS HARVEST-TIME RULE IS WHEN YOU DIG UP DEEP-ROOTED PLANTS LIKE TOMATO. THE DEEP ROOTS (BELOW 6") SHOULD BE LEFT IN--YOU'D DISRUPT THE SOIL TOO MUCH BY DIGGING THEM UP. BESIDES, THE TEMPORARY NITROGEN DEPLETION CAUSED BY DEEP DECAYING ROOTS WON'T AFFECT NEW, YOUNG PLANTS YOU PUT IN NEARBY.)

HARVESTING WEEDS IS ONLY A CHORE IF THE SOIL IS COMPACTED OR INORGANIC. WITH GOOD, LOOSE, COMPOST-RICH SOIL, WEEDS COME UP LIKE A BUTTERED KNIFE OUT OF A HOT MUFFIN. FOR LARGE AREAS, YOU MAY WANT TO USE A PITCHFORK. A HOE (THE COMMON NON-ORGANIC WEED HASSLER) IS USELESS ON GOOD ORGANIC SOIL, SINCE THE HOE JUST MUSHES INTO THE HUMUS WITHOUT CUTTING ANYTHING. WEEDS SHOULD BE HARVESTED LIKE CARROTS . . . FIRST, WAIT FOR THE "MAGIC TIME" (P. 54); THEN SIT DOWN ON THE GROUND AND GET GOOD AND DIRTY.

ONCE YOU'VE HARVESTED ALL YOUR WEEDS AND PUT THEM IN THE COMPOST, AND YOU'RE COUNTING THE MONEY YOU'VE SAVED BY GOING ORGANIC, YOU MAY BE FACED WITH A PROBLEM: LOTS OF MONEY, BUT NO WEEDS. BUT DON'T DESPAIR! LOOK FOR THE FORTHCOMING BOOK IN THIS SERIES:

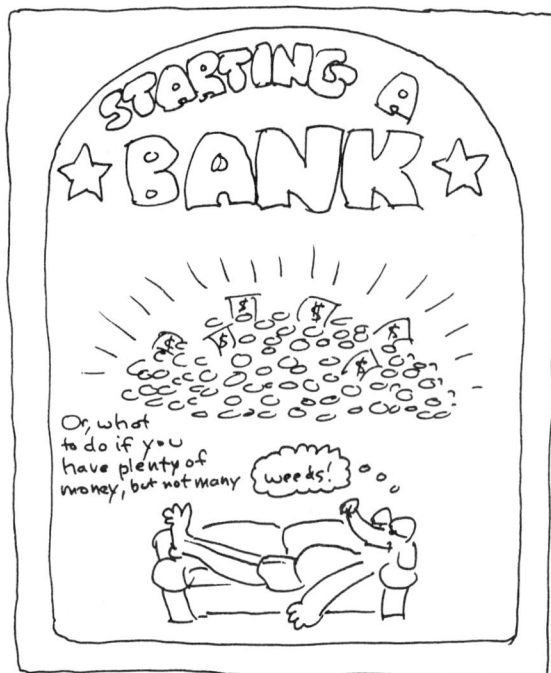

STARTING A ☆ BANK ☆

Or, what to do if you have plenty of money, but not many weeds!

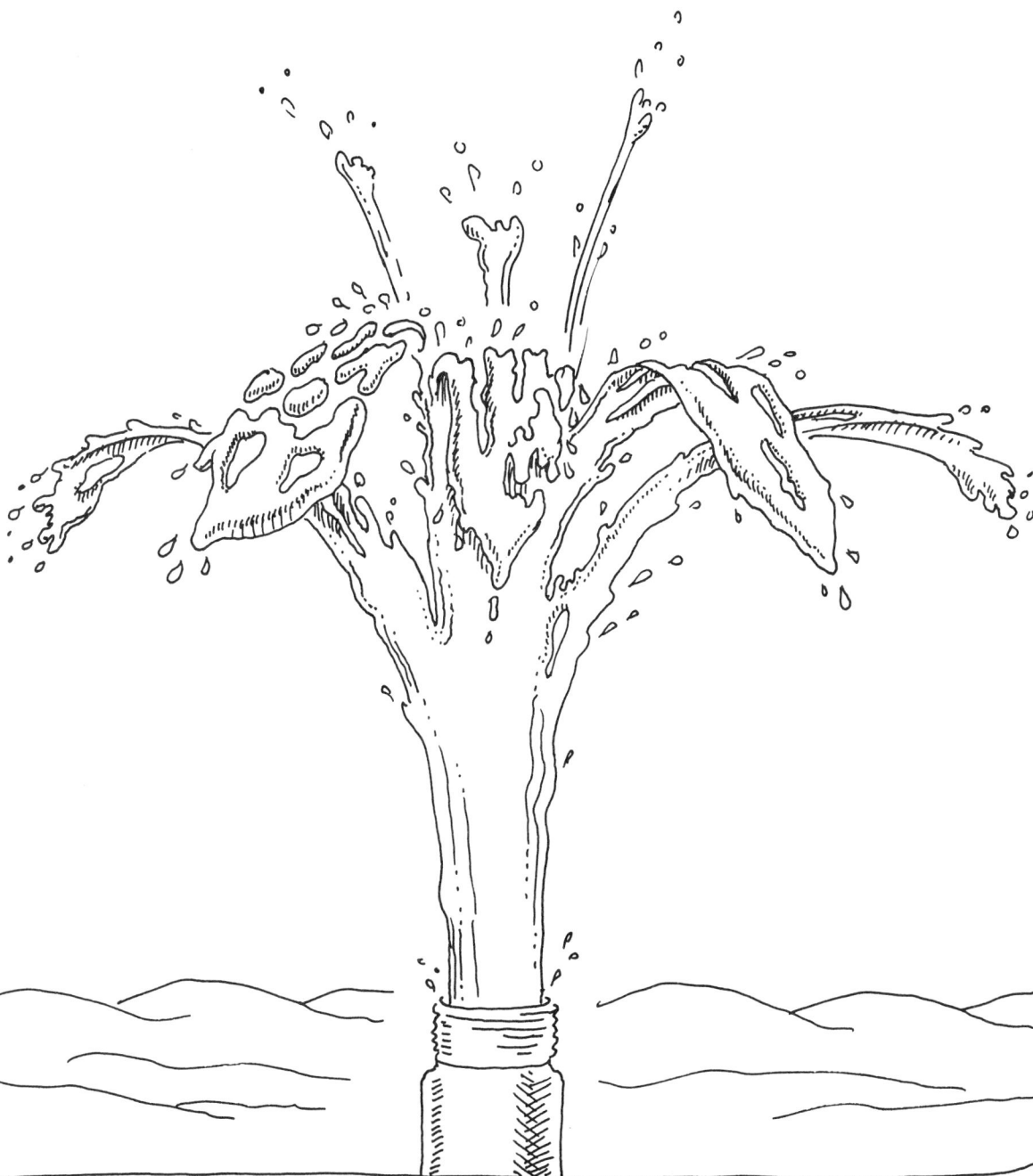

7 WATERING

WATER AND LIFE

LIFE (AS WE KNOW IT!) BEGAN IN THE OCEAN:

Gil, don't you think it's about time we EVOLVED and moved up on LAND?

Will you stop NAGGING me, Emily?

Life (as we know it) began in Topeka, Kansas in an all-nite diner!

WHEN THEY WENT UP ON LAND, EARLY ORGANISMS TOOK ALONG LITTLE OVERNIGHT BAGS OF OCEAN WATER, ALONG WITH A TOOTHBRUSH AND A CHANGE OF SOCKS. THESE BAGS OF OCEAN (CALLED "CELLS") NOW MAKE UP OUR ENTIRE BODIES:

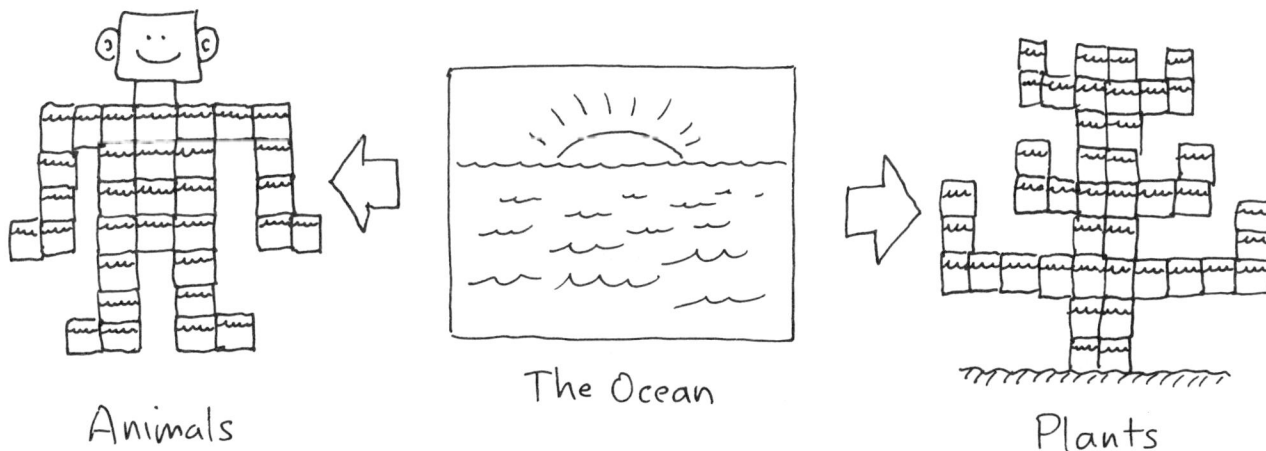

Animals

The Ocean

Plants

SO AFTER A FEW BILLION YEARS, HERE WE ARE . . . (AND WHAT A LONG STRANGE TRIP IT'S BEEN!)

PLANTS STACK THE OCEAN BAGS UP IN VERTICAL PILES, THEN DISSOLVE THE TOPS AND BOTTOMS OF THE BAGS, FORMING CONTINUOUS TUBES FROM THE ROOTS TO THE TOPMOST LEAVES:

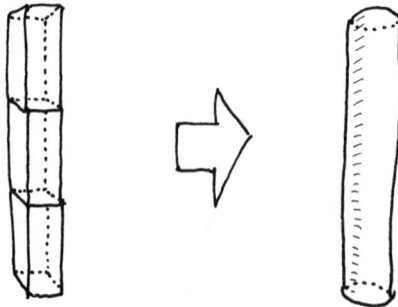

THESE TUBES ARE THE PLANT'S PLUMBING SYSTEM, LIKE BLOOD VESSELS IN ANIMALS. THEY ARE CALLED "PHLOEM AND XYLEM," AND THEY PUMP WATER FROM THE ROOTS TO THE LEAVES, AND TRANSPORT SUGAR FROM THE LEAVES TO ANY PART OF THE PLANT THAT NEEDS IT. WHEN THESE TUBES ARE FULL OF WATER THEY HOLD THE PLANT UPRIGHT, AND KEEP THE LEAVES SPREAD OUT TO CATCH THE SUN'S RAYS:

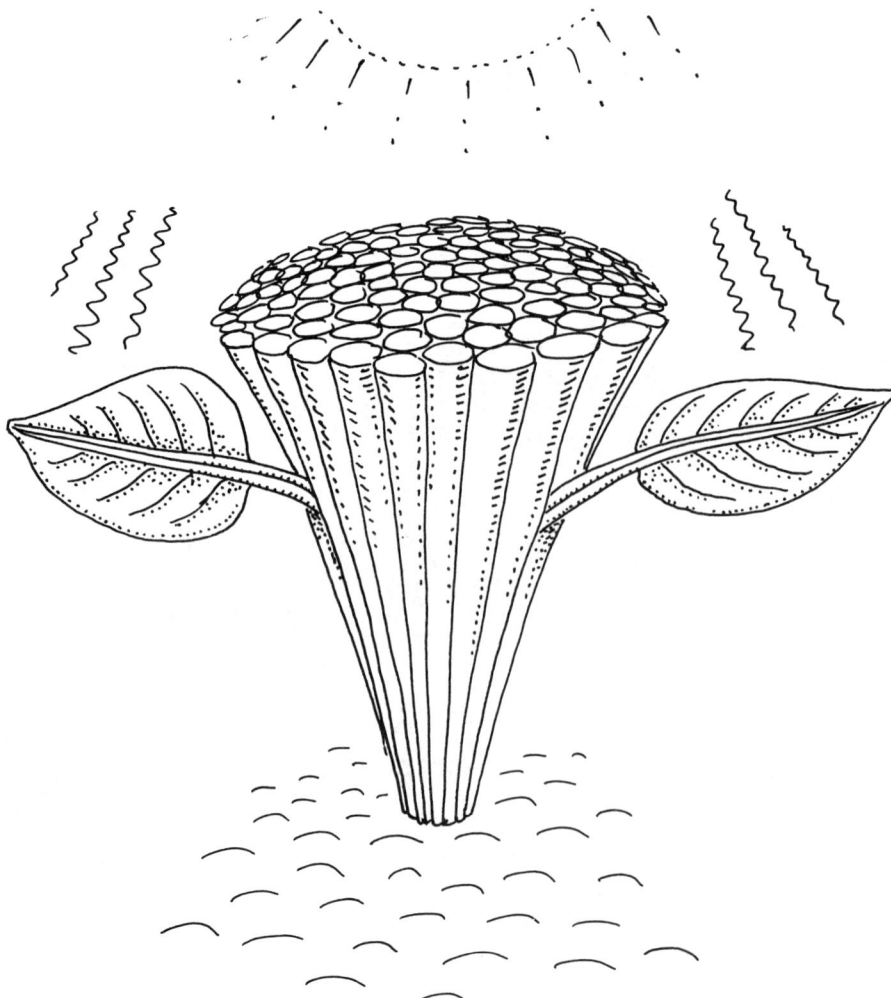

THAT'S ALL FINE AND MARVELOUS, BUT THE CATCH IS, THE LEAVES ARE CONSTANTLY LOSING WATER TO THE AIR BY EVAPORATION, THROUGH PORES IN THE LEAF SURFACE . . .

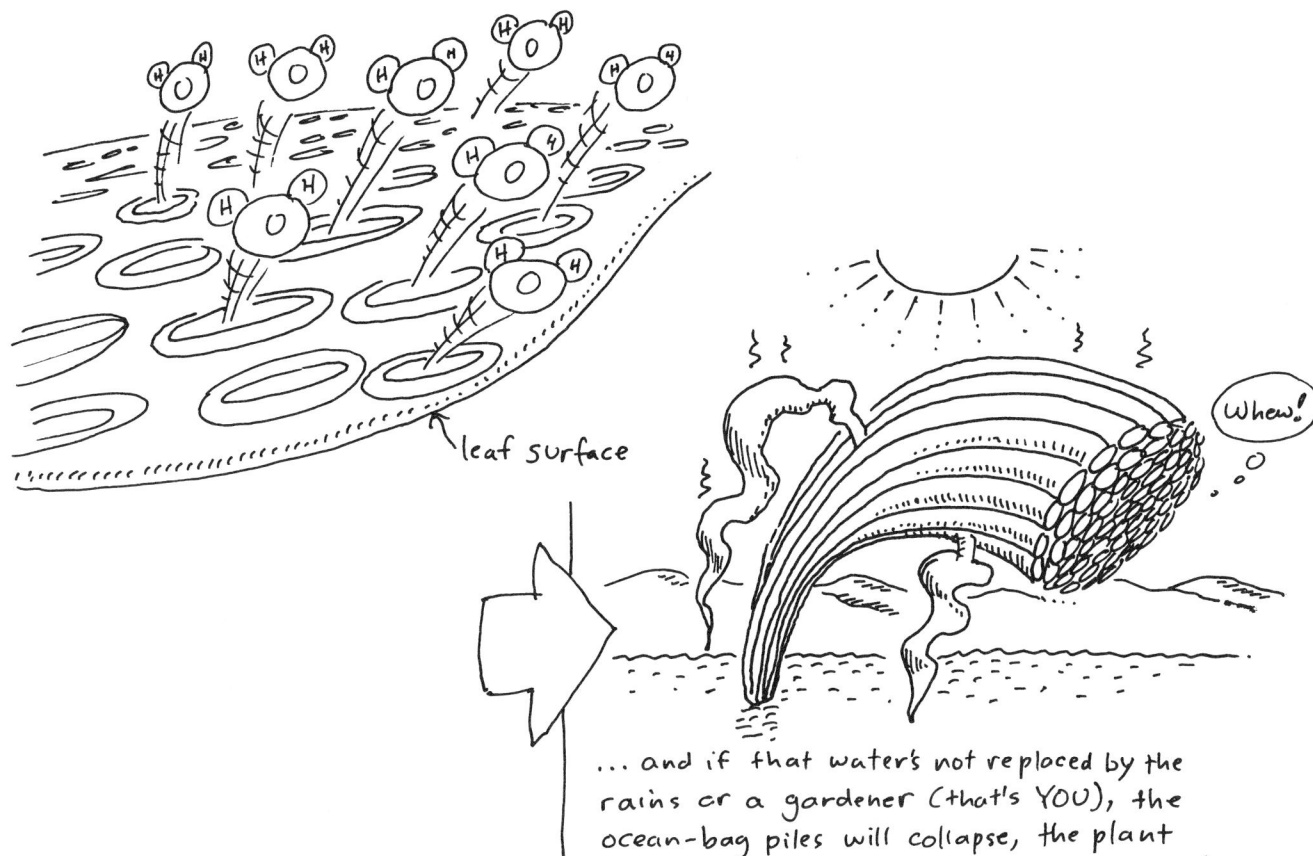

leaf surface

... and if that water's not replaced by the rains or a gardener (that's YOU), the ocean-bag piles will collapse, the plant wilts, and it's a Bad Day in Black Rock, Bunky!

Whew!

MANY OF OUR CROP PLANTS EVOLVED IN THE TROPICS OR SEMI-TROPICS (CORN, SQUASH, PEPPERS, EGGPLANT, CUCUMBER, ETC.), SO THEY EXPECT RAIN AT LEAST A COUPLE TIMES A WEEK, IF NOT EVERY DAY. OTHERS (LETTUCE, CELERY, ONIONS, BEETS, CARROTS, ETC.) EVOLVED TO MATURE DURING THE RAINY SPRING DAYS OF TEMPERATE CLIMATES, BUT WE EXPECT TO EAT THEM ALL YEAR AROUND. IN EITHER CASE THEY'LL NEED FREQUENT RAINFALL, OR THE SYNTHETIC EQUIVALENT. AND THAT'S WHERE **YOU**, AS A GARDENER, COME IN. (AND YOU'D BETTER! YOU COULD SPACE OUT IN CHAPTER FIVE––IN FACT, YOU WERE ENCOURAGED TO DO SO. BUT SPACE OUT YOUR PLANTS' WATER NEEDS AND YOU BLOW THE WHOLE BALL GAME!)

THE TWO MOST COMMONLY-ASKED QUESTIONS ABOUT WATERING ARE 1. HOW MUCH WATER SHOULD I GIVE MY PLANTS?, AND **2.** HOW OFTEN SHOULD I WATER THEM? THE ANSWERS TO THESE QUESTIONS ARE BY NO MEANS SIMPLE, BUT IF YOU UNDERSTAND A FEW BASIC PRINCIPLES, AND LEARN THE SPECIAL NEEDS OF VARIOUS PLANTS, YOU'LL SOON BE IRRIGATIN' WITH THE BEST OF 'EM.

1. HOW MUCH?

YOU NEED TO FILL UP THE PLANT'S ENTIRE ROOT-ZONE WITH WATER. THE ROOT ZONE IS USUALLY ABOUT THE SAME SIZE AND SHAPE AS THE LEAF AREA OF THE PLANT:

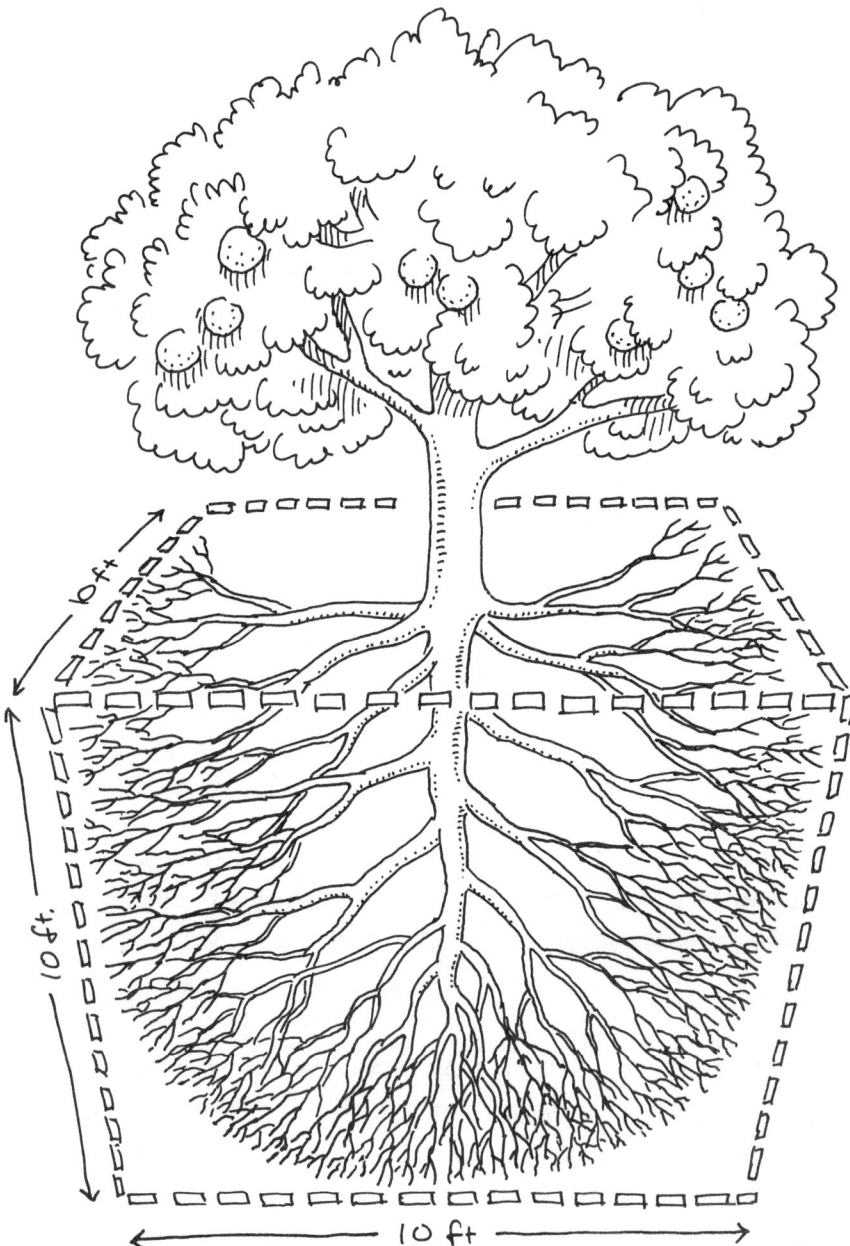

. . . SO FIRST ESTIMATE HOW MANY CUBIC FEET OF ROOT-ZONE YOU HAVE.

IT WILL TAKE ONE GALLON OF WATER TO SATURATE EACH CUBIC FOOT OF SOIL.

THE AVERAGE OUTDOOR FAUCET TURNED ON TO MEDIUM SPEED LETS OUT WATER AT THE RATE OF 5 GALLONS PER MINUTE, OR TWELVE SECONDS PER GALLON. SO THE RULE OF THUMB IS:

12 seconds per cubic foot

. . . SO FOR THE LARGE ORANGE TREE PICTURED, YOU WOULD LEAVE THE HOSE ON 2 HOURS. (10 X 10 X 10 = 1000 CUBIC FEET, TIMES 12 SEC/CU. FT. = 2 HOURS)

THE 12 SEC./CU. FT. RULE WORKS FOR ALL TYPES OF PLANTS: VEGETABLES, SHRUBS, TREES, LAWNS, ETC. AT THIS RATE, THE FOLLOWING PLANTS TAKE THE AMOUNT OF WATERING TIME SHOWN:

```
20-ft. tree — 1-2 hrs.
10-ft tree — 1 hour
4-foot tomato - 60 minutes
6-ft. corn (shallow roots) - 2 minutes
lettuce (1 ft.) — 12 seconds
lawn - 12 sec/sq.ft.
5" seedlings - 2-5 sec/sq.ft.
Seed bed        1 sec/sq. ft.
```

THAT DOESN'T MEAN YOU HAVE TO STAND THERE FOR HOURS WITH A HOSE––YOU CAN JUST STICK THE HOSE UNDER A LARGE PLANT AND GO OFF TO DO OTHER THINGS, LIKE WEEDING OR TRANSPLANTING. BE SURE TO MOVE THE HOSE AROUND A LARGE PLANT OR TREE, SO ALL SIDES OF THE PLANT GET WATER.

IT'S IMPORTANT TO GET THE WATER DOWN **DEEP**, SO THE ENTIRE ROOT ZONE IS FULLY SATURATED WITH WATER, LIKE A LOADED SPONGE. IT'S A COMMON MISCONCEPTION THAT YOU CAN JUST SPRINKLE WATER LIGHTLY ON THE SURFACE, AND THIS WILL "MOISTEN" THE SOIL (MOIST SOIL BEING THE BEST CONDITION FOR PLANT GROWTH.) **NOT SO!** A LIGHT SPRINKLING WILL STILL SATURATE THE SOIL, BUT ONLY A FEW INCHES DEEP. IF YOU DO THIS TO TREES, THEY WILL CONFINE THEIR ROOTS TO THE SURFACE, WHERE NUTRIENTS ARE SCARCE DUE TO COMPETITION WITH WEEDS, AND WHERE WATER EVAPORATES QUICKLY, SO YOU HAVE TO END UP USING MORE WATER, ULTIMATELY. SHALLOW WATERING IS OFTEN SEEN ON STREET TREES WHOSE ROOTS ARE BUCKLING THE SIDEWALK.

2. HOW OFTEN?

AS PLANTS GROW, THEY NEED MORE WATER AT A TIME, BUT LESS FREQUENTLY. A NEWLY-SOWN SEED BED MUST BE WATERED EVERY DAY, SINCE THE SEEDS ARE IN THE TOP INCH OF THE SOIL, WHERE WATER EVAPORATES QUICKLY INTO THE AIR. BIGGER PLANTS HAVE DEEPER ROOTS THAT TAKE WATER FROM LOWER DOWN IN THE SOIL, WHERE WATER TAKES LONGER TO MOVE UP IN THE SOIL TO WHERE IT CAN EVAPORATE, AND WHERE THERE IS OFTEN WATER ALL YEAR ROUND. IN FACT, LARGE TREES TAKE WATER FROM THE "WATER TABLE," WHICH IS A PERMANENT POOL OF WATER SATURATING THE SOIL, USUALLY ANYWHERE FROM THREE TO TEN FEET DOWN, DEPENDING ON THE TIME OF YEAR, THE TOPOGRAPHY OF THE LAND, AND THE CLIMATE (MORE ON THAT LATER).

WATERING TOO FREQUENTLY IS AS BAD AS NOT WATERING ENOUGH. AS YOU'LL RECALL FROM CHAPTER 2, EVERY TIME WATER ENTERS THE SOIL, IT SATURATES (WATERLOGS) THE SOIL TO A CERTAIN DEPTH, DEPENDING ON HOW MUCH WATER WAS APPLIED. PLANTS CAN'T GROW IN SATURATED SOIL, SINCE THE ROOTS DON'T GET THE OXYGEN THEY NEED TO POWER THEIR ROOT-PUMPS. (AN EXCEPTION IS PLANTS LIKE RICE, WHICH HAVE SPECIAL MECHANISMS TO TRANSPORT OXYGEN FROM THE LEAVES DOWN TO THE ROOTS. BUT FOR ALL OTHER PLANTS, YOU MUST LET THE SOIL DRY OUT BETWEEN WATERINGS.)

SO HERE'S THE WATERING FREQUENCIES FOR VARIOUS SIZES OF PLANTS:

WATERING FREQUENCIES

Seeds	— every day
1-2 wk old seedlings	— every day
2-4 wk old seedlings	— every other day
young veggies	— twice a week
mature veggies	— once a week
perennial shrubs	— every 2 weeks
small trees (under 20 ft)	— once a month
large trees (under 30 ft)	— once a summer
very large trees	— never

DEVIATIONS from the rules

HA, HA—YOU THOUGHT IT WAS THAT SIMPLE, HUH? JUST FOLLOW A SIMPLE LIST OF PLANT SIZES, AND GO OUT WITH YOUR HOSE AND BLAST AWAY? NOT SO, BOSCO. FIRST, INDIVIDUAL SPECIES HAVE DIFFERING WATER NEEDS. SECOND (AND HERE'S THE CRUSHER), THERE'S SOMETHING CALLED THE COSMIC ROULETTE WHEEL, THAT **REALLY** SCREWS THINGS UP. BUT FIRST, SPECIES DIFFERENCES:

WATER-LOVERS

CELERY—WATER EVERY DAY, EVEN WHEN MATURE

CUKES—SEMI-TROPICAL (LEAVES HAVE MORE PORES THAN MOST PLANTS)

CORN—SHALLOW ROOTS . . . WATER EVERY DAY WHEN YOUNG, EVERY OTHER DAY WHEN MATURE. SEMI-TROPICAL

CITRUS TREES—NEED MORE WATER THAN OTHER FRUIT TREES.

CABBAGE FAMILY

PARSELY

RADISH

GARLIC

ONION   (ROOTS ARE LESS THAN 2

LEEK   FT. DEEP FOR LAST SIX)

HYDROPHOBES

(OR DROUGHT TOLERANT)

TOMATOES—STOP WATERING ALTOGETHER WHEN FRUIT STARTS TO RIPEN

POTATOES—ONLY WATER OCCASIONALLY

MOST MEDITERRANEAN HERBS (OREGANO, THYME, ROSEMARY, LAVENDER; EVOLVED IN DRY SANDY SOIL OF MEDITERRANEAN REGION)

MOST CALIFORNIA NATIVES; EVOLVED FOR HOT DRY SUMMERS.

AUSTRALIAN NATIVES (EUCALYPTUS, ACACIA, ETC.)

FIG (WHEN ESTABLISHED)

APRICOT

OAK TREES—**HATE** WATER IN THE SUMMER

ALFALFA (DEEP ROOTS, 20 FT.+)

AND NOW, EVERYONE'S FAVORITE GAME OF CHANCE, **COSMIC ROULETTE WHEEL!**

AS YOU CAN SEE, JUST ABOUT ANY SOIL/WEATHER CONDITION CAN THROW THE RULES OUT OF WHACK, AND MAKE IT A WHOLE NEW BALL GAME. BUT DON'T DESPAIR--THE RULES ARE STILL GOOD, THEY JUST NEED MINOR ADJUSTMENTS, AND PRETTY SOON AFTER A LITTLE PRACTICE YOU CAN DO THIS WITHOUT THINKING.

A FEW OF THE ROULETTE SPACES NEED SOME EXPLANATION--ONE OF THEM INVOLVES SOIL TEXTURE. AS EXPLAINED IN CHAPTER 2, SANDY SOIL HAS LARGE SPACES BETWEEN THE GRAINS, WHILE HUMUS OR CLAY SOILS ARE DENSER. SO WHEN WATER ENTERS SANDY SOIL IT JUST FALLS RIGHT THROUGH--THERE AREN'T AS MANY NOOKS AND CRANNIES FOR THE

170

WATER TO ENTER AND CLING TO. LIKEWISE, IT'S EASIER FOR WATER TO EVAPORATE FROM SANDY SOIL--THERE'S LESS RESISTANCE TO THE UPWARD MOTION OF WATER. SO THE UPSHOT IS, SANDY SOIL MEANS YOU NEED TO WATER MORE OFTEN. WITH CLAY OR HUMUS-RICH SOIL IT'S THE OPPOSITE--WATER TENDS TO SPREAD OUT AND CLING AS IT FALLS THROUGH THE SOIL, AND IT ALSO EVAPORATES MORE SLOWLY.

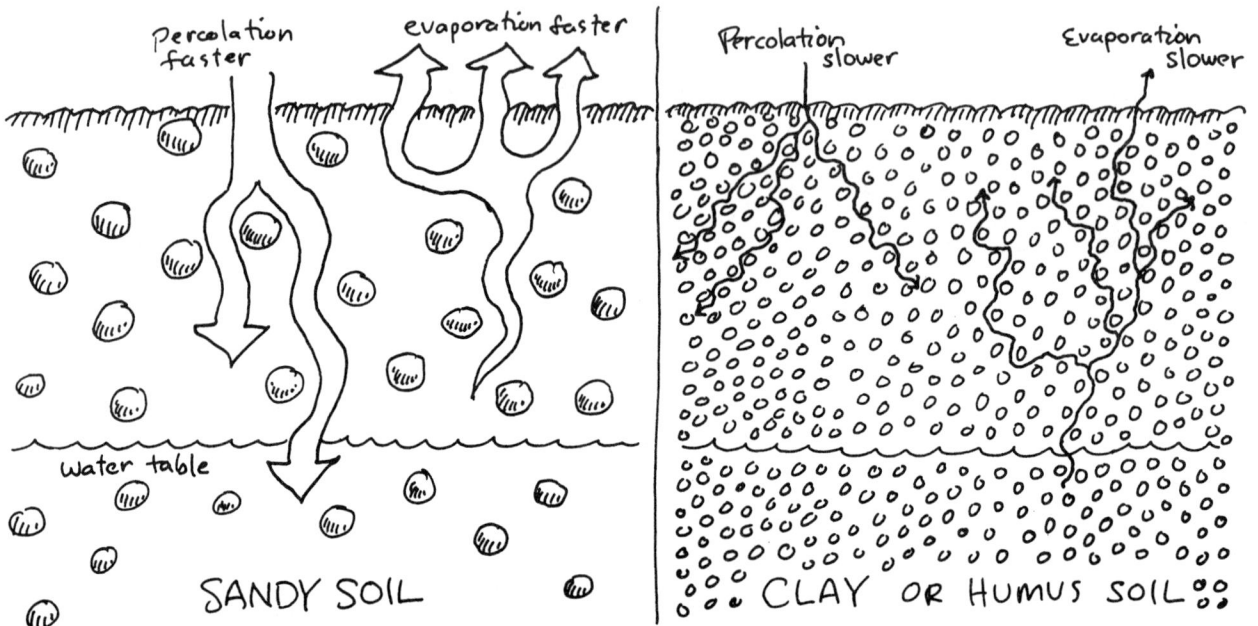

HUMIDITY AND WIND SPEED

THESE TWO FACTORS GO TOGETHER, SINCE THEY BOTH AFFECT THE EVAPORATION OF WATER, BOTH FROM THE SOIL AND FROM THE LEAVES. WATER EVAPORATES FROM LEAVES BY WAY OF THE SAME PORES THAT CO_2 ENTERS THE LEAF FOR PHOTOSYNTHESIS. IN FACT, IT'S THE EVAPORATION OF WATER FROM THE LEAVES THAT POWERS (IN PART) THE PUMPING OF WATER FROM THE SOIL. SO WATER LOSS FROM THE PORES IS A NECESSARY EVIL. BUT ON A HOT, ARID, WINDY DAY, THE PLANT CAN LOSE SO MUCH WATER THROUGH THE LEAVES THAT THE SOIL BECOMES SERIOUSLY DRIED OUT. AND UNLESS IT RAINS, OR THERE'S A FAITHFUL FRIEND WITH A HOSE NEARBY (YOU), THE PLANT'S IN TROUBLE.

ON A HUMID DAY, THE AIR IS FULL OF WATER VAPOR ALREADY, SO WATER IS RECONDENSING IN THE PORES NEARLY AS FAST AS IT'S EVAPORATING. BUT IF THE AIR IS DRY, WATER WILL EVAPORATE EXTRA-FAST.

WIND SPEEDS UP EVAPORATION, SINCE IT PUSHES NEWLY-EVAPORATED MOLECULES AROUND THE LEAF OUT OF THE WAY, CREATING A LOCAL ARID ZONE THAT NEW MOLECULES CAN EVAPORATE INTO (THAT'S WHY CLOTHES DRY FASTER ON A CLOTHESLINE IF IT'S WINDY. . . . REMEMBER "CLOTHESLINES?"—A FASCINATING PRIMITIVE CUSTOM.)

THE ULTIMATE THUMB RULE

IF YOU HAVE ANY DOUBTS AFTER CONSIDERING THE SPECIES NEEDS, THE SIZE OF THE PLANT, AND THE COSMIC ROULETTE WHEEL, YOU CAN TEST THE SOIL WITH A TROWEL. IF YOUR TROWEL DOESN'T EASILY SLIDE INTO THE SOIL (AND THE SOIL IS OTHERWISE WELL-STRUCTURED AND UNCOMPACTED), THEN IT'S TIME TO WATER. OF COURSE, THIS ONLY WORKS FOR SMALL OR OTHERWISE SHALLOW-ROOTED PLANTS (SEE THE APPENDIX AT THE END OF THIS CHAPTER FOR A LIST OF ROOT DEPTHS.)

KEEP ON MULCHIN'!

IF YOU'VE GOT A GOOD THICK MULCH ON YOUR BEDS, YOU HAVE TO WORRY MUCH LESS ABOUT EVAPORATION. THE MANY BENEFITS OF MULCHING HAVE ALREADY BEEN COVERED IN PREVIOUS CHAPTERS, SO RIGHT HERE I'M JUST GOING TO SAY A FEW WORDS ABOUT TYPES OF MULCH. CHOOSE A MULCH TO FIT YOUR SITUATION. FOR SEEDLING BEDS OR FLATS (EVEN BEFORE THE SEEDS COME UP), YOU CAN USE SLIGHTLY-SHREDDED HORSE MANURE OR SMALL LEAVES; OR, IF THE SEEDS ARE SMALL, USE SPENT TEA LEAVES OR COFFEE GROUNDS (THAT'S WHAT I CALL "PRE-EMERGENCE MULCHING."). GO OUT TO WILD PLACES AND FILL YOUR BACKPACK WITH VARIOUS LEAVES AND DUFF (DON'T TAKE TOO MUCH FROM ANY ONE PLACE). FOR ORCHARDS, YOU CAN PUT ON A FEW LAYERS OF CARDBOARD, AND THEN COVER IT WITH SOMETHING MORE AESTHETIC, LIKE STRAW OR MANURE.

WHERE TO WATER

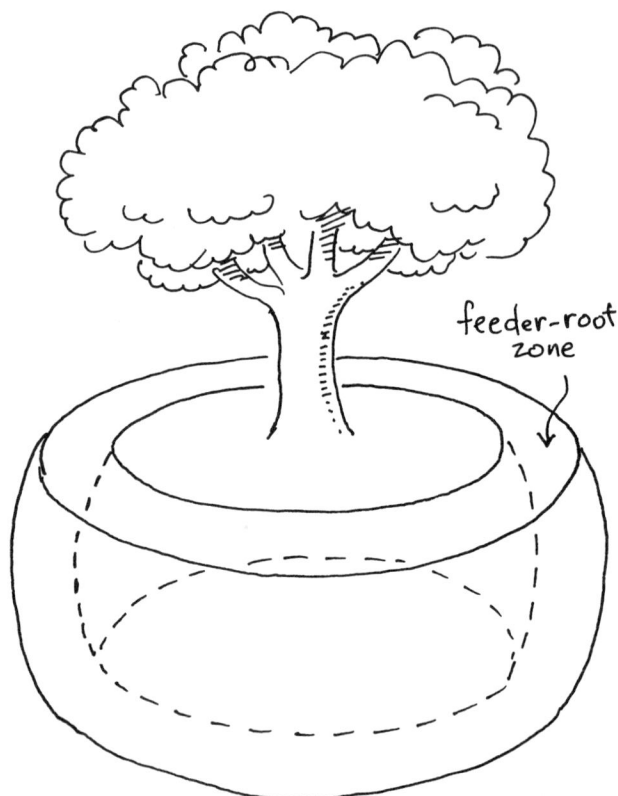

feeder-root zone

THE ROOT ZONE FOR MOST MATURE PLANTS IS ACTUALLY A DONUT-SHAPED AREA AWAY FROM THE CROWN, CENTERED DIRECTLY UNDER THE OUTERMOST LEAVES. THAT'S WHERE THE "FEEDER ROOTS" ARE: THE SMALLEST, YOUNGEST ROOTS WHICH ARE ACTIVELY SUCKING UP NUTRIENTS AND WATER. THE LARGER, OLDER ROOTS IN TOWARD THE CENTER OF THE PLANT ARE NO LONGER ACTIVELY SUCKING THINGS IN.

SO CONFINE YOUR WATERING TO THE FEEDER-ROOT ZONE. NOT ONLY WILL YOU SAVE WATER, BUT YOU'LL HELP PREVENT CERTAIN FUNGUS DISEASES LIKE CROWN ROT.

WILTING

WILTING CAN BE CAUSED BY EITHER UNDERWATERING OR OVER-WATERING, OR SOMETIMES IT'S A NORMAL PLANT RESPONSE TO MID-DAY HEAT. MANY PLANTS (LIKE CORN, CABBAGE-FAMILY PLANTS, SQUASHES, AND TOMATO) DELIBERATELY KEEP WATER OUT OF THEIR LEAVES WHEN IT'S HOT, SO THE LEAVES WILT. BY DOING SO, THEY CONSERVE WATER BY KEEPING IT IN THE SOIL, WHERE IT EVAPORATES LESS READILY.

WILTING DUE TO UNDERWATERING IS OBVIOUS: WATER IS THE HYDRAULIC STIFFENING DEVICE THAT KEEPS THE LEAVES ERECT. NO WATER IN THE SOIL, AND THE LEAVES CAN'T "GET IT UP."

WILTING DUE TO OVERWATERING IS A BIT TRICKIER. AS MENTIONED BEFORE (CHAPTER 2), ROOTS NEED AIR IN THE SOIL AS A SOURCE OF OXYGEN TO RUN THE PUMPS THAT SUCK NUTRIENTS AND OSMOTIC REGULATORS INTO THE ROOTS. THE MAIN OSMOTIC REGULATOR IS POTASSIUM (K^+). AFTER THE ROOTS PUMP IN POTASSIUM, WATER FOLLOWS BY OSMOSIS. NO AIR IN THE SOIL, AND THERE'S NO K^+ IN THE ROOTS, SO WATER CAN'T GET IN, SO AGAIN THE LEAVES CAN'T GET IT UP.

IN EITHER CASE THE WATERING FREQUENCY RULES AREN'T BEING FOLLOWED, OR THE ROULETTE WHEEL IS SCREWING YOU UP. SCOPE IT OUT AND ALTER YOUR WATERING BEHAVIOR ACCORDINGLY.

SPECIAL EQUIPMENT

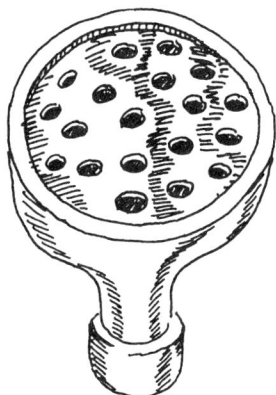

A **WATER-BUBBLER** SCREWED ON THE END OF THE HOSE BREAKS UP THE FORCE OF THE WATER STREAM WITHOUT DIMINISHING THE RATE OF FLOW. GOOD FOR TREES OR LARGE SHRUBS. (OR YOU CAN JUST TIE A PIECE OF BURLAP OR OTHER HEAVY CLOTH OVER THE END OF THE HOSE.)

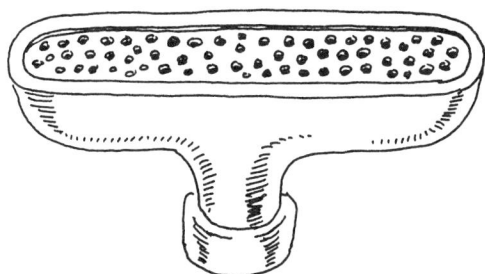

A **FAN-SPRAYER** GIVES A SPRINKLING LIKE LIGHT RAIN. BEST FOR SEED-BEDS, SEEDLINGS, AND SMALL VEGGIES LIKE LETTUCE AND BEETS.

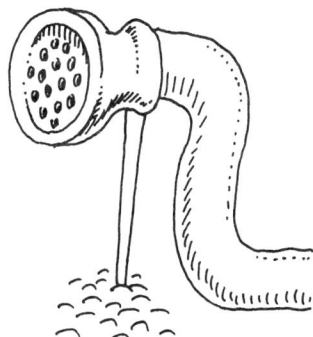

A **SPIKE-SPRINKLER** DOES THE SAME THING AS A FAN-SPRAYER, BUT YOU CAN STICK IT IN THE GROUND AND WALK AWAY TO DO OTHER THINGS.

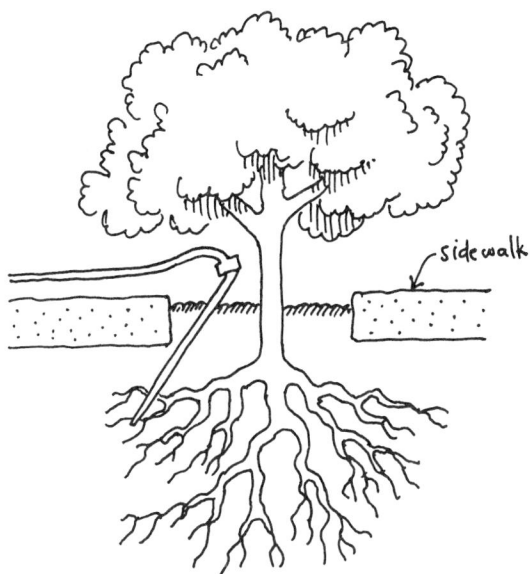

sidewalk

A **SUBSOIL IRRIGATOR** IS GOOD FOR SITUATIONS WHERE A TREE IS SURROUNDED BY SIDEWALKS OR PATIO, SO WATER SPRINKLED AT THE BASE OF THE TREE CAN'T REACH THE FEEDER ROOTS.

BASINS—A WAY TO WATER TREES WITHOUT WORRYING ABOUT RUN-OFF.

OVERHEAD SPRINKLERS ARE CONVENIENT AND QUICK, AND THEY'RE OFTEN USED TO WATER ENTIRE GARDENS OR FIELDS AT ONCE. OBVIOUS PROBLEMS ARE THAT IT IGNORES SPECIAL NEEDS OF VARIOUS PLANTS, AND VARIATIONS IN MICROCLIMATE. ALSO, OVERHEAD WATERING GETS WATER ON THE LEAVES, WHICH CAN FOSTER FUNGUS DISEASES.

SOME PLANTS SHOULD NEVER HAVE WET LEAVES: SQUASHES AND MELONS, WHICH GET MILDEW, A FUNGUS; AND POTATOES, WHICH GET POTATO BLIGHT FUNGUS. IN GENERAL, ANY PLANT WITH HAIRY OR SOFT LEAVES DOESN'T LIKE TO GET WET--LIKE TOMATO, EGGPLANT, SUNFLOWER, MINT. PLANTS WITH SLICK, SHINY, OR WAXY LEAVES DON'T MIND GETTING WET--THE WATER QUICKLY FORMS BEADS AND RUNS OFF EASILY. EXAMPLES ARE CABBAGE-FAMILY PLANTS, CELERY, CORN, LETTUCE, AND BEETS.

ALSO, OVERHEAD WATERING WASTES WATER . . . MUCH WATER EVAPORATES FROM THE LEAVES, AND ALSO YOU'RE WATERING THE AREAS BETWEEN PLANTS, WHICH FOSTERS WEED GROWTH.

SPECIAL PROBLEMS
1. Drainage

BAD DRAINAGE CAN STUNT YOUR PLANTS' GROWTH AS FAST AS ANYTHING, BECAUSE STANDING WATER IN THE ROOT ZONE KEEPS ROOTS FROM GETTING THE OXYGEN THEY NEED. DRAINAGE PROBLEMS CAN ALSO FOSTER SOIL FUNGUS DISEASES. YOU CAN DETECT BAD DRAINAGE BY LOOKING AT WHAT HAPPENS AFTER YOU WATER THE SOIL, OR AFTER IT RAINS. IF THE WATER JUST POOLS ON THE SURFACE FOR DAYS INSTEAD OF DISAPPEARING UNDERGROUND, YOU'VE GOT (GASP!) **BAD DRAINAGE!**

IF YOU HAVE ANY DOUBTS, HERE'S A SIMPLE TEST:

DIG A HOLE TWO FEET DEEP. FILL IT WITH WATER. IF THERE'S ANY WATER LEFT AFTER 2 TO 3 HOURS, YOU'VE GOT BAD DRAINAGE.

CAUSES OF BAD DRAINAGE

I. HIGH WATER TABLE. SOMETIMES YOU CAN DIG DOWN TWO OR THREE FEET AND WATER STARTS SEEPING INTO THE HOLE THROUGH THE BOTTOM AND SIDES, SORT OF LIKE WHEN YOU DIG OUT A SPOONFUL OF YOGURT, LET IT SIT FOR A WHILE WITHOUT STIRRING, AND THE HOLE FILLS UP WITH A WATERY LIQUID. IN THE CASE OF THE SOIL, THIS SEEPING IS DUE TO THE WATER TABLE, WHICH IS THE TOPMOST LEVEL OF THE "GROUNDWATER" OR "AQUIFER." THE GROUNDWATER IS A LARGE FLAT UNDERGROUND LAKE WHICH FLOWS TOWARD THE NEAREST CREEK OR RIVER, LIKE THIS:

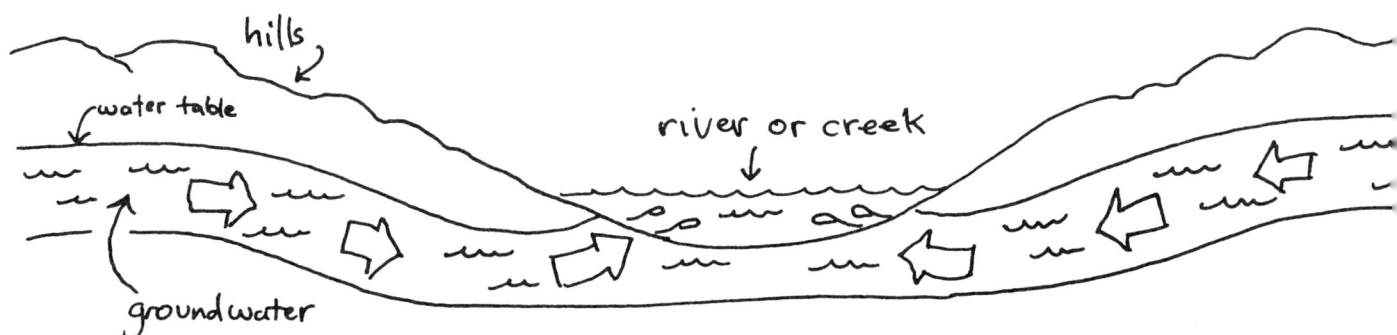

THE GROUNDWATER IS ESSENTIALLY SATURATED SOIL OR BEDROCK. IT'S WHERE WELL AND SPRING WATER COME FROM. IF THE GROUNDWATER IS LESS THAN THREE FEET UNDER THE SURFACE, YOU HAVE A FAIRLY HIGH WATER TABLE, WHICH COULD BE CAUSING YOUR DRAINAGE PROBLEMS.

OF COURSE, IT DEPENDS ON WHAT YOU'RE GROWING; THREE FEET IS ENOUGH DRY SOIL FOR MOST VEGGIES, BUT FRUIT TREES NEED A LOWER WATER TABLE (SIX FEET OR MORE). ALSO, THE WATER TABLE VARIES ACCORDING TO THE SEASONS. IF IT'S BEEN RAINING A LOT, THE WATER TABLE WILL BE HIGHER, UNTIL IT HAS A CHANCE TO FLOW INTO THE NEAREST RIVER OR LAKE (IT FLOWS RATHER SLOWLY—ABOUT A YARD PER DAY). SO A HIGH WATER TABLE IN THE SPRING IS NOTHING TO WORRY ABOUT, UNLESS THE WATER IS POOLING ON THE SURFACE FOR DAYS.

ANOTHER POSSIBLE CAUSE OF BAD DRAINAGE IS SLIPSHOD LANDSCAPING PRACTICES BY CARELESS CONTRACTORS. OFTEN CONTRACTORS WILL SCRAPE AWAY THE TOPSOIL TO LEVEL A SITE, LEAVING BARE CLAY SUBSOIL. THEN THEY'LL DUMP A THIN LAYER OF LOOSE TOPSOIL (OR WHATEVER) ON TOP OF THE CLAY, WITHOUT MIXING THE TWO LAYERS. WHEN

WATER ENTERS THE SOIL IT FOLLOWS THE PATH OF LEAST RESISTANCE, SPREADING OUT LATERALLY THROUGH THE TOPSOIL RATHER THAN DRAINING DOWN THROUGH THE CLAY:

1. NATURAL SOIL—GRADUAL TRANSITION FROM TOPSOIL TO SUBSOIL TO CLAY, SO WATER GOES STRAIGHT DOWN TO THE WATER TABLE.

2. GRADING A LEVEL AREA FOR A HOUSE . . . TOPSOIL AND SUBSOIL ARE PUSHED AWAY.

3. A NEW THIN LAYER OF TOPSOIL (OR WHATEVER) IS SPREAD OVR THE CLAY. WATER SPREADS OUT LATERALLY INSTEAD OF GOING DOWN THROUGH THE CLAY.

THE RESULT IS THE SAME THING ON A LARGE SCALE AS OCCURS WHEN YOU TRANSPLANT FROM A POT WITHOUT MAKING A SMOOTH TRANSITION BETWEEN THE LOOSE POTTING MIX AND THE DENSER GARDEN TOPSOIL. WHENEVER THERE'S AN ABRUPT TRANSITION IN TEXTURE, WATER HAS A HARD TIME GETTING PAST THE DISCONTINUITY.

BAD DRAINAGE CAN ALSO BE CAUSED BY SALTY SOIL. SALT IN THE SOIL BREAKS DOWN THE SOIL STRUCTURE, SO WATER CAN'T GET THROUGH. SEE CHAPTER THREE FOR CAUSES AND REMEDIES OF SALTY SOIL.

THE TERRAIN CAN ALSO CONTRIBUTE TO DRAINAGE PROBLEMS. OFTEN IF YOU HAVE FLAT LAND AT THE BOTTOM OF A SLOPE OR CANYON, IT IS RECEIVING GROUNDWATER AND SURFACE RUN-OFF FROM A LARGE AREA, AND CAN'T REMOVE THE INFLOW FAST ENOUGH.

OR, YOU MAY HAVE (DUM, DA DUMM-DUM!) **HARDPAN.** HARDPAN IS A LAYER OF EXTREMELY DENSE, ALMOST ROCK-LIKE SOIL, USUALLY A COUPLE FEET BELOW THE SURFACE. HARDPAN CAN BE A NATURAL GEOLOGICAL FEATURE, OR IT CAN BE CAUSED BY PLOWING THE SOIL AT THE SAME DEPTH OVER A NUMBER OF YEARS. THE "PYGMIE FOREST" NEAR MENDOCINO, CALIFORNIA IS CAUSED BY A HARDPAN LAYER. TO DIAGNOSE HARDPAN, DIG DOWN WITH A SHOVEL. IF YOU REACH A POINT WHERE THE SOIL IS NEARLY AS HARD AS SANDSTONE, THAT'S HARDPAN. TO REMEDY THE SITUATION, GET A PICK, SWALLOW FIVE QUICK CUPS OF COFFEE, AND GO AT IT.

OR, (AND THIS IS A REAL PAIN) YOU MAY BE SURROUNDED BY NEIGHBORS WITH CEMENTED—OVER YARDS, SO THE WHOLE BLOCK IS ACTING AS A "WATERSHED" FOR YOUR LITTLE YARD. THE ONLY CURE FOR THAT ONE IS TO HYPNOTIZE YOUR NEIGHBORS, BUNDLE THEM ALL OFF TO LAS VEGAS FOR THE WEEKEND, AND GO AT THEIR PATIOS WITH A JACKHAMMER.

IMPROVING DRAINAGE

THE EASIEST WAY TO DEAL WITH DRAINAGE PROBLEMS IS TO GARDEN ON RAISED BEDS. IF YOU'RE GARDENING IN A RAINY SEASON, RAISED BEDS ARE A MUST, EVEN IF YOU HAVE EXCELLENT DRAINAGE.

ESSENTIALLY, WITH RAISED BEDS YOU'RE CREATING A TINY GEOLOGICAL TERRAIN, WITH THE BEDS FORMING A SERIES OF HILLS, AND THE PATHS BETWEEN THE BEDS BEING LIKE CANYONS, WHERE THE WATER DRAINS TO FORM TINY CREEKS:

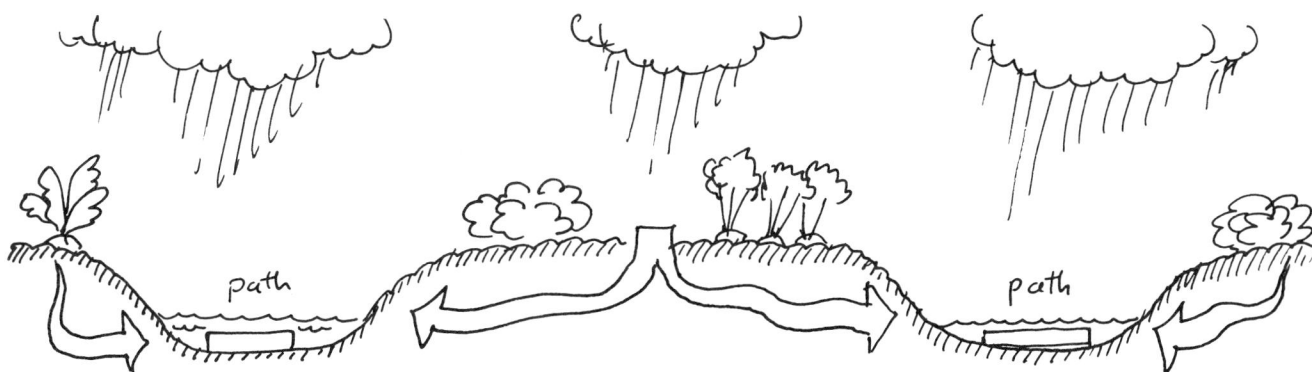

THAT IS, AFTER ALL, HOW EVEN **ROADS** ARE DESIGNED:

IF RAISED BEDS DON'T DO THE TRICK, YOU MIGHT HAVE TO TAKE DRASTIC MEASURES; THIS MEANS DIGGING DITCHES AND LAYING DRAINAGE PIPES, CALLED "TILES." THESE CERAMIC PIPES ARE LAID END-TO-END IN DITCHES, LIKE THIS:

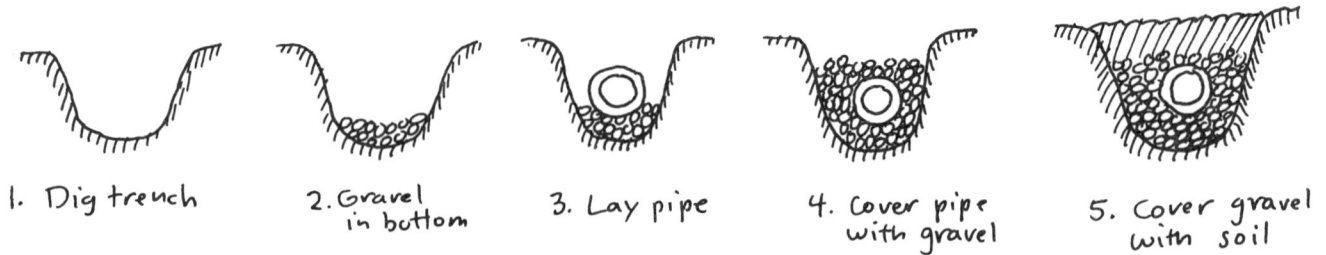

1. Dig trench   2. Gravel in bottom   3. Lay pipe   4. Cover pipe with gravel   5. Cover gravel with soil

IN THE CASE OF A FLAT AREA UNDER A HILL, THE PIPES SHOULD BE LAID IN A LINE AT THE INTERSECTION OF THE TWO PLANES, LIKE THIS:

THE ROW OF PIPES SHOULD BE POINTED DOWNHILL ON AT LEAST A ONE DEGREE ANGLE, TO HELP WITH THE FLOW.

IF YOU LIVE IN A TYPICAL CROWDED RESIDENTIAL AREA, YOU SHOULD AIM THE PIPES SO YOU DON'T JUST DUMP YOUR EXCESS WATER ON YOUR NEIGHBORS. USUALLY THE ONLY PLACE TO GO IS THE STREET, WHERE OVERWORKED CITY SEWER SYSTEMS OFTEN BACK UP IN PROLONGED RAINY WEATHER, LEAVING YOU BACK WHERE YOU STARTED. C'EST LA VIE! IF ALL ELSE FAILS, TRY GROWING RICE, AND BE PATIENT UNTIL THE DAY OUR CITIES ARE RE-DESIGNED AROUND ECOLOGICAL PRINCIPLES.

GARDENING ON A SLOPE

SLOPES CAN BE A BIG BONUS FOR A GARDEN OR FARM, CREATING MICROCLIMATES THAT HELP YOU GROW SHADE-LOVING PLANTS IN THE SUMMER (NORTH-FACING SLOPE) AND EVERYTHING IN THE WINTER (SOUTH-FACING SLOPE). BUT YOU HAVE TO PAY FOR WHAT YOU GET. SLOPE-GARDENING IS DIFFICULT, BECAUSE UNLESS IT'S DONE EXACTLY RIGHT, YOU'LL GET **EROSION** . . .

1. NORMAL WILD STATE: A LARGE VARIETY OF "WEEDS" IN DENSE PROFUSION COVERS THE SOIL SURFACE, AND TIES THE SOIL TOGETHER WITH A TIGHT NETWORK OF INTER-PENETRATING ROOT SYSTEMS.

2. THE SLOPE IS CLEARED, AND CROPS ARE PLANTED IN ROWS, WITH LARGE BARE SPACES BE-TWEEN THE ROWS.

3. GOODBYE, TOPSOIL!

PREVENTING EROSION ON SLOPES

1. DISTURB THE SOIL AS LITTLE AS POSSIBLE. ONLY PLOW OR DIG IF REALLY NECESSARY AFTER THE FIRST YEAR. (THIS IS THE WAY TO GO ANYWAY, BUT IT'S ESPECIALLY CRITICAL ON SLOPES. EVEN ON LEVEL GROUND, TILLING CONTRIBUTES TO SOIL EROSION.)

2. MULCH HEAVILY. MULCHING WILL KEEP THE SOIL SOFT AND LOOSE, REDUCING THE NEED FOR DIGGING. MULCH PREVENTS EXCESS WEEDS, SO YOU WON'T HAVE TO DISTURB THE SOIL BY PULLING THEM UP. FURTHER, MULCH SLOWS THE IMPACT OF RAINDROPS ON THE GROUND, LETTING THE DROPS PERCOLATE DOWN THROUGH THE MULCH.

3. SPACE YOUR VEGGIES SO THE LEAVES TOUCH. PLANT IN BEDS, NOT ROWS. LEAVE THE FEW WEEDS THAT MANAGE TO MAKE IT UP THROUGH THE MULCH. ADD EXTRA COMPOST IF NECESSARY TO FEED BOTH VEGGIES AND WEEDS.

4. RETURN SOIL FROM THE BOTTOM OF THE SLOPE TO THE TOP. THAT'S WHAT THEY DO AT THE STUDENT-RUN GARDEN AT THE UNIVERSITY OF CALIFORNIA, SANTA CRUZ, WHICH IS PLANTED ON A 30 DEGREE SLOPE, FACING SOUTH. THE BEDS ACTUALLY RUN UP AND DOWN THE SLOPE, CONTRARY TO ALL THE CONVENTIONAL WISDOM ON SLOPE-GARDENING. THEIR SECRET IS THEY ACTUALLY CART SOIL PERIODICALLY FROM THE BASE OF THE GARDEN UP TO THE TOP. THAT'S A LOT OF WORK, BUT IT'S AN INCREDIBLY LUSH AND BEAUTIFUL GARDEN, WITH EVERYTHING JUST OOZING HEALTH AND VITALITY.

5. IF EROSION IS STILL A PROBLEM, CONCENTRATE ON PERENNIALS: FRUIT AND NUT TREES, BERRIES, GRAPES, PERENNIAL HERBS, ARTICHOKES, ASPARAGUS, ETC. IN ANY CASE, AVOID ROOT CROPS LIKE CARROTS AND BEETS, SINCE PULLING UP THE ROOTS OF ANYTHING CAUSES THE SOIL TO LOOSEN, LEADING TO EROSION. IF ANNUALS ARE GROWN, CUT OFF THE PLANT AT THE SOIL SURFACE WHEN THE GROWING SEASON IS OVER, LEAVING THE ROOTS IN THE GROUND TO ROT. POTATOES SHOULD NOT BE A PROBLEM IF GROWN CORRECTLY (IN MOUNDS).

6. WATER AS LIGHTLY AND INFREQUENTLY AS POSSIBLE. A DRIP SYSTEM WOULD REALLY PAY FOR ITSELF IN TERMS OF EROSION CONTROL.

7. TERRACING IS A LOT OF WORK, AND SHOULD BE CONSIDERED A LAST RESORT FOR VERY STEEP SLOPES.

THE BIGGEST IRRIGATION DEVICE

RAINFALL IS AUTOMATIC, CONVENIENT, LOW-MAINTENANCE, **FREE.** THE WATER USUALLY COMES DOWN IN AN EVEN, SOFT, DELICATE SPRAY FOR MINIMUM EROSION AND RUNOFF, AVOIDING EXCESSIVE SEEDLING DISRUPTION. BILLIONS OF TONS OF SEA WATER YEARLY ARE DESALINIZED, PUMPED UP THOUSANDS OF FEET INTO THE AIR, AND RELEASED AT THE OPTIMUM INTERVALS FOR PLANT GROWTH (USUALLY EVERY 4-5 DAYS IN THE RAINY SEASONS, SO THE SOIL CAN DRY OUT PARTWAY BETWEEN WATERINGS.) THE POWER FOR THIS OPERATION IS SUPPLIED BY--YOU GUESSED IT--THE SUN.

THE RAINFALL CYCLE IS FIRST OF ALL A GIANT SOLAR DESALINIZATION MACHINE. OR, LOOKED AT ANOTHER WAY, A SOLAR STILL IS A SCALE MODEL OF THE HYDROLOGIC CYCLE:

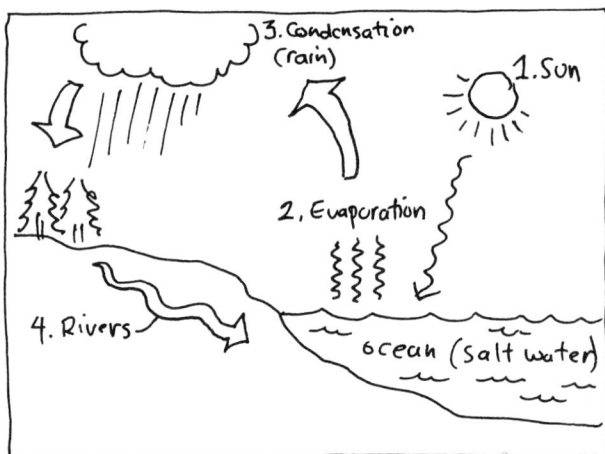

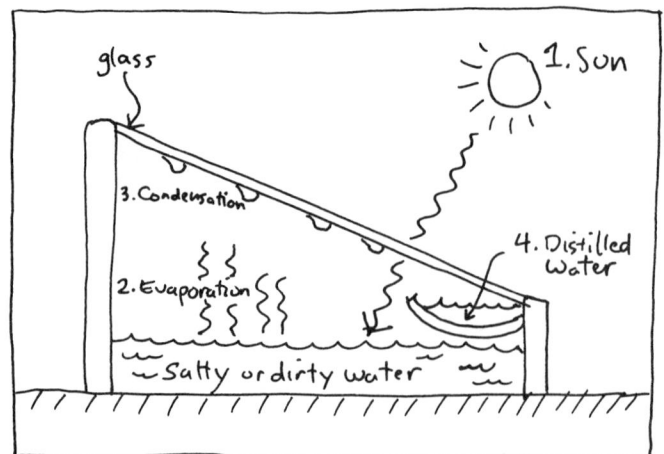

The Hydrologic Cycle

A Solar Still

THINK OF WHAT WE'D HAVE TO DO IF THERE WAS NO RAIN. FIRST WE'D HAVE TO PUMP WATER UPHILL FROM THE OCEANS TO WHEREVER THE FARMS ARE. THEN, EVEN IF WE COULD AFFORD THE PUMPING EXPENSE, WE'D STILL HAVE TO DESALINATE THE WATER, BECAUSE SALT IN WATER INTERFERES WITH OSMOSIS INTO THE ROOT CELLS, AS WE SAW IN CHAPTER 3. IN CALIFORNIA, WHERE THERE ARE FREQUENT DROUGHT YEARS, THERE ARE ACTUALLY SERIOUS PROPOSALS TO DESALINATE WATER ON A LARGE SCALE FOR HOME AND AGRICULTURAL USE. IT IS UNCLEAR WHETHER THESE PROPOSALS ARE ATTEMPTED BOONDOGGLES BY DESALINATION EQUIPMENT COMPANIES, ATTEMPTS AT BLACK HUMOR BY OUT-OF-WORK ABSURDIST PLAYWRITES, OR MERELY THE TYPICAL IGNORANCE OF POLITICIANS WITH NO BACKGROUND IN ECOLOGY OR PHYSICS.

THE REAL SOLUTION TO THE DROUGHT PROBLEM IS CLEAR: CONSERVATION, COUPLED WITH THE CATCHING AND SAVING OF RAINWATER ON A DECENTRALIZED, LOCAL LEVEL (E.G. NEIGHBORHOOD WATER TANKS, SUCH AS THOSE USED IN JAPAN AND CHINA.), SO THE DESTRUCTION OF VALLEY ECOSYSTEMS BY DAMS (LIKE THE HETCH-HETCHY RESERVOIR IN CALIFORNIA) WOULDN'T BE NECESSARY. IN MANY AREAS THERE CAN BE FLOODS ONE YEAR, AND IRONICALLY, DISASTEROUS DROUGHT CONDITIONS THE NEXT YEAR--ALL BECAUSE FLOOD WATERS ARE SIMPLY ALLOWED TO FLOW INTO THE OCEAN. THE MIXING OF FLOOD WATERS WITH THE OCEAN IS A MOST WASTEFUL EXAMPLE OF THE ENTROPY EFFECT WHICH OCCURS WHEN SOMETHING PURE (RAINWATER) IS MIXED WITH SOMETHING HETEROGENOUS (SEA WATER). THE WASTE IS NOT USUALLY APPRECIATED BECAUSE THERE IS AN IGNORANCE OF THE ENERGY (SOLAR) THAT POWERS THE HYDROLOGIC CYCLE, AND BECAUSE THERE IS USUALLY A LAKE SOMEWHERE THAT CAN BE DESTROYED (LIKE OWENS VALLEY, FORMERLY A LAKE; AND MONO LAKE IN CALIFORNIA).

GARDENERS AND FARMERS ARE IN A KEY POSITION IN REGARD TO WATER USE. ALTHOUGH MUCH IS MADE OF THE LOS ANGELES SWIMMING POOLS THAT ARE DRAINING MONO LAKE, THE FACT IS THAT 85 PERCENT OF CALIFORNIA'S WATER USE GOES FOR AGRICULTURE. THERE ARE A FEW VERY EASY STEPS WE CAN USE TO SAVE WATER IN OUR GARDENS AND FARMS. ONE IS THE USE OF A MULCH ON THE SURFACE, WHICH SLOWS WATER EVAPORATION FROM THE SOIL. SINCE AN ORGANIC MULCH IS USEFUL FOR SO MANY OTHER PURPOSES AS WELL (PROVIDES CO_2 TO PLANTS, BREAKS DOWN TO PROVIDE NUTRIENTS AND SOIL-BUILDING HUMUS, CONTROLS WEEDS, KEEPS SOIL WARM IN WINTER), WATER CONSERVATION IS JUST AN ADDED BONUS.

SECOND, WE CAN AVOID OVERHEAD WATERING AS MUCH AS POSSIBLE, ESPECIALLY ON HOT DAYS. DRIP SYSTEMS SHOULD BE INSTALLED WHEREVER POSSIBLE. AND MOST IMPORTANT, WE CAN AVOID OVERWATERING. WHILE GIVING A PLANT TOO MUCH WATER AT ONE TIME DOESN'T HURT THE PLANT (UNLIKE TOO-FREQUENT WATERING), IT WASTES WATER. AND THAT'S WHAT THE FIRST PART OF THIS CHAPTER WAS ALL ABOUT: GIVING YOU A THOROUGH UNDERSTANDING OF JUST WHAT WATER IS DOING IN THE PLANT AND

THE SOIL, SO YOU CAN LEARN TO WATER JUST ENOUGH, AND NOT TOO MUCH. THIS IS IN CONTRAST WITH MOST GARDENING BOOKS, WHICH JUST SAY "STICK A TROWEL IN THE SOIL--IF YOU CAN'T STICK IT IN EASILY, IT'S TIME TO IRRIGATE."

IF WE CONSERVE WATER AS MUCH AS POSSIBLE THERE WILL BE ENOUGH TO GO AROUND . . . EVEN FOR SWIMMING POOLS!

Appendix to Chapter 7
ROOT DEPTHS

LESS THAN 2 FT.	2--3 FT.	3--6 FT.	MORE THAN 6 FT.
BROCOLLI	CABBAGE	BEANS	ALFALFA
BRUSSELS SPROUTS	LETTUCE	BEETS	ASPARAGUS
CAULIFLOWER	ONION	CARROT	ARTICHOKE
CELERY	POTATO	CUCUMBER	MELON
GARLIC	SPINACH	EGGPLANT	SWEET POTATO
LEEK	RYE GRASS	PEPPER	LIMA BEAN
PARSELY	CORN	SUMMER SQUASH	TOMATO
RADISH		PEAS	WINTER SQUASH
		CHARD	PUMPKIN
		MUSKMELON	
		MUSTARD	
		TURNIP	
		RUTABAGA	

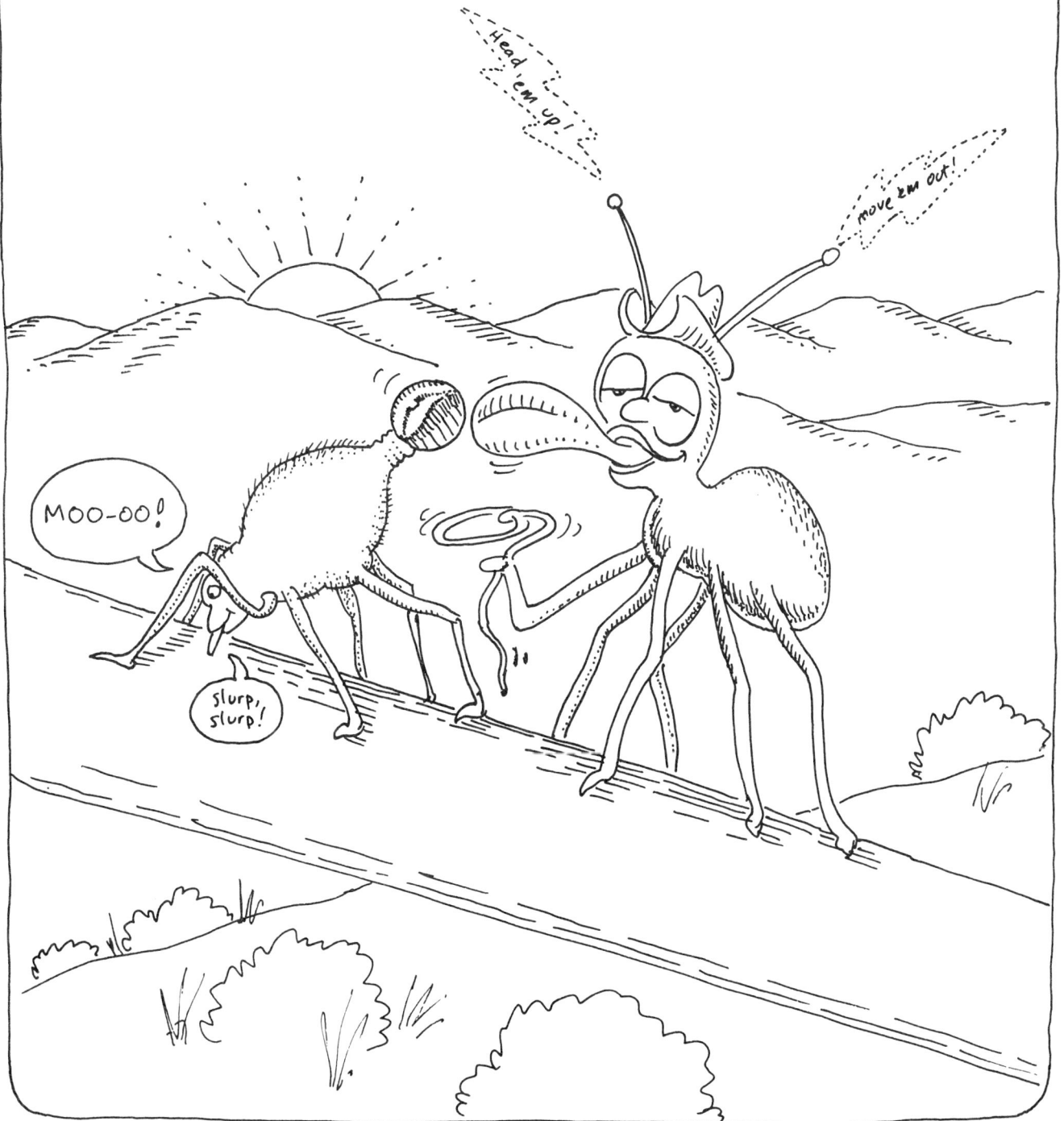

WHY PESTS?

WE BRED OUR FOOD PLANTS TO TASTE GOOD: TO GET THE SALIVA FLOWING, TO GET THE GUT-JUICES GOING, TO GIVE US THE MIDNIGHT MUNCHIES, TO INCITE ROMANTIC CONVERSATION BY CANDLELIGHT. THE PROBLEM IS, ALL THE OTHER LITTLE CRITTERS ALSO GET THE MUNCHIES FOR OUR YUMMY FOOD PLANTS.

NUMBER ONE RULE OF THE COSMOS: YOU DON'T GET SUMTHIN' FER NUTHIN.' NUMBER TWO RULE: WHENEVER YOU **DO** GET SOMETHING, THE WORLD IS FULL OF OTHER GUYS WHO WANT TO TAKE IT AWAY. EXAMPLE: LITTLE I.R.S. CRITTERS TAKE HALF OUR EARNINGS AND SQUANDER IT ON MILITARY WASTE. DO WE SPRAY **THEM** WITH PESTICIDES? MAYBE WE SHOULD, BUT WE DON'T. WE ACCEPT THIS MAJOR PEST INFESTATION, HOWEVER MUCH WE GRUMBLE ABOUT IT. BUT ONE LITTLE HOLE IN AN APPLE AND WE THROW A FIT.

IT'S ONLY NATURAL THAT INSECTS WOULD WANT TO EAT OUR FOOD. IN DOMESTICATING OUR CROP PLANTS, WE HAVE BRED OUT ALL THE BITTER TASTING CHEMICALS THE PLANTS FORMERLY USED TO KEEP FROM BEING EATEN (THE SAME CHEMICALS THAT MAKE MOST WILD PLANTS, PEYOTE, PSILOCYBIN MUSHROOMS, AND RAW CHOCOLATE HARD TO EAT). THE RESULT IS **WE** HAVE TO PROTECT OUR PLANTS AT TIMES, ALTHOUGH WE'VE GOT PLENTY OF HELP FROM SOME OF OUR INSECT ALLIES. (THAT IS, IF WE DON'T KILL THEM ALL OFF!)

FIRST, I'LL GIVE AN OVERVIEW OF INSECT LIFE CYCLES, ON THE GENERAL PREMISE OF "KNOW THY ENEMY." BESIDES, INSECTS ARE FASCINATING IN THEIR OWN RIGHT, AND IT'S GREAT TO KNOW HOW THEY LIVE, AND WATCH THEM TRUCKIN' AROUND DOING THEIR LITTLE INSECT THINGS. EVEN WHILE THEY'RE CHOMPING DOWN ON YOUR VEGGIES, YOU CAN STILL ENJOY HOW THEY MOVE AND EAT AND BOOGIE AROUND, AND THE MORE YOU KNOW ABOUT THEM, THE BETTER YOU'LL BE ABLE TO DEAL WITH THEM.

INSECT LIFE STYLES
(Micro Soaps for the Six-Legged Set)

INSECT DRAMAS ARE COMPLICATED BY THE FACT THAT INSECTS HAVE TWO DISTINCT LIFE STAGES, WITH QUITE DIFFERENT APPEARANCE, EATING HABITS, AND BEHAVIOR. THESE STAGES ARE CALLED **LARVA** AND **ADULT**.

THE **LARVA** IS AN EATING MACHINE: ITS JOB IS CRAWLING AROUND, EATING AS MUCH AS POSSIBLE, AND GETTING BIG AND FAT. (WHAT A LIFE, HUH?) THE **ADULT** FLIES AROUND LOOKING FOR ITS TRUE LOVE, CONSUMMATES THE RELATIONSHIP (OFTEN IN MID-AIR), AND FINDS A SUITABLE HOME TO RAISE THE LITTLE TODDLERS.

HERE'S THE WHOLE STORY IN PICTURES:

Oh God!

Oh God!

MUNCH MUNCH MUNCH

Eggs

Larva
(Toddler to Adolescence)

NOW THAT YOU KNOW A LITTLE OF THE LIVES AND LOVES OF THE ANTENNA-HEADED CROWD, WE CAN GET DOWN TO THE REAL NITTY-GRITTY OF WHO IS EATING WHAT, AND WHY.

FIRST OF ALL, ANYTHING THAT'S **FLYING** IS USUALLY NOT EATING YOUR PLANTS, AT LEAST NOT IN ITS CURRENT LIFE STAGE. THAT'S BECAUSE IF YOU'RE EATING PLANTS, YOU HAVE ALL YOU NEED RIGHT IN FRONT OF YOUR MOUTH, SO THERE'S NO POINT IN FLYING. (PREDATOR INSECTS, ON THE OTHER HAND, NEED TO CRUISE AROUND LOOKING FOR THEIR MEALS: ONE BUG HERE, ONE BUG THERE.) MOST OF THE WORST PESTS ONLY EAT PLANTS WHILE IN THEIR LARVAL, WINGLESS STAGE—SUCH AS CODLING MOTH LARVAE (THE "WORMS" IN APPLES), THE LARVAE OF THE CABBAGE MOTH, GYPSY MOTH, FRUIT FLY, ETC.

THE **LARVAL** STAGE DOES THE MOST DAMAGE BECAUSE LARVAE NEED PROTEIN TO BUILD STRONG BODIES. THEY CAN ONLY GET THIS PROTEIN FROM PLANT LEAVES OR ROOTS (OR FROM OTHER INSECTS, IN THE CASE OF PREDATORS, LIKE SYRPHID FLIES, LADYBUGS, PARASITIC WASPS, ETC.). THE **ADULT** DOESN'T NEED MUCH PROTEIN ANYMORE, AND THE LITTLE IT NEEDS IT CAN GET FROM POLLEN. WHAT THE ADULT MAINLY WANTS IS **SUGAR**

(FOR ENERGY TO FLY AROUND, COURTING SIGNIFICANT OTHERS), WHICH IT GETS FROM THE NECTAR OF FLOWERS. OFTEN AN INSECT WHICH IS A PEST IN ITS LARVAL STAGE IS A CONTRIBUTING FLOWER-POLLINATOR AS AN ADULT (FOR EXAMPLE, THE CABBAGE MOTH (PIERIS RAPAE), WHICH EATS CABBAGE AND BROCOLLI LEAVES AS A LARVA, AND POLLINATES THEIR FLOWERS (AND ALSO CITRUS TREES) AS A MOTH.

THE LARVAL STAGE, IN ADDITION TO BEING THE EAT-AND-GET-LARGER STAGE, IS ALSO COMMONLY THE WINTER HIBERNATION-IN-THE-SOIL FORM OF AN INSECT. LARVAE HAVE A COMPACT, ROUNDED SHAPE, WITHOUT EXTERNAL STRUCTURES LIKE WINGS THAT LOSE HEAT, AND HEAT RETENTION IS IMPORTANT WHEN IT'S COLD OUTSIDE. SO A HIBERNATING LARVA IS LIKE A PLANT'S SEED, WAITING IN THE SOIL FOR THE WARMING RAYS OF SPRING.

IN FACT, YOU CAN DRAW ALL SORTS OF ANALOGIES BETWEEN INSECTS, PLANTS, AND EVEN PEOPLE. HERE'S A FEW OF THEM:

	INSECTS	PLANTS	PEOPLE
WINTER DORMANCY DEVICE ⇒	Larva (often in soil)	Seed (in soil)	Watching T.V. football
SUMMER DISPERSAL DEVICE ⇒	Adult (wings)	Fruit, or seeds with wings or burrs. maple dandelion	Fly to Hawaii

EXCEPTIONS

ALTHOUGH THESE ARE GOOD RULES OF THUMB, LIKE ALL GENERALIZATIONS THEY HAVE EXCEPTIONS. FOR INSTANCE, THE "HOMOPTERA" (SAP-SUCKERS, LIKE APHIDS, SCALES, WHITEFLIES, LEAFHOPPERS, AND CICADAS) EAT PLANT SAP THEIR ENTIRE LIFE, NOT JUST AS LARVAE. THIS IS ALSO TRUE OF MITES, WHICH ARE ACTUALLY A TYPE OF

SPIDER. HOWEVER, ALL THESE CRITTERS ARE RELATIVELY HARMLESS, AND ARE ONLY A PROBLEM WHERE PESTICIDES HAVE WIPED OUT THEIR NATURAL PREDATORS.

THE LARVAE OF BEETLES AND FLIES FORM A SPECIAL CLASS: THEY EAT ONLY DECAYING ORGANIC MATTER IN THE SOIL. RARELY, FLY LARVAE MAY EAT PLANT ROOTS, SUCH AS THE CABBAGE ROOT MAGGOT. ADULT FLIES ALSO EAT DECAYING MATTER, WHICH IS WHY THEY'RE ALWAYS CRUISING AROUND COMPOST PILES. ADULT BEETLES ARE USUALLY CARNIVOROUS, AND THEY ARE IMPORTANT NATURAL PREDATORS CONTROLLING PESTS. THEY MAY SOMETIMES EAT PLANT PARTS (SUCH AS THE CUCUMBER BEETLE), BUT THAT'S RARE.

HERE'S A DIAGRAM OF WHO'S EATING WHAT. (SOLID ARROWS SHOW FEEDING; BROKEN ARROWS SHOW LIFE-STAGE TRANSITION.)

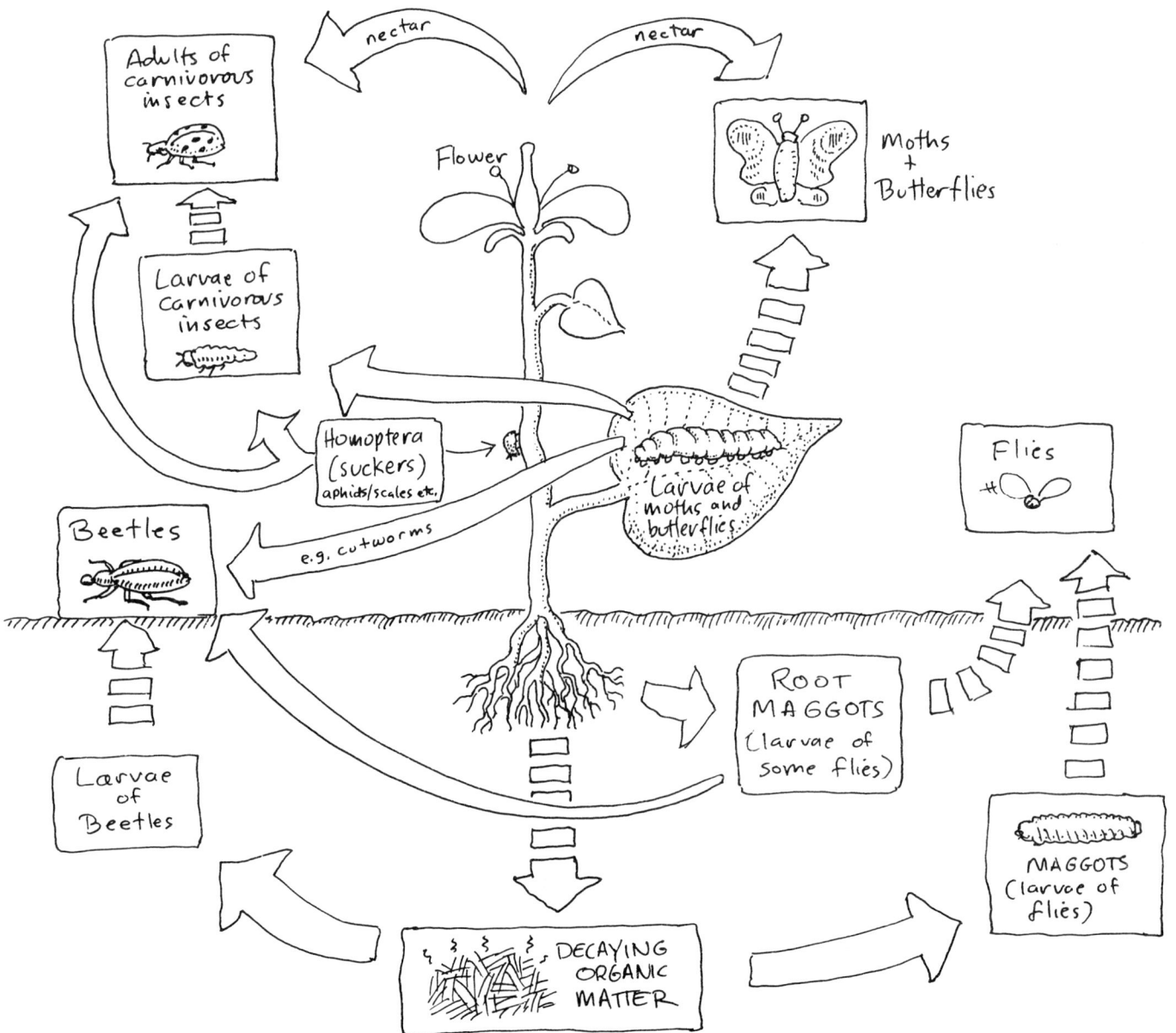

DEALING WITH THE BAD GUYS

SO LET'S SAY YOU WAKE UP ONE MORNING AND YOUR LETTUCE HAS BIG HOLES IN IT. **DON'T PANIC!** THAT'S THE FIRST RULE OF SENSIBLE PEST MANAGEMENT. IN THE FIRST PLACE, PLANTS CAN SUSTAIN A MODERATE AMOUNT OF LEAF DAMAGE WITH NO DECREASE IN FINAL YIELD. IN FACT, EVIDENCE IS ACCUMULATING THAT A SLIGHT AMOUNT OF HERBIVORE DAMAGE ACTUALLY STIMULATES THE PLANT TO PRODUCE MORE THAN IT WOULD OTHERWISE.* IT'S AS IF THE PLANT DOESN'T TURN ON FULL-THROTTLE UNLESS SOMETHING STARTS MUNCHING ON IT. MOST OF THE TIME YOUR PLANTS WILL EASILY OUTGROW THEIR PESTS, AND YOU DON'T HAVE TO DO ANYTHING.

STILL, THERE ARE TIMES (DUE MAINLY TO THE FACT THAT PESTICIDES HAVE DEPLETED THE SUPPLY OF BENEFICIAL PREDATORS IN YOUR AREA) THAT YOU MUST TAKE ACTION. SO THE QUESTION IS, WHAT TO DO?

THE FIRST IMPULSE

THE FIRST IMPULSE OF MANY FOLKS IS TO REACH FOR THE HANDY CAN OF POISON. IF YOU STILL HAVE ANY DOUBTS ABOUT THE DANGERS OF PESTICIDES (**ALL** PESTICIDES) AFTER SEEING SO MANY OF THE MAJOR INSECT POISONS BANNED ONE-BY-ONE BY THE GOVERNMENT (BUT ONLY AFTER EACH HAS BEEN DOING DAMAGE FOR TWENTY YEARS OR SO), I WILL REVIEW THE MAIN PROBLEMS WITH THESE CHEMICALS:

PROBLEMS WITH PESTICIDES

1. THEY DON'T WORK.
2. THEY KILL THE WRONG THINGS.
3. THEY ACCUMULATE IN THE FOOD CHAIN.
4. THEY CAUSE DISEASE IN HUMANS.
5. THEY WASTE ENERGY.

* ROSENTHAL, HERBERT, **HERBIVORES**, 1979. P. 279.

FLINT, MARY LOU, 1979. **INTRODUCTION TO INTEGRATED PEST MANAGEMENT**, P. 134.

HARRIS, P., **IN AGROECOSYSTEMS** 1: 219–225, 1979.

FIRST, LET'S LOOK AT PROBLEM 1, THE FACT THAT PESTICIDES **DON'T WORK** ON A LONGTERM BASIS. THEY ARE A SHORT-TERM "FIX" LIKE A SHOT OF HEROIN OR COCAINE, PRODUCING A MOMENTARY "HIGH" IN CROP YIELD, BUT FOLLOWED BY AN EVEN WORSE HANGOVER AS THE PEST EVOLVES A RESISTANCE TO THE CHEMICAL.

HOW DO PESTS EVOLVE RESISTANCE? INSECTS (AND ALL OTHER ORGANISMS) ARE CONSTANTLY MUTATING, DUE TO COSMIC RAYS FROM OUTER SPACE (WHEEEE-OOOO!) COMING DOWN AND ZAPPING THE DNA IN THE INSECTS' PRIVATE PARTS:

MOST MUTATIONS FROM THESE RAYS ARE LETHAL, BUT SOME CAN CAUSE THE DNA IN THE PEST'S EGG OR SPERM CELLS TO MAKE A **NEW ENZYME** THAT BREAKS DOWN THE PESTICIDE MOLECULES. THAT'S **EVOLUTION IN ACTION!** THERE'S A VERY REAL DANGER WE ARE ACTUALLY BREEDING PESTS SO FULL OF THESE NEW ENZYMES THAT **NO** CHEMICAL WILL BE ABLE TO AFFECT THEM.

2. PESTICIDES KILL THE WRONG THINGS. THIS WAS PRETTY WELL STATED BACK IN 1962 (**SILENT SPRING** BY RACHEL CARSON), SO IF YOU HAVEN'T CAUGHT ON YET, YOU'VE PROBABLY BEEN HELD CAPTIVE SINCE 1959 BY PAKISTANI TERRORISTS IN THE BASEMENT OF A LAUNDROMAT IN BOISE, IDAHO! HERE'S YOUR LAST CHANCE . . .

ALL PLANT-EATERS HAVE AT LEAST ONE **NATURAL PREDATOR** WHICH KEEPS THE INSECT IN LINE; SORT OF LIKE ECOLOGY'S POLICE FORCE TO KEEP INSECTS FROM EATING UP THE PLANET. THESE PREDATORS ARE USUALLY MORE SUSCEPTIBLE TO PESTICIDES THAN THE PESTS, BECAUSE THE POISONS ARE DESTROYING THEIR FOOD SOURCE, SO EVEN IF THE PREDATORS EVOLVE RESISTANCE, THEY WILL STARVE TO DEATH. (BESIDES, PREDATOR INSECTS TEND TO HAVE FEWER OFFSPRING AND A LONGER GENERATION TIME, SO THERE IS LESS CHANCE OF A BENEFICIAL MUTATION HAPPENING.*

IN ADDITION, PESTICIDES KILL HONEYBEES AND SYRPHID FLIES, WHICH WE NEED TO POLLINATE OUR CROPS. AND EVEN IF THESE BENEFICIAL INSECTS DON'T GET A LETHAL DOSE, THEY MAY BE EATEN BY OTHER ANIMALS IN THE FOOD CHAIN, AND THE POISON WILL BE PASSED ALONG. WHICH BRINGS US TO PROBLEM 3:

3. PESTICIDES ACCUMULATE IN THE FOOD CHAIN. PESTICIDES BECOME MORE CONCENTRATED THE HIGHER UP THE FOOD CHAIN YOU GO, SINCE EACH ANIMAL MUST EAT MUCH MORE PREY THAN ITS OWN BODY WEIGHT IN ORDER TO GROW, WITH MUCH OF THE MASS EXHALED AS CO_2 OR EXCRETED. YET THE POISONS STAY IN THE BODY, AND AREN'T BROKEN DOWN. (PESTICIDES WERE DESIGNED TO HAVE THESE FEATURES; IF THEY DIDN'T HAVE THEM, THEY WOULDN'T WORK AS PESTICIDES.) ONE EXAMPLE OF THIS EFFECT WAS SEEN IN THE CASE OF THE PEREGRINE FALCON, WHICH WAS DRIVEN TO THE BRINK OF EXTINCTION BY DDT POISONING.

HERE'S A DIAGRAM TO MAKE THIS PROCESS CLEAR:

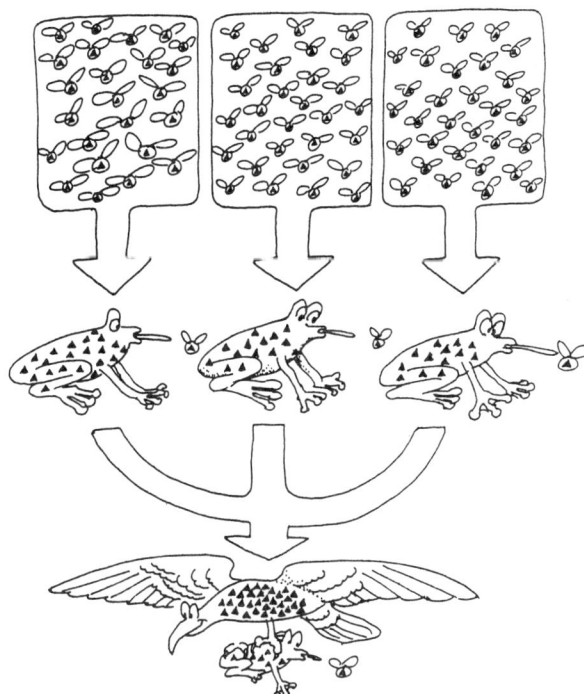

* HUFFAKER, C.B., **THEORY AND PRACTICE OF BIOLOGICAL CONTROL**

4. UNFIT FOR HUMAN CONSUMPTION. . . . AND THAT'S WHERE **WE** COME IN! WE'RE AT THE TOP OF THE FOOD CHAIN TOO, WHICH IN MOST WAYS IS A BLESSING. (IMAGINE WHAT IT WOULD BE LIKE IF WE WERE **NOT** AT THE TOP!) BUT BEING AT THE TOP OF THE HEAP MEANS WE'VE GOTTA PAY OUR DUES TOO. IN OUR CASE, IT MEANS CANCER AND BIRTH DEFECTS FROM PESTICIDE RESIDUES ON OUR FOOD (AND MISCARRIAGES, IN THE CASE OF HERBICIDES LIKE 2, 4, D AND 2, 4, 5, T.)

EACH NEW PESTICIDE IS PROMISED TO BE SAFE, AND THEN TWENTY YEARS LATER THE GOVERNMENT SAYS "HEY GUESS WHAT--IT'S NOT SO SAFE AFTER ALL." IS IT REALLY ANY SURPRISE? AS SHOWN IN THE INTRODUCTION, WE ARE ALL (ANIMALS, PLANTS, INSECTS, ETC.) MADE UP OF CELLS THAT ARE NEARLY ALIKE BIOCHEMICALLY:

NATURALLY, ANY CHEMICAL DESIGNED TO HURT ONE SUCH CELL WILL HURT ALL OTHER CELLS, EITHER DIRECTLY OR INDIRECTLY. THE OIL AND CHEMICAL COMPANIES THAT MAKE THESE CHEMICALS ARE PROFITING ON THE PUBLIC'S IGNORANCE OF THE COMMON ORIGIN AND BASIC EQUIVALENCE OF ALL ORGANISMS. TO PUT IT BLUNTLY, THEY ARE PROFITING ON YOUR AUNT MABEL'S CANCER.

ALTERNATIVES

IF POISONING YOUR GARDEN (AND YOURSELF) IS OUT, THEN WHAT'S LEFT? TO BEGIN WITH, YOU CAN USE THE METHODS USED LONG BEFORE ANYONE EVEN THOUGHT OF INVENTING PESTICIDES. THESE METHODS INCLUDE POLYCULTURE, HAND-PICKING, AVOIDING OVER-FERTILIZATION, HOEING AND TILLING (TO KILL LARVAE IN THE SOIL), AND KEEPING

PLANTS HEALTHY TO IMPROVE THEIR RESISTANCE. LATER, I WILL DISCUSS SOME RECENT INNOVATIONS LIKE THE USE OF NATURAL PREDATORS (INCLUDING PARASITES AND BACTERIA) AND PHEROMONE TRAPS.

POLYCULTURE MEANS PLANTING A MIXTURE OF CROPS, INSTEAD OF A LARGE EXPANSE OF A SINGLE CROP. IN THE WORDS OF ONE SANTA CRUZ FARMER, THE IDEA IS TO "CONFUSE THE PESTS BEFORE THEY HAVE A CHANCE TO THRASH YOUR PLANTS."

MOST INSECT PESTS FEED MAINLY ON A SINGLE PLANT, OR A CLOSELY-RELATED GROUP OF PLANTS. EVERY PLANT PUTS OUT A UNIQUE CHEMICAL WHICH IS MADE IN THE LEAVES, AND WHICH EVAPORATES INTO THE AIR. THE PLANT'S PARTICULAR PEST IS ATTRACTED TO THIS SPECIFIC CHEMICAL, AND USES IT AS A GUIDANCE SYSTEM TO FIND ITS FOOD. EVEN APHIDS, WHICH SEEM TO BE FEEDING ON MANY TYPES OF PLANTS, ARE ACTUALLY MANY DIFFERENT SPECIES OF INSECTS (PEACH APHID, APPLE APHID, ROSE APHID, ETC.), WITH EACH SPECIES EATING ONLY ONE OR TWO TYPES OF PLANTS.

WHEN YOU MIX DIFFERENT CROPS TOGETHER, YOU JAM THE CHEMICAL COMMUNICATION CHANNELS WITH STATIC, SO THE INSECT CAN'T RECEIVE THE

TRANSMISSIONS. BY FILLING THE AIR WITH A VARIETY OF CHEMICALS, POLYCULTURE EFFECTIVELY DILUTES THE CONCENTRATION OF ANY ONE CHEMICAL, SO THE PESTS ARE FRANTICALLY TWIDDLING THEIR RADIO DIALS, LOOKING FOR THE RIGHT STATION--THE ONE THAT SAYS, "HEY, YOU, EAT ME!"

Driving Insects Nuts

HERBS, ONION, and GARLIC

ONIONS, GARLIC, AND MANY HERBS NOT ONLY JAM THE CHANNELS, BUT THEY PUT OUT A CHEMICAL MESSAGE OF THEIR OWN, WHICH SAYS, "BEAT IT, YOU MEASLY SPINELESS LITTLE SIX-LEGGED S.O.B.!" MANY HERBS, SUCH AS THYME, SASSAFRAS, PENNYROYAL, CLOVE, WINTERGREEN, AND ANISE, HAVE NO INSECTS EATING THEM WHATSOEVER, SINCE THEIR ESSENTIAL OILS CONTAIN VARIOUS CHEMICALS THAT REPEL ALL INSECTS. MARIGOLDS HAVE A SIMILAR EFFECT ON NEMATODES IN THE SOIL, AND CHRYSANTHEMUMS DETER NEMATODES. (ALSO, COMPOST CONTAINS FUNGI WHICH EAT NEMATODES.) CATNIP HAS BEEN PROVEN TO REPEL 17 SPECIES OF INSECTS. (I HAVEN'T BEEN ABLE TO FIND A SCIENTIFIC SOURCE GIVING THE EFFECTIVE RANGE OF THESE CHEMICALS. PROBABLY THE NECESSARY EXPERIMENTS HAVEN'T BEEN DONE YET, BECAUSE RESEARCHERS ARE TOO BUSY INVENTING SEEDLESS WATERMELONS AND SQUARE TOMATOES. SO IT'S UP TO **YOU!**) IRONICALLY ENOUGH, THE SAME CHEMICALS THAT REPEL INSECTS HAVE THE OPPOSITE EFFECT ON PEOPLE (OR CATS, IN THE CASE OF CATNIP.)

2. Keep Your Plants Healthy

NEXT TO POLYCULTURE, THIS IS THE SECOND-EASIEST WAY TO KEEP INSECTS FROM BECOMING A PROBLEM. A STRONG, FAST-GROWING PLANT IS ABLE TO OUT-GROW INSECT DAMAGE, SO THE BUGS CAN HAVE THEIR SHARE, AND THE PLANT KEEPS ON TRUCKIN'. USUALLY THE HEAVY FEEDING STAGE OF A PEST ONLY LASTS A FEW WEEKS TO A MONTH, SO IF THE PLANT CAN GET THROUGH THAT PERIOD, IT WILL BE O.K. SO TO GET A PLANT THROUGH TOUGH TIMES, IT'S VITAL TO GIVE IT THE BEST POSSIBLE GROWING CONDITIONS— SUN, WATER, NUTRITION, ETC.

PLANTS ARE MOST VULNERABLE WHEN THEY ARE SEEDLINGS, SINCE THAT'S THE PERIOD OF SLOWEST GROWTH. SINCE IT TAKES CELLS TO MAKE CELLS, THE MORE CELLS THERE ARE THE FASTER THE PLANT GROWS (LIKE COMPOUND INTEREST ON AN ACCOUNT). HERE'S A GRAPH SHOWING THE CHANGING GROWTH RATE OF AN ANNUAL PLANT:

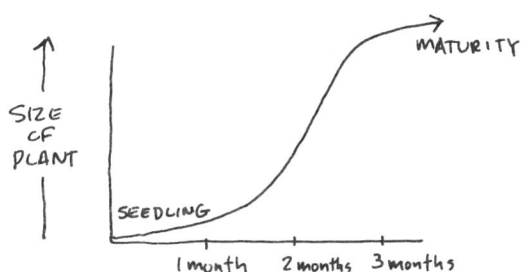

SO IT'S A GOOD IDEA TO START SUSCEPTIBLE CROPS UNDER GLASS, OR A SMALL SCREEN-STRUCTURE, OR AT LEAST ON A TABLE TO PROTECT THE SEEDLINGS FROM GROUND-CRAWLERS LIKE SNAILS.

AGAIN, DON'T PANIC. MANY PESTS (LIKE SNAILS, EARWIGS, AND CABBAGE MOTH LARVAE) MAINLY EAT THE OLDER, OUTER LEAVES:

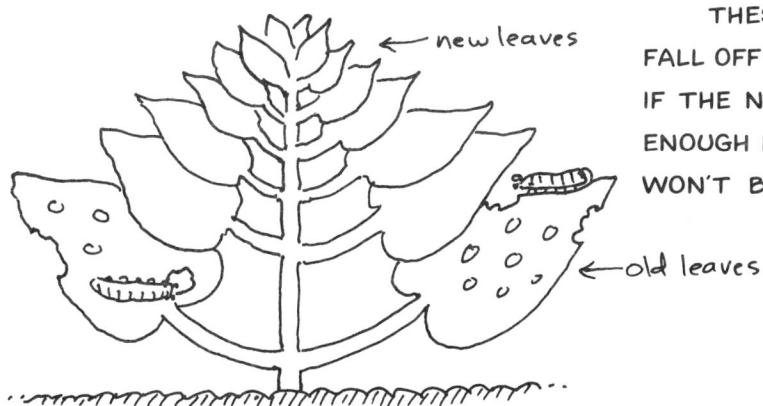

THESE OLDER LEAVES ARE DESTINED TO FALL OFF ANYWAY AS THE PLANT GROWS, SO IF THE NEW LEAVES ARE COMING OUT FAST ENOUGH FROM THE TIP OF THE STEM, THERE WON'T BE ANY PROBLEM.

3. Avoid Over-Fertilizing

THERE IS EVIDENCE THAT THE OVERUSE OF FERTILIZERS (ESPECIALLY NITROGEN) CAUSES DECREASED PLANT RESISTANCE TO RUST, MILDEW, LICE, AND MITES. SINCE THE MOST COMMON CAUSE OF OVER-FERTILIZING IS THE USE OF CHEMICAL FERTILIZERS, THIS CAN BE AVOIDED BY USING ONLY COMPOST OR OTHER ORGANIC FERTILIZERS.

4. Hand Picking

IN CHINA, TOP-LEVEL SCIENTISTS GO OUT IN THE FIELDS TO HAND-PICK INSECTS OFF CROPS. WHILE THIS WOULD BE UNTHINKABLE IN THE WEST, IN CHINA THEY ARE TRYING TO GO BEYOND THE ATTITUDE THAT SCIENTISTS MUST JUSTIFY THEIR EDUCATION BY CONSTANTLY DOING SOMETHING ABSTRUSE, HIGH-TECH, AND INCOMPREHENSIBLE TO THE GENERAL PUBLIC.

HAND-PICKING IS MOST ENJOYABLE IF YOU HAVE CHICKENS OR DUCKS TO FEED THE BUGS TO (CHICKENS GO BANANAS OVER SNAILS!). OTHERWISE YOU'LL HAVE TO SQUASH THEM AND THROW THE REMAINS IN THE COMPOST PILE. IN THE CASE OF NOCTURNAL PESTS LIKE SNAILS AND EARWIGS, DO YOUR PICKIN' AT NIGHT WITH A FLASHLIGHT.

5. Predators

AS MENTIONED BEFORE, NATURAL PREDATORS ARE NATURE'S GANGBUSTERS, CHASING DOWN THE ECOLOGICAL CRIMINALS WHO TAKE MORE THAN THEIR SHARE.

THE ACTION OF THESE PREDATORS CAN BEST BE VISUALIZED BY THE "PREDATION MANDALA." (NEXT PAGE) . . .

NOTE THAT AT LEAST A CERTAIN NUMBER OF PESTS ARE NECESSARY AS A SORT OF "PET FOOD" TO KEEP THE BENEFICIAL PREDATORS AROUND. IF NEARLY ALL THE PESTS IN AN AREA ARE WIPED OUT BY PESTICIDES, THE PREDATORS WILL STARVE TO DEATH OR LEAVE THE AREA. THEN THE FEW PESTS WHICH HAVE ESCAPED DEATH WILL MULTIPLY UNCHECKED. THE PREDATION MANDALA SUGGESTS ANOTHER TITLE FOR THIS CHAPTER: "PEST CONSERVATION."

PREDATION MANDALA

Lots of aphids, few ladybugs...

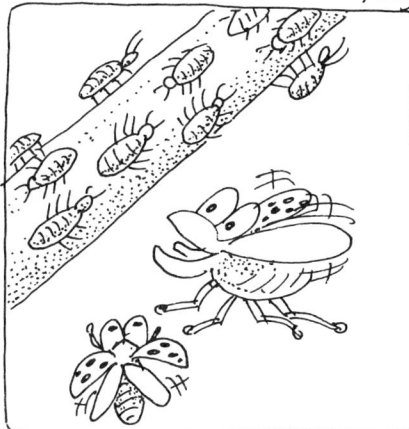

... ladybugs pig out.

Ladybugs starve or fly away...

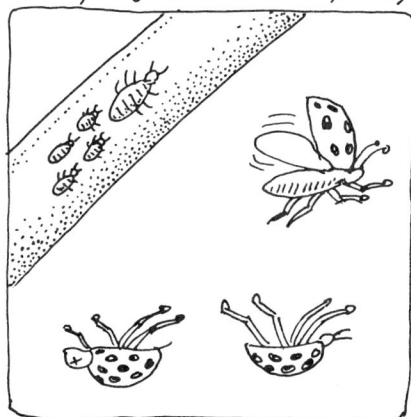

... so aphids multiply.

Fewer aphids...

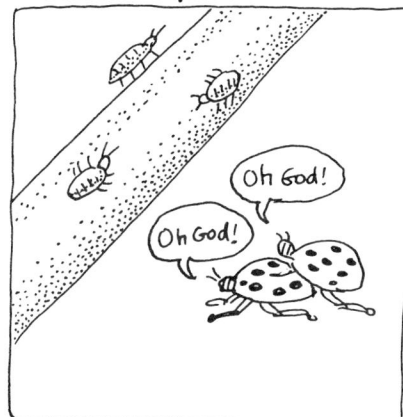

... ladybugs getting physical.

Few aphids...

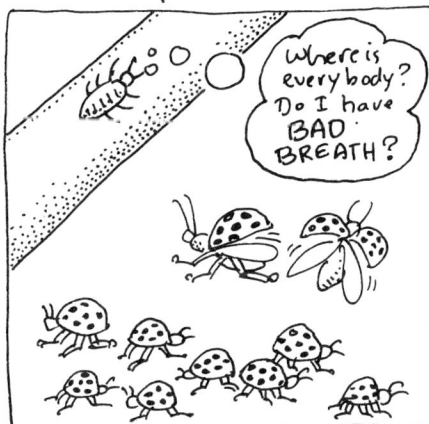

...ladybugs multiplying.

HERE'S WHAT THE MAIN PREDATORS LOOK LIKE:

THE GOOD GUYS

These insects are good all-purpose predators for your garden. They eat a large variety of pests, and many are available commercially.

LADYBUG ("12-spotted ladybird beetle")

Eats aphids and young scales, both as a larva and an adult. The larvae look like miniature gila monsters.

larva   adult

LACEWING

Eats all soft-bodied insects: aphids, mites, young scales, mealybugs.

yellow
red spots
green
larva   adult

SYRPHID FLIES

("Hover flies"/"flower flies")

Look like small bees. Often seen hovering at eye-level. The larvae eat aphids; the adults eat nectar and pollen.

1/5"
yellow or orange

PREYING MANTIS

Eats many insects, good and bad. So should be introduced only as a last resort.

aphid burger
Green

CARABID (GROUND) BEETLES

Eat army worms and cut worms (There are many species of these beetles, in various sizes. Odds are there's already some in your garden)

various

DAMSEL BUGS
(The Nabidae family)

Nabis alternatus

THESE HELPFUL INSECTS ARE BEING SLAUGHTERED BY THE UNTOLD BILLIONS BY PESTICIDES, AND **ONLY YOU** CAN HELP! XEROX THIS PAGE AND SEND IT TO YOUR SENATOR, URGING HIM OR HER TO **BAN ALL PESTICIDES.**

IN NATURAL ECOSYSTEMS, EVERY POTENTIAL PEST HAS ITS OWN SPECIAL PREDATOR TO KEEP IT FROM GETTING OUT OF HAND. IN ADDITION, THERE ARE GENERAL PREDATORS (LIKE THE PREYING MANTIS) WHO EAT A LOT OF DIFFERENT THINGS. PEST POPULATION LEVELS ARE CONSTANTLY SHIFTING, BUT THEY NEVER BECOME SO NUMEROUS THAT PLANTS ARE TOTALLY WIPED OUT:

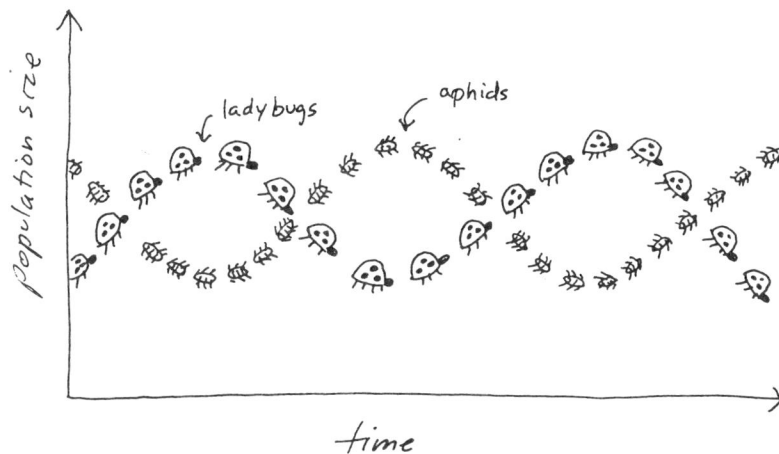

PROBLEMS WITH THIS DELICATE BALANCE ARISE WHEN A REGION HAS BEEN SO HEAVILY SPRAYED WITH PESTICIDES THAT THE NORMAL LOCAL PREDATORS HAVE BEEN WIPED OUT, LETTING THE MUTANT, PESTICIDE-RESISTANT PESTS MULTIPLY UNCHECKED. OR A PEST MAY BE INTRODUCED FROM OTHER LANDS (USUALLY BY HUMAN COMMERCE), LEAVING ITS SPECIALIST PREDATORS BEHIND. WHEN THIS HAPPENS, UNIVERSITIES MUST SEND SEARCH TEAMS TO THE COUNTRY OF ORIGIN TO FIND AND BRING BACK THE PREDATORS, WHICH ARE THEN CULTIVATED IN SPECIAL LABORATORIES, SUCH AS THE GILL TRACT IN BERKELEY, CALIFORNIA. THE APPENDIX AT THE END OF THIS CHAPTER TELLS YOU WHICH PESTS CAN BE CONTROLLED BY INTRODUCING PREDATORS TO YOUR GARDEN.

PARASITES

PARASITES ARE A TYPE OF PREDATOR WHICH LAYS ITS EGGS INSIDE THE PEST. THE EGGS HATCH, AND THE PARASITE LARVAE FEED ON THE INSIDE OF THE PEST, EVENTUALLY KILLING IT. OFTEN THERE ARE SECONDARY PARASITES, WHICH MAKE THE PARTY EVEN MERRIER:

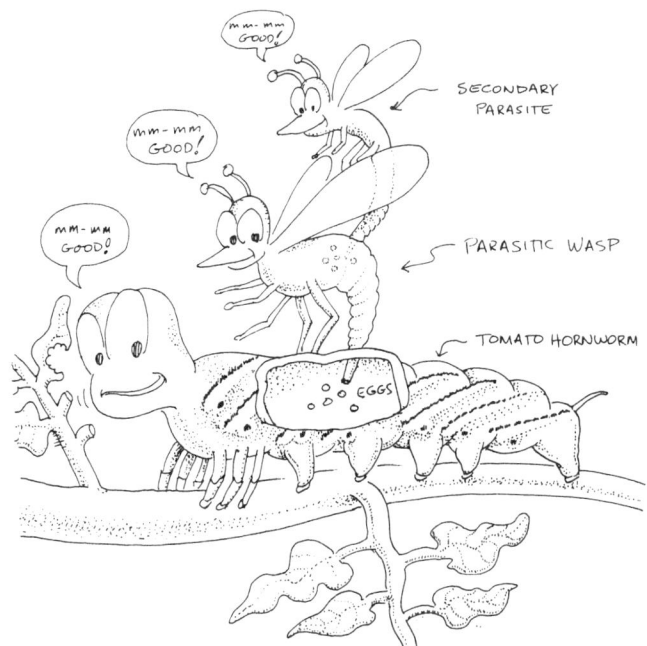

PARASITES ARE GENERALLY THE BEST PREDATORS TO USE. THEY TEND TO BE THE MOST SELECTIVE, SO YOU AREN'T WASTING YOUR TIME AND MONEY ON PREDATORS WHICH EAT THE WRONG INSECTS. PARASITES ALSO NEED LESS FOOD THAN OTHER PREDATORS, SO THEY KEEP THE PEST POPULATION AT A LOWER LEVEL, WHICH IS IMPORTANT IF YOU'RE PRODUCING FOOD FOR A MARKET WITH HIGH COSMETIC STANDARDS. (I WILL DISCUSS THESE STANDARDS LATER, IN THE SECTION ON "INTEGRATED HUMAN CONTROL.")

Attracting and Keeping Predators

YOU CAN BUY PREDATORS FROM COMMERICAL SOURCES, OR RAISE YOUR OWN, OR YOU CAN INDUCE THE LOCALS IN YOUR AREA TO HANG OUT AT YOUR PLACE. IN ANY CASE, YOU'D BETTER PROVIDE ADEQUATE MUNCHIES FOR YOUR GUESTS, OR THEY'LL LOOK FOR NEW FRIENDS WHO THROW BETTER PARTIES.

THE BEST WAY TO KEEP PREDATORS AROUND IS WITH "INSECTARY PLANTS." ALL PARASITIC WASPS AND MANY OTHER PREDATORS (SUCH AS SYRPHID FLIES) NEED NECTAR AND POLLEN AS THEIR SOLE FOOD SOURCE IN THEIR ADULT STAGE, WHICH THEY GET FROM INSECTARY PLANTS:

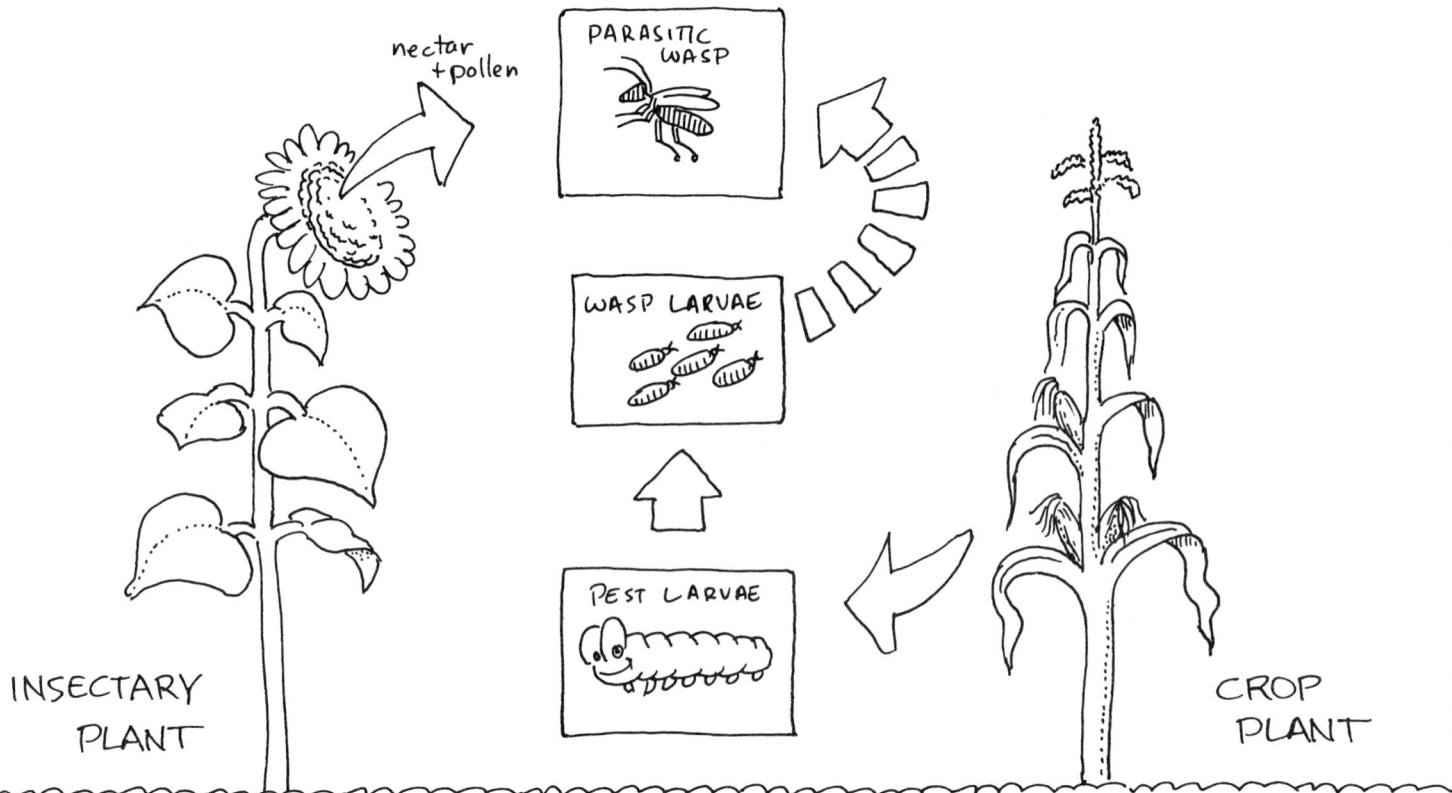

nectar + pollen

PARASITIC WASP

WASP LARVAE

PEST LARVAE

INSECTARY PLANT

CROP PLANT

INSECTARY PLANTS HAVE VERY SMALL, SHALLOW-THROATED FLOWERS, WHICH THE SMALL PARASITIC WASPS AND SYRPHID FLIES (WHO HAVE SHORT TONGUES) CAN SUCK THE NECTAR FROM EASILY. SHALLOW-THROATED FLOWERS ARE FOUND MAINLY IN THE UMBELLIFERAE AND COMPOSITAE FAMILIES:

INSECTARY PLANTS

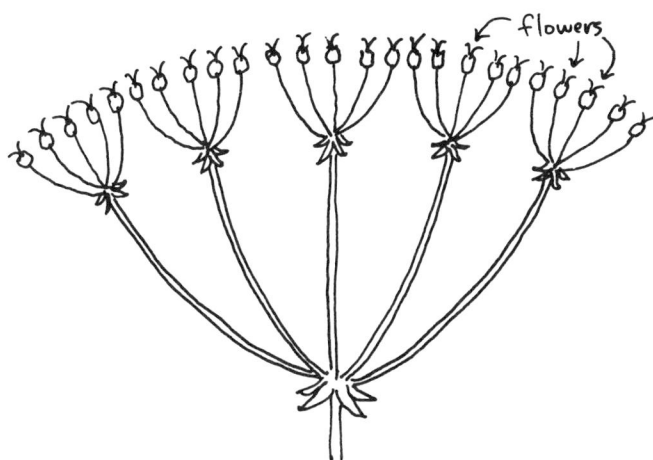

TYPICAL UMBELLIFERAE FLOWER HEAD
NOTICE THE UMBRELLA SHAPE OF THE FLOWER-HEAD. ANYTHING THAT LOOKS LIKE THIS IS A MEMBER OF THE UMBELLIFERAE FAMILY, WHICH INCLUDES FENNEL, DILL, ANISE, CARROT, CELARY, PARSELY, PARSNIP, CARAWAY, CUMIN, CORIANDER, CHERVIL, SWEET CICELY, QUEEN ANNE'S LACE, MYRRH.

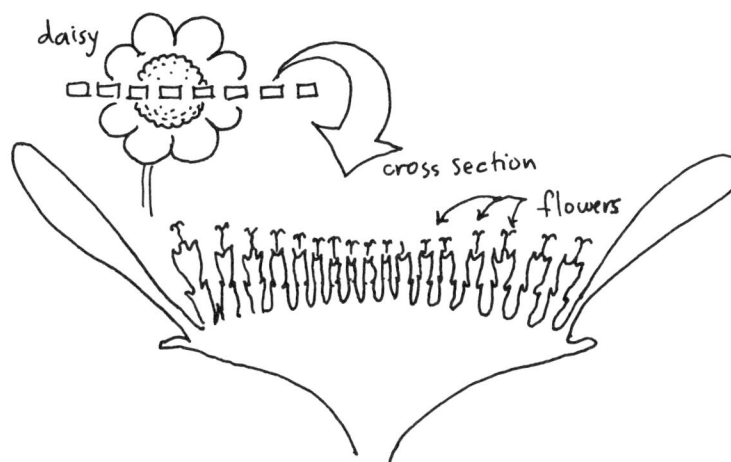

TYPICAL COMPOSITAE FLOWER HEAD
NOTICE THAT THE "FLOWER" IS ACTUALLY MANY LITTLE FLOWERS CLUSTERED IN THE CENTER OF THE LARGER MEGA-FLOWER. ANYTHING WITH FLOWERS LIKE THIS IS A MEMBER OF THE COMPOSITAE FAMILY, WHICH INCLUDES LETTUCE, DAISY, SUNFLOWER, ASTER, GOLDENROD, ARTICHOKE, MARIGOLD, FEVERFEW, CHRYSANTHEMUM, YARROW.

GERM WARFARE

YOU CAN ALSO USE BACTERIA AS A SORT OF PREDATOR ON YOUR PESTS. BACILLUS THURINGENSIS ("B.T.") IS A TYPE OF BACTERIA SOLD COMMERCIALLY AS "DIPEL" OR "THURICIDE." IT'S MAINLY EFFECTIVE AGAINST THE LARVAE OF LEPIDOPTEROUS INSECTS (MOTHS AND BUTTERFLIES), INCLUDING CODLING MOTH (AN APPLE PEST) AND CABBAGE MOTH. THE LEAVES OF THE PLANT ARE SPRAYED WITH BACTERIA; THE PEST LARVAE EAT

THE LEAVES, BECOME DISEASED, AND DIE. ALTHOUGH THE BACTERIA THEMSELVES ARE HARMLESS TO OTHER ANIMALS, THE COMMERICAL PRODUCTS OFTEN CONTAIN A LARGE NUMBER OF SYNTHETIC CHEMICALS AS "BINDING AGENTS" WHICH GLUE THE BACTERIA TO THE LEAVES. THESE GLUES AREN'T REALLY NECESSARY--YOU'D JUST HAVE TO SPRAY MORE OFTEN WITHOUT THEM. SO READ THE LABEL, AND STAY AWAY FROM SYNTHETICS.

Traps

TRAPS INCLUDE TRAP PLANTS AND PHEROMONE TRAPS. TRAP PLANTS ARE NON-CROP PLANTS WHICH THE PEST PREFERS TO THE CROP PLANT. FOR EXAMPLE, WILD MUSTARD (BRASSICA NIGRA) IS COMMONLY USED AS A TRAP PLANT FOR THE CABBAGE MOTH IN CALIFORNIA. WILD MUSTARD IS THE WILD ANCESTOR OF CABBAGE-FAMILY CROPS, AND THE CABBAGE MOTH IS ATTRACTED TO THE BITTER CHEMICALS IN THE WILD PLANT THAT HAVE BEEN BRED OUT OF THE CULTIVATED VARIETIES. AFTER THE MOTHS HAVE LAID THEIR EGGS ON THE TRAP PLANTS, THEY ARE SPRAYED WITH B.T., BURNED, OR OTHERWISE DISPATCHED. (ONE PROBLEM IN THIS CASE IS THAT WILD MUSTARD HYBRIDIZES READILY WITH CABBAGE-FAMILY CROPS, SO YOU WOULDN'T BE ABLE TO SAVE THE SEEDS.)

Pheromone Traps

PHEROMONE TRAPS ARE LIKE MODERN ADVERTIZING--THEY USE SEXUAL ATTRACTION AS A MEANS OF ALTERING BEHAVIOR. BASICALLY, YOU PUT A FEW VIRGIN FEMALE PESTS IN A SMALL CAGE, SURROUNDED BY A LARGER CAGE WITH A FUNNEL-SHAPED OPENING:

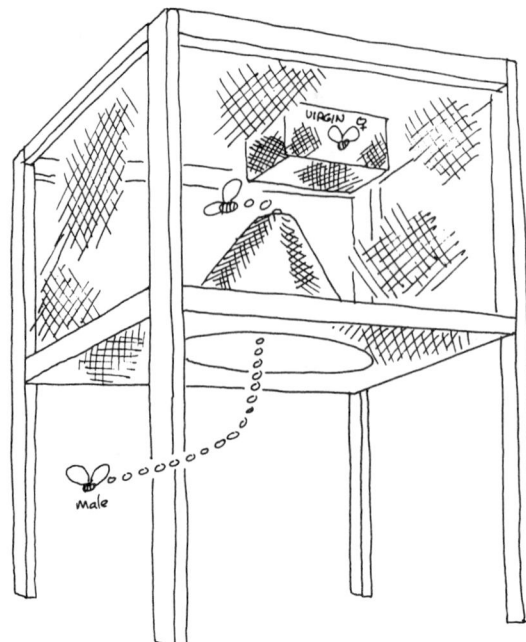

PHEROMONES ARE INTER-SEXUAL COMMUNICATION DEVICES, LIKE THE "PERSONALS" SECTION OF THE CLASSIFIED ADS. IN THE TRAP, THE VIRGIN FEMALES SEND OUT A CHEMICAL WHICH SAYS, "I'M 21, ENJOY JOGGING, SCUBA DIVING, AND CLASSICAL MUSIC, LOOKING FOR AN UPWARDLY-MOBILE MALE MOTH WITH SIMILAR INTERESTS." THE MALES CAN PICK UP THIS CHEMICAL A LONG DISTANCE AWAY—UP TO A MILE IN SOME SPECIES. THEY CAN EASILY ENTER THE TRAP THROUGH THE LARGE FUNNEL OPENING, BUT THEY CAN'T AS EASILY FIND THEIR WAY BACK OUT THROUGH THE SMALLER OPENING. BESIDES, MOST INSECTS HAVE A BUILT-IN BEHAVIOR CIRCUIT WHICH SAYS "WHEN IN DOUBT, FLY UPWARDS," SO THEY ARE DOUBLY UNLIKELY TO FIND THEIR WAY OUT THE BOTTOM OF THE TRAP. IT'S POSSIBLE TO BUILD YOUR OWN TRAPS, FOLLOWING THESE DESIGN PRINCIPLES. IDENTIFYING AND FINDING VIRGIN FEMALES IS A BIT HARDER, SINCE IT INVOLVES RESEARCHING THE SCIENTIFIC LITERATURE.

PHEROMONE TRAPS SHOULD ONLY BE USED IF THE PEST IS RELATIVELY NON-MOBILE, LIKE THE CODLING MOTH. OTHERWISE, THE TRAP MAY ATTRACT MALES FROM OTHER AREAS, RESULTING IN A WORSE INFESTATION THAN BEFORE. ALSO, THE TRAPS CURRENTLY IN USE ARE NOT AS EFFECTIVE AS OTHER TYPES OF CONTROL. ALTHOUGH THEY ARE FINE FOR HOME GARDEN USE, THEY WOULDN'T BE SO GOOD IF YOU'RE GROWING FOOD FOR COMMERCIAL MARKETS, WITH THEIR HIGH COSMETIC STANDARDS. AND THAT BRINGS US TO:

INTEGRATED HUMAN CONTROL

THE MOST DIFFICULT PEST CONTROL PROBLEM IS A HUMAN PROBLEM: SINCE PESTICIDES HAVE (TEMPORARILY) WIPED OUT CERTAIN SPECIES OF INSECTS, WE HAVE GROWN TO EXPECT SPOTLESS, UNBLEMISHED, PLAYBOY-CENTERFOLD FOOD. PESTICIDES HAVE CAUSED US TO DE-EVOLVE CULTURALLY INTO A SQUEAMISH SPECIES. IN MANY CASES THE ONLY DAMAGE DONE BY A PEST IS COSMETIC, BUT SINCE THE MARKETING STANDARDS OF MOST RETAIL STORES WON'T ALLOW ANY EVIDENCE THAT OUR PLANET IS CO-INHABITED BY INVERTEBRATES, MUCH PERFECTLY GOOD FOOD GOES TO WASTE, OR MUST BE SOLD AT A LOSS TO MAKE JUICE OR OTHER PROCESSED FOODS.

FOR EXAMPLE, THE CODLING MOTH IS A COMMON PEST OF APPLES. YET EVEN WITH NO CONTROLS AT ALL, THE DAMAGE THEY DO IS ALMOST TOTALLY COSMETIC. THERE IS USUALLY ONLY ONE LARVA PER FRUIT, AND IT EATS ONLY PART OF THE CORE, WHICH PEOPLE THROW AWAY ANYWAY. SO THE MAIN PROBLEM IS THE MERE SIGHT OF A WORM HOLE IN AN APPLE.

ANOTHER EXAMPLE IS THE CORN EARWORM, WHICH RARELY GETS FURTHER THAN THE FIRST HALF-INCH OF KERNELS, AND YET EARS WITH A WORM IN THEM CAN'T BE SOLD IN MOST STORES, DUE TO CONSUMER REJECTION.

WHO'S TO BLAME? WELL, NOBODY, OR EVERYBODY, OR MAYBE OUR ECONOMIC

SYSTEM, WHICH HAS ALLOWED PESTICIDE USE AND CONSUMER EXPECTATIONS TO MUTUALLY-REINFORCE EACH OTHER IN AN UPWARDLY-SPIRALLING CYCLE OF COSMETIC SPRAYING:

THE COSMETIC SPIRAL

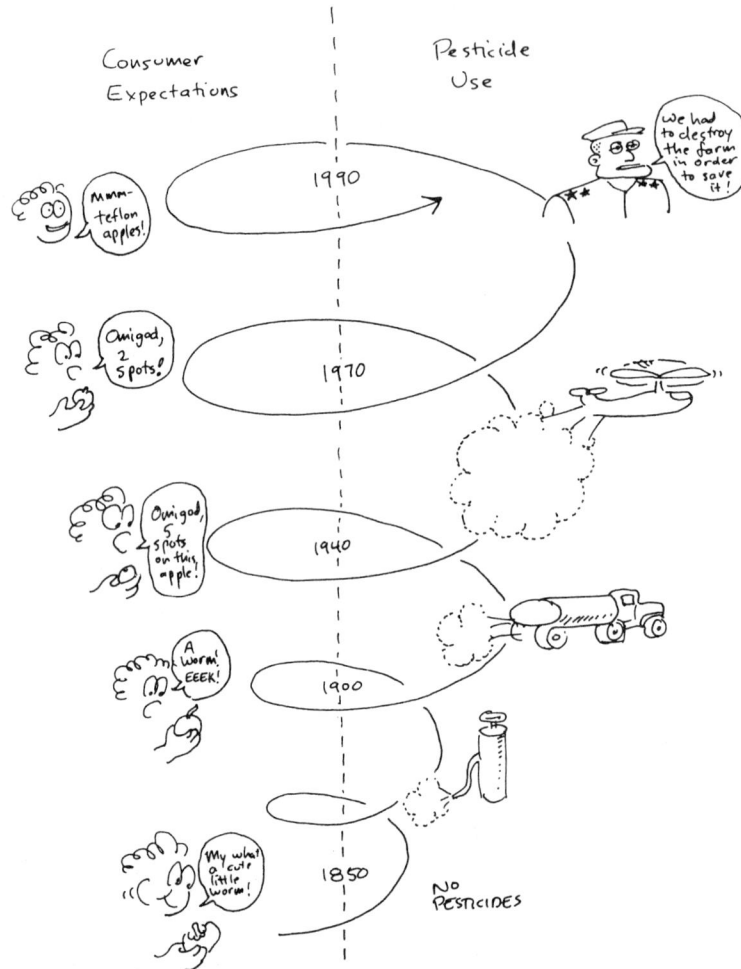

ENTOMOPHOBIA: ALIENS IN OUR MIDST

WHY ALL THIS FUSS OVER THE LOWLY INSECT? WHAT IS IT ABOUT HUMAN PSYCHOLOGY THAT REACTS SO VIOLENTLY TO EVEN HARMLESS INVERTEBRATES? THE ANSWER IS "ENTOMOPHOBIA," THE ILLOGICAL ADVERSION MANY OF US HAVE TOWARD CREEPY-CRAWLERS. INSECTS ARE DEFINITELY **WEIRD**, THERE'S NO TWO WAYS AROUND IT.

THEY ARE FUNDAMENTALLY DIFFERENT FROM ANY OTHER TYPE OF ANIMAL: THEY ARE EVEN LESS LIKE US DEVELOPMENTALLY THAN MUCH MORE PRIMITIVE CRITTERS LIKE SEA URCHINS AND JELLYFISH! THEY HAVE A SUBSTANCE IN THEIR OUTER SHELLS CALLED "CHITIN" WHICH IS FOUND NOWHERE ELSE ON EARTH EXCEPT IN MUSHROOMS, WHICH MAKES INSECTS SORT OF LIKE FLYING FUNGI. THEY OFTEN HAVE SOCIAL ORGANIZATIONS WHICH ARE ESSENTIALLY COMMUNISTIC, MAKING THEM ESPECIALLY REPUGNANT TO WESTERN CULTURES UNDER THE INFLUENCE OF THE RED SCARE. NO WONDER MANY OF OUR SCIENCE FICTION ALIENS LOOK STRONGLY INSECTOID:

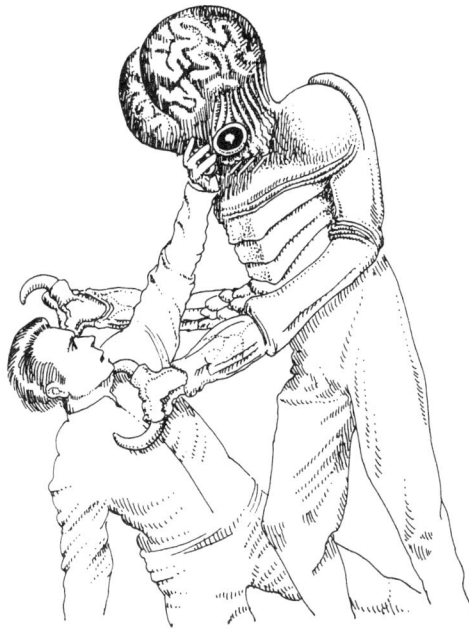

THE EGO PROBLEM

LET'S FACE IT—-BIOLOGICAL PEST CONTROL IS SUBTLE, INDIRECT, EVEN HUMBLING; A PARTNERSHIP WITH NATURE, RATHER THAN ATTEMPTED DOMINATION. ON THE OTHER SIDE, PESTICIDES ARE MACHO: "TAKE DIRECT ACTION, KILL THEM LITTLE GOOKS, NO FOOLIN' AROUND WITH NONE A' THEM "FAIRY-MOAN" TRAPS, NO SIRREE, US FARMERS IS REAL MEN, AND REAL MEN DON'T HAVE TIME FOR NO MONKEY SHINES." EVEN NATURAL PREDATORS ARE OUT, BECAUSE THEY STEAL THE GLORY: THEY DO THE KILLING, WHILE WE WATCH FROM THE SIDELINES.

CLEARLY THIS ATTITUDE HAS GOT TO GO, IF THE PLANET IS GOING TO SURVIVE. EACH OF US MUST DISMANTLE OUR EGOS, WHICH IS QUICK, EASY, AND RECOMMENDED BY NINE OUT OF TEN RELIGIONS AS THE KEY TO INNER PEACE. ALL YOU HAVE TO DO IS RECOGNIZE THAT YOU ARE NO MORE (AND NO LESS) THAN A PART OF THE EARTH, THE ONE-BIG-HAPPY-FAMILY OF PLANTS AND ANIMALS.

FINAL ADVICE: LOVING PESTS

TO DEAL WITH PESTS EFFECTIVELY YOU MUST HAVE EMPATHY FOR THEM. YOU MUST IDENTIFY WITH THEM, BY PUTTING YOURSELF IN THEIR SHOES. JUST AS THE MOST EFFECTIVE DETECTIVES ARE FORMER CRIMINALS, TO CONTROL INSECTS YOU MUST UNDERSTAND WHAT THE PEST WANTS, AND HOW IT IS MOST LIKELY TO GO ABOUT GETTING IT. ONCE YOU KNOW THEM THAT WELL, YOU CAN INTERSECT THEIR WORLD-LINE WHEN THEY ARE MOST VULNERABLE, AND BLOCK THEIR EFFORTS.

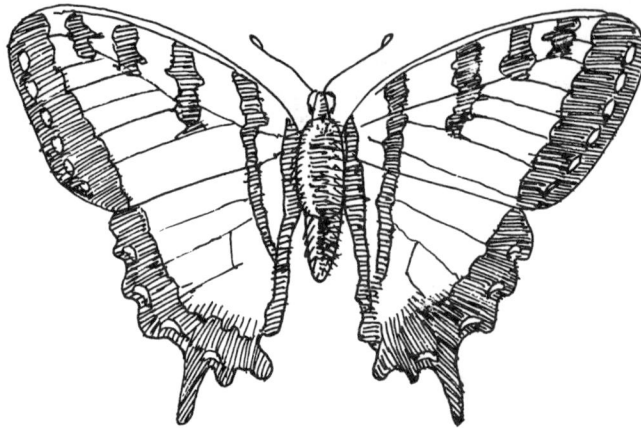

GETTING DOWN TO CASES

IF YOU'VE FOLLOWED ALL THE GENERAL GUIDELINES AND YOUR PLANTS ARE STILL ABOUT TO BITE THE DUST, YOU HAVE TO TAKE SPECIAL MEASURES.

FIRST, IDENTIFY THE PEST:

MAKE SURE YOU HAVE THE RIGHT SUSPECT. SOMETIMES IDENTIFICATION IS DIFFICULT, BECAUSE OFTEN THE MOST VISIBLE INSECTS NEAR THE DAMAGE MAY BE JUST HANGING OUT THERE, OR POSSIBLY EATING THE FUNGI INFECTING THE PLANT WOUNDS CAUSED BY THE ACTUAL PEST. IN OTHER WORDS, THEY'VE BEEN "FRAMED." IT'S BEST TO CATCH PESTS IN THE ACT, AND TREAT ALL OTHERS AS INNOCENT UNTIL PROVEN GUILTY. MANY PESTS FEED AT NIGHT, SO YOUR INVESTIGATIONS SHOULD INCLUDE FLASHLIGHT PATROLS AFTER DARK.

IF THE PRIME SUSPECT IS FLYING AROUND TOO FAST FOR YOU TO IDENTIFY IT, YOU MAY HAVE TO USE A BUG-CATCHER, WHICH YOU CAN MAKE WITH A BROOM HANDLE, A COAT HANGER, AND A PIECE OF MOSQUITO NETTING. PUT THE INSECT IN A JAR WITH THE LID SHUT TIGHT, UNTIL IT ASPHYXIATES.

THEN TURN THE PAGE AND LOOK UP WHAT TO DO IN THE FOLLOWING CHARTS.

PEST	What To Do
 Caterpillars (Larvae of moths + butterflies), such as Codling moth, cabbage worm, tomato hornworm, etc.	(1.) Hand-pick. (2) Spray with <u>Bacillus</u> <u>thuringensis</u> (Dipel, Thuricide, Biotrol) (3.) See individual pest for proper predator (usually a parasite), and other methods.
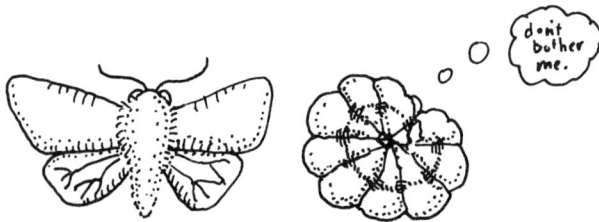 *don't bother me.* Cutworms (larvae of small brown moth. Larvae rolls up when disturbed. Often found in soil, where they pupate to become moths.) Moths lay eggs on grass blades.	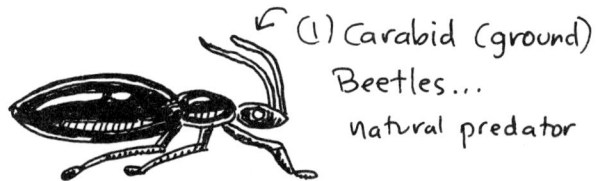 (1) Carabid (ground) Beetles... natural predator (2.) Trap moths with lights at night. (3) Clear all grassy weeds from garden. (4). Spray with B.t. (5) Tachinid Flies (parasites)
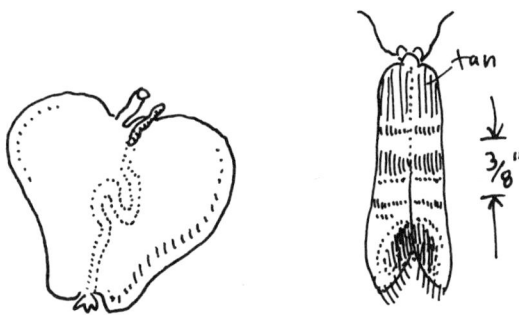 tan ↓ 3/8" ↑ Codling moth larvae ("worms" in apples)	(1) Plant bell beans under trees, and wildflowers to attract parasites. (trichogamma wasp parasitizes eggs; <u>Calliephiates</u> <u>messor</u> parasitizes cocoons.) (2) Grow <u>early</u> apple varieties: Jonathan, McIntosh. (3) Pheromone traps. (4) Spray mineral oil or rotenone to smother eggs. (5) Spray B.t.

PEST	What To Do
Cabbage Moth (<u>Pieris</u> <u>rapae</u>)	(1) The moth is attracted to host plants by odor. So interplant with onion, garlic, herbs.
← Adult - actual size. Moth lays eggs on leaves of cabbage-family plants. Eggs hatch, and larvae eat leaves.	(2) Hand-pick.
→ wings white with black markings	(3) Parasites: The wasp <u>Apanteles</u> <u>rubercula</u>; the Ichneumon fly; <u>Pteromalus</u> <u>puparum</u>.
← Larva - actual size. It's the same color as the leaves it eats — pretty tricky. Look for eggs on undersides of leaves. (light green)	(4) Corn meal dusted on leaves causes worms to leave (Essig, 1913)
	(5) A bug (<u>Phymata</u> <u>wolfii</u>) preys on moth.
	(6) Trap plants — wild mustard (B. nigra)
	(7) Spray B.t.

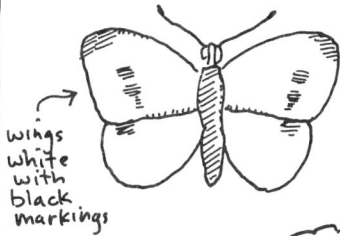

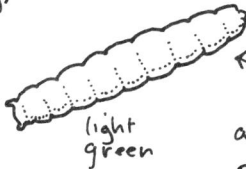

Snails and **Slugs**

(1) Don't Panic!

(2) Hand-pick (at night).

(3) Nasturtiums as trap plants (at edge of garden).

(4) Borders of dolomite lime around beds.

(5). Predator beetle, <u>Ocypus</u> <u>olens</u>.

(6) Grow susceptible seedlings on a table, transplant to garden.

(7). As a last resort, use bait (non-arsenic) (still, that pollutes the city dump.)

Spotted Cucumber Beetle

<u>Diabrotica</u> <u>Undecimpunctata</u>

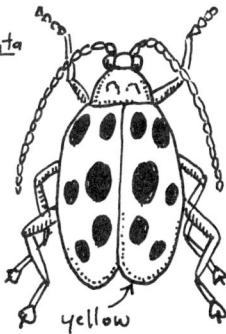

(Also called "Southern corn rootworm") Feeds on the roots, stems, leaves, and flowers of many veggies and fruit trees.

I ¼"

yellow

(1) Trap plants - have lots of yellow flowers in the garden — they're attracted to the color yellow.

(2) Preyed on by a tachinid fly (<u>Celatoria</u> <u>diabrotica</u>)

(4) Plant affected crops (esp. corn) as late as possible.

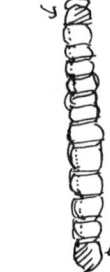

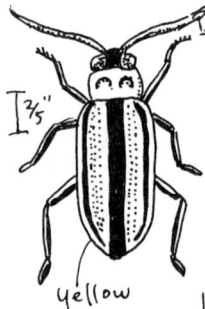

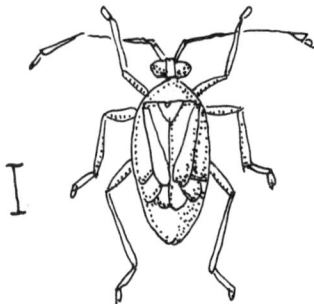

PEST	What To Do
Root Maggots _Hylemia_ genus (illustration: adult fly labeled "green", larva labeled "white") Cabbage Root Maggot _Hylemia brassicae_ Adult fly lays eggs at base of plant, Mid-April to mid-May	(1) Pile up lots of strong-smelling mulch materials (herb leaves, etc.) around plants. (Fly locates plants by smell.) Wood ashes also good to use. (Jeavons) (2) Paper collars around plant stems, so fly can't lay eggs in soil under plant. (3) Raise seedlings in cold frame, or under protective screen cones in the field. (4) Rove (staphylinid) and Ground (Carabid) beetles are natural predators. (5) Cabbage maggot deterred by garlic?
Striped Cucumber Beetle _Diabrotica vittata_ (illustration: larva labeled "brown"/"brown", beetle labeled "yellow", I ¾") Feeds on squashes, cukes, melons, peas, apples. Adult hibernates under surface mulch, emerges mid-May, lays eggs in soil around host plants.... Larvae hatch early June, feed on roots and lower stems. Adults feed on leaves.	(1) Small net coverings in field (or cheesecloth.) (2) Start plants early under glass. (not recommended for squash family) (3) Plant extra seed if sown directly in field, so beetle can have its share (Essig, 1913) (4) Plant seed directly in field, but put cloches (gallon jugs with the bottom cut off) over each seedling as it comes up. (5.) Clear away mulch in winter (6) Various soldier beetles are predators.
Lygus Bug (illustration: bug, I) Pest on strawberries; also pear, apple, other fruit trees. Pale-green to grayish-brown, with yellow, black, and red markings. Adults hibernate in surface mulch, and in crown of plants.	(1) Nicotine Spray (not recommended) (2) Predators: Big-eyed bugs, damsel bugs, assassin bugs, crab spiders. (3) Alfalfa is a trap plant... plant it a month earlier than the affected crop. (4) Clear away mulch in winter.

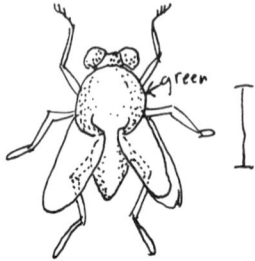

PEST	What To Do
Mites 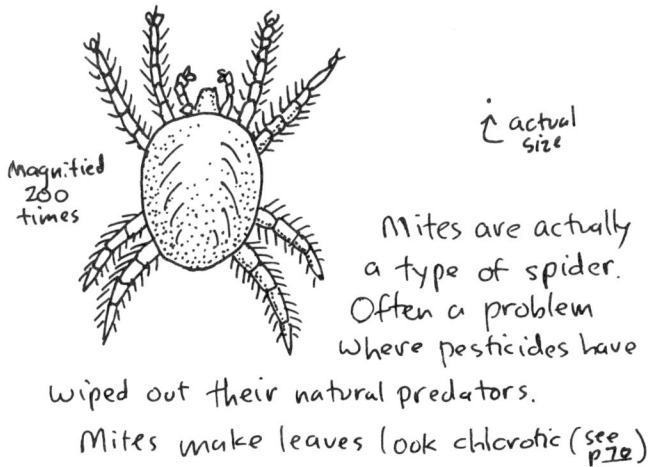 `actual size` Magnified 200 times Mites are actually a type of spider. Often a problem where pesticides have wiped out their natural predators. Mites make leaves look chlorotic (see p 70)	Many insects eat mites, so they're usually only a problem indoors or in greenhouses, where predators are excluded, or outdoors if pesticides have been used. ① Indoors, keep windows open during the day, so predators can come in. ② Increase ventilation — strong air currents disturb mites. ③ Predatory mites — e.g. <u>Metaseiulus occidentalis</u> — release before leaves are chlorotic (indicating mite damage.) ④ Lacewings.
Whiteflies (<u>Trialeurodes vaporariorum</u>) 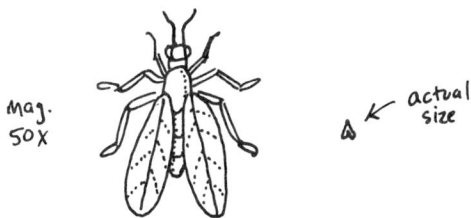 Mag. 50x actual size Common in greenhouses if windows kept closed.	Nearly everything eats whiteflies — especially ladybugs. Common in greenhouses when pesticides are used, and doors kept closed. So, ① Don't use pesticides. ② Open doors. Parasite: <u>Encarsia formosa</u>, but that shouldn't be necessary.
Tomato Hornworm (Protoparce sexta) 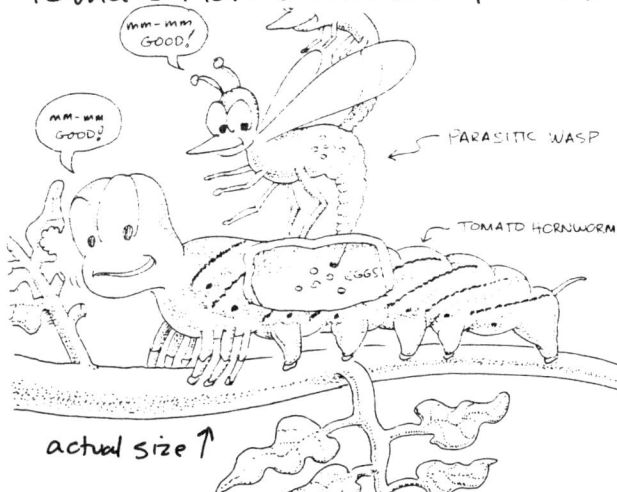 mm-mm GOOD! mm-mm GOOD! PARASITIC WASP TOMATO HORNWORM EGGS actual size ↑	① Don't panic — these dudes look worse than they are. ② Hand-pick... there's usually just a few of them. ③ Parasites: Braconid + Trichogramma wasps.

PEST	What To Do
Cottony-cushion Scale (Icerya purchasi)	... They were only able to stop it with the Vedalia (Rodalia cardinalis) ~ a type of ladybug. (From Australia, 1880's)

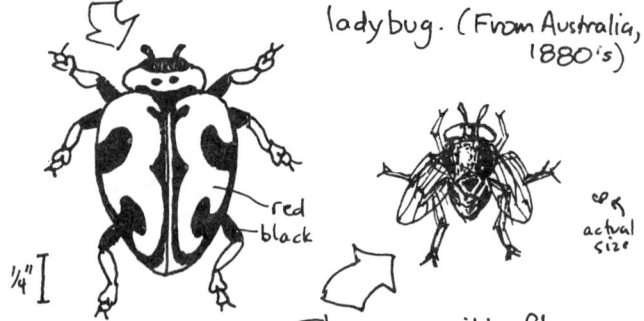

Cottony-cushion Scale (Icerya purchasi)

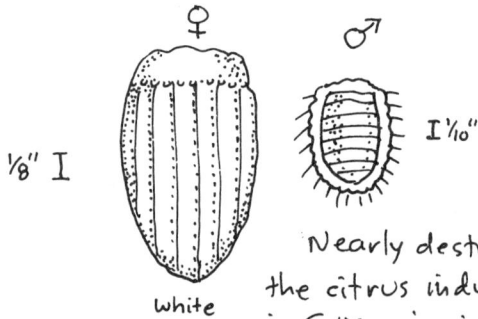

♀ ♂

⅛" I   I 1/10"

white

Nearly destroyed
the citrus industry
in California in the 1800's

Introduced at Menlo Park, Ca. in 1869,
from Australia.

... They were only able to stop it with the
Vedalia (Rodalia cardinalis) ~ a type of
ladybug. (From Australia,
1880's)

red
black

¼" I

actual
size

This parasitic fly
(Cryptochaetum icerae) is
also effective.

Mealybugs (Planococcus spp.)

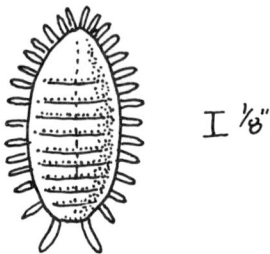

I ⅛"

Planococcus citri (Citrus
mealybug)

Another early success for biological control:
A ladybug from Australia, Cryptolaemus
montrouzieri.

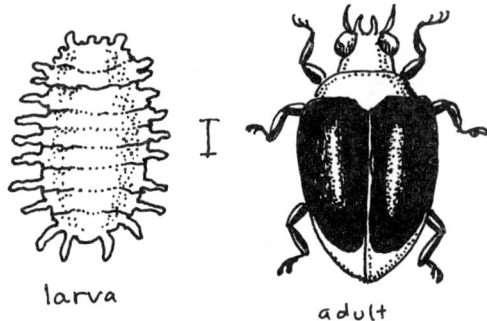

larva   I   adult

Black Scale (Scissetia Oleae)

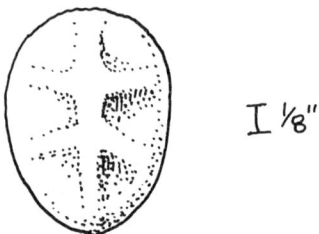

I ⅛"

A pest on citrus trees in
Coastal Southern California.

Metaphycus helvolus, a parasite

PEST

WHAT TO DO

California Red Scale

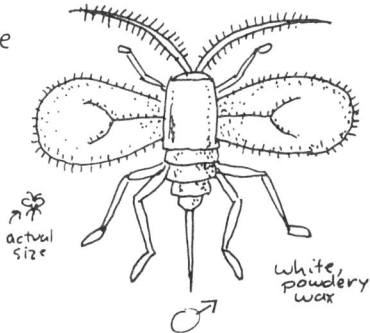

← actual size

← actual size

white, powdery wax

♀   ♂

The most important citrus pest in the world. Found in Southern California's citrus belts. Introduced from Australia around 1870. Aonidiella aurantii.

(1) Spray with dormant oil in spring.
(2) Chalcid wasps are parasites... various species, including Aphytis lingnanensis, A. melinus, Prospaltella perniciosi.

← orange

← scales

Mildew

SAMMY SPORE SEZ:

Wheeeeeeee

ptui!

sporangia

leaf surface

suck!   suck!   suck!   suck!

A fungus which looks like a coat of white spray paint on the leaves. Screws up light reception & photosynthesis. Common on squash- family plants, especially in late summer, or in summer-fog areas.

Avoid overhead watering, since the fungus spores need drops of water on the leaves to germinate.
Make sure squash-family plants are getting enough sun.

← Actual size

Nematodes.

Tiny soil critters causing root knots.

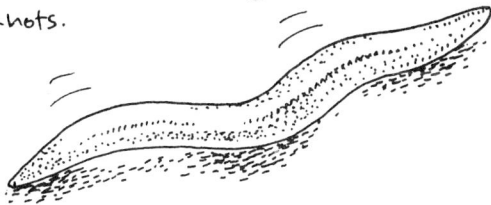

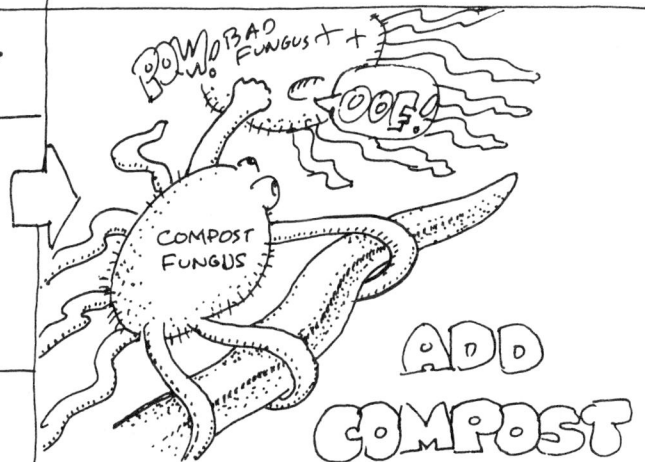

POW! NO! BAD FUNGUS! !

OOF!

COMPOST FUNGUS

ADD COMPOST

Verticillium & Fusarium Wilts

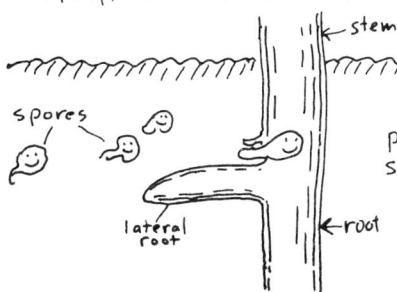

← stem

spores

lateral root

← root

A common fungal problem with tomatoes. Spores hang out in the soil, enter roots and plug up water channels, so the leaves wilt.

Your soil doesn't have enough compost in it. Compost contains beneficial fungi that feed on nematodes, and out-compete bad fungi (such as Verticillium + Fusarium) for nutrients.
Marigolds also deter nematodes.

PEST	What To Do

San Jose Scale (<u>Quadraspidiotus</u> <u>Perniciosus</u>)

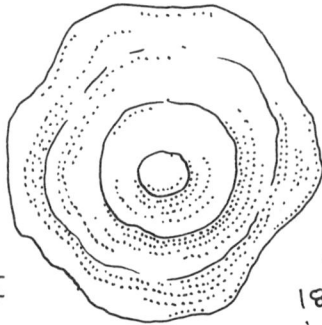

Found on deciduous fruit trees like apple, pear, plum, cherry, peach, pecan.

    Came from China to California around 1870, threatened to ruin the fruit industry. Still troublesome.

I

SIDE VIEW insect shell

leaf surface

---

(1) Ladybugs (Huffaker)
(2) Spray with dormant oil emulsion in early Spring before blossoms open.
        (Carr)

Leafhopper

Blue or green

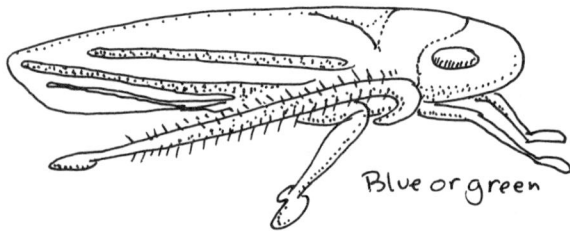

Can transmit viral diseases to plants. There is a different species for each type of plant, although some species are generalists.

    Usually not numerous enough to cause a problem. If your plants are getting viral diseases, then:
  (1) Spray plant with a forceful jet of water.
  (2) Dust with diatomaceous earth.
  (3) Cover plants with netting in early summer.

Pear psylla, <u>Psylla</u> <u>pyricola</u>

Does damage by: (1) secreting honeydew, which feeds a sooty black fungus on the leaf surface; (2) transmitting viruses to the plant, causing Pear Leaf Curl and Pear Decline.

1/10 I

nymph- black, white, pink.

adult- brown

Introduced from Europe ~ 1832

---

(1) Chalcid wasp~ <u>Trechnites</u> <u>insidiosus</u>)
(2) Spray with dormant oil in Spring }Carr
(3) If established, dust with limestone.)
(4) Predator~ <u>Anthocaris</u> <u>antevolens</u>
    — native to Coastal California
("Natural predators are only able to reduce psylla below economic injury level in trees not susceptible to virus diseases." — Huffaker)

Cabbage White Butterfly
Pieris brassicae

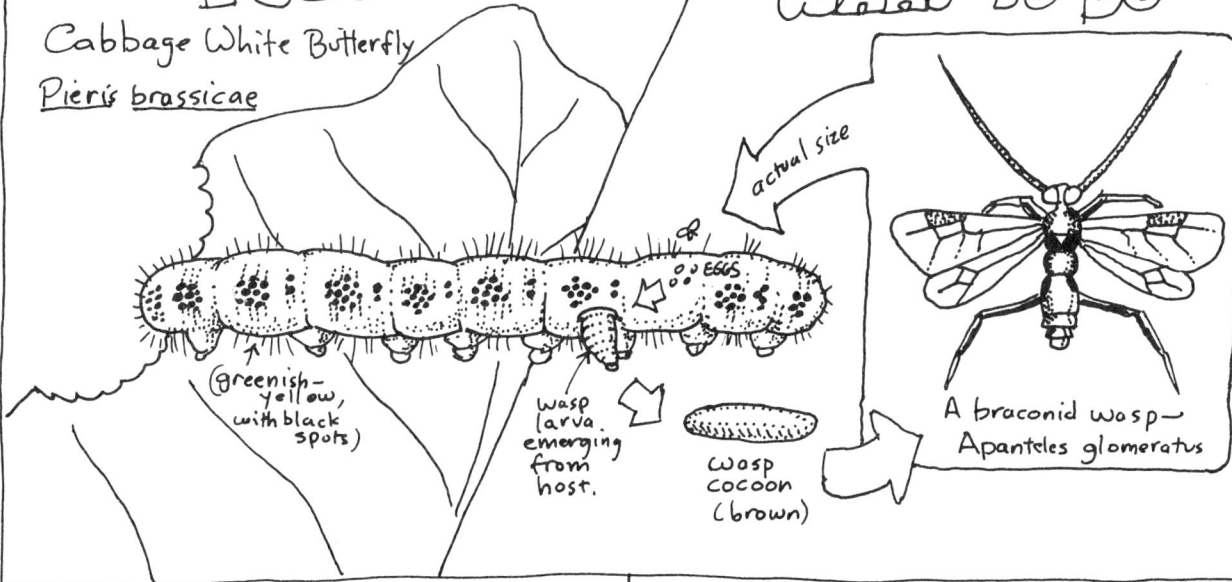

actual size

(greenish-yellow, with black spots)

EGGS

wasp larva emerging from host.

wasp cocoon (brown)

A braconid wasp— Apanteles glomeratus

Gophers

Mmm— Thanks for the celery!

Gophers are just trying to make a living, and they have the humblest possible profession: crawling around in the soil, grubbing for roots and rooting for grubs.

(1) Macabee traps:

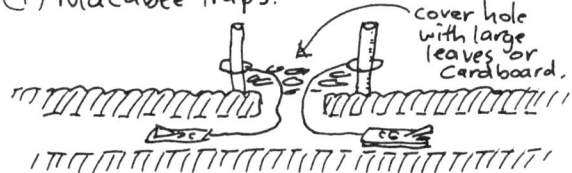

cover hole with large leaves or cardboard.

You need 2 traps per hole. Tie the traps to stakes so the gophers don't drag them away. Bait with banana peels.

(2) Male urine in their holes pisses them off.

(3) Repellent plants: "Gopher plant" (Euphorbia latyrus); Squill (scilla bulbs)

(4) Windmills vibrate the ground - this is said to disturb gophers.

(5) Put especially vulnerable plants (celery, parsley, etc.) in pots.

Asparagus Beetle

crioceris asparagi

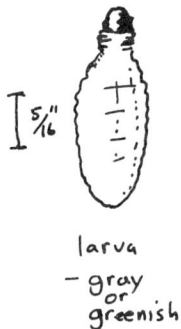

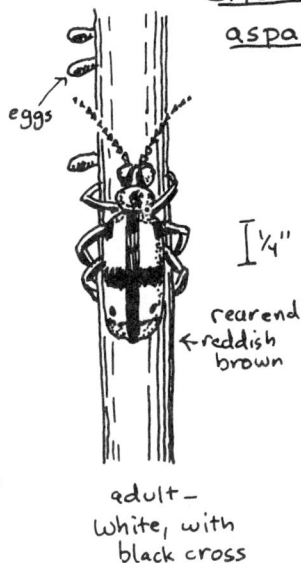

eggs

5/16"

1/4"

rearend ←reddish brown

larva – gray or greenish

adult— white, with black cross

(1) Ladybug larvae.

(2) Chalcid wasps.

(3) Clear off mulch in the winter (the adult overwinters in plant debris)

(4) Rotenone for severe infestations.

PEST	WHAT TO DO

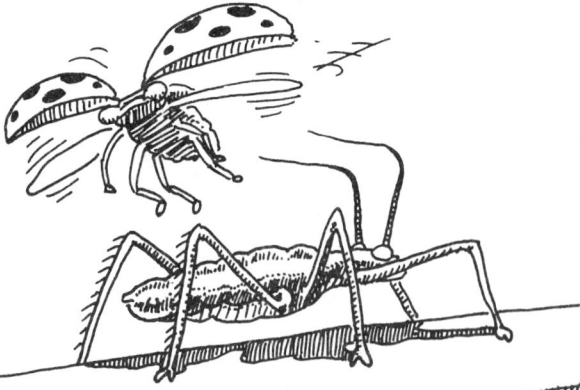

Aphids

Usually not numerous enough to be a problem, unless natural predators have been wiped out in your area.
  Predators: (1) Ladybugs
  (2) Lacewings (5 larva per plant, in JUNE, 5 more in July) (Huffaker '76)
  (3) Gall midge larvae.
  (4) Syrphid fly larvae.
 Aphids are attracted to the color yellow... keep this color away from affected plants.
  Daisies can be used as trap plants.
  Interplant catnip and tansy (Lockeritz).
  Discourage ants. (see below)
 Parasite: Aphidius metricariae — good for greenhouse aphid control.

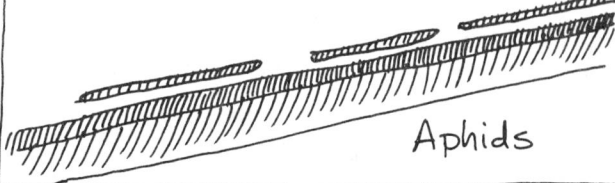

Ants

honeydew

MOO-OOO!

slurp!

head 'em up

move 'em out

Do nothing, unless you have a severe aphid problem. Ants and aphids are like ranchers and cows... ants transport aphids from plant to plant, and aphids produce "honeydew" for ants to eat. In return, ants protect aphids from predators.
  Pyrethrum or "Stickem" can be used to keep ants off aphid-infested plants.

Corn Ear-worm

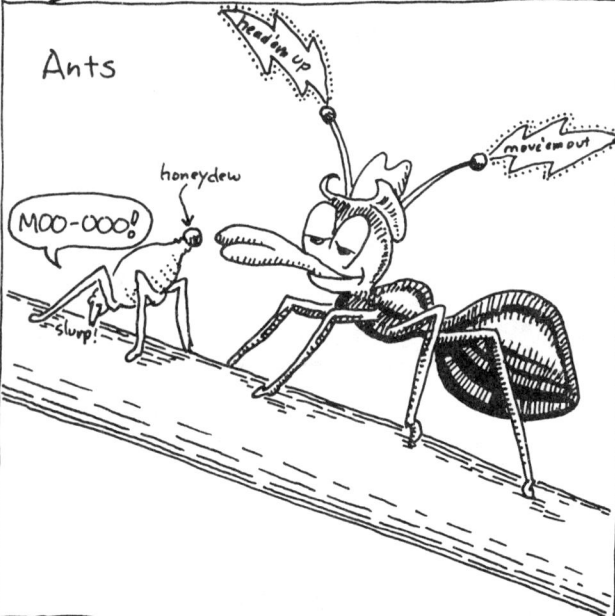

pupa

A big problem in large-scale monocultures, but easily managed in gardens and small farms. You must time your harvest so the worms have only eaten a few of the kernels (see illustration). Then the tip of the cob can be cut off, and the worms added to the compost.
  In large scale situations, or if you are growing corn to sell, you can spray with B.t., and/or introduce Tachinid flies.

INNOCENT BYSTANDERS

Most garden critters are neither good nor bad. They just hang out in the garden, munching on decaying matter or weeds, and minding their own business. They're fun to watch, and have metaphysical discussions with.

Sowbugs (Pillbugs)
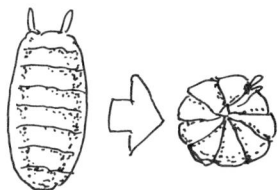
Actually not insects but crustaceans, related to lobsters. Sweet, shy little things.

Earwigs

Eat everything from plants to decaying matter to other insects, including aphids. Rarely a problem. (Don't prod their rear end with your finger, though.)

Jerusalem Cricket
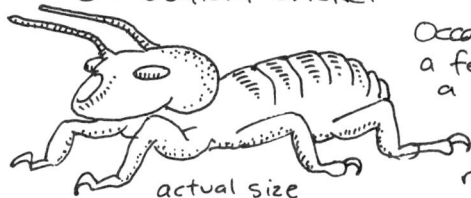
actual size

Occasionally take a few bites of a potato. Their heads are remarkably humanoid.

Spittle-bugs

Tiny bugs hidden by a frothy mass of secreted bubbles. Suck plant juices, but not enough to harm them.

Crickets
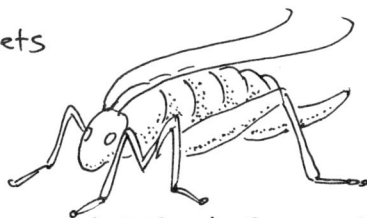
(California Camel Cricket.

Most butterflies + moths

Buckeye (_Junonia coenia_)

Most flies

← Housefly _Musca domestica_

Cats

Who, me... "innocent"?

SOURCES

CHAPTER 1 - COMPOSTING

GOLUEKE, CLARENCE. 1973. **COMPOSTING, A STUDY OF THE PROCESS AND ITS PRINCIPLES**. A DEFINITIVE SCIENTIFIC VIEW.

RODALE, J.I., ED. 1960. **THE COMPLETE BOOK OF COMPOSTING**. THE DEFINITIVE HOW-TO BOOK.

-----. **PAY DIRT**. WRITTEN IN THE 40'S, THIS BOOK CONTAINS MUCH INTERESTING HISTORICAL INFORMATION, PLUS SOME THEORY.

WAKSMAN, SELMAN. 1952. **SOIL MICROBIOLOGY**. A CLASSIC BY ONE OF THE TOP SOIL MICROBIOLOGISTS.

EHRLICH, PAUL AND ANNE. 1977. **ECOSCIENCE: POPULATION, RESOURCES, AND ENVIRONMENT**. A BEAUTIFUL BOOK ON BASIC ECOLOGY BY TWO OF THE BIGGIES IN THE FIELD.

INTEGRAL URBAN HOUSE STAFF, BERKELEY, CALIFORNIA. I CALLED THEM UP ONCE AND ASKED THEM VARIOUS OFF-THE-WALL QUESTIONS. THEY WERE VERY HELPFUL.

FARALLONES INSTITUTE. 1979. **THE INTEGRAL URBAN HOUSE**. INCLUDES HOW-TO INFO ON COMPOSTING, ALONG WITH JUST ABOUT EVERYTHING ELSE.

LECKIE, JIM, ET. AL. 1975. **OTHER HOMES AND GARBAGE**. LIKE THE FARALLONES BOOK, WITH SLIGHTLY MORE DEPTH ON FEWER TOPICS.

HATTORI, TSUTOMU. 1973. **MICROBIAL LIFE IN THE SOIL**.

ROSEBURY, THEODOR. **LIFE ON MAN**. ABOUT THE BACTERIA-HUMAN INTERFACE.

CHAPTER 2 - SOIL PREPARATION

BERGER, KERMIT C., 1965. **SUN, SOIL AND SURVIVAL**. EASY-TO-READ PRESENTATION OF BASIC SOIL SCIENCE.

U.S. DEPT. OF AGRICULTURE. **1957 YEARBOOK**. A SPECIAL ISSUE ON SOIL. PROVES THE GOVERNMENT AIN'T ALL BAD. TAKES A LITTLE TRANSLATING TO UNDERSTAND.

UNIVERSITY OF CALIFORNIA, DIVISION OF AGRICULTURAL SCIENCES, COOPERATIVE EDUCATION PAMPHLETS, 1979. "MANAGING COMPACTED AND LAYERED SOIL," ETC. THESE PAMPHLETS ARE FREE! UNFORTUNATELY, MUCH OF IT MUST BE TAKEN WITH A GRAIN OF SALT, IN LIGHT OF THE UNIVERSITY'S ENTANGLEMENTS WITH INDUSTRY.

FARALLONES INSTITUTE. 1979. **THE INTEGRAL URBAN HOUSE**. DESTINED TO BE A CLASSIC.

WAKSMAN, SELMAN. 1952. **SOIL MICROBIOLOGY**.

OELHAF, ROBERT C. 1978. **ORGANIC AGRICULTURE**. ONE OF THE FEW SCIENTIFIC LOOKS AT THE ORGANIC-VS.-CHEMICALS SQUABBLE IN TERMS OF SOIL FERTILITY.

STEVENSON, F.J. 1982. **HUMUS CHEMISTRY**. MUCH UNINTENTIONAL SUPPORT FOR ORGANIC GARDENING.

220

CHAPTER 3 - SOIL CHEMISTRY

BRADY, NYLE C., **THE NATURE AND PROPERTIES OF SOILS**. A CLASSIC IN ITS FIELD.

U.S. DEPT. OF AG. **1957 YEARBOOK**. GOOD INTRO TO CLAY AND CATION EXCHANGE, BUT VERY WEAK ON SOIL BIOLOGY.

MENGEL, KONRAD. 1978. **PRINCIPLES OF PLANT NUTRITION**. ADMIRABLE ATTEMPT AT A PURELY LEFT-BRAIN, REDUCTIONIST UNDERSTANDING OF SOIL FERTILITY AND PLANT GROWTH. MORE UNINTENTIONAL SUPPORT FOR ORGANIC METHODS.

CHAPTER 4 - FERTILITY

FUKUOKA, MANASOBU. 1981. **THE ONE-STRAW REVOLUTION**. BY THE PROPONENT OF "DO-NOTHING" OR "NATURAL" FARMING, THIS BOOK IS ALSO ABOUT NUTRITION, PHILOSOPHY, AND RIGHT-LIVING.

CHADWICK, ALAN. **1972 LECTURES AT U.C.S.C.**, ESP. LECTURE NO. 6. AVAILABLE AT MCHENRY LANGUAGE LAB, U.C.S.C. GOOD INTRO TO RUDOLF STEINER'S CONCEPTS OF THE RELATION BETWEEN THE SEASONS AND LIFE CYCLES. VERY INSPIRING.

JEAVONS, JOHN. **HOW TO GROW MORE VEGETABLES**, ETC. PROBABLY THE BEST INTRODUCTORY GARDENING BOOK. BIODYNAMIC/FRENCH INTENSIVE.

GARDENER, VICTOR R. **PRINCIPLES OF HORTICULTURAL PRODUCTION**. A GOLD MINE OF ASSORTED DISCONNECTED INFORMATION. HARD TO SIFT THROUGH, BUT WORTH THE TROUBLE.

CUTHBERTSON, TOM. 1978. **ALAN CHADWICK'S ENCHANTED GARDEN**. MORE BIODYNAMIC-FRENCH INTENSIVE-ISM; THIS ONE MORE PRACTICAL THAN CHADWICK'S LECTURES. FOR ADVANCED GARDENERS.

FITTER, ALASTAIR. 1981. **ENVIRONMENTAL PHYSIOLOGY OF PLANTS**. UNINTENTIONAL, UNWITTING SCIENTIFIC CONFIRMATION OF STEINER AND CHADWICK'S INTUITIVE INSIGHTS.

CARSON, E.W. 1971. **THE PLANT ROOT AND ITS ENVIRONMENT**. AS CLOSE AS WESTERN SCIENCE GETS TO A WHOLISTIC, COHERENT VIEW OF WHAT'S GOING ON WITH SOIL FERTILITY. AT LEAST IT'S INTERDISCIPLINARY.

ALSO, MOST OF THE SOURCES CITED FOR CHAPTERS 1, 2, AND 3.

CHAPTER 5 - GARDEN PLANS

GEIGER, RUDOLPH. 1965. **CLIMATE NEAR THE GROUND**. THE CLASSIC THAT EVERYONE REFERS TO--RATHER TECHNICAL AND HARD TO GET THROUGH, BUT IF YOU TACKLE A LITTLE BIT AT A TIME, YOU'LL BE AN EXPERT IN NO TIME FLAT.

BAER, STEVE. 1975. **SUNSPOTS**. ACTUALLY A BOOK ABOUT SOLAR TECHNOLOGY BY A MASTER ENGINEER AND ALL-AROUND GENIUS. CONTAINS MANY USEFUL PERCEPTIONS ON SUN ANGLES, HEAT FLOW, AND ENERGY PSYCHOLOGY.

MOLLISON, BILL. 1979 AND 1982. **PERMACULTURE ONE AND TWO**. WHAT CAN YOU SAY?-- THE MAN'S RIGHT AT THE CENTER OF THINGS. MICROCLIMATE, ECOLOGY, APPROPRIATE GARDEN TECHNOLOGY, AND SAVING THE WORLD.

ADAMS, GEORGE. 1980. **THE PLANT BETWEEN THE SUN AND EARTH.** GOOD INTRO-
DUCTION TO RUDOLPH STEINER'S VIEWS ON COSMO–AGRICULTURE; SPACING OUT TO
ZERO IN.

PLUS FUKUOKA, JEAVONS, GARDENER––ALREADY CITED.

CHAPTER 6 - PLANT PROPAGATION

GILL, NORMAN T. 1966. **AGRICULTURAL BOTANY.** ONE OF THE BEST, EASIEST–TO–READ
TECHNICAL BOOKS ON THE SUBJECT, WITH BEAUTIFUL DRAWINGS.

ROBBIN, WILFRED. 1975. **BOTANY OF CROP PLANTS.**

RAVEN, PETER. 1975. **THE BIOLOGY OF PLANTS.**

BLEASDALE, J.K.A. 1977. **PLANT PHYSIOLOGY IN RELATION TO HORTICULTURE.**

TILTH. 1983. **THE FUTURE IS ABUNDANT.**

BEEVERS, LEONARD, **NITRATE METABOLISM.** P. 26–34. DENSE SCIENCE, BUT I FOUND IT
USEFUL FOR ASSESSING THE FERTILITY NEEDS OF SEEDLINGS.

JANICK, JULES. 1972. **HORTICULTURAL SCIENCE.**

HARTMAN, HUDSON. 1975. **PRINCIPLES OF PLANT PROPAGATION.**

HAYWOOD, HERMAN. 1938. **THE STRUCTURE OF ECONOMIC PLANTS.**

SUNSET GARDEN BOOKS. 1969. **PRUNING.**

CHAPTER 7 - WATERING

MOST OF THE SOURCES FROM CHAPTER TWO.

CHAPTER 8 - PEST CONTROL

ESSIG, E.O., 1913. **INSECTS OF CALIFORNIA, INJURIOUS AND BENEFICIAL.** THE CLASSIC
ON WESTERN BIOLOGICAL PEST CONTROL, WRITTEN BEFORE THERE WERE ANY
PESTICIDES, SO NO FOOLING AROUND. WHAT UNIVERSITY SCIENCE USED TO BE (AND
STILL IS SOMEWHAT, FOR EXAMPLE AT U.C. BERKELEY'S ENTOMOLOGY SUB–
DEPARTMENT AND GILL TRACT RESEARCH FIELDS) BEFORE THE ONSET OF
CORPORATE MANIPULATION.

FLINT, MARY LOU. 1979. **INTRODUCTION TO INTEGRATED PEST MANAGEMENT.**
BEST ALL–AROUND INTRODUCTION TO BIOLOGICAL PEST CONTROL.

HUFFAKER, C.B. (ED.) 1976. **THEORY AND PRACTICE OF BIOLOGICAL CONTROL.**
SLIGHTLY ADVANCED––HAS A GOOD CASE–BY–CASE ACCOUNT OF WHICH PREDATOR TO
USE IN WHAT SITUATION.

VAN DEN BOSCH, ROBERT. 1982. **AN INTRODUCTION TO BIOLOGICAL CONTROL.**
DETAILS ON HOW TO FIND AND REAR SPECIFIC PREDATORS.

LINSENMAIER, WALTER. 1972. **INSECTS OF THE WORLD.** UNBELIEVABLE DRAWINGS.

POWELL, JERRY A. 1979. **CALIFORNIA INSECTS.** A GOOD REFERENCE/FIELD GUIDE.

RICE, ELROY L. 1983. **PEST CONTROL WITH NATURE'S CHEMICALS.** MOSTLY
ABOUT ATTRACTANT AND REPELLENT PLANTS.

ROSENTHAL, HERBERT. 1979. **HERBIVORES, AND THEIR INTERACTION WITH SECONDARY PLANT METABOLITES.**

CALLAHAN, PHILIP. 1977. **TUNING INTO NATURE.** CALLAHAN IS AHEAD OF HIS TIME--A HOLISTIC SCIENTIST WITH A NEW APPROACH TO PEST CONTROL USING RADIO WAVES TO ATTRACT AND TRAP PESTS. POSSIBLY THE GALILEO OF ENTOMOLOGY.

CARR, ANNA. 1979. **HANDBOOK OF GARDEN INSECTS.** RODALE PRESS.

BLANEY, WALTER M. 1976. **HOW INSECTS LIVE.** GOOD PHOTOS.

DEBACH, PAUL. 1974. **BIOLOGICAL CONTROL BY NATURAL ENEMIES.**